A Place To Call Home

The Forensics

By

Filomena Almeida Bruno

Dedication

I thoroughly dedicate this Book to my late husband, General Joao Almeida Bruno who always encouraged and supported me where writing was concerned, being - A Place to Call Home, The Forensics - the book that he also loved after watching the series. Having said that, it goes to my two older brothers, Noel and the late Henrique who was looking forward to read the book, unfortunately this was not to happen, however, I am more than happy that my daughter Noella will love to read it, my two grandchildren, my son in law. Is also a pity that both of my beloved Parents now late uncle Natalino are not here to treasure this book. I am also here to thank all of those who supported me, pushing me and going with me the great length. Bevan Lee for starters who was enthusiastic about my Book, and the stars of APTCH who backed me up excitingly…thank you. More over, being such a hard fan of APTCH, i am also dedicating this book to all of the APTCH who followed the series and demanded more. Here's proof that there is always more. Please enjoy this reading, thanking you all for I had a whale of an excellent time writing the first Edition. I will see you all with the Second Edition.

Acknowledgment

Hello and good afternoon. I have been writing this Book since 2014. But it all came about when I attended the Gala Dinner in October 2018 where I actually got to see and visit the grand Estate of AshPark hence the whole scenario fired up my imagination where I could see and follow the trails of my Book. The feeling was surreal and even more from a farcical estate of a series. Now I was there in person experiencing the whole thing one hundred per cent. For every step a scenario from the APTCH flashed in my mind, and the ideas surfaced altogether, making me sit down and re-write this book. Writing this book rejuvenated me one hundred percent. The memories flooded of my childhood in Macau, the foreign policies worldwide and a new country which brought even more closer to this book being in Australia. The setting is in Sydney. The time/s were in the early fifties, the family a very guarded dynasty where Elizabeth Bligh ruled with her own iron thumb…it was either her way, or the highway. This book symbolizes the utter strength of what a woman can go and her determination nonetheless. The Blighs women are a force to be reckoned with and in this no one doubts it. For all of you I am grateful for the pushes, the support, the backing up and in particular all the stars that I have met, commented on and reunited on that fun day in 2020 before the hazards of Covid 19. Without further ADO please entertain yourselves with this First Edition Narrative of A Place to Call Home, the Forensics and the ironic part is that this Book is published, thirteen years late. (September 2013 - March 03-2026)

Yours gladly

Filomena,

Australia's Golden Angel.

Table of Content

Dedication..3

Acknowledgment...4

Chapter 01: Anna Bligh: The Reluctant Fundamentalist 1

Chapter 02: Doris Collins. "A Fool such as I." 48

Chapter 03. George Robert Bligh...80

Chapter 04: Caroline Bligh. The Colourful Bligh. The Reel Bligh. *(Part One)* 101

Chapter 04 George Bligh: The Essence of the Bligh Empire *(Part Two)* 129

Chapter 05: Sir Richard Bennett. The Smooth Operator...................138

Chapter 06: Between Two Worlds. 155

Chapter 07: Roy Briggs 187

Chapter 08: The Femme Fatalle 224

Chapter 09: Dr Jack Duncan. The Lost Boy....................................268

Chapter 10: Sara Adams: Florence Nightingale. 308

Chapter 11: Olivia Bligh: The Princess in the Ivory Tower..............334

Chapter 12: Hitler's Furies 369

Chapter 13: Elizabeth Bligh. Queen of Camelot of Broken Dreams. 398

Sponsors 422

Chapter 01: Anna Bligh: The Reluctant Fundamentalist

Based on the APTC Home TV series.

To the world outside you are a Bligh, Act like one, Bellows Jack Duncan angrily admonished his "daughter" with Caroline Bligh. Hard and pressed feelings... harsh. Controversial words of a caring and loving father who had seen hell and lived through it all. Now he was going through it all over again, this time with his own daughter. Anna Bligh, whose career and marital life, and life itself had taken a terrible turn over. Or is it?

Anna, refusing to give her baby away, it was her business, exactly what her tante, Petite Lizzie, always said. And now the beautiful, blonde, petite *papillon*, the youngest Bligh, was at a crossroads again and again. She would always be a controversial personality and, like her mother Caro and tante Petite Lizzie, a thorn in the side of the Bligh family.

The world outside sucked. Now the spoiled young Anna Bligh found that not all was a confectionery of sweets and sugar dandies, with colourful butterflies lightly pausing here and there, always fluttering around, just like Anna did. There was a time when what young Anna wanted, young Anna got, with or without anyone's approval.

You have guessed it, young Anna Bligh was the RELUCTANT FUNDAMENTALIST of *de facto* reasoning, her self-explanations being all about her own status and she would maintain her own status, which she would stubbornly keep or so she thought. Against her stood the Blighs. She was solo in her own endeavour. Yes, you read that right... SOLO.

Unbeknownst to them, what they failed to observe, was that Anna, though the youngest, was a Bligh through and through. She had inherited the beauty, the fun personality, the wealth, the status, and also that true fundamentalism, the self-rigidity so much like her grandmother, her mother, and her rebellious tante Petite Lizzie. They were all alike in that respect, indomitable, grand women, and young Anna was one who almost like her and no one noticed.

But what all of them failed to notice was that for all of Anna's rebelling and being a fundamentalist, now the reluctant one, she was a Bligh. And as Gino once put it to James, "...and everything that comes with it. She's a Bligh?" "And that's a lot to put up with?" James asked, or words to that effect. Of course, it was the real thing, not kosher, but Gino's own "woke-his-way". For him, it was a wake-up call, or was it? Perhaps not. Maybe. Yes.

Anna had no illusions, no babble or blubber. Even though Anna Bligh was a dreamer, a writer, a novelist that would produce great works and become a national fodder for it, she grew cynical in the process: smoking, drinking, and being promiscuous. Some people said everything came with the territory, and the spoilt princess was no angel.

As Sir Richard Bennett once remarked, "I hear that you and your publisher share more than publishing rights, perhaps it's time to share them around." He called her all sorts of names, comparing her to Caro, Anna's mother. The question was, how did he know that, and who was he to judge or criticise?

Delectable young Anna was deeply hurting, bitterly. The reason? Anna would bristle at anything tied to society's harsh rules and regulations. She was now a "law" unto herself. But one could not deny she was forever caught in an emotional pain from which she would never recover, simply because she wouldn't let go.

Already, and effectively, the RELUCTANT FUNDAMENTALIST… she covered her pain with cynicism and imperious rebellion, accentuating her own self, eccentricity, self-absorption, selfishness, narcissism, discomfort, bitterness, sorrow, all of which Anna used as her own self-defence.

Being the youngest of the Blighs, and as with most youngest children, she absorbed everything and sometimes, would be in her own world, because, in many ways, the adult lives she witnessed were living nightmares: reaching towards the Apex one moment happy, and the other, down and out, and of course Anna being loved, tendered cared for and nurtured by her own Grandmother Anna immersed into it but got confused by it all.

Who doesn't want a little girl to spoil rotten, to love, to dress up, to play with like a doll, to care for, creating that special bond through shopping sprees that many mothers cherish with their daughters, shopping until they drop? But Anna grew up without either mother, Caro, her biological mother, and Elaine, her "make-believe" one. Her grandmother Elizabeth adopted Anna as her own daughter, and again as her granddaughter, hence James becoming her older brother.

Anna was no push over alas this kind of family melodramas did get very complexed, insidious. In the end, she knew what she wanted, fundamentally, radically. And one really questions if these alone were the things that shaped someone like Anna.

Anna oh yes, was born into such wealth, such prestigious status... into such a respectful family... wait... powerful too... her family. Theirs was a world of small pleasures, expensive tastes, and near-royal status. Her grandmother, the indomitable Grand Elizabeth Bligh, had servants at her beck and call, and in her case, two different sets of parents. Odd but it happens... but with Anna, nothing was the term and condition of anything odd still that her

Still, Anna's birth registry named her true parents. Now you see why she is *The Reluctant Fundamentalist*. It is, after all, self–explanatory... but with Anna apart from being SELF, it was very complex.

The BLIGHS revolved and evolved but stayed out of, or stayed in, any kind of involvement of any kind..sometimes it looked like they were cursed. It was bad mojo for the Bligh's family. Everything was possible or impossible. The Blighs could not really afford scandals, yet at any breaking point the scandals were there.

Anna was also one of the Bligh's... so whatever was going to happen, Anna made it possible. To the sad state of the Blighs' affairs, and being always controversial and complex, Anna, being colourful and bountiful, would always be caught in the middle of the main storm. But then again, so were the Blighs, her own family.

The proverbial daughter and the trademark of what her privileged status could afford Anna, but that she was a fundamentalist and very much a reluctant one, made things extremely difficult and troublesome. No one understood, much less the outsiders, that everything could be applicable to such a little darling living in a world of fairy tales. And she was. But by the same token, to the chagrin of this mademoiselle, this Reluctant Fundamentalist needed to face the facts.

Whilst she sympathised with the pain and suffering of many people, looking at the basis of their own laws and restrictions, which she believed, Anna was hard put to follow these same rules and regulations. The thing is, for her, their laws did not affect her, would not even rule her, much less regulate her. She refused to be dictated to by stickybeaks and badly intentioned society. She would do what she wanted to do, with or without their permission, and that is why Anna Bligh became her own pesky enemy, saying one thing and doing another, her own words, which goes against each other plus having a loose tongue harnessed into her hands in the mounting of her favourite horse, heralding more trouble that she wanted to consider or even imagined.

Anna, being a reluctant fundamentalist, should have known that nothing in this world moved in one direction. Naïve as she was, the world and society were not as formal or easily disposable as her ways of thinking or manners of function. To that or other effect, this included or excluded her family. Yet her own family could betray themselves with so many "colourful" personalities, and some would say "deviants". Or is it?

The commandments were set up so that the world knew the "rights" from the "wrongs", the instructions in the respective associations where law and chemistry were abided by. But our own Anna, the *joie de vivre* of the Bligh family, the *belle petite papillon* with her beautiful, refreshing frocks, would never comply with them. Showing her youth, her own freedom, her self-expressed liberation, she wore her rebellion in her clothes.

For many others those same frocks, those beautiful rock-around-the-clock dresses that Anna wore... the same that existed during the fifties, becoming the world's trademark during the fifties, and Anna made them her own. To some they were a sign of superficiality, a statement that she was free from all of society's shackles. A Bligh temperament, or simply a capricious young girl spoilt enough to defy all logic, explanations… going against and incredibly, her own indomitable grandmother, the grand Elizabeth Bligh, and both of her sets of parents. It was her way or the highway.

THE BLIGHS are an old traditional Australian dynasty. Anna Bligh was one true-blue Australian Bligh.

The CAMELOT'S KINGDOM's matriarch, held such shocking secrets, with revelations that young and delectable Anna Bligh harboured such a nefarious state of mind, all negative and precociously harmful. One must be kidding, but then again, the BLIGH WOMEN, in their own way were rebel-rousers, distinctive, pronounced, but modern and defiant.

With Matthew Goddard administering the following: "You Bligh women... it's your way or the highway," as he walked away from the Bligh family, returning the key to his father's house to Elizabeth. Aye.

Anna was of medium height and slim stature, blonde, with high cheekbones and wide brown eyes. With a sun-kissed complexion, she was fun to be with, full of crackers and jokes, the epitome of a beautiful young lady of fine and delectable style, brimming with grace and oozing charm, whether among Blighs or otherwise. We all fell for that youth and freshness. Beautiful and so recalcitrant. Young and so damned intent. Resolute? Hmm. To her own detriment, yes.

Young Anna's lively, refreshing, and colourful nature combined perfectly with the beautiful frocks that depicted the time and its fashion, a time when rock and roll brought love, hate, and rebellion. These were the main elements that defined young Anna's story... classified being a new vibrant and colourful yet loud, and social.

She was, of course, *très chic*, *nouveau riche* in style but not in origin, being the youngest beautiful and so extravagant *petite fille* of the Blighs.

Take notice: she was rich, and she inherited it from the BLIGH'S trousseau and her own BLIGH'S SAVINGS TRUST inheritance. Not a *nouveau riche*.

The BLIGH'S ARE AN OLD TRADITIONAL AUSTRALIAN DYNASTY.

Young, delectable Anna Bligh was, for certain, a true-blue Bligh.

And she was right on... or wrong.

Some people psychologically hide their pain and bitterness in the way they all dress up and wear their clothes with expensive taste and *haute couture* fashion. Doubtful, full of grievances, yet for us who were once young and free, Anna's dresses revived the pleasure, excitement, passion, and freedom we all had in our own youth, especially yours truly.

When I saw Anna's frocks, the epitome of the great time of the fifties, I thought about the young, schooling free days of our own lives. No responsibilities, relying only on our parents' love, tenderness, and care. But Anna did not have the normal life we all had. It is highly doubtful what kind of schooling she had.

She was orphaned by her adopted mother. Her biological mother was far away. Her foster father was also drowning in his own pain, mending his broken heart after losing Elaine in the Japanese bombing on 19 February 1941, his first wife. Anna's real father, Jack, was ignorant of her true identity as his daughter, believing that Anna and James were actually George and Elaine's biological children.

Anna's frocks showed, to a large extent, that she was also a young, pre-eminent girl growing up at all costs, and that our carefree ways, our spontaneous personalities, our defiant and challenging ways of life, were once, when it came, the new dawn of breaking all the rules, the epitome of what we would have called *joie de vivre*, bountiful, full of fun, a breath of fresh air.

Who in her perfect, or imperfect, world... Tante Petite Lizzie would call young Anna *la belle petite papillon*. Aunty Lizzie was right. All of Anna's frocks depicted a time long gone, but not meant to be carefree.

(*Ashpark de Rêves Brisés.*)

"Une social enchantement dans le monde de rêves et des arts, tout est un délice."

(*A social enchantment where, in a world of dreams and the arts, everything was delicious.*)

And her Tante Petite Lizzie knew what it was to be a Bligh. For a lot of them, without the 'B', only *light* meant *lumière* in French. Oh yes, the Blighs were the beacon light of Inverness, where the exquisite Camelot ruled its own kingdom by hook or by crook, and the Blighs, whether they wanted to or not, were always caught in the middle of everything. Hence, the Blighs were the *lumière*, the light.

"Anna Bligh, la belle petite papillon colorée et sociale, était un enchantement dans le monde de Camelot et des rêves non accomplis, pauvre jeune petite fille riche."

(*Translation: Anna Bligh, the beautiful little butterfly, colourful and social, was an enchantment in the world of Camelot and of dreams that were never fulfilled. Poor little rich girl.*)

Exactly right. Young Anna was the social butterfly and a storm that came and went, leaving her mark. Anna hovered and flew from here to there and landed lightly among all the budding flowers in full bloom throughout the years she lived at Camelot or elsewhere.

She was flighty, fanciful, and fun-loving, colourful and charming, one moment here, the next there, flying in every direction, to places where the fierce wind or gentle breeze would take her, and of course to the far, remote recesses of her highly imaginative mind, where romance happens, love conquers all, and marriage is forever. Or is it?

"Dans le monde de rêves et des arts, tout est un délice." (*In the world of dreams and arts, everything is delicious.*) And it was for Anna anyway, a motto of Petite Tante Lizzie, the aunt that Anna would one day meet, but had yet to meet.

Yes, Anna was perfect, for us all, a dreamer, as most young girls were. She was young, incredibly naïve, not much different from any rich girl.

For the more stuffy Blighs she was exuberant, a breath of fresh air, and very much the social butterfly she was becoming, the lively essence of the BLIGH'S DYNASTY. She was heard but not seen... or seen but not heard? Alas, we could all compare ourselves to her.

Young as she was, as we were, we all thought about pure love and believed that love would conquer all and that marriage would last forever. We were so young and naïve, at the hands of fate. But Fate… ahhhhhh Destiny could play such unfair games with all of us. Anna would be one of them.

To some degree it might have been. But still, there are many questions that allow us to sit and wonder, mine especially.

Gino, in the next book (*Book 2: A Place to Call Home – The Forensics*), and in the GINO POLLETI, THE FARMER WANTS A WIFE) was exactly everything the opposite of what young, beautiful, that young Anna was and even more... rich and spoilt.

(Please note that these reasoning are very much well applicable to this book. Both are the basis of what is intended to be written and why, naturally you are all free to express your opinions and your reasoning). Making sure that they resonate and make sense.

In the series, it does not tell where Anna attended school or what education she had. It was such a disappointment when she married so young, though it had a purpose and a logical explanation, and she missed out on her Bligh *de rigueur* DEBUTANTE BALL, in Inverness, like her mother Caro, her grandmother, and the coming-of-age event that her "father" George had. James did not have his own birthday's emancipation..rather, it was more of a *fait accompli* for Elizabeth Bligh when James Bligh got married.

But I guess Bevan Lee had his own motives and reasons why Anna married so young, and to a farmer. Gino was a farmer. He was traditional but not cultured. He spoke Italian and English, but with a heavy accent. Gino was a *paysan*, antisocial, with old family traditions and attachments. Whether he wanted to or not, Gino was a peasant, pretty much anti-social and with old family traditions attached."

For many, he had not cut the apron strings from his mother. For others, he was cold, distant, and cruel. And for us, being the only male child in an Italian family, he was also the king. Anna was virtually his "slave", so to speak.

Sometimes opposites attract. Others, opposites distract. And that was exactly what fate had for both of them, and more. But in this case, fate did not play a hand in their love. There was no condescending love, only pride and honour. Gino was of strong Italian stock. Whether peasant or not, he was bound by his own pride and character. Two against one. Anna never stood a chance.

Gino was of tough Italian stock. He lived and breathed the farm. Gino inherited the farm from his family and wanted, in the rural place of Inverness, to continue his lifetime's inheritance… and his *rêves* were big and audacious. He wanted everything he could get… even Anna. *(Rêves means dreams in French.)*

"Did Gino Polletti really marry Anna for love, or just to defy all conventions and challenge the might of the indomitable Elizabeth Bligh?" There we are… the "flickering in one's eyes" states the veracity of it all… the truth. ((If you wonder, I added and beautified the words of Sara Adams.))

Everyone would have a purpose in life… period. Gino's was to be a farmer all his life. But was he meant to be married to Anna, or was it for an even more detrimental purpose? Supposedly, he wanted to get involved up close and personal just to see how the other half lived and functioned… fair question?

I think that might have been his purpose. The novelty of being accepted into the Bligh family had worn off by then. He saw the Blighs, as he cruelly put it to Anna: "Your family is sick… a baby dies, and you buy another." Confirming that the Blighs were indeed a very complex family, Gino regretted it more than anything else… now he wanted out. Now the Blighs, in Gino's mind, were nothing… just a prelude of their ancestry…The realisation that nothing the Blighs did—or would do—was part of his ideal life… the question is: what was his "ideal" life?

"It has nothing to do with us… or with me…" or words to this effect, made great sense, as we could sense Gino was getting fed up and would do anything to rid himself of his "sick" wife and all of her perversion… *malle*, *patsos* (evil, crazy). So he intentionally took his wife abroad so she would get used to him and their marital stability. Instead, she went off and returned with a book titled *House of Lies*, and more to it… (please read on… if not in this chapter, then Chapter 1 in Book 2).

Gino, who never wanted anything to do with the Blighs' money, did travel the world with Anna, using the money from Anna Bligh's trust. Still, the man was not happy. Like Anna, he said one thing, meant another, then did something else.

Clearly, Gino's life revolving around the Blighs, in and out, was coming to a regretful end. The more he intended to be agreeable with his wife's "patsos" family, the more he concluded it was not worth it. And Anna? Gino thought that Anna was now used by date. It was his time out and to move in a different direction.

Gino accused Anna of lying to him about her inability to conceive a child… his own child… what about the child that she miscarried, conceived through their love and affection?

Whether Gino knew it or not, Anna was vulnerable, as most young girls were. Besides being rich, Anna was a dreamer. This emphatic desire to have a normal life and be married into the "other" people… to be included in their side… in Anna's case, she was encapsulated in a small world: her own novels and others' novels—one such as Barbara Cartland, the Queen of Romantic Novels. She built in herself a romantic notion and elusive phenomenon: love triumphs at the end.

That was Anna's desire: to be happily married. Actually achieving her solo side… hers being determined and as good as her willpower would make her do… she cooked Italian, spoke Italian, and wanted very much to become a proper Italian farmer's wife and an Australian top novelist, authoress—a terrific writer.

Dreams of becoming a writer were, at that moment, null. Gino did not want her to be anything except his wife… a farmer's wife. But that would come out later, when both of them struggled to be what one wanted while the other wanted something else. Rich or not, a rich young lady such as Anna… one would know that after the death of her mother, Anna would have been very much protected within the stern, solid but cold walls of Camelot's Castle Kingdom. Especially in those days, when kidnappers abounded. Times were hard, difficult. One would find something about the Blighs and their vulnerability… plus chivalrous beneficiaries… and Anna Bligh was, of course, in this position. What I meant is that… pure and simple… the social…

Status would have never allowed both Anna and Gino to be together. Anna definitely was not born to be a farmer's wife, no matter how hard this reluctant fundamentalist, beautiful social butterfly was, all ready and gung-ho to face it… typical of her grandmother, the indomitable Elizabeth Bligh. But Anna was also like her mother Caro: a free spirit.

As for Gino… well, his days might be over with the Blighs and everything that came with them… including Anna. But he was Italian. Gino would never, ever forgive or forget the Blighs and their ill-intentioned mistreatment of him. The time would come when "justice" would be done.

Anna was a delectable, innocent romantic… far-off romances, where the man was always strong, enthusiastic, full of ardour, dynamism, fiery, dominant, heroic… and handsome was an added plus. But was Gino all of this?

Anna's fiery passion, and being passionate about her "inamorato," as trustworthy and devoted as she was, with empathy added to her highs and lows of morality… she was being driven into a spot. But whilst all of these were full marks, her major downfall was that she trusted too much and couldn't keep her mouth shut.

For Anna, it was all or nothing. It never occurred to her that things at home with the Blighs—Gino's other family—should stay at home with the Blighs. She was now a Polletti and should have conformed to this, keeping the Blighs' business private… but she blabbered to Gino.

The Pollettis were far and remote. Plus, they were the new Daegos in town. They were Europeans, refugees, and nowhere near the same status as the Blighs. Hard to find a footing where they could stay and establish roots… a place to call home. This was particularly challenging, as most of them were refugees. That added even more complexity, not only finding their footing but trying to fit in.

The Pollettis

were employees of the Blighs… as his Mama Polletti put it when she tried to warn Gino: "Everything that we have, we owe it to Anna's family, Gino… everything."

At the time, it was highly repugnant. Social status could not only divide, it could also tear and break anything solid, hard-edged, and even move or shake the recipient, leaving them reeling to no effect whatsoever. Once kicked out of the more solemn and sublimed state of the rich affairs, they could become highly vindictive. Gino would be caught in this whirlwind of prejudicial and unjust systems. More so… in Gino's mind, he was used and abused, cast out by the Blighs when they had finished with him.

Thoughts… venomous ones and of non-existing affairs… not alone in this disposition of facts and fictions. Gino pretty much ignored the facts; he only believed his own fictions. Anna could not have any kids with him… Anna lied to Gino. Anna preferred to be a writer than a farmer's wife… "being tied to the stove, working her nibbling fingers to the bone." It kept coming to him… these bitter flashes… and he called the Blighs "patsos," when he was far more "patsos" than them.

On the other hand, Anna's big mouth continually gave Gino full ammunition to hate and abhor the Blighs. A fed-up Gino told Anna: "If it's not one thing, it's another… there is always something happening… I've had it… no wonder you are not expecting," roughly and without any piety. A drunk Gino told Anna. He needed something to rest his conscience so he could find a reason to drown his frustration… His dreams were now all gone. Nothing on the farm was working for him…

his marriage was in tatters. He had Rose, and it was easy to manipulate her.

There was so much at stake… the weirdness of Andrew Swanson… Anna's big mouth kept shooting off, and in her haste, she also didn't see that Andrew Swanson, for all that he was, could be something for her… of course, I could be wrong. As he was also wealthy, his father knighted, he could also be capricious, flighty, expansive. But one also notices he was brought into this charade due to the manipulative Grand Elizabeth Bligh, who wanted Anna distracted to the point that her ideas of marrying Gino would stop. If Andrew Swanson didn't have any purpose, then for her ex-sister-in-law Olivia, he would. But one tends to consider all points. Was Elizabeth Bligh right in having Andrew Swanson as the one to make her granddaughter happy, or was it another dream that would end in tatters? Was Anna doomed or jinxed in love? The Bligh women seemed cursed… none of them lucky in love. Maybe it was the *ashpark of broken dreams*. All the women had their hearts shattered, marriages broken, or died terrible deaths.

But, as we know… young Anna went ahead and did what she wanted. Meanwhile, we take it up as her impetuosity, happy that Anna, for what she was, stood up and accounted for herself… defying everything, including prohibiting her own indomitable grandmother from attending her wedding. Having said that, we all looked the other way, forgiving and forgetting Anna's folly, admiring her love and determination.

What about James being gay… what has that got to do with Gino, and to what extent would Gino understand it? More so… what evidence or proof could be afforded to show Gino? It was no one's business, nor should anyone interfere in what James was/is/would be. As Gino pointed out: "James is a happily married man." Whatever it was, when the right time came, James showed Gino his true colours as the older son, brother, and a Bligh… gay or not.

"You make up with Anna, or you'll answer to me," or words to that effect. One really admires James. I admired James Bligh for all that he was. But how many of us felt how James suffered and went through the ups and downs of it all? James stood his ground, with Gino relenting. James was a Bligh and showed his mettle.

It worked. But through it all, it was Anna's lies and noncommittal attitude that were her undoing. Gino left Anna. Anna wanted a divorce. Finally, the burden was lifted and ended.

Gino was reeling from one secret discovery to another… with the frequent harassment of knowing about James being gay… then Andrew Swanson, about James' son little Georgie. Anna found it "improper" but proper to tell Gino about her older brother's son. That was bad mojo. Then it was her mother Caro and her father Jack. If so, George Bligh was only her uncle. Therefore, Anna might have been rich and powerful, with thousands of pounds in her trust, but that was not what Gino and she wanted. You may think Gino married for love; I am more inclined to think he never married Anna for love, rather he married her to challenge Elizabeth defiantly… and the Blighs per se.

He admitted this to Regina Bligh when she asked: "Your point?" "I took on Elizabeth Bligh," he stared right and deeply into Regina's eyes… and stated: "I can take on you too." Now he totally admitted what I've always suspected, and now it is proven.

But the question that thoroughly intrigues me:

Was Anna covering for herself… trying to distract Gino by telling him sordid tales about other people's business so she could avoid feeling pressure and guilt about not being able to conceive? Psychologically, she was creating a diversion, trying to move Gino's mind in other directions. Gino was already under stress… he owed money to Carlo, the tractor broke down, Anna's horse cost a fortune, bills were stacking up, and the farm was not functioning as expected—the vines ruined by frost. Gino pawned a watch to his *vicini*, suffering from stress and loneliness without the support and love of his absent parents. One questions how he could raise a baby under these circumstances… how he could keep the farm running, maintain the family status quo… Gino might even have had more, maybe a brood. Europeans historically had large families. But anyone's thoughts aside, as I could be wrong, I do not wish to be prejudicial or biased… but Anna complicated things further in Gino's "modus operandi."

Andrew Swanson was a frequent visitor to the sprawling Camelot Kingdom, invited by Elizabeth Bligh, who wanted Andrew to marry Anna so she would forget her dependent love for Gino. So, both her grandmother and Anna were manipulative and liars, leading double or multiple lives. But did Anna also confide to Gino that her grandmother, the indomitable Elizabeth Bligh, never truly understood love? Elizabeth, the grand matriarch, was bitter and disillusioned. Anna observed that Elizabeth lacked empathy; love always eluded her. Anna never thought the same could happen to her. The world might change… yet history repeats itself. The pattern would revolve again… and nowhere was it truly 'kosher.'

Until the day her grandmother, the grand Elizabeth Bligh, the bitter, lonely, sad lady, met Mr Douglas Goddard, who proved himself a real gentleman, though previously betrayed by other elements of the family. Though he loved Elizabeth dearly, and perhaps Elizabeth met the true love of her life (not forgetting Jack Duncan's father), Douglas confirmed that he and his wife shared mutual love and affection. Elizabeth told Douglas that Lewis Bligh never showed her affection, to which Douglas Goddard finally came to terms. Yes… that's my Lizzie. He was correct. Did Elizabeth really find her true love?

Douglas told Elizabeth Bligh what, in fact, was the state of his relationship with his late wife, primarily with both of his two sons… one died… but the pain showed on his face as he recounted it. Respectfully, Matthew Goddard personally told Elizabeth how bitter the father–son relationship had been. The elderly Goddard never saw fit to reveal what was so heartbreakingly painful. But the son did, until he was found out; his character—non-smoking and non-conformist—came into question. In fact, Matthew Goddard came through as a fake.

It was not long before they met Matthew and, to their regret and disappointment, discovered to their detriment what a pain in the butt Matthew Goddard was… and would be for the Blighs… along with Gino. The phrase "two peas in a pod" sounds very appropriate, but that alone is not enough. Along with them, there is the family portrait painter/artist… remembering Lloyd… adding to the Bligh dynasty's pain as Lloyd returns to Inverness… flat, broke, and nowhere to go… so the gravy thickens even more.

Unfortunately, the Blighs' lives were always intermittently infused and diffused with these dire elements, and Anna aided and abetted them, multiplying more embarrassing details. These might be sore points, ones anyone would notice; however, Anna never did, was not in any position to do so, nor did she want to try. For a social butterfly, as her petite tante Lizzie called her: "La mode de l'opérateur à la mode était si 'séduisante' où et quand La Jeune Anna Bligh se levant avec aplomb." ((The fashion of a trendy operator was so "smoking" hot that young Anna Bligh would rise with great aplomb.))

Anna was living in her own new world… a married life meant to be succinctly sweet and without drama. Meanwhile, she was going to write novels and become one of the most acclaimed novelists in Australia. For Anna, the die was cast… she was now writing the full "biographical" story of the librarian who committed suicide—meaning Regina Bligh. It was funny, but while she was making plans to harm poor Reggie, who was, for starters, the *fait accompli* friend of Grand Elizabeth Bligh, sharing the same hatred and loathing for the "Jew" nurse/sister Sara Normand, they were all set to actually destroy Regina.

The question is… when did she begin to loathe Regina? I saw for myself that Regina used to love Anna and was proud of her dealings. So what happened? Even in the mental institution, she told the specialist that "her niece" was now a famous writer. Anna was a Bligh, but under no circumstances did she associate with Regina. Anna was the daughter of Caro and Jack Duncan… so she would have been Anna Duncan, née Bligh.

But nothing went Anna's way. She and Gino fought for what were supposedly their own rights. Yes, she had the right to pursue her career as a writer, or anything she wanted. I felt bad when she informed Gino: "Don't be angry… but they want my novels." Angry at her writings.

Absolutely ridiculous. She was a Bligh. And she feared her husband's reaction to what her dreams might bring. Incredible.

Gino, being an old Catholic and of Italian descent, would receive the Blighs' shocking revelations… and being Italian, there was room for him to take revenge on those sick

Blighs. It was a wonder that in his mind he did not seek compensation, considering he badly needed money.

At the time, Gino was working hard to have his farm ploughed and developed his own wine brand. He told the Blighs about the *camara de provare* (the tasting room), where his new wine venture would be showcased… with so many dreams at stake. His own wine industry, two different dreams… one would succeed, the other fail. So many lives and hearts would be broken. Anna would live to regret it, turning Gino into a volatile, obsequious, belligerent, and revengeful man, who would seek to destroy the Blighs. Period.

The interwoven lives through the

Blighs… one notes that it was impossible for Anna to accomplish her dreams as a writer while married to Gino… exceptionally and tyrannically selfish. Gino set out to make his own dreams come true: growing his vineyard. That alone made him bitter, destitute, and poisonous. Someone needed to pay.

When Gino, Rose, and the kids met Sir Richard Bennett, the Blighs' days were numbered—that was the start.

But

Anna had not yet realised two things. One, if her marriage was to be successful, she could never accomplish her dream as a famous writer, which she eventually did.

But what of the

Pollettis? Where are they now?

Doing what? Is the father with the bambino he always wished

for? More importantly… is he happy now?

(L'écrivain de roman romantique, mais comme sa grand-mère amère, Anna souffrait aussi de l'impact de l'amour perdu, et encore plus.)

(The writer who writes romantic novels... but like her bitter grandmother, Anna also suffered the impact of lost love, and even more.)

For all intents and purposes, Anna Bligh was an innocent growing up in a forbidden palace during turbulent times, looking out windows to imagine, in a major or minor way, what a wonderful or sad world might be. She should have looked around her. She lost her mother, Elaine, which could have been heartbreaking. We never hear her speak of her mother Elaine... was it painful, or did she not remember her at all? Somewhere around it, Anna did honour her passing by naming her daughter Elaine.

The lives of others were outside those eerily creaking, hard, cold iron gates. Small tours around her own mini-kingdom of Camelot allowed her to observe the outside world. She had taken short tours, trips, and long journeys with her parents. At one time, her mother Elaine was visiting... dying in the Japanese bombing in Darwin. Little Anna then came to live with her distant, cold, manipulative grandmother. But later, she came to love and respect the formidable grandmother, the indomitable Elizabeth Bligh, who delighted in showing off her grandchildren and occasionally took Anna on shopping sprees and short trips to Sydney's CBD.

Being a Bligh Belle Petite Papillon, Anna had full permission to roam Ash Park on horseback (she was given her first horse as soon as she could walk, following predecessors, especially Tante Petite Lizzie, or la bella piccolina Elizabeta, who was an equestrian champion and loved picnics and bathing in the clear river).

Young Anna did the same, unaware that her family had once enjoyed the same freedoms. Later, she came to meet her beautiful Tante Petite Lizzie.

The Blighs' name represented an upmarket existence and luxurious industry. Everything Anna Bligh indulged herself in... but as with everything, she also had a paramour, or so she thought... a newly arrived refugee, which could become her downfall. In those years, everything was prohibited and shamed.

The Blighs were under the radar of many, politically and otherwise, mainly Sir Richard Bennett, who always called Anna's grandfather a great stick in the mud. In many ways, Bennett was right, hence why he hated the Blighs so much. The real modus operandi of love was the reason behind his own vendetta. Sir Richard Bennett was highly unforgiving, but never to be called a peasant or a waste of the Bennett media empire. He thrived on scandals and notorious media exposures, gleefully accepting whatever came.

As he once said, if George Bligh passed wind, he wanted to know. Time would tell when Bennett would return, and the Blighs would be fighting against all odds and the terrible vendetta Dickoboy was to inflict. The media mogul had no restraint of time or period, and the bitterness he would inflict…

His target… the Blighs.

His job… the Blighs.

But to do so, he needed to organise. A new plan was now being devised.

His plans in the past did not work… so why would they work now?

But as far as Gino was concerned, he would find a way to hurt the Blighs. Now that they were in their sixties, life could be easier. He was thinking of the best way to extract money from the Blighs. Compensation was out. But to thoroughly exterminate them, callously… that was the fitting and proper course.

The temptation was great… but staring at his two kids, thinking they could starve… was not a proposition; it was reality.

He also had Rose. She knew about the Blighs, about their rough treatment of Regina Bligh… if Regina went mad over what they did to her, Rose would tell all.

Anna could afford it all.

What were a few quid? They all needed more than spoiled, petulant Anna Bligh.

Young Anna Bligh and her flights of fancy… Gino smiled bitterly. "Yes," he thought… "very fancy."

So Anna grew up in a world of fairies, magic, and pixie kingdoms, lakes… into a most tight and private environment. Unlike young Olivia, the Ivory Tower Princess, Anna was the Blighs' princess… perks included being doted on by Grandma Elizabeth, who took care of her grandchildren. Love flourished towards Gino… a "faux pas."

One afternoon…

Placid and calming, with breezes suavely brushing her face, Anna played some songs. Dressed in her nightie and sipping iced tea, she sat on the porch, drinking and soaking in the cool atmosphere that Camelot, the Blighs' kingdom, afforded. She was getting accustomed to, and loving, the scenery and the serene side of town… away from Sydney's hustle and bustle. It was her time to enjoy tranquil waters, benign spacious air, and the freedom she left behind when she married Gino to pursue her writing career.

Of course, being beautiful and trendy… a "séduisant, très chaud" ((smoking hot)), Anna had picked a few lovers along the way and enjoyed rendezvous with them, including her publishing manager.

Anna was suffering from the curse of writer's block… let's face it, we all go through that. She needed inspiration to complete her novels, but nothing worked. Her mind was empty. Desperate, she played songs from a record collection she had never used before, from the fifties rock-and-roll era. The beat was energetic, and she enjoyed it. Noisy, seductive… the wild voice of Elvis. Anna smiled, thinking about the King of Rock.

One of the cooks and some maids ventured onto the porch, curious about the music. Some were ready to dance; others were softly moved, reminded of golden memories. Anna noticed their expressions.

"Aww…" said the first cook. "We thought the young mistress was back home."

The other looked around. "Same records… but she isn't here… how sad."

One cook added, "It's high time this place had music and dance again."

"No, the young mistress is not home," replied another, turning back to the kitchen. The cooks had served at Camelot for years, seen everything, and remained loyal to the Blighs. They prayed that one day the little darling would return.

Anna assumed they were referring to her mother, Caro, and didn't ask further.

By now, young Anna was growing into her adolescent years. Heartbreaking memories were still part of her life. Anna had a daughter, like her mother had with her young Anna. She was without a partner, essentially a single mother. She wisely stayed away from social gossip, which tried to uncover her daughter's father. Few knew that Elaine's father, the handsome, athletic Dr Henry Fox, was living with another man.

Anna's daughter was well cared for, either asleep or fussed over by the maids, allowing Anna to indulge in her writing. Her novels were now selling like hotcakes.

She enjoyed tea, sampled morsels, and savoured small privileges

. Barefoot, in her nightie, hair undone, wearing no makeup… waking after sleepless nights, living the life of the rich and famous, Anna sat drinking coffee and eating breakfast. Camelot Kingdom provided her a state of tranquil elixir. Dreamily, she watched smoke rise, mingle with the air, and vanish. She marvelled at the vast greenery, manicured lawns, and vivid flowerbeds. Awaking from a long undisturbed sleep, she noted the raw beauty, the smell of rich earth, the deepening blue sky, and the strong sun. Nothing mattered except her peaceful, tranquil existence, calming her anxiety and occasional desperation.

After feeding little Elaine and enjoying quality time with her, Anna beamed. Little Elaine was her best creation… her own flesh and blood. The baby Gino left her for another, Rose… Anna wondered how Gino would feel seeing her now, with her daughter.

But Gino was closer than Anna expected.

The 1960s were a new era of fashion, hairdos, politics… it was a decade of freedom and power... it added a huge explosion at the time to everyone who rebelled and wanted a better time, a better life and everything that money could buy and to be accomplished.

Equal payments for the minority of women. Women now attended universities, colleges... with majordomos, cooks, maids... an agency to protect their interests. But more audaciously, now not only did England have a woman sitting on the British throne... but the screams were of having a more ladylike woman in the Prime Ministerial Office. But that was in Britain. That wish would come at a later stage, many moons and moons after… another new decade yet to be formed in the seventies in the shape and form of Thatcher, who was to be Prime Minister from 1979 to 1990. Australia still lagged behind until the eighties, with Joan Kirner officially becoming the first Premier belonging to the Labour Party.

But, whilst the economy was going up and down, the census was that the scandals continued to pile on... if it was not Britain, it would be the USA or, per se, here in Australia.

In the glowing charts of the USA, a very young and handsome man was completely elevated and elected to the prime position of the **Commander-in-Chief of the United States of America**. He was young, charming, debonair and spoke with an interesting Irish accent. With him was his charming wife, the beautiful, effervescent and effectively modern First Lady.

Both of them made a very and highly prominent duo... where the state and the fame were grandeur and the 60s epitome of what an American family was and portents of what an American family was to be. His name was none other than President John Fitzgerald Kennedy and his much more modern and beautiful wife Jacqueline, who was a trendy fashion lady.

For the moment, her dark good looks and eccentric fashion module catapulted her into the iconic First Lady of the USA. The new White House family was beautiful, private and a glittering promenade of fashion, dramas and also minor scandals.

In the United Kingdom, HRH Princess Margaret Rose got married.

The intensity of the 60s sparkled throughout Australia.

New bands were created, and by then Australia was easing on and allowing more Europeans and Asians to take refuge in Aus.

Now slowly… things were changing.

Now the pound was no longer in existence... in its place was the **Australian dollar**.

The gastronomy was relaxing. The food was becoming a pleasant alternative... all was coming into a good time. THE SIXTIES... were on.

...and after so much of the hard lines by the 50s... now most the era and the time was more relaxed... Women's power was now riding high.

Now, ladies were showing their strength, vitality and independence, now working full time for the government and business plus industrial places... freedom without the need of their husbands' signatures to travel.

"The times... they are a-changing," so sang our own Bob Dylan, who would go on singing *"Mr Tambourine"* about drugs... we were evolving... we were developing, and young Anna was the one who also enjoyed taking these little trips.

Young Anna Bligh. Little Lizzie. aSHpARk of broken dreams.

Around the world, wars of independence in the Portuguese colonies in Africa were now preparing to fight a cold war of independence. The French abandoned Vietnam, but now that the 60s started, it would collate with an old war, the continuation of Vietnam, whose name causes shivers down anyone's spine... VIETNAM. One name... many lives... many deceptions... many, many things that would go down as wastage... a war that simply did not make any sense at all. Now the American army was going into it. Australia was also joining in.

But that would not affect Anna Bligh in her way of thinking, behaving, or socialising... she was now a famous celebrity in her own right… winning many awards and was by now the top novelist, infusing in it the incomplete and broken shards of yesterday, complementing it and extending it. Her novels were all about fundamentalism, broken hearts… with the same reluctance of what then she went through… one recognises her semblance in writing without even knowing who wrote it in the first place. That would be highly indicative of what's-his-name, Sir Bennett… Dicko, thank you very much… he was enthused in reading Anna's flowering sexual innuendos, revealing how much society could be a sick place to live… but nothing about her own "brother," the "fag" as he Bennett boy called him, and also that Foxy guy…

Many tears will fall... so the song would go by… and how true this was... as Dean Martin drummed on suavely... he was well known for being really a gentle, suave, debonair crooner.

Being a famous writer, her books were now the incentive stories and drama featured in

All the radios and their programmes, in doing so she had won a great many competitions... she was now the Queen of Romance. In the Australian fictional lives, with that in mind, Anna attended official interviews talking about her trendy fashion galore and her own cynical quotes, her favourite food, family life. Her new hairdos… the brand of her cosmetics and perfumes… she was featured in posters with her beautiful face and those dark eyes staring bluntly out of the books and magazines.

As far as writers went, all of them, at one time or another, would suffer from the same malady… the present condition of what we all call "the writer's block," as I mentioned above.

Right now… the lifestyle she was used to, the opulence, the grandiose style, eventually grew in status, where Anna now completely changed and modified her own likes and dislikes… it was a new factor in her modus operandi for what she presently became… appreciating whatever there was in her own domain… her domain… she was still a Bligh no matter what.

Anna's make-up was heavier, with added fake eyelashes and the heavy slash of black eyeliner, Cleopatra's style… heavy on the eyes, but the cheeks and lips were painted pale pearly pink lipstick. The fifties hair was gone, now they were much more of a beehive, 60s style. The dresses went from the full "Rock Around the Clock" swirling skirts, now to a much straighter, shorter style, and instead of high heels she wore flat boots. Other times she teamed short tops with pants with crisscrossed laces. The colours were bright, orangey, happy, psychedelic style... modern, no-nonsense... with heavy trinkets adorning both ears, and thick amulets with the double V, begging for peace, hanging from her chest. Chunky jewellery was worn around her wrists and fingers. Overall, Anna was heavier. She had put on a few kilos. Drinking, smoking, and swearing like the European farmer's wife, she by now realised she would not or ever be that... no matter how much she did love her Gino. Anna Bligh had come a long way.

The sad days of her marriage and her broken heart were replaced by longing for what could have been. Anna was so guilty and so unconscious of what she was doing and thinking... her ideas ranged from: "if I did this, or that... if I told Gino the truth... if I was far more honest, frank and open... if I sought treatment..." with all of these "suggestions of her guilt, lack of confidence... a desperate attempt to actually find the reason for something that has never happened and, if so, would only be happening in her own mind..." Yet it did not solve any of her problems. Gino was gone. Period. Anna now was like her grandmother... bitter... sharply cynical... disappointed... a recluse... but more to it... she had become highly impossible and temperamental... irritable... debatable... sometimes highly irritating to those concerned.

From one little young girl to a beautiful young teenager, and now young Anna, she had transgressed from the rural farm wife to a newly elected, famous, and successful novelist. Fame came at a cost... she preferred to be alone and solo... her days of hopping in and out of different beds had ceased... she found tranquillity and peace a better medicine in the throes of the **CAMELOT KINGDOM'S** natural raw beauty and paradise. Here, in the absence of her older brother James, her mother Caro and Dad Jack who were overseas, and her grandmother's comings and goings... of course, the fact that she would always be visited by her "beau" Henry Fox, along with his partner, the also dashing and handsome Harry Poulson, were plusses. She, for once, now reaching a certain age, her own age, enjoyed their company and **AshPark of broken dreams.**

But still… Anna could not stop thinking about the possibilities of her being happy and married to her now defunct husband, Gino… she would ask where and what Gino would be doing now.

Anna couldn't help feeling, at one moment thinking back, that she was deliriously happy, supposedly married to a DAEGO; the next… bitterly disappointed… divorced. Pinning and still heartbroken for her Gino… now far and distant, whereabouts unknown.

Gino and Rose disappeared into the air. The Blighs had no more patience for Gino, nor did the Polettis for the Blighs. But Papa and Mama Poletti were still reeling from it all. They were living a real nightmare… the fear of what the powerful Blighs could do to them, the mere refugees… but their fear would be even greater if they had known or could actually predict the stauncher stance that Gino and Rosa would take in their attacks on the Blighs. Mama Poletti saw herself as the person who should have stopped this madness… Now they had nothing. They were back to square one, with nothing to prove or show for.

Watching and following Anna fulfilling her dreams with success, the Polettis witnessed glimpses of Anna's young daughter Elaine in the more manifest magazines and newspapers. They would stare at one another, both completely speechless. Anna was filthy rich… and even richer now… a complete star… glitzing it up, shining like a diamond… all decked up in the latest fashion, with contracts for her books growing grander, bigger… but she was still a BLIGH… left, right and centre… with her was her young and beautiful Elaine… blonde and cute, still making her mark in the world. Where to next? The Polettis were thoroughly perplexed… completely flabbergasted. Seeking reasoning.

Gino and Rose… were struggling with penury. Their ordeal was such… It seemed that the moment they left Inverness, selling their farm, no improvisation was made… money was gone as quickly as they got it, now fighting to stay above water, counting their losses, with more questions to ask… Gino and Rose were shaking in fear for the answer, especially Rose… who wanted to know who the father was… thinking of herself… if, and if so, could it happen… if little Elaine could be Gino's daughter… Gino now burning with the beginning of his own incensed fire, a thorough hatred for Anna and the Blighs, a deep resentment and now… hatred… nothing more surfaced.

("Many a tears will fall... and it would be falling still.")

Anna's own "inamorato"… the father to her daughter Elaine, yet he kept himself with professional companies, more so with his own "inamorato." If Gino found out that James' boyfriend was the father of the little girl that Anna once told Gino she could never conceive… and a gay man did that? That would be a real blow to Gino… Gino, the all-time macho man, yet Anna could not conceive with him… but…

More anger and irritation built in Gino, with Rose and Bennett reading some of Anna's novels, predominantly featuring fiery sexual and brutal innuendoes, including the hard lovemaking and forbidden love, which made them ever the popular thing to have happened. Luckily for Anna, now, after so much of her own youthful regrets, the bright and colourful swinging 60s changed the ancient ways of people thinking… as they clambered to buy her books, where literally the sexual revolution was exploding. Apparently, Anna's books, the filler of the decadent SIXTIES sexual time, came at the right time and in the right place… the timing was highly precious and of supreme essence. The 60s couldn't have come at a better time. Now, our Anna Bligh, the ebullient and fundamentalist radical, was not only the pride and joy of AUS society… she was the darling buds of May, with her popularity going from strength to strength… and the good thing was her books had no censorship. But… Gino was hardly amused. Even her own grandmamma was not… but that comes later.

The petite social et belle papillon outgrew herself, and she was now the hot property in the social status of Australia, wildly setting tongues a-wagging, with a huge bonfire being bombed into the fire where her love life, or lack of it, was concerned. It was Anna's formidable BLIGH'S style… **ALL OR BUST**… and this was the young lady who championed her causes and defied her own indomitable grand-mère Elizabeth

Bligh… how much would anyone find out how much both of them were so much alike? It was unfathomable… both were the extensions of each other… of course… same blood, same roots… and now same fate.

Anna's love life, what one terms the "road to perdition", was hell on earth, setting the stage on fire… as cynical as it could be, maybe in the words of her grand-mère… steamed and vacuus. If anything goes by, one questions if life was imitating art or the other way around. One gets a bit confused here, there, everywhere… but one also knows that with a more mature, beautiful Anna, nothing could be confirmed. For and with this reluctant fundamentalist, there were no lastings of forever or remaining forever. Testimony of Gino's betrayal. But her days of being a beautiful social butterfly were coming to an end. Somehow, her wings were being clipped, and like it or not… someone was now replacing her, and her years were beginning to show on her beautiful features. Anna lived hard and, of course, played hard… drank hard and chain-smoked. It was not surprising to see her seated in any place, dressed up to the nines, with her coiffure in the viper's shape, smoking endlessly, and her wine glass being filled and refilled. If not with the rarest of champagne, then by the hard liquor…the golden one… they replaced Anna's main meals. It felt so liberating… and it also softened the edges of her forever unconditional pain. After all, it was the sixties… any excuse to be what one wanted, relieving her from her soulful pain, which was still alive, devouring her soul, consuming her.

The sixties were the sole incentive of the **SEXUAL REVOLUTION**, with the "Day Tripper," sung by the Beatles, with drugs being an exponent. Enjoyed. Anna Bligh was going through her own evolution, with no control over how things would turn out… Anna Bligh, trying but throwing convention and tradition to the wind, was after all a woman **with flesh and blood**… she was striving for love, either sweet or all decadent love. One noticed that her promiscuous affairs were only a cover-up for the replacement of her downfall, disappointments, regrets, and her own guilt. She was starving for so much love, understanding and attention… unlike the champions and heroes of her novels… with her often moodiness, a composition of sex, her own delusions of what could have been. Poor Anna, so cheated out of her own beneficial love.

They were hard, exhausting years, fighting off everything and then fighting back for everything… they were hard lines, now etched visibly in her once beautiful face. Her blonde tresses were now greyish around her temples. Reinventing herself with new beehives with constraint, followed by trips to the hairdresser, beauty salons, to the modiste for the new fashions, the shoes… whatever kept her busy and going. Currently, her hair was growing long and straight. She wanted the vampish look, with the peak in the middle of her face, the hair straight down her shoulders. Then there was always… Elaine. The major reason for her own living.

Elaine was born through her own upbringing with hardships, cruelty, and the bad motivational factors… an innocent baby caught up in the midst of all the storms through, and thorough, raging… raging… and raging… the storms from everywhere… personally, climatically, and in the family… that brought in Anna, the Blighs' blood… staunched, firm and detached. But Anna was happy. She probably had everything. Her dreams were all accomplished… being a mother, which made her more approachable and understanding. Two dreams… being a writer, Anna was still living under her own shadows, albeit sour, bitter… regrets… all smoke and mirrors… living in her own fantasy world is not an easy deed. The thought could be fed, with Anna Bligh going down the steps into deep depression mode… it was plausible… the thought being fed, but lucky for all of us, the thought never crossed her.

Over the years, time was not going to ease up on her, neither would the past with Gino be forgotten. The good thing was that she was always supported by her own family through thick and thin, with the help of a very honest man who also helped her by caring for and taking good care of her daughter… or, to this effect, their own daughter. However, Anna could not and would not give up her own reluctance in being the fundamentalist. Somewhere along the line, it still was that love conquered everything, and this was again her dream, a most disastrous one… but virtually her own hopes, wishes, rêves (dreams).

Let's define what a reluctant fundamentalist is… it is when one is unwilling to really concede or submit to one's rules and regulations and shows oneself to follow suit in other ways… their ways. In this, Anna Bligh did, going against her grandmother's wishes when she married Gino.

Being a fundamentalist triggers the effect, to my understanding, that Anna Bligh, who was a writer, believed in the basis of all things that could happen, and even more, being what she wanted and being in love with her Gino. But being reluctant meant that she was not willing to give up her rêve and become just a farmer's wife. (Rêve means dream.)

These were her choices… Anna could live the life of a farmer's wife and be happy with Gino, maybe have a few kids with him, running the farm happily and forever, which was not her fate. But that was just that. A plain farmer's wife. Cooking, washing and looking after the husband and the kids. Thoroughly depending on Gino's money, and Gino's love and support… tendering and caring to Gino's more wanted things. Even then she would never have been happy, as Anna's heart was set up to be a writer, and in doing so, she went and became one. Through fire, hell, and damnation. These were her own choices. One or the other, and for that, she would have to live it through, sorely and painfully, as she explained to her mother Caro.

Being this, the excuse that Gino left everything connected with the Blighs, as he told James, "he married a Bligh and with everything that came with it…" minus his own child… but Gino omitted the fact that Anna did fall pregnant with his child, but it was miscarried… either this, or he fails to remember it. But there was another… "You've lied to me…?" I still see his ashen face… and his sour words rippling and tearing beautiful Anna to shreds… "Tell them to leave now… I don't want them in my house." No one could ever have done something like that to a Bligh… and Gino Polletti did it. Was it guts or did he have enough? Now the true character shines through… he could be so cruel.

One wonders why Anna, being who she was and what she was, did not in the beginning try and see why she could not have any kids… One miscarriage in the mainstream would not have stopped her or anyone from falling pregnant. However, it was meant to be, part of it, no kosher… no way… but it is the major reason for Gino and Anna to go their separate ways. But Gino had a motive… and Anna, so inamorata, saw the motive. Too late for both of them. There was hardship… there was resentment… there were misconceptions… at the end, there was nothing…

It was her fate… the choice was hers… not Gino's… and the marriage was doomed right from the start. Gino would never have relented… he made good fun of the Blighs… but he thought otherwise.

Gino now had a new life with Rose, and Rose gave him what he wanted, and even more…

A new beginning with fame and fortune, being blessed with a daughter. Yet typical of ANNA BLIGH and where all of the BLIGHs were applicable, Anna was still failing to see the benefits and riches, along with her dreams that were fulfilling, about and without Gino. If he ever returned, it would really be her undoing, to the regret of both of them.

Loving Gino and being cruelly rejected by him, Anna still thought of what could have been and what would have been… she would have never understood this side of the equation, only her love for the Italian handsome man, which she was missing so much… but the question now was: did Gino actually miss Anna? And this is the question… did Gino ever love Anna? He remembered her alright, but for all the different reasons, mainly the wrong ones.

The world changed, and everyone changed with it. Ones emancipated… others got older… the new genre and the new generation was being created and now existed. Others expired… life went on… and then passed. Some others enjoyed the new 60s… the extravagance… the new freedom… everything. It was a new decade… things had to change and were forever changing.

As her grandmother, the indomitable grand Elizabeth Bligh, stated: she was tired and exhausted with so many changes. The 60s were a new kettle of fish, and as for Anna's novels… they were pure and simple… "steamy and vacuous."

Now the Beatles rocked, the Ventures, the Shadows. A new singer was emerging, the new rock and roller to replace the more famous Elvis

Presley… his name was Cliff Richard, and the influx of British rockers was now a new novelty, as they took off and controlled the world. Australia followed suit… we had our own bands and singers.

If Elvis, draped in a leather jacket, blue jeans, and a white t-shirt, with his duck-tail and side-lobster smile, gyrating hips, was scandalous, the Beatles' new hairdos, suits, and shoes were detrimentally another fashion to be accounted for… which, for the ancient and the elderly, was another shocker.

With all of that, we still had Sir Robert Menzies as our long-serving Prime Minister, and in 1966 Harold Holt succeeded Menzies as Australia's Prime Minister… and our boys were conscripted to Vietnam.

Along with it came the war of independence in the African countries, the Profumo scandals, and Elizabeth, Queen of Britain, giving birth to another two princes, Andrew and Edward. The first James Bond movie heralded all over the world. It had the best professional and updated versions of guns, gizmos, and even far more sophisticated things to carry with oneself, including girls… and it all heralded in the Portuguese beaches of Estoril.

James Bond was inspired by British espionage… and the novels written by one alone who was also a spy working for the British Government… his name was none other than Ian Fleming. His novels that became movies were a real success all over the world, including Macau, the tiny peninsula in South East Asia that was prominent Portuguese, where there was a small stint in the Macau Palace Casino, filmed then in 1974/75 under the name *The Man with the Golden Gun.*

However, on this note, James Bond heralded in Portugal's sunny, sandy beachside of fabulous Estoril, based on the rich playboy who owned casinos, hotels, and businesses. Therefore, as one of the producers was reading *The Man with the Golden Gun*, the idea of creating James Bond came right on, based on the gentleman's character.

The famous Australian band The Seekers was also promoting Australia with their lively, fancy, but beautiful songs. Along came authors, writers, and singers that lent their names to this 60s world.

The fashion was totally different from the 50s… the skirts got shorter, the make-up heavier, the lips paler, and the hair worn as a beehive with so much hairspray that not even the strongest typhoon could blow it.

Most ladies wore long boots with their multicoloured mini dresses, and the world was never going to be the same when the Vietnam War started, after the Geneva Convention divided North Vietnam from South Vietnam, and the French left Indochina for good. The sixties would bring many changes, many revolutions, many deaths, scandals, dramas, and so much political uncertainty and horrible exposures. Meanwhile, Portugal fought on three theatres of African wars.

It was a powerful revolution… one sexual revolution, as in the East, the Rose of Vietnam gave birth to… so many people were infected with venereal disease, and the spreading of it all.

The sixties were also called the SATANICAL years. Cults were created and imbued with their senses of belonging, which amounted to a killing spree, as in the Manson cult.

(The Swinging Sixties and Anna Bligh.)

The decade would trigger assassinations… with John and Bob Kennedy, not to mention King, as in Martin Luther King, along with Che Guevara… not only Cher was betrayed but assassinated, and his hands cut off.

In Australia, the disappearance of our Prime Minister Harold Holt would remain a cold case and a real mystery, still being talked about.

In the Asian countries now, with the death of Shan Kai Shiek, Chairman Mao Tse Tung led one cultural revolution after another, with attacks in Hong Kong and Macau. December 1966 was obvious and evident for all to see, as the Vietnam War raged.

The Communist Cultural Revolution spread worldwide, particularly in Hong Kong, where strikes and revolutions were happening almost every day. But it was deadly, an inferno in Vietnam, and the same could be said in the three theatres of the Portuguese Colonial War. where rumours of an independence rebellion began in 1959, escalating in 1961 with the death of a Portuguese farmer's wife in March of that year.

Australia was also involved in the Vietnam War, but that was the last thing on Anna Bligh's mind.

These days, Anna fought to find mental peace and the calming waters, residing in her own Camelot's Kingdom. She felt protected after the sexual attack from Sir Richard Bennett. Anna reasoned that she was too fragile to live alone, to be destitute, especially after the early frazzling stages with Dr Henry Fox, who again referred to her for "not being able" to fall pregnant, a bitter issue exacerbated by her outspoken nature, which had caused her more trouble. Now, both she and Dr Fox felt a sense of wellbeing returning to their roots. For once, she knew how she was loved, spoiled, and appreciated, even by her present "inamorato," Dr Henry Fox, who was over the moon at the news that he was the father of little Elaine.

Food, coffee, and tea were always served at her summons. Alcoholic drinks, wine, liquors, champagne, spirits, were plentiful. Maids were at her beck and call, and she had full use of the mansion. She could also ride her new purebred horse at ease, teaching her own daughter to ride as well. Right now, the little princess was asleep, and her darling was already growing bigger and cuter, calling Anna "mama," smiling, gurgling, glowing. She walked and talked; Elaine was a joy to be with, to hold, the best thing that could have happened to Anna. Being a mother ultimately. Anna would melt thoroughly, thanking God for all the pain and hard work she endured to have Elaine. Hugs and kisses flowed freely, with outbursts of tears of sheer happiness.

George, Sara, and little David were absent. Sara had been sent back by the Australian authorities, charged for her illegitimate entry into Australia, along with charges for officially marrying George, who faced bigamy charges with more still to come. His previous wife, Regina Bligh, might have been dead, but her shadow still prevailed. Regina Bligh was exacting thorough revenge on the Blighs, though they remained married.

Roy Briggs was in charge of their Camelot's Kingdom, overseeing matters that were not always going as intended. Unusual happenings were the norm, and though he was getting older, he was wiser. Now, he supervised the whole of Camelot's Kingdom, a place he had come to love and, against all odds, would fight for everything so dear to him. He had done it once, he would do it all over again if necessary.

It was July, and the winter days were gloomy, long, and bitterly cold. For Anna, it was a most depressing time; it was always raining, always dark and grey, and always cold.

The sun was absent, and the days grew darker with rain, wind, and hail.

Anna sat at her desk, typing away. She would type and type, and each time she looked out the window, the day perpetually turned darker. By midday, before lunch, the whole of Camelot's Kingdom was grey and black. The rain continued slowly, drizzling, the sound welcoming and relaxing. Nothing was better than the sound of the rain with the windows open; Anna was blissful with the raw smell of the earth assailing her nostrils.

Damn, the blockage was severe. She went on and off her writing, having lunch and dinner in between, but she also spent quality time with Elaine, supervising her bath. Now, having finished her own bath, she tucked Elaine safely into her bed, peacefully sleeping with her beautiful eyes shut, long thick lashes fanned. It was her daily bedtime. Outside, the day grew darker and stormier, the wind stronger.

The light rain tapped suavely on the window panes. One of the maids lit the fire, it was cold. The gentle singing of the rain grew heavier, stress-free, combining beautifully with the sounds around her. It relaxed her tense mind as she drank liquor and smoked. Once the drink was finished, she poured more into her glass. She ate a light supper in her office, dressed in her nightie.

The food was dry and tasteless. Lately, her diet had suffered setbacks; nothing seemed to agree with her. She would visit her father, but he was serving a life sentence.

She poured another drink and dreamily watched the rain change to hail, punishing the grounds at Camelot. Her endless supply of cigarettes went on and on, the butts piling in the ashtray, a testimony to her determined focus on daily journeys and flights of fancy. The radio warned Inverness City of an approaching wild storm, which Anna could see growing strong and hard. What began as light rain and soft winds now intensified.

Now hail pounded Camelot, hammering the roof of the sturdy mansion. It was still early afternoon, but darkness enveloped the entire mansion and its extensive grounds. The wind grew stronger, and the first sounds of thunder were heard. Anna jumped and went to Elaine's bedroom as lightning flashed. The rain and wind became ferocious. The strong foundations of the tall, stalwart building shook; hail stripped the walls. Lightning flickered on and off, as if someone was playing with switches. Thunder roared audaciously, horrifyingly.

Within Camelot, employees gathered the animals into shelter to prevent them from being frightened by the lightning and the tremendous sound of thunder. Mother Nature unleashed her powers terribly, and all the lightning in Camelot's Kingdom ceased. There was no electricity.

LITTLE LIZZIE.

The horses were whining inside the stables, and the employees were now in a state of panic. It was going to be a long, hard day, but the promise of a stable and a fitful evening and night would be hard to comply with. Everyone knew the signs that were coming.

The darkness now cast shadows all over the immense, wide mansion. The wind, along with the heavy rain, badgered the magnificent building that was the mansion. Thank goodness Elaine was fast asleep in her own *la petite princesse* chambre… (in her own little princess room).

Anna went to play some records. Maybe the happy-go-lucky voice of Doris Day singing *Que Sera, Sera* would liven up the whole place and make the atmosphere lighter and playful.

Anna Bligh. Little Lizzie. Camelot's Kingdom of broken dreams.

Little Lizzie.

It did the trick. Now Anna was dying to do something fruitful and to keep herself occupied.

She remembered that for some time she had wanted to go up to the attic and see if she could find something to write about. Her mind was totally blank. She couldn't concentrate, and there was nothing compiling inside her beautiful head. Anything… she was so idle that she was really bored to tears. Maybe the attic would be the correct place for her and Elaine to stay for a while. Sometimes Elaine's crying in the middle of the night would wake up the others, so the attic would be a welcome relief until Elaine grew up. Elaine's bedroom would still be on the ground floor until further changes.

The lively singing of Doris Day continued to serenade the whole house. The cooks and maids again turned up to see what was happening, and again they were left disappointed. The young mistress was not coming home for a long time. Maybe after the terrible ordeal of the mother and daughter fighting like hell for the last time, the fight between them was never resolved. Worst still, the young mistress packed her bags and left. No one knew where she went. The household employees, mainly the maids and cooks, knew of the harsh and cruel ways Grand Elizabeth Bligh, the Camelot Kingdom's matriarch, imposed on the youngest Bligh, but they'd failed to do anything for fear of losing their placement and jobs. Nowadays, jobs and work were hard to find, and they sorely missed the goodwill, youth, and harmless attitude of the young mistress. It seemed that whatever Grand Elizabeth Bligh touched… something bad happened.

Right then, a tremendous thunder echoed around the whole house, deafening Doris Day's voice. Anna could only hope that Elaine didn't wake up. She stood still to listen, but no… so she leapt up the stairs two at a time. Once there, she tried to push the door open. It had been some time since the attic had been tended to, and Anna was so right.

The door opened slowly and eerily creaked. It was cold and frightening, but what would one have expected? There was a cold draft, freezing even. She tried to compose herself. She was not going to be afraid. Anna was dying to get into the room.

The room was pitch dark, stenchy and mouldy. It had to be. She could only distinguish white sheets all over the place, covering the furniture, toppling others. The place was messy. And oh… there was a huge green velvet heavy curtain or drapery covering the left side of the wall. No wonder it was so dark and smelly. From where she stood in the middle of the door, she could see through the dim light coming from the two dirty, stained windows on her right side.

Little Lizzie. Camelot's Kingdom broken dreams.

She tried to switch on the light. Finally, the light was on. It was so weak that once lit, it made the place a wee lighter, but it was still dark and dank. Now she could touch the white sheets covering the furniture and the dust covering the white sheets. Whoever and whatever used to be there, it was clear to Anna that once "someone" lived in this room. Her belongings were still there, a testimony of what it used to be.

Anna could distinguish the closets, the dressing table, a desk, trinkets that were expensive. Now, uncovering one white blanket at a time, she realised the place was huge, doubling in dimension, and at the moment very uninviting. But Anna was curious, and her curiosity got the better of her. She sneezed countless times. It might have been damp, left at its own expense. The stale air, along with the dust everywhere, affected her. There were other oddities too. As she walked through it all, she kept tripping, bumping over here and there. The dim light was still not strong enough for her to make heads or tails of it. Her first idea was to open all the windows so fresh air could come into the room, but the windows wouldn't budge.

The room reeked of everything. The dust overtook the whole wide room, and one could see the remains of them all. She looked up at the ceilings, they were covered with spider webs, hanging from their heights. Others were stretched from one wall to the other. The dirt and dust piled high and terribly. The floors were covered with so many things scattered across them. The walls were yellowish and stained. It was a lost cause.

Anna's sneezing was terrible. She now felt the ordeal keenly. Curious and stubborn, Anna continued on her journey of discovery. One by one she removed the white blankets, throwing them onto the floor. From underneath, beautiful antiques of porcelain décor belonging to decades of old tradition and furniture still painted gold from Queen Anne's time were revealed, as she slowly and carefully removed the extra white sheets.

How romantic. Queen Anne's furniture. Whomever owned this room was a romantic at heart, and everything suggested that the person had great taste. The white wardrobe still held dresses and shoes. The dressing table was dainty and delicate, with a beautiful box that, when opened, made a little ballerina dance while a song played. She thought it sounded like the Blue Danube.

The desk had horse pictures and trophies, awards from horse racing competitions. Anna felt good and loved every single moment of her discoveries. It was a BLIGH'S TREASURE TROVE. She coughed and sneezed again, her eyes welling with tears. The dust created a thin fog, and Anna fought to clear her sight. She loved the full scenery and was enjoying it. Wow… what a streamer, she thought. This was really something. Some people found treasure troves in the deep oceans. She was lucky enough to find them here, the awards for the best equestrian: Elizabeth Bligh. Her own grandmother, or so she thought… then she saw something written on the desk.

Something was written on the desk: *Little Lizzie*. Her grandmother's nickname, by Douglas Goddard, was just plain Lizzie… Little Lizzie. Remembering that her grandmother's time was in the early twenties, she might have been born in the nineteenth century. Now she was so curious that nothing would deter Anna from continuing her marvelous adventure of new discoveries. She already wanted to keep the ancient trinquetes and delicate porcelains. The more she observed the little ballerina dancing before her eyes, the more determined she became to continue.

Outside, the darkness grew heavier, enveloping the whole of Camelot's farcical KINGDOM. Its towers of strength and the beacon light of the Blighs were pelted heavily by torrential rain. Anna was afraid that the hails were so fierce they could break the windows. The building shook.

The horses kept whining, and it was now a madhouse as the employees rushed to and fro. The storm had triggered panic.

The thunder was heard constantly, louder each time, terribly strong and noisy. Lightning struck, cutting the air with razor-sharp flashes. It was mayhem and chaos at every turn. Much to Anna's chagrin, the lights went out. She had nothing to survey as darkness took over, and the storm outside was not helping. What was she to do? She was not going to leave this "world." She decided that if she drew the curtains from the other, now right, side of the room, it might make it brighter. Anna continuously strove, tripping to reach and pull the cord to separate the heavy velvet curtain. It was heavy and covered in dust, but Anna would not budge.

Especially now that she was in the attic, she felt at peace. She loved it. A faint smell of perfume emanated through the heavy, stenchy air. She grabbed the long cord of the curtain.

She pulled and pulled at the cord, cursing how hard it was. Tripping over here and there, bumping along, crying foul and in pain, she tried every other way. She decided to pull the cord at the other end. No way, the cord remained stubborn. But Anna was not going to give up. She was not going to leave the attic without discovering more treasures. Now, even more so, with Elaine asleep, Anna thought it was now or never. Elaine would be awake with all this terrible noise. Anna had very little time to continue; it had to be now.

It was now. With one strong, stiff pull, using all her strength with both hands, she struck it rich. Finally, the cord broke. At the same time, the green velvet drapery fell to the ground.

What it revealed made her stifle a cry. She stood there for a long time, still sneezing. Each time she sneezed, she could not believe what she was seeing. She was totally speechless, completely lost. She didn't even know what else to say or do. For a moment, time stood still. Outside, the storm raged violently, but inside, everything was unmovable, steady, and still. Fingers of coldness enveloped Anna.

In front of her… she confronted a huge, well-decorated, vivid painting she had never seen before. She had never come across anything like it.

It revealed a breathtaking, vivid painting, done exquisitely by a professional painter. It featured all her glory and beauty: a young, innocent but beautiful little girl. At that moment, she was brought back to reality as heavy thunder shook the sturdy foundations of the edifice. The storm battered Inverness mercilessly.

The wind whistled uncontrollably, and the rain belted heavily on the window panes. Lightning cut through the air. In some parts of Inverness, it would have started fires, but the strong rain easily subsided them. Each time lightning struck, the thunder grew louder and stronger.

Even though Anna was distracted by nature's force, she did not turn away from what was in front of her.

The little girl was extraordinarily beautiful. She sat with her dog on the fabulous velvet green lawn of Camelot. A long-haired black collie kept her company, with extraordinary long mahogany locks tumbling in huge waves of curls, staring with slanted green eyes straight into Anna's dark brown eyes. The face was fragile and elongated, with high cheekbones adding to her exotic look. She had a generous mouth, a perfect nose, and porcelain-like skin, soft and silky, peachy under the strong sun.

The sun shone brightly behind her. The sky was a startlingly clear blue. The painter captured the essence of the time, the penetrating beauty, and the surreal mingling of colours with the splendid surroundings of Ash Park, Camelot's Kingdom. Now, more than ever, Anna could appreciate the magic of this marvelous kingdom. Behind the girl stood tall and mighty the Camelot's Kingdom magical palace, the famous and popular beacon of light that had become the Bligh dynasty's trademark.

The young girl was ethereal in looks, belonging to a far time… long distance… a fairy magical place. She wore a beautiful mandarin high-necked red dress, and as one of her hands held the dog, Anna noted the watch and a fine gold bracelet. But more to it… she looked so calming and accommodating. Comfortable even.

For a long time, time and space were lost to Anna. Everything stopped, and momentarily Anna seemed uncannily enveloped in that magical kingdom of a bygone era. Never in her life had she seen something so vivid and elaborate, the smell of the green velvety lawns, the perfumed roses so lovingly tended by her *grand mère*. One could hear the buzzing, happy sounds of summer, insects flying about that they all missed. She could feel the sun's strong rays heating and permeating her body, giving her energy, while admiring the lively, vivid, and colourful scenery. The ethereal-looking little girl was strikingly beautiful. Anna had never seen her before. But she was a BLIGH, definitely. She reminded Anna of her grandmother, Elizabeth Bligh, though it was either too dark or there was nothing to imply the young lady's identity. Could this be young Elizabeth in the prime of her life? But no, her grandmother didn't have green eyes, blue more likely. On the desk bore the stamped name: Elizabeth Little Lizzie Bligh. LITTLE LIZZIE. Unheard of.

The more she stared, completely taken aback, speechless and dumbfounded, the more the little girl's slanted green eyes seemed to beckon Anna into her world, into the painting, inviting her to enjoy the day, the time, and everything connected to it. Anna's senses were working overtime. Her mind raced, her heart kept pounding. Yet no words came out of her mouth. Time and space stood still. Seconds ticked by. Anna had no idea how long she stood there in front of the painting, mouth gaping, staring at the vivid, invitingly surreal painting.

Anna was brought back to reality when a huge thunderclap shook the whole foundation of Camelot's majestic edifice for the second time. She heard Elaine's faint crying. Anna shook her head as if to balance her mind. Time ticked by, the painting seemed to tell her not to go, for they had plenty to talk about. Now it was raining terribly, pounding the windows with full strength. The wind howled, and lightning struck, creating havoc and electrifying parts of Inverness. Anna was jolted into the present. Hearing Elaine's now hard crying, Anna ran down from the attic into Elaine's bedroom.

Being with Elaine was one of the maids tending the little one. Anna thanked the maid as she held her daughter in her arms, reassuring her there was nothing to be afraid of, soothing her, kissing and rocking her. Elaine needed her afternoon feed and her daily bath. Later, after bathing and feeding Elaine and happily playing with her, Anna, after her own supper, would review again what she had seen earlier. Anna's mind kept wandering to the attic, firmly entranced, captivated by the extraordinary piece of art. Nothing would stop Anna; she would need to return to the attic to explore what she had seen. Strangely, no one had ever spoken about the lady in the painting. But at this moment, Elaine came first.

Power failed as the storm raged on.

Now more than ever it was cold, even colder with the dropping temperature, and the manor completely without power. Outside, rain lashed, causing floods. Lightning struck continually, devastatingly, causing damage, with some people taken to hospital suffering electrocution. The wind whistled wildly, sending shivers down one's spine, followed by the huge sound of thunder. The storm was not easing; if anything, it was intensifying.

Heavy floods covered the area; the lake burst and dams overflowed.

It would take a long time for everything to return to normal. As the maids heated water and milk, a very happy Elaine was ensconced in the warmth and love of her mother. Anna held Elaine, walking her through the manor, soothing her with love and tenderness. Elaine smiled, her baby talk sweet and tender. Anna was thrilled to pieces having her daughter with her. Elaine was her everything. Anna wanted someone to love badly, and Elaine was that love.

She had her own supper late at night, drank, and kept an eye on her daughter beside her. After the relaxing sleep, little Elaine wanted to stay awake and play with her mother, which Anna enjoyed, keeping an eye on the terrible storm outside. Chaos exploded outside; inside, the maids prepared to evacuate. Things were getting bad.

Anna's mind was on the painting and the remarkable estate they resided in. She realised how beautiful and magical Camelot's Kingdom could be, but the storm dictated otherwise.

She also prepared bags in case evacuation was needed. Water had flooded the kitchen, and the maids and cooks had to find another place to cook, but they too were afraid and preparing to evacuate.

Camelot's Kingdom was now alone, except for Roy, who ran around keeping everything in check. Jack was absent, and Caro was in the Inverness hospital.

At times like these, accidents could happen; others could be struck by lightning, causing havoc.

Briggs was doing his best for Camelot, restoring power and ensuring all was well at the stables and with the employees. Many had gone home to care for their families; others stayed overtime. When raging storms hit Inverness, all hell broke loose.

No one was around, not even Elizabeth Bligh, the Camelot matriarch. She was at her late husband's home.

After a few hours with Elaine, Anna thought it was time to retire. Her sneezing had stopped, and she now had some liquor and one last cigarette before calling it a night. Elaine would sleep with Anna in her bedroom; there was no way she would leave her alone.

If Anna could not concentrate during supper, then when night fell, she could not sleep at all. She watched her daughter fall asleep peacefully and beautifully in her arms. It was pure sweetness and innocence. The long lashes, soft baby skin, curly blonde hair, Elaine was her daughter. Anna understood how and why a mother could be so worried.

Elizabeth Bligh, the matriarch, tried to call, but each time she couldn't get in touch with Camelot. She rang the hospital and tried to contact Caro to find out when George would return to Sydney, expressing concern for Anna and Elaine.

"When is George returning home, your brother, Caro?" Elizabeth inquired, drinking her port.

"Mother, things are moving… but not the way we expect," explained Caro.

"George should have checked the fine details before marrying," Caro stated matter-of-factly.

"I never believed in Regina's kindness… she set all of us up," Elizabeth replied irritably.

Caro was more worried about Jack than anything else but continued answering her mother's questions, though a solution seemed far away. Elizabeth could complain endlessly, and nothing would come of it.

Anna made provisions to ensure Elaine was snug, cozy, and warm. She ensured her daughter was safe and comfortable. Anna could be highly indulgent but was never a pushed-over damsel in distress; she was her own mistress.

That night, being so elated and excited about the vivid painting in the attic, Anna had questions: Who was she? Why was she there? And more importantly, why had there never been any mention of the young girl?

Grand Elizabeth, at the end of the other line, was so much into her own problems that she failed to notice how terrible the storm was… and she was not a tidbit suspicious of the goings-on and the discoveries that Anna had. But then again, she was on the other side of town, and Anna was on this side.

On the other hand, at every glance, Anna only saw the painting and everything related to it. If she could, she would go up to the attic all over again. She might need to do a thorough cleaning of the room, but the thought of her sneezing like there was no tomorrow stopped her in her tracks.

Anna started a new chapter in her book. Next to her, her beautiful daughter slept peacefully. But again, as much as Anna tried, nothing could be written extensively. Her written composition remained completely blank. Now Anna was deep into the night. She could hear the clock ticking slowly, and the soft sound when it hit the 12 mark heralded the night's visit. Outside, the night was coal black. Nothing was visible. There was no light. Now Camelot's Kingdom was terrifyingly deep and coal black. One could hear but see nothing, not even shadows… just noises of incoming and outgoing things. The creaking of the rusty big gates was overheard all the time.

Anna could not sleep at all. As she sat up in the darkness of her bedroom, with Elaine sleeping next to her, the storm raged endlessly, violently shaking the whole of Camelot's Palace's sturdy foundation. The wind continuously whistled and blew. The storm was on. It caused nothing but chaos and mayhem, maybe even destruction due to the flooding. Anna and Elaine were well kept safe and sound… for now.

Elaine started to cry again, awakening due to the enormous thunder. Anna comforted and snuggled her little daughter, singing and calming her. Anna started to worry, as the high winds and rain whipped hard against the mansion, and she could hear it cracking. Down in the kitchen, water had already flooded it and was pouring into the house.

Little Elaine hugged her mother and slept smilingly in her warm, cosy, and loving arms. While Elaine slept happily, Anna could not sleep at all. What's more, with Elaine sleeping with her, she couldn't smoke or drink… but drink she did, summoning the maids for her liquor. The maids were busy with many things but brought Anna liquor to keep her warm. Now that Anna wanted, she had some sandwiches to go with her drink. She needed to wait as the kitchen had moved and food was being cooked elsewhere.

The night went on. It was terrible. Doubtful that anyone slept under these horrid circumstances. Giving up on sleep, Anna sat in the darkness, watching the savagery of mother nature's terrible, violent unleashing. It was frightening. All she could see and feel was this terrifying situation, winds blowing, thundering, and the frightening slashes of lightning. Anna went back to the hot, calming time captured in the vivid painting in the attic. She would have loved that day, decades ago, that perfect and beautiful day. Again, the painting beckoned her.

During the raging storm, trees tumbled down, floods were everywhere, some houses crumbled, people were in dire straits. Cars and other objects were submerged. No one was safe. Inverness Hospital was filled to the brink with people seeking refuge and being brought in with injuries. Elizabeth was now utterly worried about Anna and Elaine. The phone could not be reached as it was out of order. Lines were cut off. Nothing worked under the fierce fury of mother nature, lashing terribly, inflicting huge damage. Her fury was felt and heard all over Inverness. It was devastating, heartbreaking, and deflating. It would take time to fix everything.

Anna, who spent the whole night awake, was tired. Sleep evaded her. All she could see was the vivid painting and the young girl's slanted green eyes, smiling and inviting her into the entrancing paradise of that world. She could hear, in her broken sleep, the young girl's soft whisperings, bewitchingly, enchantingly calling her. It was one of the maids.

It was early in the morning. The maids were bringing her brekkie. They took Elaine with them. Finally, Anna succumbed to sleep during the raging storm. It had been a wild, terrifying night. Now it was morning. The rain continued to lash with power. The winds were more subdued, but every now and then thunder still roared, and lightning eased slightly. It was still freezing cold. Some windows had broken from the fierce wind. It was more like a hurricane.

Anna would soon find out who the fine lady in the painting was. But now she wanted to sleep. The maids looked after Elaine, exhausted and tired from the night before. Anna sank into a deep sleep, though she would never be the same again regarding the vivid painting. Sleep brought her nightmares; in her dreams, she was told to pack up and evacuate. Camelot's mansion was crashing down.

Chapter 02:
Doris Collins. "A Fool such as I."

"Indeed, Indeed. Oh Mrs Bligh, do my eyes deceive me..." she loved Elizabeth Bligh.

In Tarot cards, or to this effect in every single deck of cards, the FOOL usually turns up. Its presence could mean an explosion of things that are going to happen, or, to this effect, things or people are coming into your life. It is usually a card that can fulfil many purposes. In any deck of cards, and in Tarot, it is inconceivable not to have the FOOL in them.

The FOOL is very much the prominent card, and he is the Jack of all trades. He waves his magic, the know-how... the popular one, the workaholic, the fun and the entertainer. They boast several faces or outlets in their working and daily life. They are the JOKERS for many people, the CLOWNS. One can either love them or hate them, but one can never ignore them.

They are so popular that, once upon a time, they were the right-hand officials of the more respected Kings, Emperors, Queens, and Empresses around the world, where their mutual work was considered an entitled right, showing how they could best serve high-ranking officials. For some unknown reason, their ways and deeds were often required by most people. In the Royal Court, as mentioned above, the FOOL or the JOKER was usually the closest element to the royals, but on the other hand, the farthest too. More so, should the King, Emperor, Queen, or Empress need to know anything, the FOOL would, of course, be the one summoned to investigate, it was the person for it.

One could either love them. Their **vêtements** were crude and funny. Their shoes were immense and big, their hats a labour of work with feathers hanging from one side to another, and the white painting on their faces, sometimes with a dark star on one eye, gave them a slightly sinister look. The wide, colourful **vêtements** were, for many people, loud and highly extravagant. The Fool was merely for fun, recreation, and entertainment. One had enough of the busybodies, and the Fool, with his usual antics and fun, could easily collect everything. The FOOL was the Jack of all trades, and none at all. But when the FOOL arrived, everyone would sit up and take notice.

One such person was Mrs Doris Collins.

Doris was by far the most loved and also popular in Inverness City. By the same token, some people could not stand her at all.

Doris could be highly judgemental, penetrating, and, of course, a city's living nightmare. As nightmares go, one also knows the answer… she was a busybody. She was always in the thick of everything. She had to poke her nose in, whether she was wanted or not. However, everything had to be the way Doris was meant to know, ignoring the more intimate details. As the grand Elizabeth Bligh once said, "She's a kind dear soul… sometimes highly irritating…" to which her own husband, Douglas Goddard, quipped, "That's my Lizzie." Both women were extensions of one another, one that Doris Collins would never ever imagine crossing paths with. But crossing Doris was just another case. Where would Elizabeth Bligh be without the information that Doris collected, sometimes misjudged, and gave to the grand Elizabeth?

Without the help of Doris Collins, for the lady in her ingénue with the whole idea of always trying to help others, one could imagine how lost Inverness would be.

Doris lived in what we would now call a suburban house in a familiar neighbourhood of Inverness. She ran a boarding house to supplement her own income, taking in girls who were working at Inverness Hospital and living far from home, as transport at the time was hard to come by. Meanwhile, she also protected all of them from nefarious and profane stories that could easily circulate in Inverness.

Doris was a homemaker. She looked after the wellbeing of her two-storey, five-bedroom house, with kitchen and dining area, a huge lounge, bathrooms, laundry, and a beautiful tender garden that she lovingly cared for. She did the cooking, washing, ironing, shopping with the girls, and sometimes driving and introducing newcomers to Inverness Hospital. Doris made things easy, more so for those who resided with her. Life was easier and tailor-made for all of them, yet Doris was incapable of staying away from being a gossip monger.

Doris was a hands-on lady. Helping around the hospital, offering spiritual guidance and love, always spreading goodwill, with her faith in the Bible, she firmly helped read the Bible's verses and psalms, praying with them and taking local trips to the Church, where she would assist in keeping it up to date, bringing flowers, and keeping it tidy and formal. For Doris, nothing was too much. She loved entertaining, helping, catering, and moving forward without hesitation. She could be a force to be reckoned with.

Doris made countless contributions for fetes and fairs, by baking and cooking excellent food and cakes, to sell or share. To be fair, this beautiful lady was also a PERSONA GRATA in Inverness City. But many did not welcome her, as Doris was a real busybody. Some thought that she used her fool such as I persona as a cover to uncover personal secrets, suspecting that her modus operandi was just this. Doris, on the darker side as was known, was overwhelmingly judgemental, with tunnel vision, and often thought of the most obscure and highly ridiculous ways of the malicious that intertwined the good and the bad, her ways of thinking.

Doris also had a lighter side. Her endearing, helpful, and warm character shone through. Being just plain Doris, she was, in many unequivocal ways, harmless, but she had a knack for putting her foot in it when it came to her mouth.

During the Second World War, Australia's men voluntarily served King and Country.

Whilst men enlisted, Doris felt lost and deeply down. She was completely crestfallen with so many things to endure, and her nightmares were only beginning. It took her a long time to recover from the sadness as she watched her beloved man leave the shores. As she began to settle down again with prayers and motivation, she contributed as usual, always alongside her mother, doing the best for Inverness families: providing support, accommodation, food, help, and slowly healing them.

Mother and daughter healed themselves in the process. Every morning, Doris would bake hot bread, with milk, butter, and cheese churned, then cart them to the local market or distribute them to many families. Fine. Mother and daughter pulled their weight together, and Inverness City took notice.

Little Doris did have a nice and moderate family life. For many, a most moderate life. Growing up in Inverness at the time was not easy, but for a simple family of three, it could be plenty and good.

It was a city slowly growing. Time and again, if they were lucky, the Circus would come and entertain them. While the fun and creativity of the Circus attracted many people, one young, cute lady with curly dark hair and beautiful, expressive dark brown eyes thought to herself how hard it would be to perform all that athleticism and fly through the air as most trapeze artists did. But she loved the ice creams, the sweets, and, most of all, the fairy floss.

The circus would come to Inverness during summer and leave in autumn. Doris had other hobbies and places where she and her parents spent summer vacations. The cute, beautiful girl was the only one in the family but was also loved and spoilt in many ways.

She went to a public school. It was no big deal. But Doris was brought up religiously. It was always the Church's way. She was taught the Bible, learned verses by heart, prayed, and quoted psalms and scriptures as was proper. Doris was indeed a faithful, loyal churchgoer. She would never intentionally miss mass on any Sunday. Yet there were many lessons to be learnt, and the odyssey of life continued, vast and strewn with obstacles. Many were the times Doris tripped and stumbled during her long journeys over bridges above raging rivers.

Winter's time, young Doris would be a busy bee, concentrating on her studies at home. But one takes notice that she was far from being a top student. At home, warm and cosy, she'd love the pumpkin soup with hot bread and butter. For the time being, and during the time of what may come, Doris still remembered the nights when people, including herself and her parents, were frantically glued to the radios so they could know what on earth was happening worldwide… as you would know by now, the war was on. However, the critical time had not yet arrived; life was still good when she returned to school the following morning. While young Doris did not excel at her studies, she knew the Bible, the verses, and the psalms according to whatever was befalling the world at that correct moment. But her father continued to work as the Australian Government's public servant, and her mother was collecting vouchers for them to keep abreast of the times. Food was beginning to be scarce, and milk was beginning to become hard to get by and was getting expensive… but all was good at school. The children would still get their supply of milk in public preparatory, primary, and secondary schools.

Young Doris. The Young Debutante

During the autumn season, during Sundays, the atmosphere would expand into a more belligerent family attendance. During Easter, fetes, fairs, and bazaars, depending on where one could call it, the Church they attended would hold all of these diversions so they could collect money from donations and make it into charities. On the other hand, there are times to be appreciative and also to enjoy. During the Second World War, life was at its extremities, harder and difficult, and getting by.

One would find the young, big-eyed, beautiful young Doris in the prime of her increasingly social development. Doris noticed everything around her… it seemed that help was around, and people were helping with everything they could. The ladies would make wool coats, knitted shawls, blankets, woollen gloves, and also hats. The war was going on and promised to continue at full scale. Times were hard, and little Doris was happy that, unlike many unfortunate people, she still enjoyed the benefits of having a roof over her head, warm clean clothes, a warm bed to snuggle in at night, food and water, and the Grace of the Almighty.

Little Doris was growing up. She had problems really grasping things in school, but slowly her mind was developing intelligence. She not only took notice but felt too the pain, sorrow, and suffering that were going around her. Even then, though young Doris was empathetic, the feelings of misery were overwhelming her… still her big dark expressive eyes wondered what, in fact, she was able to actually do or make to help the more unfortunate.

Doris was growing up, by developing slowly. It wasn't long before she became a beautiful young lady. Of course, as a teenager, she had her loves and hobbies… but being popular was still a stigma inflicted on the young girl. Some people grew to loathe her for her over-the-top judgemental personality and sticky-beak notions that, in the long run, would drive anyone to distraction. She was not a popular girl in school due to many things that came from her own character.

Although she finally finished her schooling and was not one to excel brightly, young Doris far more than made up for it. Now that she had finished secondary schooling, two things were on her parents' minds. One would be a small gathering for her eighteenth birthday, which now was the unprecedented task of becoming the DEBUTANTE after Doris' bright and sunny school finishing, announced as Doris' debutante. Young Doris had a few friends over for her small party. Her parents were delighted to see how much she had grown into that sensible young girl, and now her eighteen years of Springs were there to mark the fun. On the night of her small eighteenth birthday party, it was announced that Doris would descend the stairs of Inverness Secondary School as a new, refreshing debutante. There were applauds, smiles, and toasts. The day after that evening, mother and daughter would be highly busy going shopping so they could select a proper dress, shoes, and all the accoutrements for the young girl.

Unlike the Bligh girls, debutante balls and wedding gowns, where the materials were bought from overseas, taken home, or flown home as in the case of Elaine's wedding, Doris and her mother got the material in the local flea market during one of their trips into Sydney's CBD. The trip proved fruitful. They practically got everything they wanted, and now they needed a seamstress to sew Doris' debutante dress. Meanwhile, her mother went to Inverness Secondary School to check on all the things that would happen on the day.

Young Doris. The Debutante of the Year

Debutante balls were de rigueur at the time. They had a long and distant flavour, and were highly held by the King, who made it possible for Queen Charlotte, a Portuguese lady who captured the King's eyes. Every single girl who came from a respected family would be looking forward to this exciting evening, but as usual, it was really hard work. Originally, it used to be for the rich and elite. However, throughout the years, it became something official and not so expensive.

Music would have been the first priority. Then came the decorations inside the school's gymnasium, with everything being cleared and cleaned. Meetings and gatherings were held to brainstorm what new and relevant things would be put on display and what could actually be classified as entertainment. Every year things were different, and this year was to be even more different… they were at war.

They also needed the proper attendance of elite and official personnel. But, more important than anything, money, green paper with the huge dollar sign attached to it.

Of course, there would be canapés on arrival for the guests, as the starters would all be met outside in the main school grounds before being allowed into the building. The food would be served as a five-course meal, with desserts, coffee, tea, and beverages.

But for that, money needed to be in. The Church would prop up the gallant decorations, and for more effective reliance, the money collected at the service the previous week would go for the ball.

Still, money was barely sufficient to cover the costs. Therefore, they decided to hold a winter fete to collect funds, selling their wares: coffees, cakes, fried donuts, lemonade stalls, and again the ladies from CWS collectively made garments to be sold. Some other ladies made bath salts, home perfumes, and some beautiful, sophisticated wrappers. It was sold, but money was still short.

During the Church service four weeks before the actual date of the debutante ball, the mighty Blighs turned up in full force for the services.

During the sermons, the priest leading the mass pleaded loud and clear for everyone to really donate. The debutante ball was just around the corner, and they all barely scratched the surface… and without the money donated by anyone, then it might as well be forgotten about.

Grand Elizabeth Bligh, the Ash Park matriarch, heard the pleading from the priest and shook George, bringing his attention to the more relevant side of the Church. The Blighs donated three hundred pounds, and more were to come. By the end of the week, there was money not only for the ball, but for gifts for the girls and the guests…

Gladly, the Swansons also donated one hundred pounds, and Mrs Pang from Macau was more than happy to join in… She happily donated fifty pounds. The rest collectively added up to one hundred shillings. It was a small fortune at the time, but it did the trick. The hall, or the gymnasium, was renovated with fresh paintings, and the floorboards were replaced. On the night, the refreshingly replaced and well-polished floors were so polished that, much to everybody's amusement, they could see their own reflections.

The money came in handy that season, for the school could now afford new tables and chairs. The food could now be ordered, and again the Blighs paid for the beverages, gifts, and for many families, work that paid.

Now… all that was needed was for the girls to turn up to be introduced to the more selective and elective personnel, being accredited with what they were capable of doing, with their CVs being more reliable about being, or not being, the role models. But it all came down to their hairdos, arrangements, jewellery, gloves, shoes, and, of course, their debutante gowns, which would score the best… or the worst.

Everything was to be related, starting from the heads to their toes. The girls' beauty would also be a thorough imposition: minimal makeup, showing their own candour, innocence, and refreshing youth. Their hard work would also be rewarded, as each one of the debutantes would have made an effort to collect money for donation. Lives were at their best… not normal. The talk of deaths and the wars did not bring anything good, but one needed to keep a positive mind, that alone would be a plus.

The debutantes' work was never done. After collecting money came their composure, confidence, and manner of conduct, well, behaviour, to be exact.

Everything was at stake. It was not a beauty contest, if one thinks about it… far from it.

Debutantes always had to maintain their own status quo. Even a pin falling on the ground during their walk down the "aisle" would be enough to lose points. Efficiency was everything, and one could lose a great deal, even losing the DEBUTANTE OF THE YEAR award, which consisted of the silk sash, the beautiful flowers donated by the Church, gifts sponsored by anyone in an elite position, and vouchers. During the Second World War, vouchers for food, clothes, and beverages were very much the in thing.

Struggling families… internationally, the world received them. Therefore, the Debutante Club in Inverness, as in any other clubs, had their respective official delegates, and each one did their best for the Debutante Club, whether it was for gatherings, receptions, gala dinners, or the most important event: the DEBUTANTE BALL. These potential and powerful ladies worked hard, checking and reviewing every single detail. Their observations were as sharp as an eagle's eyes.

On the day that arrived, young Doris was driven to the school and kept inside along with the other girls, with everything catered for them.

In the school's big gymnasium, music played for almost all day as the girls rehearsed for their night. The girls kept on rehearsing how to enter, right from the main double doors, as their names would be announced one by one when they were called and introduced to the elite and publicly prominent Inverness society. Everyone in Inverness lived for this day. It was a night that rich or poor would not miss. It was so special.

Inverness was coming alive and kicking. The talk in town was only this: THE DEBUTANTE… THE DEBUTANTE BALL. The newspapers kept on singing it in bold black letters, celebrating it as something akin to a status symbol. There were even bets on who would become the DEBUTANTE OF THE YEAR. The names of the girls were listed, and bets were placed. Whoever won would donate the winnings to whatever charity they wanted, though not all were inclined to do it this way, some kept their money for themselves.

A Place to Call Home

It began with a glorious day. The sun emerged, the king of the world, and its harsh rays embellished the coloured fields but parched Inverness, sending sharp kaleidoscopic multicolours swirling in and out. It shone like a diamond with multiple facets strongly shining down on Inverness, and all were more than happy to enjoy briefly one sunny and celebratory day. The ladies went about their own accoutrements boisterously, happily chatting on a friendly basis. The gentlemen were eager to dress up for the occasion, and this one was for their "rendezvous" for the evening: broad smiles, happy that even during war, it was a brilliant and fun time. Everyone who was anyone was brimming with joy, excitement, and happy anticipation.

The school gymnasium was embellished with beautiful shades of lights. The place was colourfully animated with flags and other extravagances that meant so much to everyone.

The tables were all set up. The white tabletops were brightly arranged for when the guests turned up. They would be served straight from the menu that was already stipulated, with drinks. The canapés and light drinks would already be served outside before the guests entered the gymnasium. The decorations were delicate and fancy, certainement très élégant, et les couleurs complétées avec brio, splendide et très magnifique. L'effort was well applauded. A good time was something everyone was anxious to have and share.

The ladies were highly occupied and distracted with their goodwill in helping; however, some were still wearing their daily outfits and aprons. When the time came, the other ladies guests were the new goddesses of the silver screen: immaculately dressed, with evening gowns, without a single hair out of place. The cosmetics were incredibly well applied, the hairdos à la forties. They were a pretty picture not to be ignored.

The flowers and the sashes were being taken care of by the ladies of the delegation and spread onto the tabletop on the right side of the gymnasium.

The dainty boxes of gifts were now being accounted for and spread amongst the other goodies at the side tables inside the gym, for the debutantes, with the stage well accommodated for singing, dancing, and entertainment… with jokes creating so much great fun, and the high spirits were a good token from all the present guests. It would not be long before the stronger and brighter lights would shine in the gymnasium on all of them… it was time to celebrate on a grand scale with the extra lights swirling around.

Until the time that would actually start the ball, apart from the ladies in the debutante delegation's committee, besides the preparation and setting up of the tables as elegantly and sophisticatedly as they could, the rehearsals played by the organist stopped as the band or the orchestra were allowed to set up on the stage, with anything they needed for the evening. Only the ladies of the Delegation Committee were then allowed to get in.

Outside in the garden, volunteers, such as the gentlemen, would serve the starters. The drinks were already set up on the tables, and the canapés were selectively collected onto the silver plates. The white wine and champagne were already filling the tall glasses.

"Thank goodness it will be inside the school's gym," one was heard mumbling as he watched the sky turn from the blue, clear, cloudless expanse to a darker one. What was a welcoming breeze that everyone cheered on earlier in the day was now becoming crisp and cold. Someone shivered, and a lady said, "Someone just walked over your grave." The gentleman smiled and said, "I should be so lucky." The jokes and jests continued. It had been a beautiful, but long day, and they were all wishing to enjoy it, having the greatest time of their lives, to forget their troubles and tribulations, and, for once, to forget about the cruel and freezing war.

"Did we have a weather forecast today?" asked one of the ladies as she was overseeing the tables, canapés, starters, drinks, and outside décor.

One of the men responded, "It will be all right… nothing is going to happen. By the time the rain comes down, we will all be happy and content with our servings and drinks inside the gym." He smiled and winked, but he too was worried.

"If the guests arrive early and on time," the lady said, sadly, taking one of the canapés and tasting it, "Now this is really food from the gods." She smiled and took a sip of her lemonade. "Can't drink at the moment," she laughed. "When I am inside, I will let my hair loose and put my feet up." The man laughed. "Terrible manners if you ask… and hopefully your feet don't smell." It was funny, but the women were getting a bit nervous, as all ladies do.

Doing voluntary work… by now that they were getting into the gymnasium, they would have changed and were already all dressed up for the occasion. The men had replaced their comfortable loafers with the highly convenient, patent black shining shoes. They were not comfortable, but luckily the ladies and gentlemen were all smiling, as they proudly contributed to the biggest "affaire de la cité de Inverness."

The official guests now entered the gymnasium. For many, this was a good-luck token, as it was such a terrific opportunity to rub shoulders with the rich and famous. These were also official personnel… and, you've guessed it, among them was the beautiful Grand Elizabeth Bligh, shining in her own power and glory in a beautiful satin silver ensemble. The diamonds sparkled in the midst of her black raven hair. The bags, shoes, and wrappers made the lady an awesome, dignified figure. She had been a widow for a number of years. Her husband was said to have been accidentally thrown by a horse off a bridge. Along with her was her older son George, all dapper and debonair, with his tall frame cutting through, and not to be outshone, George's beautiful wife Elaine, who glittered in a gold lamé ensemble. Her dark hair was beautified with gold specks and a light feather, with a black and gold veil. The gold lamé dress shimmered and glowed the moment she moved and had a touch of the 1920s. With her was a beautiful shimmering shawl. Her mini high heels were T-bars and made of satin gold.

Elaine's beautifully made-up face, with thin painted eyebrows and red-painted lips, completed her wardrobe. Elaine looked a treat, a million-dollar lady. She held her gold clutch and also wore long gold gloves. The Blighs always knew how to be the centre of attention.

The Blighs were treated with great respect and reverence. The priest arrived in the company of other priests and officials gathered at this special time. Roy Briggs, with his wife and their two boys, along with his older brother, also turned up. His wife Millicent was delighted with all the regalia and treats presented to them. She wore a beautiful, simple, petal-coloured dress of light organza material, light and beautiful. Millicent was just the normal girl next door. She also wore her hair in the coronation braids, topped with some fancy clips adorning her tresses. She wore the same material shawl, black shoes, and carried a clutch bag. Her ornament was her strong, no-nonsense, handsome Roy. She also wore light makeup and red lipstick.

Roy's mother was the person who had made the canapés and was delighted that everyone appreciated them and couldn't stop talking about the lovely easy bites and morsels that were so becoming of the elderly Mrs Briggs. Roy's father took a few samples and grinned from ear to ear… his girl was really the best.

They were all handsomely and beautifully attired. No one was disappointed. Everybody respected the rules and regulations. All of them dressed up to the nines and were glowing and glittering as they were supposed to be. The war was raging, but at this moment, one forgot the rigid, difficult life outside Inverness. Except for Roy, no one knew about the private lives of the Blighs. He was very much their best friend and the thorough Blighs' best friend.

Elaine was still a new and beautiful bride. She was now the real Bligh, the pride and joy of George and Elizabeth. Fresh from giving birth, Elaine could never put a foot wrong. With her, a little beauty came with her parents too. Little Reggie made heads turn the moment she arrived, stepping out from her limousine with her parents. She wore an indigo-coloured ball gown. Her hair was styled long and braided onto the right side and beautified with brilliant stars-studded hair clips. She wore makeup, was daring and ostentatious, and a huge flirt. Who could really rival her beauty, apart from her? Only Reggie's older sister Elaine. The sisters reunited, kissing each other on the cheeks along with Reggie's parents. What a colossal team Inverness was having.

The new arrivals were being summoned to take their seats. The organ played all the suitable songs and diversified it. The guests had their own place cards with numbers, being shown to their tables. Champagne was poured into their tall glasses. More canapés were being served. They were deliciously eaten and marveled at.

They were glad with the beautiful settings; the Gymnasium was decorated with beautiful dainty flowers, with placed beautiful organdie white curtains, balloons, and colourful banners. The tables were covered with dainty white lace tablecloths, and everything on them suggested good taste. The porcelain gold plates and the cutlery were placed from left to right, to be served from left to right. There were about three glasses sitting on the left of the individuals. There were baskets with hot rolls and butter. There were silverware holders where salt and pepper, plus vinegar, mustard, soy sauce, tomato, and tartare sauce, were all set up in this six-item silverware holder. In the middle sat the trio of candles with fresh flowers surrounding it. There were silver water jugs and extra glasses for the guests to drink from. It might have been an event in the old traditional city of Inverness, but for the money they'd acquired, there would be nothing for anyone to criticise about the event.

The menu was simple. The committee decided that Australian good tucker would suffice for the evening. Therefore, the menu was all Australian, with a five-course meal.

The first serve was crème de chestnut soup. It was the chestnut season.

The main course was divided into three settings:

A: Fish and chips.

B: Beef tenderloin, with mashed potatoes and veggies.

C: Fried chicken with Diane sauce, with fragrant steamed rice with veggies.

D: There was also food for the vegetarians.

The sweets were the new dessert in the City of Inverness, as Alaskan Bomb was the treat of the time, followed by coffee, tea, cigars, port, and whisky.

Each time a serving was done, there would be a fifteen-minute interlude for speeches, entertainment, jokes, fun, and of course the counting of money that the debutante girls collected, now being donated to their own Club.

Young Doris. The Debutante of the Year.

When the right time came, the "L'organisateur honoraire or Le Maître de Cérémonies" welcomed all the honoured and official guests, the committee thanking the volunteers and especially Mrs Briggs for the beautiful morsels and bites that she made, and then went on to introduce the conductor and le Chef d'orchestre for being present and providing all of them the sounds of the good times. Everything was perfect. A thunderous clapping was overheard.

They, of course, thanked the Bligh family for their kind donation. Elizabeth and George donated three hundred pounds previously, and tonight another three hundred were added, plus the in-laws, which added another three hundred pounds. Altogether, the Debutante Club was the thrill of their own time. All the elites were paying double dividends, and it was not only a night to be remembered but also to be celebrated with all the incoming benefits, and for once all was forgotten about what was happening in the outside world. There was laughter aplenty, and money from the auction now reached its peak. The Master of Ceremonies, who was to start inviting the Debutantes to be introduced, highlighting their efforts by nomination, and of course the girls now all dressed up, happy and so excited, waited for their names to be called.

That was the start before the meals were served.

"And now…ladies and gentlemen of this Debutante Event, without further ado…" he pronounced really excitedly, "we are now approaching the good times where we are introducing the beautiful girls in Inverness."

A deafening, thunderous ovation rang around the whole of the gym. It echoed back, and all in there laughed, shaking the walls.

"Please, Mrs Betty Black, would you do us the honour?"

Mrs Black approached the microphone and gave a sign for the main door to open, and both doors were then opened. One of the males, dressed up in the old version of the ancient times, with a white curling wig, powdered face, and dressed in red coats, red breeches, long white socks, and buckled black polished shoes, surfaced and smiled. He loved being the mascot and hitting the ground as the names of the girls were called.

Mrs Black was dressed in black in an open-shouldered black long gown. She had a diamond brooch on the right side of her breast. Her hair was pulled back in a bun, exposing her ears that now glittered with diamonds. She wore dark-rimmed glasses, but her make-up and red lipstick were the statement of how a lady improvised herself and elegantly dressed for the occasion.

She started off by saying thank you and how vehemently she was so honoured to actually introduce the girls. Therefore, she would start: "I bring you Miss Norma…her parents live in the beautiful City of Inverness…" and she would carry on. Her voice would usually be drowned amidst those vivacious whistles, cheers, and clappings. The girls smiled and clearly were enjoying themselves too.

Then it was the second, the third time…until the beautiful young girl's name of Doris was called.

Doris, with her long hair all curled and waving down to her waist, had a fringe that softened her face, making her look feminine and fragile. Her huge expressive brown eyes, her statement feature, shone, with her lips painted with pearl pink lipstick. Her dress, which had been paid to be made, was long and flared from her waist down. The more elaborate bustier closed her waist, giving her an hourglass figure. It was an open-necked bustier, and she wore her dainty gold necklace with her D's initials along with the number 18, her eighteenth birthday gift. She also had a homemade pouch with the same material and a fan with flowers sewn into it, which she now held ornamentally. Everyone smiled and thought Doris to be perfect. She was the tenth lady to be introduced to society, and another five were following.

The ladies in the committee were the judging panel. They kept on writing every single detail about everything they were surveying. Whenever they met aside, it was usually to discuss the pros and cons, until the final decision would be made before midnight.

Meanwhile, the fun continued: speeches, music, dancing, storytelling, jokes, donations, and raffles.

The five-course meal was a real treat. The dessert, the Alaskan Bomb, was served with tea and coffee. The night was championing for more debutante balls, as everything went without a hitch.

Then the time came to announce the lady who was predominantly named the Debutante of the Year in Inverness.

Mrs Betty White went back onto the stage along with the other ladies. One had the sash ready in hand, another held the huge bunch of flowers, and the last one had little boxes of gifts, not only for the Debutante of the Year in Inverness but also for all the girls who attended, rightfully recognising their efforts in raising donations for the Debutante Club.

The ladies' names were called, and up to the stage they went as the official Master of Ceremonies congratulated them one by one and gave them their respective certificates and gifts. They accepted and lingered a little longer, waiting for the nomination.

"Now…the moment that all of us are waiting for, with our hands in our hearts…" everybody laughed. "And I am more than excited…it has been a terrific evening…beautiful to a certain degree," as he stared out the window and saw that outside it was now raining. "But outside seems to be entertaining themselves with their own singing…Mother Nature at her best," he teased. Indeed, the sounds of the rain beating the steel, the potty, and the pans made another think they were playing a tune.

"Well then…before the stroke of midnight…we are now very happy to nominate the name of the lady…" He took a deep breath, smilingly showing his white teeth.

He took the paperwork and read from it, in a very well-versed and written composition, the name of the lady who would now be nominated as the DEBUTANTE OF THE YEAR in Inverness.

"…and…" someone rolled the drums. "…and ladies and gentlemen…the DEBUTANTE OF THE YEAR IN INVERNESS…is…" The drums rolled, and once they stopped… "Miss Doris."

"Miss Doris…would you like to approach and join us all?" There was so much "ahhhhh" and "ohhhhhh" as Doris blinked, speechless. She approached the MC, and at this time the Committee's ladies' delegate kissed Doris on both cheeks and brought out the sash, while the other ladies helped attach it to Doris.

After the sash came the beautiful bouquet of flowers.

One by one the gifts were given to Doris, and once finished, the Master of Ceremonies declared: "Ladies and gentlemen...our Doris is the nominated Debutante of the Year in Inverness." A standing ovation was heard. For some, she was well selected; others shook their heads. They knew the perverse side of Doris, who could be highly judgemental, unforgiving, and also a real busybody.

Before anything else, this very Australian gentleman stood up and, in front of everybody, yelled: "Doris… I have always been in love with you…will you honour me and my family by being my wife?" From his pocket he removed a small box, climbed the stairs to the stage, and knelt, asking Doris for her hand in marriage. It was sudden, but the result was good. Doris, with tears in her eyes, said yes, and the ring was placed on the third finger of her left hand. They were now betrothed. That was the ULTIMO surprise and blessing…over the top.

They both kissed on stage, and another standing ovation was heard. The Master of Ceremonies asked everyone to drink to the two lovebirds.

What a magical evening and night.

Young Doris' betrothal.

Doris was still dreaming all the way home, in the arms of her boyfriend. Herbert was the typical Australian bloke, conservative, hard-working, traditional, and a homebody. He was also tall, blonde, and blue-eyed. He had a very good disposition, worked as a public servant for many years, and still lived with his family. His family and Doris were the best of friends. He came from, by and large, a good, big family, whilst Doris was the only girl in her family. For years he had watched her grow and develop into a beautiful young girl, always giggling and whispering. For him, she was of such sweet nature. He also observed how she helped in the local community, which overawed him. The girl was blessed with so many good things, and one day he told his family that on the evening of the debutante ball, where Doris was to be, he would propose. It took him a few months to find the ring, and when he found it, he thought it would really fit her. Now his dreams were fulfilled. On their way home, the rain pelted against their windscreen. Doris cozily snuggled up against her beau.

Soon, their official engagement would follow after Christmas and New Year.

On the same evening, their wedding day was also announced.

For Doris, after her DEBUTANTE, where her photos were all over Inverness depicting an eighteen-year-old beautiful young girl staring out of magazines and newspapers, one could only imagine what an enchanting life the beautiful young lady was now having. Nothing she could do could dampen anybody's spirits, and hers was on a high. Jealousy is indeed a curse, but don't let anyone tell Doris this. Some of the girls did not have the same fate. Unlike Doris, they went to the city to study to become secretaries. The time of being maids, serving the elite, was now a thing of the past. Others did not find anything and later married into a life they alone chose.

Young Doris' wedding.

The forties heralded a new era, and young girls wanted to be glamorous and independent. Some were now eyeing big university degrees, to be solely dependent on themselves. Whatever hardships were presented to them, there was a solution to every problem. Their parents would sacrifice for them, and they would have to work part-time to get extra money to attend uni and find boarding.

On their wedding day, Doris wore the same debutante gown, with the same gloves and shoes, now with a veil and a glittering comb holding her long curly locks. The flowers were collected fresh and aromatically. It was hard to get the materials, and now that the war was frantically raging, everything was difficult to obtain. Therefore, she chose her debutante gown so her family could save money, which would instead go towards food, drinks, table arrangements, and anything else needed. The wedding was held on the outskirts of the chapel. The guest list again included the Blighs, the Briggs, Dr Jack Duncan, George and Elaine with their two kids, handsome little James and the new addition to the Bligh family, little Anna.

Again, the wedding was a huge success. The newlyweds, after a brief honeymoon, decided to live with Doris' parents. Doris seemed to be leading a charmed life, anything she touched turned to gold.

Doris, now a married lady, tried to emulate her mother's deeds. She helped her mother with baking and cooking, and to be truly a lady of the house. She accompanied her mother wherever she went, helping with everything that needed to be done. She was diversifying her skills, and now more than ever she was pregnant. They were all over the moon.

Officially Mrs Doris Collins. A blissful wife and pregnant.

For a time, life was normal, and everybody was living each day the way they were praying for the good Lord to bestow on them. Doris was so happy…and so was Herbert.

The charmed life that Doris was enjoying now came crashing down, as the radio announced that Australia was now joining the war, the Second World War. Herbert was conscripted. Roy's older brother was going. Now his two sons were also conscripted, and Jack Duncan was already serving; he had left months ago.

As much as Doris tried to explain to the health authorities that Herbert was indeed a very sick man and that he didn't work anywhere else but only as white- or blue-collar in the public service, saving hard to buy their own house, nothing would dissuade the health authorities or the Australian Army.

On the day that Herbert departed, full of bitterness and sadness, Doris lost her baby.

The family was in mourning. But six months later, during Christmas and New Year, Herbert was granted furlough leave and returned home to the sad news of his own baby.

Mrs Doris Collins. A Young Mother.

He stayed for the next two weeks. For Doris, those days were a treasured trove. Doris never knew that love could be so wonderful but also tear you in halves. They'd spent colossal times together, he as traditional, with no doubts about his own love for cooking and the homely atmosphere, but again he had to leave.

Not overseas, but still working around the docks. Doris breathed a sigh of relief. She applied herself to her work and volunteering. She helped with knitting and crocheting while her mother baked cakes and cooked soups for the Inverness more dependent personnel, especially at the hospital.

Herbert rang and sent telegrams. He was home for another furlough, and this time, before he left Doris for the second time, she found herself pregnant. She was over the moon.

One day, she was volunteering in Inverness. Not being able to see with all the tasks piling up, she tripped and lost consciousness. By the time she left the hospital, she had lost the baby for the second time.

She was devastated. She simply couldn't believe it, one moment she was living the dream life, and now she was hitting the skids. But lucky for her, Doris had her parents, who doted on her. They still made a fuss when Herbert returned. Crestfallen and devastated, she thought how lucky she was to have her parents. Herbert felt bad. He requested AWOL leave, which was without pay and by consent. However, he was granted leave with pay due to his wife being sick and the loss of their child, with this time allowed to stay with Doris. Six weeks became extended to almost three months.

Mrs Doris Collins. A young widow.

Singapore fell to the Japanese.

The news came like a thunderbolt, with the Japanese completely occupying all of Singapore and much more. Hong Kong was their next stop. British and Australian troops were taken prisoner.

The Japanese now occupied all over the Orient. They had occupied the whole of Malaysia and the Philippines and were riding high and mighty in Hong Kong.

Macau was under the Red Cross, so no harm came to the Portuguese there. Any bombing did not come from the Japanese but from the Americans. Later, Portugal sought compensation and was paid over twenty million USD.

On the day Herbert left, Doris was elated. For the third time, she was pregnant. She was over the moon. But she couldn't shake an uneasy feeling. After hugging and kissing Herbert nonstop, with tears in her beautiful big brown eyes, the moment he turned his back, a strange morbid feeling overtook her. She suspected that she might not see him again…ever. She prayed to God not to let this happen.

Life went on. Her parents were now listening to the radio and following news from Asia. Her parents looked after Doris, this time she was confined to staying home. She was determined not to lose her baby for the third time. She hoped.

She was careful and did her utmost to carry the baby safely.

Herbert would ring mostly at night, knowing they would all be home for dinner.

Then one day he gave them the sad news that the army was sending him overseas. He said goodbye and kissed the baby, whatever the sex, assuring them the child would always have a loving father.

Every now and then they received Herbert's long letters and sometimes telegrams. More than six months passed without hearing from Herbert.

One wintery, cold morning, the doorbell rang.

It was a telegram delivered by the Army officers themselves.

Her mother called out to Doris, who was lounging in bed. Doris was in a fitful sleep; in her dreams she wanted to feel the baby inside her. She imagined the times she and Herbert and the baby would have had, picnics, circus outings, and what she experienced, she would give it all to her own child. She imagined Herbert returning home from work to sit at the table with their child. It was sublime. Her mother woke her, and Doris was dazed.

Doris came down to the door in her gown. Her mother handed her the telegram. As she opened it, she screamed. The officer had to hold her before she hit the ground. Both parents were there for her, they rescued her.

From a magical time, the family was now faced with living nightmares.

Mrs Doris Collins. Death comes in threes.

Doris was taken to hospital and sedated for a while with a drip attached.

She wouldn't eat; the food tasted bland or had no taste at all. She threw up. When she left the hospital, she found to her horror that her father had succumbed to a heart attack.

The funeral was held while she was still in hospital. When she came home, she also found out that being a mother was never going to happen. The feelings were deep, sour, and terrible.

Returning home was a hard pill to swallow for both women. Everything that once spelt happiness, joy, and endless laughter, with so much love, tenderness, and caring, now seemed gone. Someone had shut the tap, showering both of them with hellfire, leaving only torment and pain.

She lost her baby, she lost weight, it was a wonder she did not lose her mind. Her lively and beautiful face bore nothing but dark circles under her eyes. The lines seemed etched onto her face. Doris looked older, almost ancient. For a time her face looked insipid, pale, and sickly. Even worse, it was now only her mother and Doris alone. The tragedies the war brought were endless. The sorrows and bitterness of not knowing the future were etched on their sad, sleepless faces, as they wondered about those who left Australian shores and were in alien territory, and may never return, the others: mothers, brides, wives, sisters, daughters, fathers, brothers, sons, left behind, never to see them again.

Doris and her mother still resided in their own home. Her mother inherited her husband's pension. Doris inherited everything from her elderly and sick husband. It was a fair and good amount. Herbert also had his investments; as wise a man as he was, even though he didn't look it, the amount was close to twenty thousand pounds plus his collection of old cars. Doris could also receive back the money allocated to her through the Army and the sole deposits Herbert made while in the army. Young and widowed, Doris was now a very rich lady.

But, as the saying goes…Death Comes In Threes.

It was during dinner. Her own mother fell and hit her head. The poor woman was suffering from anaemia and lack of vitamins. Her bones had no resistance; going through menopause had made things worse. Her bones were either broken or cracked, leaving her totally weak and unable to sustain herself by standing or walking. Doris was again at her lowest ebb. She visited her mother twice daily. She prayed for her mother to get better and return home as soon as possible.

During one of her Sunday services, Doris was called. The news made her faint.

During the night, her mother suffered a stroke, and despite everything, by the time all efforts ran out, they realised that Doris' mother was never going to make it.

Recovering from her fainting, she was surrounded by the Blighs and Roy's family. "Geez, woman," cracked Roy, "we were wondering when you were coming a-calling…" His broad smile made Doris laugh… but only for a moment.

He said that the funeral arrangements were done and they could proceed without Doris' presence.

Doris Collins. Alone.

Doris kicked up a fuss, screaming, "NOOOoooooooooo." Then, between her sobs, Roy calmed her down. "All is going to be alright, Doris…just rest…we will postpone the funeral," he said calmly but sadly.

On the day of the funeral, Doris could hardly walk, let alone give a speech or eat. Doris seemed to have aged terribly in the few years, it was barely three years since she became the elected Debutante of the Year. Then her betrothal. Then her wedding. Doris was barely twenty-five years old and had been through a living nightmare within those three years.

Everything collapsed around her. Roy Briggs and the Blighs, along with others, gathered to help Doris. Inverness was a tight community, and when something happened, they did reunite and help. Doris, however, could have been denied that. Some people in Inverness resented her sticky beak and, even though they felt sorry for her, some refused to help her. So it was up to the Briggs, now solo and a widower, along with the Blighs. Like Doris, Elizabeth Bligh had also lost her husband in an accident (we all know better), and in a matter of months both of her daughters left Camden, much to Elizabeth's grief.

Just plain MRS DORIS COLLINS of Inverness.

Doris was re-starting her "new" life. Doris would never lose her faith in God. Whatever happened, if it was His will, it would be done through Him.

After the funeral and reception, Roy told Doris that the lawyers were at her home.

Doris tried to avoid it. It was too soon, too early. She had just bid her mother goodbye, and now she had to face the lawyers. When would this terror and horror finish?

It was good news. Her mother left her everything. The house had no mortgage, and her parents' savings were all left for her, as she was their own daughter. The house alone would have brought her a handsome sum. It was wide, beautifully maintained, with spacious bedrooms, a suitable lounge, a small study, the kitchen and dining room, powder room, laundry, and bathrooms. Few people could boast such a house, but her father worked hard and was proud to provide for his family. Such hard work…she would rather not have the house and everything connected to it but to have both her parents, her husband, and her three babies. Now she had the material things, but not the tender love and care of her family. Her face twisted in pain, her eyes moistened, and tears ran down her cheeks. She could not speak. She was choking, not only for the faucet of tears to be opened and flooded but for the terrible pain.

This was her fate…her destiny. Through her tears, she stared in wonder at the three lawyers, the first one, the assistant, and the secretary. It was all hers. The codicil.

Roy asked Amy to keep an eye on Doris. In days to come, Amy and Doris would become friends, but now it was high time for her to return home. She never wished it this way. She had always thought that love would stand by her no matter what.

Amy drove Doris to her home. Even though she thought the house was beautiful, Amy felt so sorry for Doris. Amy helped open the door and carry her luggage into the house. She sat with Doris for a cuppa and then made sure everything was in order before she left. Doris was now alone, and a very, very rich lady.

Doris went through the house for the first time alone…solo…in the same house where she was brought up. The memories screamed at her, the fun, the happiness, the joy, the love…everything in that house suggested everything that many people did not have.

She surveyed the smiling pictures staring back at her. Some were in black and white, moments frozen in time. She could hear the lively laughter of her childhood and remember how much her parents had doted on her.

Just Mrs Doris Collins. Now the rich lady of Inverness City.

They loved her…she was their everything. She grew up going to school, her mother would take her and pick her up. On Fridays, her parents would take her shopping, and sometimes on Saturdays there would be matinees. There were always parties, always places to visit. Oh, those Summer vacations, those Winter visits, friendly and family gatherings. Where they…? Herbert's family moved away, leaving Doris alone too.

She stared at her Holy Communion pictures, a spiritual journey. Doris looked back at her features, the white pristine dress, the face of innocence.

Then, taking centre stage and the pride of her family, sat the prime and proper picture of a very elegantly dressed lady, beautifully attired for her debutante ball. The sash, the gifts, the certificate, all there for anyone to witness. Awww…those were the good-looking days of joie de vivre. Pictures of her appeared in some magazines and official newspapers.

One lived to the fullest; it was a time of quality, not quantity. Then came the engagement, those two little lovebirds. Another picture saw her and Herbert holding each other, showing the diamond engagement ring.

Then the happy day…her wedding. Her parents had her wedding pictures all over the house. The house crackled with life, the smell of her father's pipe and tobacco, her mother's delicious morsels, hot steamed food.

Not many people drank coffee, but her family loved it with biscuits. Her mother was a whizz at making and baking cakes and always had some when Doris came home from school.

Once, the house was warm, welcoming, family-oriented, simple, and so loving. Where was the tenderness, the caring, the devotion and dedication once afforded in this house?

It was her first day back home. Her mind swam with countless dubious questions.

Everything there broke her heart. She felt frozen and hostile. She had nightmares. She was in terror. Indeed, "rien ne fonctionnait pour elle… comment triste… ce qui va lui arriver maintenant?" (Nothing was working for her…how sad…what will happen to her now?) She switched on the radio, and again the brilliant, laudable, vivacious voice of Doris Day sang "Que Sera, Que Sera" (What will be, will be). Doris thought how funny some thoughts could be in relation to one's questions. She imagined Doris' face, her happy-go-lucky ways in dancing and singing, and moving forward.

It was the End of the Line.

She needed a shower and to actually re-educate herself. She was being reborn. She was a new person. She was going through the hard and punishable process of changing. She cried.

The next day, gathering all her strength, force, and praying hard for God's blessing not to abandon her, she woke up, showered, looked at her long curly dark hair, at her wide awake dark brown eyes, and saw how much she had aged during these few years of desolation, failure, and thorough disappointment. Then, as she moisturised her face, painted her eyebrows, applied maquillage, rouge, and red lipstick, sprayed l'eau de parfum, and combed her long hair into a coronation of braids, wearing a petite chapeau, she put on a lavender suit, black shoes, grabbed her handbag, and went out to meet with a Real Estate Agency. She made up her mind to sell her family home. Too many great memories, she could not take it all. The memories were slowly killing her.

Mrs Doris Collins and the Purpose.

It was terrible returning to an empty house. The house echoed nothing but the good times that had gone by. She was haunted by the shadows of the past. Perhaps her first step towards her own future was doing herself justice.

Meanwhile, she was also looking for a brand-new house. It had to be fresh, new, as she was now upright in organising her own life. If she did not, no one could. Her decision to sell the house was a good one, as she observed other people living in inferior conditions. The war was still raging. She saw suffering everywhere, famine, hunger, homelessness, and she was feeling sorry for herself. No more piety, no more self-service. She was now becoming another "casualty" in a new world of post-war. But the war was still raging; this news was cold comfort for anyone going through the ravages of war.

She had the money…she had the efficiency…she was also very empathetic towards the feelings of others. First, she was to sell her house, that was midstream. Now she needed to find herself a new house too, and she saw one that she was immediately taken by.

Mrs Doris Collins. Finding the whole Purpose to her life.

With the sale of the other house, she could accommodate herself in this new house without the worry of mortgages and have a fresh beginning. She hoped that her parents and Herbert would understand her decisions. It took her those sad days, then the following weeks were spent making do with her new house, and then came the following months.

And, of course…those few years when she would celebrate Christmas alone after midnight Mass…going through New Year's.

Everything was now taking shape around her. Selling her house was perhaps the main thing holding her back to the past, with all those memories, however sweet. In the new house, which Roy Briggs and others in Inverness helped her move into, Doris decided that the time would come when she would set up her own photos again. At the moment, she wanted to free herself from all the pain, and even though she was healing, the scars still reminded her of a good past and a nightmare that enveloped everyone. Then she burst into tears. By now,

she could have shared her small fortune with her three children…all three that she had lost.

She wrote down the pros…forget about the cons…she was her own boss and would thus far do what she wanted. She had the means; practically fortune always smiled on her. Of course, no one could lose everything in three years and remain the same. Doris had lost more than anyone could account for…or so she thought. Others thought that for a busybody she would have taken into account that most people lost practically everything; some even lost their long-standing countries, their families, their fortunes, their pride, and integrity. War had never been good for anyone. All was now going well, but of her own PURPOSE…she needed a sole purpose to conduct her life, something she could wake up for in the morning and put herself into: *les travaux quotidiens qui deviendraient son* (the daily labours that would bring her alive). But for the moment, she had her life to put into *l'horaire quotidien* (the daily timetable). After that, she would worry about the PURPOSE.

Most of Doris' furniture was donated to the Salvation Army (founded 2 July 1865)…the clothes of her parents and Herbert's, along with shoes, some covers, shawls, and coats, were all taken to the Salvation Army as well.

Then she settled into her own new domain. She would still be Mrs Doris Collins and live in this new residential place, a double-storey house with two bathrooms, five bedrooms, and a study; a laundry, a kitchen big enough for breakfast, lunch, dinner, and even supper. There were two huge lounges, one for visitors and the other for entertainment and parties. It also had a separate dining room. The garden was beautiful, and Doris would have people cut the lawn. Her front garden was also nice and beautifully manicured. She loved her roses, like the grand matriarch Elizabeth Bligh.

After years of torment and death, her luck was finally changing.

The good news continued. A new family saw Doris' old house and bought it for a handsome sum of ten thousand pounds. The family reminded Doris of her own. The buyers also had a daughter, their only little girl. Doris thought about how much the little girl would be loved and spoiled, living in Doris' former house. For others who knew of the new owners, it would be their own problem. But for Doris…well, being Doris, one would know her by now, curious as ever, she had to constantly ask and find out.

Mrs Doris Collins. Finding THE PURPOSE.

On one side of the world, the war raged, inflicting the worst penalties and torture against the Jews. Many ran for cover, and one Portuguese, who was then Consul to France, against his own official rules and regulations, his honourable Consul Aristides de Sousa e Mendes Abrantes e Amaral, with the help of others, allowed and granted visas to thirty thousand Jews to escape the Holocaust that so assailed them. His motto was simply: "I would rather be with God against men than with men against God." He needed to return to Portugal, being punished, losing everything, and his family going through poverty and penury, suffering many distressing things. But he was a strong man with firm principles, kept his faith, and defied all conventions. Today, he is recognised, and there is a foundation under his name.

Food was scarce. A piece of bread cost millions of dollars. Milk, and people were fighting for a stable lot. With so many obstructions and difficulties, one could hardly find food, which was hard to come by.

Food and other necessities were controlled in South East Asia and the Pacific, where the Japanese controlled the rice.

Flour was the only thing Doris could find, but milk, eggs, cheese, and lard were rationed. Being a busybody, Doris knew where to look and how to get them. She was very industrious, she knew she could get anything she could afford, so long as she could pay good money, and since she had the means, everything was fine.

She also obtained supplies from convents and the church. Her motto was to help and aid, and cooking and baking became her forte. Doris, as the French would put it, *"quelle idée, qu'elle était maintenant remue"* (what an idea...Doris was now brainstorming).

Bread was now treasured gold. Doris baked and cooked, delighting in delivering fresh loaves to schools and hospitals, cakes to fairs, and making soup for the needy.

Doris developed her own business by crocheting, sewing garments, and knitting. Her forte became an inspiration. Soon, she was the loving but gossipy, bicycle-riding lady who collected herbs for tonics, cooked, and baked delicious cakes, *les gateaux, bonbons et desserts* (cakes, sweets, and desserts).

She also engaged in counselling, reading psalms and Bible verses, becoming a source of healing for herself and others.

One day, as she measured flour for cakes to deliver to local schools and hospitals, she met some nurses who complained about not having decent meals, accommodation, or a place to rest during shifts at the Inverness hospital.

That was it...she found her PURPOSE. She didn't wait. She advertised her house as a boarding house for young girls. Queries and questions came in. Doris was now the lady of her own house and took great care of the girls.

It was a delight to have them. She cooked, washed, cleaned, baked, knitted, crocheted, and sewed. Doris Collins, the Inverness busybody, had come a long way.

It was also wonderful to have someone in her house. The girls were the source of her work, and if she had her own three children…well, that is another story.

Now she was in her element. No sooner had that happened than she became the ambassador and speaker for Inverness. Sometimes God takes us on endless journeys, and we find our own purposes, as Doris did. As the saying goes: "The good Lord works in mysterious ways."

But what comes after…would she betray the Blighs and go against them, including Roy? Or would she remain aloof, out of the bickering and the lawsuit against the Blighs?

One thing was certain. David Bligh would follow in her footsteps. He would move himself and his family from the curse of Ashpark. The Blighs came to reside in a new place, just as Doris did…thirty years before, 1944–1974.

Chapter 03.
George Robert Bligh.

Caro's Return

George Bligh sat in front of his employees, presiding over them, depicting a very smooth, dapper figure, one that resembled a gentleman holding a meeting.

A phone rang, breaking the silence. The lady, looking every single inch of a very proficient secretary, shorthand-noted the details about the caller. This done, she resumed her work, waiting until George finished the meeting. The Vice President handed the secretary a pile of papers, annotated. The secretary smiled and sighed… more work for today, and it was a Friday. He saw for himself the misery that the war had damaged the people.

Each meeting being conducted, the same problems kept arising. The Australian economy was still recovering, slowly, with shares always being on tender hooks, as they could crash at any time. The problems in raising money were due to the Great Depression. With that in mind, being an honest man with qualities and principles, he was torn between his wealthy world and the present one. He saw for himself the misery that the war had caused and the major trauma and suffering inflicted on the people.

The cattle prices needed to be raised. George thought deeply and felt it was fair enough. After all, they were all in business, and he really needed the money for a number of things: to pay his employees, to continue the preservation of CAMELOT'S KINGDOM, or Ashpark, to its former glory, well, sort of, the mansion and its upkeep amounted to soaring costs. Each day there was food to be accounted for, new electricity installations, gas, water consumption, and so much more than he could ever think of. But they were there, and there was no point avoiding or ignoring them. Things needed to be done, and slowly. If done fast, then he would need to borrow money, which George wasn't keen on.

It was a time growing into the inevitable. Being George Bligh, the rich cattle baron, he was not immune to anything. One slight and bad manoeuvre and the Blighs would be out of their estates.

His kids were growing up, and his son was getting married, and soon enough. James had dispensed with his emancipation party and wanted things done his way. He was in London, staying with close friends of the Bligh family, another aristocratic British family. Exactly what his mother, the proud, non-negotiable Elizabeth Bligh, was.

It never struck him as strange that James was shipped off to London. He found out when he returned home to tend to his family's business. With him, his lovely daughter was waiting… oh yes, she had grown into a lovely young lady. His mother, the indomitable Grand Elizabeth Bligh, was taking good care of his two children, her grandchildren, James and Anna.

Not long to go now for his daughter Anna to move through her refreshing youth, and while that was happening, George was thinking about Anna's coming out, looking ravishing in that beautiful debutante ball gown. It was a dream for so many young ladies to be introduced to society's gentry and to be included among them, so rich males could call upon them. Maybe he could be wrong. There were beautiful young ladies having their debutante moments; however, they were not rich or wealthy or whatever.

His mother would be ecstatic. He remembered when his mother and his younger sister Caro spent three months in Paris, smiling, the two ladies, his mother and his sister. Then his smile disappeared… and little Lizzie. Where could she be now?

Now that the meeting, which went for hours, had ended, he and the others were sharing some light refreshments. His throat was parched. In the meeting, he was met with so many guidelines, some were easy instructions, others were new business deals and the reason behind the price rise. It was a moment of hard decisions, but it was all voted into one YES vote. Democratically, they all won. No one negated the possibility of it not being done.

Now that he was in his own office, he surveyed everything and checked everything. There were papers to be signed and calls to be made.

The secretary knocked at the door and handed over the message that had been taken hours before.

His tired face broke into a wide smile. He was happy now. As soon as he signed a few papers and gave some instructions to his secretary, he picked up the phone and dialled the number scribbled on the paper.

The phone rang a couple of times on the other side of town, and a female picked up.

"Hello…" the voice came through.

"Oh…" George stated, "…and how is my beautiful sister?"

He heard the lively, crackling laughter. Oh yes, his very colourful sister was back home. It was nice to hear her voice and her *joie de vivre* personality. She was really something, and he was proud to call her his sister.

"George!" she screamed. "How is it going?" Caro asked.

"What do you think?" he replied.

"We will need to meet for dinner. Tonight?" Caro stated.

"As a matter of fact, I was going to return home to Mother and Anna for dinner."

"Nothing's wrong with Mum, I hope, and nothing's wrong with Anna?" Her voice turned serious.

"Nah… nothing like that. It's just that the house is pretty empty without you, James, and little Lizzie."

A deep silence. A long pause. "What… has Lizzie not returned home as yet?" Caro asked seriously.

"No… nothing. We have not heard from her for a long time. Mother has been really worried. Hardly a day goes by without seeing Mother crying silently. Mother, for what had happened… still, little Lizzie is her daughter and our younger sister." Then he fell silent.

"The youngest Bligh," murmured George. On the other side of the phone, a deep, dry silence remained, as if both were meditating and reflecting on the same thing.

"Okay, we can discuss this at a later stage," Caro said. "Do come over for dinner. I will be ordering some Chinese."

George laughed. "Chinese? You do have Oriental tastes… Chinese, indeed."

"I've had them by the pocketful of all the rainbows," Caro laughed.

"A Pocketful of Rainbows, wasn't that our little Lizzie's favourite song?" George asked. He was tired, exhausted. He seemed to be finding it hard to manage his giant estate, and he had not yet trained his son to do it.

Before hanging up, they made time to see each other.

He met his sister, and after a long, brotherly-and-sisterly hug, they sat down comfortably on the couch, throwing away convention, having dinner free from the usual constraints and etiquette of home. They sipped champagne and truly savoured the Peking duck wrapped in the doilies, dipping it into the warm, delicious sauce, then sharing Chinese fried rice with sweet-and-sour pork, vegetables, and other tasteful morsels. They had never enjoyed this kind of privacy, colourful atmosphere, and warm ambience. Caro's exotic place, with its Buddhas and extras, added an extra layer of happy contentment and the pretence that they were somewhere outside Australia. It was cosy and beneficial. Make-believe and fantasy could exist together.

His sister was always full of surprises. Caro brought back dessert, leaving it warm on the coffee table, then put on some soft, gentle melodies of yesteryear. Both were thrilled to pieces at being reunited once more. Both had been through a wringer of ups and downs, but being Blighs, they would always fight for the benefit of the family.

Caro had grown older, much older. Some light lines delicately showed on her perfect dark skin. Her beautiful, dark, curly hair had specks of grey. She had put on a few kilos, but all of that only added to make her far more beautiful, enticing, and sophisticated. Caroline Bligh was simply beautiful, wild, self-accomplished, younger once, now older, but George shrugged inwardly… still not wiser.

She was a Bligh, after all.

Caro was so different from him. He was all traditional; some would say he was too perfect, bordering on dull, but he never wavered outside his own comfort zone. Whereas his far more cosmopolitan, colourful, and rebellious sister was a real rebel. Nothing was ever the same, sometimes like Anna's make-believe novels, where imagination and living standards blurred into another world's segment. Yes, Caro was flexible and entertaining, and sometimes very out of line. She was dubbed the Blighs' black sheep. Then he raised his own eyebrow, some even went the distance, calling her sordid, embarrassing, and shameful names. But George ascertained she would always be his sister, warts and all, and he would fight tooth and nail for her, which he mainly did. In her own ways, she too did and would do the same.

They both caught up on the present and the local gossip. The only touchy and sensitive subjects were their own mother and their little sister. They knew about their mother, but they never found anything about their younger sister, little Lizzie. At this precise moment, Caro's attention was towards Anna and James.

"Oh, James' wedding will be sooner than anyone can think of," George stated matter-of-factly. They spoke to one another for the entire night. By the time they realised the hour, it was the early hours of the morning, and the sun was already peeking. It was going to be another glorious day, and for once, George felt good, confident and self-assured. Everything seemed to be going well, and after the Second World War, whilst there was still a great deal to be done, this was the major reason for the rise in his cattle prices. But that alone was not an isolated case.

Their devotion and love for one another were open for anyone to see. Now, he said, "Before I go to sleep…" He laughed. "Are you coming with us to James' wedding?"

For a moment, Caro hesitated. Then she answered, "No… I'd better not. Mother should enjoy the day, and everyone else. I hope James chose a woman… who is good."

George looked at Caro, and her words made him feel tired and drained. *I will take that sleep now.* He got up and headed into her bedroom. "By the way, please call my office and tell them that I will not be in today or for the rest of the week. They know what to do," he said, making himself comfortable and falling asleep. The room was inviting; it smelled of incense, and the curtains now covered the bedroom. The moment he lay on the bed, he slept like a baby.

Caro went and had a shower and made herself a cuppa. She sat down on the couch, stretching her legs long, extending them all the way across, then removed a cigarette, lit it, and took a long puff, shutting her eyes tightly.

From where she sat, she could see the vibrancy of Sydney as the sun rose, showing the world the natural and raw beauty that Sydney was. She could hear the hustle and bustle of the early hours, the sound of cars, the screams and voices. Sydney was never a sad place to be; it was wonderful, bright, and so cosmopolitan, just like her.

Now Caro threw her head back in deep reflection. "So, her nephew was getting married," she thought, and then succumbed to sleep on the couch.

Her dreams were highly contradictory. One moment she saw herself in Camelot, having fits of laughter. Then Jack's face appeared, she jolted a few times. Then she heard little James calling her, and then a baby crying. A face came through, a tiny, dainty face with long, long locks, then Elizabeth's face peering in. She woke in a state of panic, sweating. Her heart beat furiously. George, who had finished his shower, watched her and took notice, so he asked if she was okay while filling a cup with percolated coffee. He also noticed the panic etched across her beautiful face. Within a few minutes, Caro had smoked more than half a packet of ciggies.

She nodded, but still frightened, and answered that she was okay. She took the cup from George's hand and slowly began to sip the delicious coffee. As it turned out, George travelled to London with Elizabeth and his daughter Anna.

"Finally," thought Elizabeth Bligh, the grand matriarch of the Blighs' powerful Australian dynasty. At least her family were altogether, and she was enjoying it. Keeping the secret, and everything connected to it, was a must. Woke. *("Woke" is used intentionally here as slang, coming from a Jewish word meaning melted gravy.)*

They were not the surmises of blank blubber. Elizabeth Bligh's search for hope amidst a repressive and totalitarian society was something the younger Elizabeth, the present and the future, would never have understood, comprehended, or tolerated. She fell in love but was harassed by the reminders of her own heinous crimes, of hers and theirs, crimes of the mind, which could have happened, or, by the same token, may not have happened.

The Blighs' office was the same as anyone else's. Girls did the typing, and the secretary was constantly at the beck and call of the boss. But they could relax for a few days with the boss travelling overseas. He was going to Britain to attend his older son's wedding. The boss's son was a real dish, tall, dark, and so handsome that he had the girls in the office talking and dreaming whenever James turned up to discuss something with his father, which was a very common occurrence. Other times, it would be the grand Elizabeth Bligh with George's younger daughter, Anna.

George also had his own secrets, as a matter of fact, plenty, about his father, about his mother's affair with Jack Duncan's father. He never bothered telling his mother, the indomitable Grand Elizabeth Bligh, because his sister asked him not to. His mother had terrible mood swings, and he simply wanted to maintain the status quo, quiet and peaceful. Little Anna also had her own pursuits and ideals of being a novelist. He smiled. She was growing up, and she was now a pretty young lady.

The following week, his older son married the lovely Olivia. She, with black, short, curly hair and an English rose complexion, looked a treat in her beautiful wedding gown.

She looked prim and proper, speaking in that old Cockney British accent. She looked so becoming, the princess in the ivory tower, fragile and spoiled, but all the same beautiful, more so when she walked down the aisle, radiant and bursting with love.

Both families had been good friends for many years, and now even more so. When someone married into the Bligh family, they married into Australian royalty, a family that stood the test of time, where time itself seemed to stand still: the wealth, the respect, the status quo. She was now Mrs Olivia Bligh, or Mrs James Bligh.

James Bligh was tall, dark, and handsome. George wished his late wife could have been there with the family to see James in his tall and glorious form, how much he was now the pride and joy of the Bligh family. George wavered. There were tears. He felt emotional.

George was happy to stay in London for a few days. Elizabeth was even happier. Finally, she got to do some shopping, meeting people she had not seen for many years. Soon enough, they would need to return to their beautiful ancestral home in the middle of Inverness, what they called CAMELOT, the Blighs' Kingdom of Power and Glory. For some, it was Ashpark of Broken Dreams.

George was a very soft, undeniably understanding sort of bloke, but when he lost his beloved Elaine, he almost lost his soul.

He grew up in a world where everything was handed to him on a silver platter, or worse still, a 24-carat gold platter. Of course, George was the son and grandson of the Blighs. Above all else, he was the heir apparent to the Bligh dynasty.

Naturally, nothing he had earned ever came easily. Being a Bligh had its complications, but it also had good, even excellent, moments. George's life was not as easy as many perceived, nor so hard that others wanted to share its responsibilities. He knew his father's secret. Yet it was through his father that the family fortune came, and through his mother's as well. Both were wealthy. This was the major reason for their marriage, which George observed over the years became a tortuous, tormenting, nightmarish reality, something he could never fully shake from his mind.

George was born into a family whose pride was always to keep up appearances, at any cost. His character had finally emancipated.

As he reflected deeply on what it meant to be a Bligh, he thought about his own mother, who was hard to deal with. Both he and Caro knew her as a far-off, distant, inflexible lady. They met and conversed only during breakfast, lunch, dinner, and supper, if there was supper.

George learned to live with the angst of his Bligh family. There were full marks where he stood as the older son, the heir apparent, no, the heir.

With the surname came few rewards and many reluctant responsibilities: trying to be the best at school, trying to behave himself, the strain and stress multiplying in double digits.

His father "committed suicide", so they said. George remembered that day well. Whatever his father was, he was still George's father. Whatever his mother was, she was still George's mother. Whatever his sisters were, they were undeniably his sisters. Nothing could ever divide them. In the mainstream, they were the Blighs.

He was sent to boarding school soon after his father's death. It seemed his mother could not rest until he was supposedly safe and sound there. If life was tough, it only made him stronger and more resolute, though his ways could sometimes be deceiving.

For George, everything had its timing. Some things could not be controlled. Others, if they were going to go wrong, eventually would, and there was no point forcing or stopping them.

As calm as he was, as his sister called him, "sweet, kind George", he was still a Bligh, fully in control of his senses and his character, never dubious or uncertain.

He was well educated, spent time learning the Bligh business, and enjoyed overseas travel. Each time he returned home, his place was waiting for him. He was the boss, after all.

People often assumed a rich man like George would be presumptuous, outdated, bossy, and demanding. After all, he was George Robert Bligh, heir apparent to the Bligh empire, or was it dynasty?

George mixed with the rich and famous. He had to. His place was among officials, politics, and diplomatic circles. He was a VIP, someone everyone wanted as a friend, a son, a father, a brother, and a husband. He was a predictable gentleman.

Back in his Sydney office, pictures of his late wife Elaine and his two children sat on his desk. Behind him hung a large black-and-white photograph of his mother, the austere and imperious Elizabeth Bligh. To the right, the imposing image of his late father, Lewis George Bligh, sat upright in a dark grey suit, hair neatly greased, staring out proudly and majestically. A farcical and sad state of affairs.

The good news was that the Blighs were returning home to Inverness, to their Camelot Kingdom. The Blighs were a force to be reckoned with, and cruising back to Australia became a delicious adventure. Olivia was now the new Mrs Bligh, and George found himself unexpectedly captivated by a blonde, blue-eyed nurse aboard the cruise ship, tending to his mother. Her name was Sarah.

For once, minus his two sisters, the Blighs were together, returning home with one additional lady, the new Mrs James Bligh. Questions arose about whether Olivia would manage life in such a rural, remote place, but George dismissed the doubts. Positive thinking.

The voyage was indulgent: fine food, beverages, entertainment, the ocean changing colours, the salty breeze. It was a privileged experience. He observed Olivia, hoping she would enjoy her honeymoon. His thoughts briefly wandered to the nurse, Sarah, but his attention returned to Olivia.

Why would Olivia feel frozen out? She would be well looked after. The Blighs had servants; she would live a wealthy, privileged life. The fateful day came when the Blighs and the new bride departed London for Sydney.

"Please… don't misunderstand me."

George Robert Bligh, the older son of the Blighs, was a sight for sore eyes and a good catch.

The man exuded goodness. Tall, dark, handsome, always impeccably dressed, with varied suits and ties. At his most relaxed, he was effortlessly debonair.

He was never seen unkempt. Everything about him suggested style, philosophy, and principle. He asked many questions. Most were answered; others he pursued through study and self-challenge.

He was well versed in current affairs, intelligent understatement.

George found good in everyone and everything. A conservative, he harboured no malice. Though born wealthy, he knew Camelot needed colour, people like his sister, whose spontaneity brought laughter and life. He himself could not tolerate a stifled environment. Her return made life brighter and more entertaining.

As a gentleman, George was once voted the ultimate Australian True Blue...he was not complicated and things could be easily resolved due to his deep analytical personality...and he was never in any position to put a foot wrong...this is one reason that his

Mother the mighty Elizabeth trusted him implicitly even though when he was young and having those sexual hormones driving him deeper into his impulses creating limitless control of his hormonal effects.. of course having some illicit affairs...he drank..he smoked..and sometimes he gambled. Yes George Bligh was in the throes of his manly emancipation and women played a major role in his life. George shone like a true Bligh, and sometimes got himself into trouble.

His mother paid his debts, until the day she made it clear that his time was up.

The Queen's bastion needed to be passed down the line. He was next to hold that bastion, which was meant to be upgraded to an honorary status.

Elizabeth was happy. Her son would one day inherit everything. Now, if George could avoid those gold-digger women and find himself a decent woman, that would be the second instalment.

George Bligh, for me at least, reminds me very much of British royalty and the establishment of status quo. In so many ways, he reminds me of

Prince Charles, and Caro of Princess Anne, no offence to the British Royal Family, for this is surely a surreal Australian enchanting fairy-tale story.

Now, anyone would know how fairy tales unfold, with everything at its best, and by the same token, the worst of it all. It has everything: the good, the bad, and notably the ugly.

George Bligh, after his emancipation, became the heir presumptive to the Bligh empire or dynasty, officially the Blighs' dynastic cattle baron. He was no emperor, but the heir apparent, and after his father falling off the bridge, George assumed the responsibility.

Now they were hunting for a beautiful bride. The wife would be the new lady of the family, but no queen. During this time, George was fancy-free and footloose.

In those days, Débutante Balls were *de rigueur* (details in Roy Briggs, Chapter Four), and the Bligh family were, of course, invited to the various official balls, events, inaugurations, etc.

But the first meeting where Elaine and George met, nothing could have stopped them from falling in love. By the time Elaine's debutante ball came around, it was inevitable to notice how much George and Elaine were already in the throes of love. During the debutante ball, George announced his engagement to the beautiful debutante Elaine. They were now betrothed, to the wide, immense cheers and thunderous clapping that shook the ground and even the walls of Sydney Town Hall.

The next day, the newspapers officially had a field day. George and Elaine's faces, staring at each other, made the headlines.

Six months on, the engagement was officially announced once again. The party, like all others, was fabulous and entertaining, with exquisite food and champagne continually flowing. Bands played romantic music, and guests danced away the night under a multitude of sparkling, twinkling stars as dark clouds replaced the sun's strong rays. The breeze brushed their cheeks, decorations swayed gently, and the evening was perfect. Everyone was enjoying themselves, including Elaine's younger sister, Reggie. Shoes off, sipping champagne, she sat comfortably on the porch, overseeing everything.

Reggie loved what she saw, continually surveying the scene and smoking. Then her eyes met the sparkling blue eyes of someone else. He raised his champagne glass, eyes twinkling mischievously, saluted her, and drank the last of its contents. He never lost sight of the beautiful, flirtatious girl, smoking like a chimney and drinking, but happy. Finally, someone had noticed her. The man was none other than Dickie Boy, Sir Richard Bennett.

George continued with his life. Now that he was engaged, more things needed to be addressed, things needed to be redone and renovated, as he was bringing his beautiful wife home. He could not wait for the wedding date; it would be notified, and the invitations would be sent soon enough. George could have been well educated, being brought up in one of the most exclusive private schools, but he loved literature. He also loved open spaces. Being an avid reader, he found solace in the more nitty-gritty world he was in. With books, he learned more about the world and adventure, things that, once upon a time, boys his age would have loved to undertake. With George, it gave him elementary wisdom and insights, but also a deeper influx into other worlds, which was profound and greatly furthered his self-education. Where his development, or plain development, in the near future would take him, one could classify him as an intellectual. For a male like George, who had good looks, height, intelligence, and a pleasant disposition, this was notable.

George Robert Bligh: wealthy, without the upper-crust attitude. Anyone would have thought that George's credentials were rare and impressive. Being the heir presumptive to the Bligh dynasty, the cattle baron, and the owner of vast holdings was indicative of everything one could aspire to be.

Therefore, George Bligh, the heir apparent, now the heir, very much had both of his feet well planted on the soft, refreshingly green lawns of his own Camelot's kingdom.

His knowledge and understanding would never sway him from anything mundane or abnormal. Nothing was going to stop him now from getting married, starting a family, and being a proud husband and a good father. But life, as it is, has a way of turning day into night and vice versa. Fate can really play us for the fools we are.

George was always well organised, but that was because he had his life totally mapped out in everything. The man was always impeccably well versed. He never left anything to chance. But he was no God, and neither could he change the course of his own destiny. He tried hard to comply with what fate dared him to go, but alas… fate had its ways of redirecting anyone. George then accepted what he had to do, directing himself to the trails he must follow. First, he saw his father dead, but now he was facing the direst of all events, his beloved wife's death. It was simply sorrowful, painful, and bitter.

George Bligh: widower.

"Have him wait in the hallway, please," George instructed the maid when it was announced that Dr Henry Fox was at the door. "…surely… now… HOW," he muttered, referring to his "daughter" Anna.

"Father," Anna pleaded, completely taken aback by such questions. He should have known better. How does one get pregnant? Naturally, by making whoopee. But Dr Henry Fox was not that kind of man.

"If I see him right now, Henry has no choice but to ask you for your hand in marriage, and you have no choice but to accept it. That is the way the world works. If he were not injured, I would knock him off his bloody block." George at his worst, throwing his principles aside. He was normally a man who followed rules and regulations, but now… George Robert Bligh, the man many saw as sweet, kind-hearted, and able to see good in people, revealed his protective side. Those who tried to take advantage quickly learned who was in charge.

He moved cautiously in a world of peace and quiet, afforded the chance to spend quality, and quantity, time with his family and catch up on his readings. For the record, he knew the sting of being bullied by his own late father, who kept skeletons in the cupboard. George was a determined, resolute man, with a hard personality. Now, more than ever, after the trysts he had with Regina, Sir Richard Bennett, and the fight for survival, he occasionally flared, letting others see exactly who wore the pants and who was the boss.

This side of George was something Anna, his so-called daughter, never saw coming. It really shook her foundations.

George lived by the rules and regulations of a harsh society. The Blighs were considered Australian royalty, with immense wealth and status, radiating power. Yet they were not true royals, bound by strict protocols and etiquette. Though the palatial Monégasque-style building gave that impression, George was only heir presumptive to the Bligh dynasty's wealth and the well-known cattle empire. By and large, he was a free Australian citizen, with generations on both sides boasting centuries of history. Family tales of their journeys into this fabulous country were often shared on cosy winter evenings around the table with relatives, in the gardens, or wherever the family dined. The crackle of the fire, the aroma of logs, the flow of wine and food shared, all painted a vivid picture of warmth, comfort, and togetherness. These moments, fleeting yet perfect, were what made a place a home.

George Bligh was no pushover. Very much his mother's son, the indomitable Elizabeth Bligh. True blood ran in his veins.

Though he forgave and forgot, things beyond his control sometimes forced him to take ferocious stands. Unlike his mother, however, he was warm, calm, and affectionate, showing empathy where she remained distant, austere, and icy, a figure to be respected and kept at arm's length.

George showed his emotions openly, whereas his mother controlled hers. She was so afraid to show weakness that many times she cried alone… senselessly and without anyone understanding the pain, the sorrow, and the sadness that went with it.

But like his mother, who was stricter about any kind of rules, and afraid of scandals that could actually ruin the good Bligh family's name… he too never committed a "faux pas." He was the perfect son, and he was the pride and joy of his mother's love and pride, even if it came with utter and deeper condescension.

For a long time, grand Elizabeth Bligh carved herself a niche for her own empire or dynasty and governed it. She also managed her own office. With them, she had her own set of lawyers, and some employees who served her blindly, as her word was just that… after the death of his father. But for the cold and distant Elizabeth Bligh, it was business as usual. Thus, everything in Camelot's Kingdom was going really well according to all the rules and regulations… inside, outside, or around Camelot's Kingdom.

But George shuddered at the implication of what Camelot's Kingdom was really all about. Some people called it Ashpark of Broken Dreams. He had no answer to it.

Many of the decisions were solely made by her "royal highness," and they stuck. But more to it… Elizabeth had ears everywhere. Good or bad, she believed them to be nefarious. Nothing went through without investigation… even her daughter-in-law Elaine. That, my friends, was the correct process.

Elaine's family was wealthy and respectable, and Elaine was a "good" girl. She did not smoke, drank occasionally, and was as beautiful as she was. There might have been hundreds of admirers seeking her hand, whether she was the smart one or not, she chose George, of course. If you wonder… then… he was a good catch.

In their younger days, Elaine, Regina, and their parents were frequent visitors to the sprawling, immense, large, and pretty much gigantic estate of the fantabulous Camelot's Kingdom. But then again… who in their right mind could ever resist the magnificent, majestic, and stately architecture of such a handsome building? What might have been a dream for others… now it was turning out to be a "fait accompli" for Elaine.

Unbeknownst to Elaine and her family, two things would soon come out… her younger sister, the beautiful, fiery, sophisticated, and elegant Regina, and the subsequent extra "investigations" that the Blighs sought hard and intelligently. They got word: yes, she is a virginal, beautiful, young, exciting lady, worthy of a Bligh marriage. That done, it was all systems go.

So there was another lady being added to the Bligh family. Elaine was the first to reign, for a short while.

Meanwhile, back at the "ranch"… George was now responsible for his deeds, businesses, and of course the name Cattle Baron had to come from somewhere. He was cursed for rising the costs of his cattle, and more so… now he needed to reapply for a new registration.

What is a "cattle baron"? It is a title or term used for a local businessman and landowner who possesses great power and influence through operations on a large ranch or homestead with many beef cattle.

Baron is a rank of nobility or title of honour, often hereditary through royal ancestry. The female equivalent of a baron is a baroness. It is the lowest rank after Duke and Duchess, Count or Countess, which can also be Baron or Baroness, then Earls or Marchionesses, and then Ladies and Knights, which are also referred to as Dames for ladies, followed by Ladies-in-Waiting or, per se, Lady such and such of a royal title, ending with the names of the husbands, brothers, etc.

There are other meanings: Baron could be "baro" or "baron," derived from old French and Latin, meaning "manservant," "soldier," or "mercenary" (barus).

In Portuguese, "barão" or "baronesa" are both nobility titles, implying a lower nobility class in many monarchical countries, lower than a viscount but superior to a knight. In Portugal, this is called the "Baronia," also found in Spain, where dignity and jurisdiction fall under the title.

The term "cattle baron" started in the USA. Many powerful ranchers (sons and daughters of wealthy English nobility) sought a New World in the Old West. Their ranches were similar to the homesteads owned by the French and Spanish. The difference was that these landowners were English with aristocratic backgrounds. Their "fazendas" (Portuguese), "haciendas" (Spanish), and "fermes" (French) were usually owned by them, not forgetting that there were also slaves working on their plantations.

References for the export of livestock: inquiries 1800 900 090.

In Sydney: Australian Agriculture, 195 O'Riordan Street, Mascot, NSW 2020.

Telephone: 61 2 8334 7444. Fax: 61 2 8334 7555.

In Melbourne: Australian Agriculture, C/Custom House, Corner of Grant Road, Melbourne Airport, VIC 3045.

Telephone: 61 3 8318 6700. Fax: 61 3 8318 6701.

Office locations in Canberra:

Mail to Department of Agriculture, Water and Environment,

GPO Box 858, Canberra City, ACT 2601, Australia.

Chronology of livestock export – 18th century, 1889 (Foot and Mouth disease).

https://www.aph.gov.au/About_Parliament/Parliamentary-D

Australian National Library, Sydney, NSW

Lawson Crescent, Acton Peninsula, Canberra, ACT 2601

Telephone: 1800 026 132

Australian National or State Library, Melbourne, Victoria

328 Swanston Street, Melbourne, Victoria, AUS

George's life at that time was an enchantment. It seemed that he could never put a foot wrong. Naturally, he could… after all, George Bligh was only human.

He was also marred by tragedies, the sad realization of what in fact his father was.

He had problems communicating with his mother.

He had not one sister, but two, who actually left the household.

One created only scandals and was the black sheep of the family.

The other disappeared without leaving a trace.

He lost his wife, whom he adored, in Darwin's Japanese bombing.

He had a son.

His son was gay.

He took care of his sister's Caro'a daughter, passing her off as his own daughter.

His mother never told him about Dr Jack Duncan's father, but he found out anyway.

Why in fact Dr Jack Duncan was actually part of the Bligh family.

He had just been through the First World War, but he was a baby.

He had seen suffering from the bad economy assailing the country and also the Great Depression.

Now they were going through the Second World War, only this time he was a lot older.

He not only saw suffering… but he lost his wife.

He was shot. He was charged for impunity. His bigamy.

He was also set up by Sir Richard Bennett.

He was also set up by Regina, his present wife.

He had to struggle to keep his grandson with the Blighs.

He had to struggle to find that his grandson was not a Bligh.

He had to fight and fight for his own son David.

He had to fight to get his divorce, which never came through.

He had to fight for his new love, Sara Adams.

He had to fight for Camelot's Kingdom.

He had to fight to find out that Sara Adams, who carried his son David, wanted to get rid of it.

Both times, it had been nothing but a big struggle to continue their businesses and to actually keep themselves above water.

The Blighs were slowly recovering from the hardships that the Great Depression brought them. Now, they were all returning home to Sydney, but his mother, the irrepressible Elizabeth Bligh, was not feeling one hundred per cent, as she was weighed down with cumbersome ill health. George only thought it was due to all the excitement about the journey to and fro, the wedding… the accumulation of everything. By the same token, James was also feeling blue, but logically, George thought James was probably suffering from seasickness. Most people do, so he left it at that.

It was during this trip home to Sydney that he would meet his future wife.

The lovely and efficient sister/nurse Sara Adams: blonde, blue-eyed, pretty, confident, and direct. He loved the simplicity of her being dressed in her nursing uniform and her bright, amicable smile.

For George, something shook him violently in his feelings.

He loved her demeanour as he found ways to lead Sara while taking her to meet and check on his mother, the indomitable Mrs Elizabeth Bligh.

Slowly, George fell in love with sister/nurse Sara Adams. Or was it love at first sight?

The nice, snug, and cosy life that, for the time being, George thought he had a grip on would bring him nothing but jealousy, resentment, and betrayals… a life fraught with troubles and obstacles, where it was virtually impossible to make heads or tails of it all.

But trouble started right on during their back trip home… women. It had to be between the amazing nurse Sara Adams and his dominant and tough mother.

"Mother is tough…" he worryingly stated to Sara. She replied confidently, "I am tougher."

For his understanding… his mother started the cold and frozen war against Sara, and she subsequently came to loathe and despise Sara so much that she wanted Sara expelled virtually from Inverness, Inverness Hospital. Elizabeth wanted Sara out… full stop.

Throughout it all, George remained true to his heart. He knew what life was about when one loses the person one loves. He married her… or so he thought.

George would never have thought what his “marriage” to Sara Adams could actually bring.

The shadows of his first wife still followed him ever so lightly… through his second wife Regina… still remained the forceful shadow, forever following George, thoroughly laughing at him for still being naive and innocent to the methods that Regina would use to hurt him.

Right now… he was speculating on the rigidness of his life, as always dominated by everything. Wouldn’t a day go by that George did not think that even though the Blighs were so wealthy, it was hard to maintain their status? One name only… Sir Richard Bennett. His premonition came through.

The phone call that he so much dreaded came through. George thought he heard Regina laughing… Sir Richard Bennett was back with them all over again.

But this time, Sir Richard Bennett was back with a vengeance. For once, George Robert Bligh was powerless to do anything.

But his son David Bligh had a brighter idea. Ashpark of Broken Dreams would be sold… and the Bligh family would have a new place to reside. Maybe they would be free from the curse.

Chapter 04: Caroline Bligh. The Colourful Bligh. The Reel Bligh. *(Part One)*

Colour me blind, with the pink-tinted glasses, and the world will look better.

Elizabeth Bligh was enjoying her afternoon, doing her knitting… it was a placid spring day. She was listening to the days gone by in *A Summer's Place*, as it suited the essence of the time, calming, peaceful, and relaxing.

The maids opened the door, helping a very happy and busy bee come into the lounge room with bags and packages. She had spent the day shopping and doing her hair the SIXTIES' way.

Elizabeth stared at her daughter and blinked twice. There would be her daughter… there… her peaceful day was gone. **PERIOD.**

Caro had a new hairdo, the beehive of the Sixties. She also wore a most garrulous, knitted, shapeless but colourful short dress, with those big sunglasses according to the Sixties fashion, and dangling from her ears were two huge triangular earrings. Her lips shone with the palest pearl-pink lipstick. She was loud; her fashion was loud. Everything was loud. It was Caro's way, and the fashion befitted her to a T.

With her came two VOGUE magazines featuring the '60s models, dresses, and Twiggy.

"Ohhh Caro…" Elizabeth scoffed, "what are you wearing?" She was astonished, looking at her once-upon-a-time elegant daughter now replacing her then-elegant dresses with these… loud, extravagant outfits. Maybe it had always been Caro, so attention-catching, and Elizabeth could not stop staring at her own daughter… the hair… what kind of hair was that?

Caro plonked everything down on the ground floor and removed a few records. She went to her record player and changed the record… it was The Beatles. The tune of *A Summer's Place* was gone. Now it was *A Hard Day's Night*. Elizabeth's brows lifted. A hard day's night?

Then Caro removed her sunglasses. To the detriment of Elizabeth, the make-up was also loud and expressive: thick eyeliner with heavy blue eye shadow and a face pasted completely white. The lips were painted a pale pearl pink; the red lipstick was gone.

"Oh, for God's sake, Caro. That is terrible." Elizabeth looked in horror at the new cosmetics trend her daughter was wearing.

"It is Mary Quant's, Mother." Caro opened the make-up case and showed her mother the palette of colours and perfumes. "They are all here for your inspection, Mother," she said, checking herself in the reflection of her compact. She removed the puff and powdered her face. "Ta-raah… what do you think, Mother?" Caro's voice was jubilant and full of fun.

At that moment, the maid arrived with afternoon tea and sandwiches. Caro and Elizabeth were leafing through the pages of the magazines and re-examining the goodies from the new Mary Quant cosmetics collection, and Elizabeth would say in high agreement how very nice they were, as she leafed through the magazines. The models were shown beautifully and expensively dressed.

"Anna would love them…" stated Caro matter-of-factly.

"And maybe Olivia too…" added Elizabeth sarcastically.

"Mother, don't be so Presbyterian. If Anna loves it, most probably Olivia will too," Caro said.

"…Samantha Swanson and also Elaine would… not forgetting Lady Prudence… she of colourful character and worse off than Mrs Collins when it came to the subjective innuendos of her own social circle… she was full-on with everything… she knew the ins and outs of her brilliant social and anti-social circle. The Lady had a systematic way of inducing everything that was or was not probable, but it was there… she was full of mischief and gossip, including about her own ex-husband and her son

Andrew, who now was happily married to the lovely, fragile Olivia, and father to the spitting image of Sam, their daughter. And so did Lady Prudence, the grandmother.

Everything was big… enormous, but short of the woman's touch… so skinny… as in the case of the beautiful model Twiggy, with her doe-eyed expression, big fake eyelashes, and pouting mouth… she was a winner for many girls.

"Mother, we are now in the SWINGING SIXTIES… almost everything goes."

"Caro, what kind of hairdos are these?" Elizabeth asked irritably.

"Mother… they are the new hair fashion trend… called BEEHIVES." Caro brought out hairspray and sprayed her hair, gargling with laughter.

Elizabeth watched in wonder at her amazingly strong and independent daughter as Caro cooed and laughed, playfully cracking wild jokes, sipping tea whilst eating sandwiches.

"Goodness…" thought Elizabeth. How much her daughter had changed… now she laughed at ease, cracked jokes, and nothing was too sore or taboo to talk about, certainly not the Sixties fashion. "Careful, Caro…" she warned, "you might choke on a few morsels." Mother and daughter roared with laughter.

Caro was still her child. Elizabeth reflected on how tough it had been to deal with Caro and the terrible time when she was pregnant. It was hard for her, for her older son, and more… her own husband, the cold and stern Lewis Bligh. Perhaps Sir Richard Bennett was right. Lewis Bligh was a real stick in the mud. He was always stiff and stern. There was hardly a time when he smiled or cracked a joke. His time away brought nothing but more worries to Elizabeth, such as: what if he was found out? Now he had a good excuse. Elizabeth was pregnant and couldn't accompany him on his trips, which was understandable.

It should not have been hard giving birth to the second child. But it was. The pain was terrible, as any mother would know… but being alone with your husband away… was a hard pill to swallow. Caro was born on a placid, calming, and peaceful morning, where the sun happily blinked its rays of sunshine. It was a most fulfilling time. Her daughter… she came with the name of Caroline.

Perfumed roses were brought to the hospital by Mrs Doris Collins. Elizabeth couldn't thank Doris enough. Along with her was her older son, barely two years older than Caroline, but Mrs Doris Collins took good care of him along the way. Roy Briggs also helped… mentioning both made Elizabeth sigh in relief.

Lewis made an effort to pick them up and drive them all home when he returned. He was proud of the new baby. Two weeks later, Lewis departed on another short trip. His excuse: the baby and older son took all his wife's time. He was doomed to travel alone, a very good, though ancient, excuse.

The Blighs and the Swinging Sixties

But Elizabeth knew of his double life. Lovemaking was something he duly performed. It was plain and fast—no love, no tenderness, no coziness. Lewis was far from any romantic interludes. She was lucky to be married into the Bligh family and should be happy. She thought of Olivia, who had everything—money, wealth, status—but not her husband's love. That was the reward for being the dutiful little and beautiful wife that little Elizabeth was. Elizabeth was far from dutiful. She was determined to make her own moves, and she succeeded, but she felt pity for her husband. He often said he felt "disgusted" by what he was and did. She swallowed what came to her and soldiered on.

Elizabeth sipped her tea, watching and observing her daughter Caro—unaware that Caro was beaming with delight and happily enjoying herself. Caro and Jack were happily married and enjoying everything that life and love had afforded them. It was high time. Caro and Jack were also grandparents to a bouncy, beautiful baby girl, Elaine. Precious. Elizabeth was proud as punch.

"Damn this society… damn their hypocrisy," Elizabeth thought, reflecting on young Anna and then again on her relationship with Caro, venting her frustrations and taking them out on her daughter.

Poor Caro. She had so much to live for, but a cold, stern, distant mother stopped her in her tracks. She barely knew her late father. One day, Elizabeth came home after visiting the Swansons—and no one sat with her at the dining table. Elizabeth, being so vicious and venting her frustrations, ended up alienating her own children. Caro left.

For everyone else, Caroline Bligh was simply… CARO. That alone said everything. She wanted to belong, to be one of them, in her magnificent, vast palace. She felt alone and lonely. Caro drowned her sorrows and her own pain by drinking and smoking heavily from a very early age. It numbed her emotional pain and allowed her to cry out what she felt, physically, spiritually, and deeply.

Caro could also be loud, colourful, shameless, and very much out of the ordinary. She was, after all, CAROLINE BLIGH, throwing caution to the wind and damn the society. She knew what she lacked and demanded attention, love, tenderness, and care.

Growing up in a world of coldness, austerity, and rigid rules and regulations, she relentlessly rebelled against everything. She became the black sheep of the Bligh family. But if the pretentious high-class society called her that, she would proudly showcase what sterner stuff she was made of.

But for the Australian society, Caro was the laughing stock of everybody… they wondered then, amongst her riches, if everything handed to her came on a silver platter… or perhaps 24ct gold. It seemed that her birth was akin to a royal one, except there was no twenty-one-gun salute to herald her arrival… neither was her older brother honoured with such a deed. One could wonder if, in fact, Elizabeth, the matriarch of Ash Park, had a difficult birth when Caro was delivered. Of course she did, after all, believe it or not, Elizabeth Bligh was only human. But Caro… hmmm…????

Growing up in the Bligh mansion, stoically built, the mansion had two sides to it. Caro remembered the pleasant times when both her parents made an effort to spend quality time with George and herself…

… It only bred anxiety and sadness, the unfeelingness, the cold and distant relations between her parents, creating a heavy, unassuming air. No one could deny that it was also the place that belonged to the Blighs, with Caro born into it… the place breathed goodwill and bespoke practically everything connected with wealth, status, privileges, and a very closed yet inviting social life.

But a highly manipulative mother and the lack of her father's figure accumulated into a sense of absence for Caro, making her feel the bitter taste of being an outsider. The neglect of her parents, particularly her mother, reinforced this. On top of it, she constantly lived under the shadow of her older brother George. He was the real deal. He was the Bligh. He would inherit all the Bligh's inheritance, leaving her with mere crumbs. George did everything right… whereas Caro… was "between Blighs." She now had a little sister, Little Elizabeth.

Caro, as always, was prone to committing "faux pas." Her gullibility played a part, as no one could ever judge her harshly… she was not the type to raise her stiff upper lip high and mighty, looking down on everyone else. There were many mistakes she made… but a time came when the haughty Caro would learn hard lessons. She indeed learnt one of the harshest, delivered open-handedly by the haughty elite Australian society. They all diminished her for being "loose." A slut, as Sir Richard Bennett called her. Society could talk.

Caro was a living, breathing socialite, but her actions and manners for the upper class led her down a dangerous road. If she were not a Bligh, one could have seen her in the colourful clubs, drinking, smoking pot, having highs, wearing headbands, bell-bottoms, gypsy tops, painted with Peace and Love, wearing platform shoes or none at all… saying, "Hey man, that's so cool, peace be with you, brother," smiling incredulously at everything, however ridiculous. But Caro was a REBEL with a deep cause.

Caro was an early teenager when Elizabeth gave birth, but complications arose as the baby was delivered. Elizabeth almost died giving birth to the last of the Blighs. Her distant father was usually away, but this time he took her mother's health very seriously and was present to witness the birth. He cried for days, witnessing the terrible pain of giving birth. By the time he returned home with his wife and baby, he was almost a changed man. But after a few months, he went on his own merry ways… leaving Elizabeth confined to her bedroom for a while. All Caro heard was the faint crying of the baby and the maids hurrying to serve the newcomer.

Caro was told it was a girl and that her father gave the little girl the name Elizabeth Alexandra. But it would be months before she could meet her younger sister. This was announced matter-of-factly by her father at the dining table. He spoke to George, her older brother, and happily took him out on errands, lunches, or Boys' Clubs, strictly for males only, he said repeatedly. He seemed to live in a world of his own, forever, impartially living in and out of Camelot. Father and son went on their own self-discovery journey, with bonding effects, while Elizabeth tended to her youngest baby. Caro was virtually forgotten.

Caro found herself wanting… with her own maids, cooks, and chauffeur. One day she returned from school to the news that her father had died in a horse accident, the horse threw him over a bridge. Now more than ever, she was alone. She had nothing to remember him by, and the funeral was a sad affair. Not even the sun could lighten the day; the weather seemed a sombre hostess, implying that Lewis Bligh was now resting. It was hard to see her mother through the heavy veil, and her older brother… the three of them were simply the Blighs, representing the entire family.

She always wondered if she had cousins through her maternal and paternal uncles and aunties. If there were, no one mentioned them… the youngest of the Blighs were nowhere to be seen. Hardly anyone knew about her.

Life in the vast, spacious mansion in Camelot became even sterner… somber. The cries of the baby girl filled the empty, dark corridors. The death of her father made it even worse. Caro's memories returned slowly and painfully… to her younger days and how completely out-of-this-world her mother could be.

Her mother subjected Caro to humiliations, embarrassing moments, anything to trigger Elizabeth's disagreeable instincts or irritable moods. Elizabeth was like a switch, on and off. No one could understand her mood swings… and Caro felt it intensely. The three of them were anxious, desperate, and searching for solutions. Baby Elizabeth continued to grow, her cries always audible, sometimes glimpsed basking under the sun in the gardens.

Craving motherly love, Caro was beset with doubts and insecurities… loveless, devoid of her mother's affection. The tough, disciplinary persona always found reasons to criticise Caro. There was always something highly unpleasant that Elizabeth would take on… full stop.

After months, the time came to meet her little sister. But that did not stop Caro and her mother from being at loggerheads.

Grand Elizabeth Bligh never bent the rules. But Elizabeth Bligh did… Caro was unaware of it.

For once… or anytime… and in Caro's mind, rules were meant to be broken. One should have tried to tell Grand Elizabeth that, the hard way. As her older brother once put it to his soon-to-be wife, the nurse Sara Adams, "My mother is tough." To which Sara responded, "I am tougher." Nothing would change Caro's mother. She had the iron will of a woman who denied no one anything, being herself also a law unto herself, hence her essence as the ruling queen of her own kingdom, which she ruled by her own thumb. She now ruled Camelot… she was a defunct widow. Her words became her own. Caro wondered if her mother actually had any feelings and whether she was ever capable of love. Caro was so blindsided by her own pain and suffering that it never occurred to her that her mother cared deeply for her children and was enduring the same kind of pain.

Caro's feelings of rejection were harsh and damning, containing so much self-hatred. She judged her mother harshly too. Elizabeth never complained and tried to prevent Caro, who was left-handed, from punishment at a time when society condemned left-handed children. In some countries, being left-handed meant exclusion, and in more exotic restaurants, it could be seen as insulting to eat with the left hand. Elizabeth never belittled Caro for that.

She had beautiful soft brown eyes, a delightful face with high cheekbones, an upturned nose, and a soft mouth. Her face was oval and well blended with her dark wavy brown hair. She was slim, charming, and fun to be with. She now lived dangerously, a most scandalous, but colourful, life.

Caroline Bligh was beautiful. She took dancing lessons and attended the best private schools for ladies of her pedigree and high status, but hated it.

Money was no problem. One only had to bear the BLIGH surname, which carried weight. But life in the mainstream was not so easy. Caro might have attended these prestigious schools, but they were not suited to her tastes… or perhaps her tastes were too expensive.

Schooling was mortifying. Caro hated it. She wanted to return home the moment her feet touched the boarding quarters. She suffered from a nervous disposition, had tummy aches, and life at both places could be so bitter that it left her feeling lost, without purpose, and lacking in everything. Caroline Bligh was at the time a lost cause. One wonders what psychological malady afflicted her. To relieve herself, she drowned her pain and sorrow in frantic drinking. She was always with a glass of hard liquor in hand. She smoked endlessly, and there were times she was so confused, her mind fogged, that chaos followed. Others would find her drunk in public, wrecking rooms with smoke. Her health was threatened, but Caro could not have cared less. At times, anyone could share her bed. She would also bring a flask of "coffee" to class, until teachers discovered it contained hard liquor.

In high society, where socialites bedded anyone, Caro was patronisingly classified… but she was highly promiscuous, sexually indulgent, perhaps even kinky, belligerent, defiant, controversial, sour, cynical, and despondent. One day, she would see the same reflection of herself in her daughter Anna, regretfully.

Her slim shape and beauty spoke volumes, but it was her audacity and challenging personality that confused many. Caro could be highly private, yet she knew how to charm and cultivate friends. As she grew older, she tempered her moods and became popular, but her rebellious streak soon dominated her schooling.

It was quickly apparent how scandalously Caro shook the grounds she walked on, and how the colourful Caro emerged, loving the limelight in a society that both condemned and encouraged her superficial boldness. To some, she was an arrogant slut. Caro never cared; it hurt badly that none offered sympathy, love, or even condescension.

Caroline Bligh found it hard to deal with the outside world. Even harder was life at home with her mother. Grand Elizabeth Bligh, the matriarch, was like Queen Victoria: distant, cold, removed. It was extremely hard for mother and daughter to coexist, especially now with Little Lizzie.

Grand Elizabeth Bligh's attention was often called upon for interviews about her daughter's conduct. Caroline Bligh's report card read:

- English: D
- Maths: D
- Science: F
- Foreign Languages: F
- Typing and Shorthand: required
- Home Crafts
- Science: D

Caro had been:

- Suspended for drinking
- Suspended for smoking
- Suspended and sent home multiple times
- Found swearing
- Uniform incomplete: missing buttons, hat, bow, socks

- Hair uncombed and untied
- Wore lipstick and makeup
- Failed homework
- Did not make her bed
- Late for classes
- Bringing boys into dormitory

Caro did everything… and none of it suited the conventions of the private, elite all-girls' school.

The private secondary college Dean told Elizabeth Bligh, in a terse and no-nonsense manner, that Caroline was either too wild… or there was a reason for her morbid, dilettante behaviour. "Your daughter," said the handsome, stiff-upper-lip gentleman, eyes blazing, "is either WILD… or simply a basket case. Something is psychologically wrong with her." He was tense, irritated, and angry. Nothing seemed to work with Caroline Bligh.

"The Second Assistant Dean, the School GP, and the nurse have noted details that are worrisome and troublesome," they said, looking at Elizabeth with brutal honesty. "Caroline is sick, mentally, physically, possibly spiritually. She is difficult to understand… and constantly suffering. What is going on at home in your forbidden palace?" asked the school counsellor, joining them. She was late, but apart from all others, she understood best.

They all sat opposite Elizabeth Bligh, a formidable group, ready to pounce upon Caro. Like Elizabeth, they were raised in a strict, harsh society. They looked cultured and well-educated, but appearances were deceiving. Elizabeth thought sardonically that with their backgrounds, they should have shown more understanding. The world did not centre on Caro or themselves alone. Granted, reputation mattered, but Caro was not the only girl in such a position. Others were dilettantes too, with colourful "adventures," yet no one spoke of them. Caro was a Bligh, and she flaunted her lifestyle. She loved scandalising, giving the elite high-volatility shocks, watching their mouths drop, and often leaving them speechless.

Even with their hair now grey, and a bit on the heavy side… one would be silly to dismiss them as mere old goats. What they said made huge sense… and more too. They also told Elizabeth that whilst Caro was unwell, something had triggered the effect on her. The GP and the nurse had already commented on this. It seemed Caro's pain was more psychological than anything else, leading them to believe she badly needed psychiatric treatment. Elizabeth pouted. "Oh my God… not this. Not my daughter." And then the freezing cold words came:

"We will take your daughter up until the last few months of her studies. We cannot refer her to higher education… we cannot refer her to any universities here or abroad. These are the sad news we need to inform you of. We are not sorry… but we apologise for this lack of respect to you, Mrs Elizabeth Bligh… we do apologise." They looked as though they meant it.

Caro's school days hung over Elizabeth's mind like a cloud… the future seemed numbered. Reading Elizabeth's thoughts, the Dean softened his approach. "We are sorry. Your daughter is intelligent. Beautiful… that much we have noted. But," he said dramatically, "Caro badly needs help. We don't know what is going on in your lives, but we are very worried about anything deeply affecting your daughter…"

He sighed, his wavy grey hair pulled back, his moustache absent, his craggy, unsmoothed face marked with lines. His nose, mouth, and dark, glittering blue eyes reflected anticipation and sadness. He perspired heavily, his crisp white shirt drenched. Perhaps he should see a specialist, Elizabeth thought wryly. It was a hot day and almost the end of term, one last year before Caro's debutante ball, which, Elizabeth thought morbidly, was the only thing fit to do. Caro would leave the boarding school officially in a few months, for Christmas and New Year. "How quaint," Elizabeth smirked.

Compared to her older brother George, who earned the best school marks, bursaries, and rewards, Caro had come close to being expelled time and time again. Hence, the final meeting with Caro's mother was definite.

Another troublesome year for Elizabeth, as Caro was concerned. Now she had to be content with Little Lizzie. George, of age, had enrolled Little Lizzie at a Catholic college, of course, a private one. When Elizabeth heard, she was furious. That was an understatement.

Her own son was betrothed to a beautiful young lady. George's emancipation party had been a success, and he had never given her cause for worry. Elizabeth glowed with pride and joy, George Robert Bligh, her own flesh and blood.

Finally, Caro's years at her private, prestigious boarding school ended. The teachers breathed a sigh of relief, but Elizabeth Bligh was confounded by the truth and saddened by the reality: even though the Blighs had everything, Caro had been so disappointing.

Caro was coming home to stay at Camelot.

Poor Caroline Bligh… damned if she did, damned if she did not. She could not win. The stiffness, coldness, and austerity remained. If one harsh, disciplined school could not repair what was broken, what made Elizabeth think her own frozen austerity would make Caro adjust to her ways? Ash Park now revealed its dark side, three Bligh women. Oh dear.

Now that Caro had returned home, Elizabeth wanted her to have her debutante.

- Invitations were sent out.
- The organiser for the event was arranged.
- A… catering for the exquisite food.
- B… bands, singers, entertainment.
- C… beverages, with champagne playing a central role.
- D… everything needed to be perfect, with colourful surroundings embellishing the place.

- E… magazine and newspaper editors, the movers and shakers, were invited.

It was an official date and event. After all, Caroline Bligh was the daughter of Grand Elizabeth Bligh, the indomitable matriarch of Camelot. Some likened Elizabeth to Queen Victoria, for her austerity, coldness, and icy temperament. The difference: Elizabeth loved multicoloured dresses; Queen Victoria wore solemn black.

At times, Elizabeth was the butt of jokes. Anyone thinking she cared were mistaken. But her children were fair game. Now it was Caroline Bligh's turn. "Debutante Ball… ohhhhh I am so pure and virginal," whispered the onlookers, rapturous about Caroline's immature life, whispering innuendos.

To decorate Ash Park, the brightness, fun, and inviting atmosphere had to be chosen carefully, adding sophistication and elegance. Elizabeth thought about her daughter's pain, delusions, and disappointments… What sorrow? What disappointment? Elizabeth resolved to make up for whatever Caro had endured. This was the Blighs' terrain, they would do as the Blighs do.

Mother and daughter selected the songs and bands together. Elizabeth integrated everything with Caro's choices. The rest was left to caterers and professionals to decorate.

Everything would be as Caro's mother, Grand Elizabeth, wanted, measured up and paid for.

As with her older son, it was now for her daughter. Nothing but the best. A lavish debutante ball would be held, and everyone would have a whale of a time. As a debutante ball, Grand Elizabeth wondered who would be brave enough to ask for Caro's hand. She gazed across her magnificent domain, sipping tea, wondering where Caro was.

Mother and daughter needed time to bond. Elizabeth, ever innovative, had a new idea.

Regarding the dress, her ladyship told Caro that nothing but the best would suffice for a Bligh. The next day, Caro found herself seated next to her mother, flying first class to Paris.

The trip promised to be beautiful, with the soulful and historical attractions of the City of Love. Mother and daughter would bond well.

But it soon turned into a battle of wills. Heated debates led to arguments; both wanted their own way. One followed traditional protocol; the other, her free-spirited ways.

The modiste, a professional haute couture model with her own shop in the romantic heart of Paris, tried hard to please both. Full credit to her, she carried on with aplomb, distinguished, well-informed, highly dedicated, and with a soft, sugar coating, crisp French accent. Though Caro's French marks were poor, both mother and daughter understood the modiste's efforts, leading to a peaceful solution for the two strong-willed ladies.

"Tout ce que la jeune mademoiselle a essayé est tout simplement magnifique..." the modiste said, trying to express how beautiful the gown would be on Caro, while also making sure that Grand Elizabeth, the matriarch, would see the effect it would create on Caro. "...pour vous, d'accord Madame Bligh?"

She went on to explain, showing the fine details of the selected materials. "Le matériau est vraiment fin..." she smiled. "Est de la soie et est léger. C'est une très belle combinaison... et la lumière... pour sera pour la belle peau de votre fille... votre fille Madame Bligh est très belle, fine et très féminine... votre fille devrait être un modèle." Caro blushed, and Grand Elizabeth smiled politely. Her daughter a model? Yes... she would not answer.

(Translation: The material is indeed fine... it is silk and very light. The light will also bring out your daughter's beautiful skin... your daughter, Mrs Bligh, is truly beautiful, delicate and very feminine... your daughter should be a model.)

That alone did the trick. All three ladies were now talking and agreeing.

For the next few hours, they discussed designs and fashions, going through most of the classic gowns for Caro's debutante gown. One day turned into another, then weeks passed, and soon they were preparing to return to Inverness City, NSW.

Paris was such a delectable place. Even though they were together most of the time and invited to formals and official functions, mother and daughter found ways of bickering and opposing each other, from one subject to another, nothing seemed to fit either of them.

Finally, the day came to visit the French modiste to collect the robes de bal, chapeaux, gants et chaussures, and pay for them. The French modiste was pleased with the payment from the Blighs, plus the generous tip. Elizabeth knew how to treat anyone loyal and efficient in their work. "Travail acharné," the modiste smiled, bidding them au revoir, stating it was a pleasure to do business with them. She was already thinking about Caro's wedding gown.

The following week, mother and daughter arrived in Sydney, where the gallant Blighs' adopted son, Jack Duncan, picked them up.

The sight of the handsome Jack Duncan delighted both mother and daughter. Caro's heart skipped a beat when she saw him. She tried her utmost not to show the love she felt for Jack. For some time, they had known how compatible they were and how much they loved one another. The lonely days at boarding school and the three months in France had made them ache to be together.

Now reunited, their love was still forbidden. Grand Elizabeth Bligh hoped Caro would marry into a wealthy Australian family, perhaps one like the famous Swansons.

Upon arriving at Ash Park, Elizabeth's domain, Jack was invited to dinner. The gathering was amicable, with Jack and Caro stealing furtive glances and, when possible, smiling secretly at each other. Elizabeth either did not notice, or chose not to. Her mind wandered to her youngest daughter, Little Lizzie, who was nowhere to be seen. Elizabeth was fuming silently.

At least the family was gathered for a special dinner. George was happy, he was going to be a father. The news was terrific. But no one spoke about Little Lizzie.

Grand Elizabeth retired for the night; George returned to Sydney. Caro and Jack were alone, and they could not have been happier.

Little Lizzie returned in the early hours, feeling as lost as Caro had.

Now it was time for the two lovers to enjoy each other's company. Their lovemaking was deep and endless. They had missed each other terribly. They cared little for the world outside, resting in each other's arms in the softness of the hay, making love in the Ash Park stables. Still, Elizabeth was always a shadow over them.

Caro whispered, "Oh… I missed you so much…" Her face showed a shadow of sadness. "Mother does not know anything."

"I fear the day she finds out," Jack said seriously, looking shaken. A shiver ran down both their spines.

"Oh… three months of hell…" Caro said, still lying on the soft hayloft. Outside, night deepened and the wind gently stirred. The dim light of Ash Park gradually gave way to daylight, with the birds singing and a distant kookaburra calling.

"In Paris… the City of Love?" Jack smiled as he listened to hooves approaching the stable.

"It might be the City of Love… but I was with my mother," Caro said thoughtfully, elbow across her forehead.

"What do you think mother will do when she finds out about us?" Caro asked, worried. The Debutante Ball was just a few weeks away. The hooves drew nearer. They held their breaths, covering themselves. Little Lizzie's sweet voice was heard calming the black stallion while removing saddles and feeding the horse.

"Au revoir… mon beau étalon noir," she said before leaving the stables.

Please include.: "Caro would marry into a wealthy Australian family, perhaps one like the famous Swansons… (is already in the manuscript) so add this…. paragraph please…but would hell hath no fury should Elizabeth find out about Jack and Caro and so…. but Elizabeth was not being scorned.

Jack said, "Little Lizzie would suit herself very much if she went to Paris… her French is so colossal," he said. He never knew how predictive his words could have been. Then… Jack shrugged and asked when they would see each other again. "You know how much I do love you and how much I missed you… but unfortunately, as things are…" He stopped, mainstream. "I had better be going. I will shower in the hospital… it will not do if your mother finds out or sees me sneaking out of the stables… we were almost found." He gathered his clothes, his shoes, and went out through the wee hours of the light morning, getting into his car. "Your mother has huge ears," he said before he leapt out of the hayloft, smilingly. Then came the sounds of his car and the tyres leaving the rough ground of Ash Park. Carol was thinking about Ash Park… so remote, so alone… such a cursing place… whatever had happened here for all of them to suffer so much.

They made time for a get-together the following evening. They both couldn't wait… each time, each minute… they needed to steal. Both did not trust tomorrow, as outside the Second World War coldly and impishly raged.

The new day brought sunshine, clear blue skies, and the green lawns of Ash Park looked lusciously velvet green. Elizabeth's roses were blooming in full view, and the perfumed garden with its beautiful marbled statues depicting different positions, each one a myth, were the silent witnesses of what grandeur and wealth could mean to everyone. In the middle of it all, residing inside the manor, was the tall, immense building, stalwart in its magnificent position and something that one would stop in awe to admire even for a second. The mystery of Ash Park, or the Kingdom of Camelot, remained secretive, bright, and a splendoured piece of artwork.

Elizabeth sat at the end of the table. She was being served breakfast, and Caro joined her too. She looked around and asked the maids where Little Lizzie was. One of the maids stated that Little Lizzie was training for another competition. Little Lizzie had risen early and was on the training tracks with her Oncle Roi.

Grand Elizabeth sighed. "She could at least have been here last night," Elizabeth quipped angrily. "...and the sounds of the car last night..." Elizabeth stared at Caro and asked, "Was that Jack leaving Ash Park in such wee hours of the morning?"

Caro poured coffee and replied, "Mother, we really need to talk about my debutante ball." She changed the subject.

Elizabeth frowned, looking at her own daughter. "What about the debutante ball?" she continued. Drily, she asked.

"I thought that the debutante ball is now heading for the final chapter... is already organised... there is no secret about that. They will be coming for the outdoor décor, and we will need to prepare the rooms for the guests. Also, we will need to double up on a great many things." Caroline finally put the tees on the eyes.

"Exactly right," Elizabeth agreed. "Still, what was that... the car's..." Elizabeth inquired seriously.

Facing the silence, Elizabeth, in her usual way, went on. "So Caroline... what is it that troubles you? Come on, girl, say it." Elizabeth insistently inquired again.

"You don't have many friends from your school that you so much would have wanted to invite?" It was a dumb question that Elizabeth knew the answer to.

"What about the Dean... he retired... the Assistant Dean... now the present Dean... the GP, the nurse, and the College Counsellor?" asked Elizabeth again. "For sure, you would love to let them know how well you are faring... without them and the college." Elizabeth quipped. Then she got the toast and drily spread the cheese and butter on both of them. One of the maids poured coffee, then filled the sugar, and finally the milk.

Caro sipped her coffee, took a bite of her toast, and remarked, "Those frumpies?" She shook her head. Then she said, "If they were so colossal,

Mother, they would have backed me and supported me all the way." The pain showed on her beautiful face. Caro was so beautiful.

"Maybe they were jealous of me," she laughed. "Per se… they should have been wet nurses in a hospital for the sick and the disabled," she said. "Those poor souls having to put up with nurses and aids like that." She bit the toast, then broke the eggs, starting to sprinkle salt and pepper on the food. Then she picked up the fresh salmon, sausages, and the ham. "Delicious," Caro moaned. Then she added,

"My family will be enough. At least George, Elaine, who is pregnant, you, Jack, Little Lizzie, Roy, Mrs Collins, Bennett… so much more," replied Caro. "Our own social circle… eh?" She thought in amusement, however…

"Ohhhh… ohhhhhhhh," moaned in delight Elizabeth. "Yes… my first grandkid… and for you, your first nephew or niece." "Awww…" Elizabeth cooed in utter delight. Now she was going to be a grandmother. Then she looked around and summoned the maids. One of them entered the dining room. "When Miss Little Lizzie returns from her training, make sure she comes and sees me," Grand Elizabeth commanded with gritted teeth. They all knew when Elizabeth was angry.

She had not seen her youngest daughter for about three long, hard, sour months. She only saw George. Elaine could not come over due to her impending pregnancy. Roy was very busy with his own cottage to be renovated from head to toe..., and sadly Little Lizzie was nowhere to be seen. Was she the Grand Elizabeth Bligh so hard to put up with? Elizabeth thought, her face showing disappointment. Her mouth as usual twisting in sheer spiritual pain.

Caro told her mother that she was going out for the day and would not be back for dinner. Elizabeth nodded. Now she was worried about Little Lizzie.

The morning was beautiful. The Polletis family hovered around, being busy bees and working hard around Ash Park. They went to pay their respects and greet Grand Elizabeth, as usual bringing their weekly boxes of vegetables from their farm.

A flower in bloom.

Caro left the moment she saw fit. Kissing her mother on both cheeks, she could not wait for the time and energy to be all out with her honey bee, Jack Duncan. She was looking to make up for lost time… everything.

Caroline Bligh was so happy being back in Sydney's suburbs, and using the key to Jack's small, cute apartment, she found herself well accommodated. It was not luxurious or anything that suggested money or power; it only showed the hard work of a very macho man, a man who actually struggled to get everything, and everything that he acquired was through knuckles, sleepless nights, and sometimes asking where he was going, where from.

If Jack was not in his own domain, however small and cramped it could be, that he loved so much… Jack spent his nights in Inverness Hospital where he was still an intern doing graveyard shifts.

Whatever it was, Caro was always finding ways to be with Jack, hence one of the major reasons why she was so sad, depressed, missing Jack so much when she needed to board the infernal school. She waved it about. None of them had the warmth and elements that she sought. Still, even though she preferred her own company, she made it her business to be friends with some of them, and one of them would be ready to meet up with her in London.

Caro and the tough disciplinarian teachers were her deepest dislike, and it was hard to see Caroline Bligh somehow feeling humane with teachers she deeply disliked. There were some kind of unimaginable misunderstandings on both sides, with Caro giving the issue a little pad, thinking, okay, so they were only doing their nefarious jobs and trying hard to complete their unimpressive work. If being a teacher was like that, Caro would never be a teacher if that was the way teachers went about mistreating their students.

For the teachers, Caro was simply damaged goods. A wild, insincere, damaged goods with the surname Bligh. She was the shame and the uncultured daughter of the Blighs. So the dye was cast. Caroline Bligh was nothing but the black sheep of the Bligh family. Now Caroline Bligh was portraying herself as the dutiful, well-sophisticated daughter of Sydney's society which for many, it was a big laugh.

Or was she, in reality? You make your own opinion.

Elizabeth thought otherwise, for she too was brought up in a harsh, disciplined era, taught that ladies should be highly hardworking and culturally quiet in their ways of thinking, actually pretty liberal. What made sense for the maybe older and wiser "Queen Elizabeth of Camelot's Kingdom" did nothing for her own daughter. Worse still, Caro would not donate a thing to that infernal college anytime soon. The thing is, who needed such discipline, such harshness, such coldness when she had all of these at home? Nobody at the college suspected, much less would know about it. But their ignorance was bliss.

The only thing that drove her home, to paradise, was returning home to her "amant," whom she loved with all her heart and feelings. For her, Jack was everything. That was the reason why she hated being away from Inverness and Jack's place, this pure carnal feeling of love, comfort, her own pleasure, their own pleasure, fused into one.

But it was more than pleasure that both had for one another. With Jack, sexually, lovingly, they both were unstoppable. Their love was so deep, it was undeniable. Nothing could break them apart, not even Elizabeth, the indomitable Grand Elizabeth Bligh. As Matthew Goddard would one day quip, "You Blighs' women… it's always your way, or the highway." Therefore, it was either Elizabeth's ways, her ways… Elizabeth was the main obstacle, the huge blockage. That, as Elizabeth crying tears of regret would one day admit, "…and the tragic of it all… is that I would have thoroughly approved…" It had never occurred to either of them that Elizabeth Bligh would have allowed it to happen. If love was so sweet and beautiful, all the sore points and the pros would far outweigh the cons. Caro and Jack were then on the right path. Now we all know their own paths… would Elizabeth melt her ways and stop being the stronghold in everything and, in doing so, destroy everything with her own bitterness?

Elizabeth's ideas of the debutante ball were the major reason for her daughter Caro to, one, benefit from all of it, and two, for the benefits to be Caro's marrying into one of the richest and most respectable families in the marvellous Ozzie society, the elite, the officialdom, the rightful privileges, the high status, wealth, money, and power. Such dreams that a delusioned mother would cater for her own daughters. What Elizabeth Bligh never knew was that the private college and her so-called friends had actually branded Caro as the black sheep of the Bligh family, and for a time, the poor darling's reputation was spreading wild and free. Still Elizabeth found a good motive or motives to invite them.

She was deemed to be a drunk, a chain smoker, a shameless wanton woman. She was mad as anything. There she was publicly, throwing caution to the winds. She was always the life of the party, always a fashion follower. Anyone would always find her usually with a drink in her left hand and smoking. Many would have loved to be in her shoes. Many were in her shoes. But no one ever created such colourful entertainment in the social circles of Sydney's societies.

Every time, day or night, Caro would sneak into Jack's cosy little apartment.

But fate could always be such a cruel twister, and the blow would be terrible for both of them, bringing down Elizabeth Bligh. But would their love go to the extremes?

"The tragic reality of it all..." said a regrettable Elizabeth Bligh to Jack and Caro, crying tears of repentance, "...is that I would have approved," or words to that effect, when she finally told both Caro and Jack about her feelings where their love was. Too late.

With so much on her mind, with the caterers coming and going, the decorators, the bands and the musicians, Grand Elizabeth Bligh was so occupied that she never gave a thought to her daughter Caro. Presently, she was busy with Little Lizzie.

That year would be one of those many the Blighs would love to forget, but for one down, others up would come.

The grim news of the Second World War raging was enough to dampen anyone's feelings. But for the Blighs, the sun continually shone on, and for Camelot's Kingdom… the good news was that Elizabeth was a grandmother to a bouncy, handsome baby boy, whom her son George and daughter-in-law Elaine named James. George was smiling from ear to ear, proud as punch. Elaine was now the real Mrs George Bligh, having secured her position as the new and grand lady of the majestic mansion. The surname Bligh shone like the strong, sturdy, majestic, and imperious palace of Camelot's Kingdom.

It was one party after another. Grand Elizabeth would not stop at anything too lavish, anything that she, as the grand lady of the Blighs' kingdom, could and would bestow on her own blood and flesh. Nothing was too expensive and nothing was too much of a burden.

Thus, very soon, her dour and stuffy name of Queen Victoria would change to Queen Elizabeth. She was now thinking about Little James' baptism, still highly preoccupied with Little Lizzie, who made all the excuses not to meet with her own mother.

The Christening of Little James was an affair to remember but i private one. They all had a whale of a good and enjoyable time, and Jack and Caro found the blessed time to really express their undying love to one another. Now their lovemaking increased, and both were audacious enough to sneak into the barn, as previously, wildly making love in the horse stables. Now that one would be off the stables, but nothing would be so wild and romantic ever in making love in the wild of the immense hay stacked up, and nothing was so deliciously outright and highly defying and challenging. More so, they both delighted in really going all out. Under the full moon, after swimming and having their supper, they slept under the stars, the moon. They professed their undying love this way and every other imaginable way. Caro and Jack would die for each other. Still, the shadow of Caro's mother and Jack's adopted mother was always there, actually hindering their love, or so they thought. How wrong could they be? But one must take into consideration the times, the era, and to some degree or all of it, that, by and large, where status galore was at, Caroline Bligh was royalty. Jack Duncan was still working to get his GP certificate or diploma. He had no money to his or anyone's name, and if he had, it would have come from his own adopted mother, who was the mother of Caroline Bligh. Get the picture?

But the war was still raging, spreading all over the world. Asia and the Orient started off with the Japanese invasion, beginning in Nanking in 1935, with the Japanese establishing their bases and headquarters there.

Now the Debutante Ball, which was a few weeks away, was taking hold at Ash Park. The enchanting fairytale of this beautiful Camelot castle was coming alive, with colourful decorations, banners, flags, balloons and Chinese lanterns fluctuating in the breeze. The place was enchanting, and the guests were arriving one by one in their luxurious and expensive cars. The ladies twirled around in their fineries, with their chapeaus, little clutch bags, high heels, perfect makeup and hairdos, adding their fine touches to their fashion wardrobe. All glitter and glamour, all silver and gold. As the French modiste in Paris, France, would have detailed: robes de bal, chapeaux, gants, chaussures et petits sacs à main… quelle beauté! Les mesdames et les mademoiselles et les messieurs étaient quelque chose à regarder, se demander si c'était si beau… et les cavaliers étaient aussi très élégants.

With them came the young, handsome, rich, dignified younger gentry of Australian society. They too were keen to ask the young and beautiful Bligh lady for her hand. They also had betrothal rings for the ethereal young dark-eyed Bligh beauty, the ethereal Caroline Bligh.

And with them, sadly, was the forlorn, far-away, and distant Dr Jack Duncan. He looked beautiful and magnificent, all dapper and debonair in his black tie and suit. He looked sophisticated, elegant, and so handsome that he would melt any lady's heart within sight.

Caro looked devastatingly beautiful in her French gown, the little pearl tiara adorning her long, curly dark hair. Against her beautiful dark brown skin, the gown with its glittering and glowing setup created a most sophisticated combination. It brought both of them together, much to the pride and joy of Grand Elizabeth Bligh, the grand matriarch of Camelot's Kingdom, exactly as the French modiste had expressed earlier. Caro looked divine, an ethereal beauty.

Jack had tears in his eyes. He was even more teary when the news of young Caro abounded and of Grand Elizabeth Bligh's dreams of finding the perfect suitor for Caroline.

Before anything, with Jack Duncan now denominated Doctor, a small party was given by Elizabeth. Caro and Jack stayed together to continue their celebrations. Their selfless, soft, and gentle love bespoke everything. They were one now, and their love flourished, developing immensely.

Amidst all the hahhhas and awwwws, the sighs, Caroline walked softly, gently, and sophisticatedly with the bouquet of fresh roses, everyone watching and cheering for her. One of the men surveying the whole "scenery" was none other than Sir Richard Bennett. But Caroline Bligh, for all intents and purposes, looked a treat, well, a vision. A trademark belonging to all of Bligh's women.

Now that Caro was establishing herself as a socialite, the Australian elite society were more than welcome to come and ask for Caro's hand. Champagne flowed, the delectable bites, or what one would call petites bouchées de nourriture, the band played beautiful, soft, and suave music. Dancing went on, gifts were taken to the lounge. It was a beautiful sunny spring day. It was crisp and cooler, as the breezes were getting icy. The cold weather was arriving sooner than expected. Whilst the party went on without any hitch, Caro unfortunately took sick and was confined to her bed for a few days, at the same time and on the same evening where she was the beautiful, charming, and dream debutante. Her days were literally numbered.

Meanwhile, Dr Jack Duncan was conscripted and left within two weeks, with the sole blessings of Elizabeth Bligh, to fight for king and country.

Two weeks later, much to the disappointment of Elizabeth, the news that Caro was pregnant came through. Elizabeth suffered her first heart attack.

That alone, and precisely, was the darkest time for Elizabeth and her daughter Caro. First, it shattered Elizabeth's plans of Caro ever finding a suitor and marrying into the elite and high Australian society. It smashed and broke Elizabeth's grand purpose. For the second time, she was to become a grandmother; however, Caro would not say who the father was.

When Caro gave birth to her own flesh and blood, Elizabeth and Caro had a terrifying all-out quarrel, the biggest fight that would occur, leaving both mother and daughter in dire conflict to the point of not speaking to one another. Two months after that, Caro packed her own luggage, bought herself a ticket, and flew overseas.

She stayed in London, and on her return her colourful, rebellious nature was well spotted all over Sydney's society, again, again, and again, much to the delight of Sir Richard Bennett, who by now was great friends with George Bligh.

By now, Caroline Bligh was the scandalous social butterfly that shamefully and audaciously coloured the more integral newspaper headlines of Sir Richard Bennett. He could never have enough of the Blighs. The more outrageous the behaviour of Caroline Bligh, the more he had something illicit, embarrassing, highly shameful, and degrading to write about them, in particular Caroline Bligh. She was well known to be promiscuous, sex-crazed, insatiable, so different from her own mother, the cold, far and distant Elizabeth.

"For years, you've treated your daughter as the slut that she was…" Sir Richard Bennett would taunt and torment Elizabeth Bligh one day, as he callously insulted, demeaned, shamed, and humiliated the Grand Elizabeth Bligh. "Your daughter loves a good time," he would insist, and it would be his excuse for why and how he actually raped Caro.

But the triumphant return of beautiful Caro would now be a predominant force against everything that dared to rule the indomitable Camelot's Kingdom. Then, and it still is, becoming thus the Ashpark of Broken Dreams.

But not before Caroline Bligh embarked on more colourful experiences, taking lovers, whether female or male. One thing came up. Now that she was alone in a very colourful but deviant world, Caroline came to understand what education was. She took a course on art and began living for her own dreams. Alone as Caro in a diversified apartment, infused with her own ideas and her own art, Caroline Bligh came a long way through thick and thin.

Until then, so many changes to this still young, cosmopolitan, adventurous lady would occur.

Returning home to Camelot's Kingdom, would it benefit or totally destroy her and her family, the Blighs? Camelot's Kingdom or Ashpark could be a doomsday place, the Ashpark of Broken Dreams, or a brand-new time, refreshing and Jack. Still Ashpark or Camelot, always and would always play the duality of life. The black and white. The female and male gender. The Sun and the Moon. The forces of both sides, that could be good but bad and lethal and terrific. The Yin and the Yang.

But would Camelot's Kingdom destroy their own myths, their own lives, and, towards the end, destroy everything? One remembers the mythological Camelot with King Arthur Pendragon, Guinevere, Merlin the Magician, and Morgana la Faye (as in Fata Morgana, an illusive map) … please read on.

In years to come, David Bligh, the sole inheritor of Ashpark of Broken Dreams, after living through such terrifying ordeals and tragic events, and one so horrifying that Ashpark suffered badly from a terrible, heavy flooding with the kitchen exploding, would, having enlightened himself during his long journeys of self-discovery, move all of his family and sell the Ashpark that he came to dub the Ashpark of Broken Dreams, and into a newly built mansion they will move???

Chapter 04
George Bligh: The Essence of the Bligh Empire
(Part Two)

George Bligh was at a meeting when a phone call came through. He couldn't take it, telling his secretary to either ask the caller to call back or, incidentally, get the person's name and number. Once this was done, he continued with his meeting. The project was to raise money for his cattle. The Second World War had certainly diminished his beef enterprises, or business to that effect.

The meeting went for about two hours. Meanwhile, they had some refreshments, which were called for, as George's throat was parched from giving so many guidelines, directions, and instructions, explaining the reason for the price rise. Once it was finished, his secretary handed over the message: the number and, more importantly, the name, scribbled on nicely written paper. The name was simple: Caro. And the number. George's hands trembled. His sister, the black sheep of the family, had returned.

Jolly good. His sister had finally had the good sense to return home to Australia and to contact him. He was glad. He had been worried about his sister and her so-called wild ways wherever she settled. He thought of his own mother, the formidable matriarch of Camelot's kingdom, Grand Elizabeth Bligh. She would be glad to know that Caro was home. His smile soon twisted into a bittersweet one, for the other sister was still lost to all of them.

His mother was never known for her subtle ways, but he came from her, and he knew that sometimes Bligh women were made of the same stock, liberally and literally. They were not supposed to tangle with others to begin with, and to actually undermine them would be a real mistake. The Bligh women, eh?

What to do? He had grown up with Caro, and to say he actually missed her would be an understatement. He had come to recognise his sister's strengths and weaknesses—at least to his comprehension and thorough understanding. In his mind, Caro stood on her own, and for him, she had his backing and support.

On his desk sat pictures of his wife, Elaine, and his children, James and little Anna. At the back sat an imperious picture of his equally imperious mother, the grand Elizabeth Bligh. On the right side sat the picture of his all-time dominant father, Louie George Bligh, in his grey suit with neatly done short hair. His father never wore a moustache.

But these were good news, if not excellent. Someone was needed to brighten up Ash Park. Even though he had two little cheeky monkeys to practically drive him nuts, they made the place sunny and brought him a real sunny disposition—and so did his imperious mother.

Not all was as it seemed, but then again, nothing ever was.

Don't let me be misunderstood.

For many, including his own sister, George Robert Bligh was meant to be sweet, very understanding, a man who followed the code and its principles.

George always found good and positive things about everything and everyone. Being a conservative, he provoked no malice towards anyone. Born rich and wealthy, he was also handsome and debonair. The added plus was that he was a real gentleman—those sorts of elements multiplied in his ways.

The older son of the Blighs was a joy for anyone's eyes. He was kind, honest, highly impressive, intelligent, and well educated. More than that, he was popular and well loved by almost everyone. Yes, a man everyone would be proud to introduce to their parents.

In his life, George always knew that position, wealth, and timing mattered. His deep analytical personality meant he proceeded with caution in everything, ensuring he never put a foot wrong. But that didn't mean he didn't drink, smoke cigars, and have his share of women. Of course, he might have been a Bligh, but he was human after all. He ate and drank, and his sexual hormones were like anyone else's. George Bligh was in the throes of his manly emancipation, and women played a major part in his life.

We cannot help but liken him to Prince Charles of the UK. In many ways, George Bligh, like Prince Charles, was the heir to his own Bligh empire and the reigning cattle baron. George, like Prince Charles, was born into Australia's "royalty," with immense wealth, status, and fortune. His regal mother was the imperious Grand Elizabeth Bligh, exactly like Queen Elizabeth II—minus the official title. While the Queen resided in Buckingham Palace, Grand Elizabeth Bligh made her own kingdom, power, and glory, creating Camelot in Ash Park.

Even though the grand mansion in Ash Park was nothing compared to Kensington Palace, it was clear enough to be a similar kind of palace. George Robert Bligh, in so many ways, mirrored the cleverness and stakes of a royal family. This is a surreal fairy tale, one that shows what it takes to survive in a royal court: the hierarchies, the glooms and dooms, the pleasant moments that all the money can buy, the extreme luxuries, the dramas, and the scandals. For the royal family, life could be both glamorous and dismaying. All that shines is not necessarily gold—mostly fakery, and in this case, fiction.

So George was born into these pleasantries: love, promise, and fortune. In fact, he could have and did have the world at his feet, servants at his beck and call. His position demanded attention—maybe even a bow—but no one called him "sir." It was either Mr Bligh or simply George. He also had his own books and readings. A private upbringing in an exclusive, expensive school made him a lover of literature. He found solace in books and in the nitty-gritty world he observed. Through them, he gained elementary wisdom, insights, and a deeper understanding of other worlds—a huge perspective for his self-education and personal development. Like Prince Charles, he was a deep thinker, an intellectual, a man of good looks, medium height, smart and rich.

Most men in his position in Australian society would have had credentials stemming from expensive education. George Bligh would one day inherit the entire Ash Park estate, all of which were his legal birthrights. But as in every major history, romance, or dalliance, there would come a time when he would need to fight for what was rightfully his: his honour, the right to love a woman, and the registration of his newly born son as Ash Park's master, the legitimate heir to the Bligh empire. Naturally, along comes his new wife.

The Bligh Fortune and Empire

As with any family, big or small, rich or poor, there comes a time when someone like George Bligh must confront the skeletons in the closet.

For his father, Louis, George was too calm, too quiet, a dreamer. He wanted his son to be tough, social, and outgoing. George preferred a quieter life, spending time with himself and nature. Nothing was wrong with that.

His father's tactics weren't getting anywhere. George also had a resolute streak. His strong personality would come to the fore, showing a determined man who would not submit to verbal bullying or anything more.

Unlike Prince Charles, George Bligh lived in a world bound by many things, including rigid protocols, etiquette, and formalities. George was not only like Prince Charles—he was also a man who bloomed in his own way, something most people failed to notice due to his sensitivity and sense of duty. While Prince Charles needed to serve the British monarchy, George Bligh was a free man, a mere Australian citizen, with generations of family stories that could be shared on cozy winter evenings around a crackling fire drinking and smoking. How deliciously beautiful.

George Bligh was no pushover. Behind that cool, calm, and collected demeanour, he knew what he wanted. And alas, he was very much his own mother's son, but far more liberal in many ways, especially in ways that required caution. His calming and collected personality helped him carry on with his duties, guided by direction and experience. One would be mistaken to think that George ever put a foot wrong. True, he was the honour and pride of his mother, the grand Elizabeth Bligh, Ash Park's matriarch—not to mention that he was also her joy.

George Bligh grew up in a time that little prepared him for his battles, psychologically and philosophically. But he was a man to be reckoned with. In his position, he had informants dishing out both positive and negative information—good or bad, black or white, left or right, up or down. But, as always, he often found such news arrived a tad too late, and usually the hard way. This led him into deep confrontations and exposed dramas, which he faced with his mother's brave spirit. He confronted adversaries and even personal demons, including discovering that his father was homosexual. He did not reveal this secret to his mother immediately, but he knew how to resolve problems. For every problem, there was a solution, and he would achieve justice or triumph in due course. But he never accounted to the fact that fate could be really cruel and things could change easily.

To outsiders, George's bountiful and wealthy forums made him seem to live a magical life. His business was booming, and his love life was exciting and romantic.

When he returned home from boarding school, until the death of his father, life in Ash Park slowed, becoming quiet and measured. His mother was often at home, carving herself a niche within her own empire, directing it, maintaining her office, managing lawyers, and overseeing employees. She delivered well and dealt with everything. Business continued as usual, according to the rules and regulations of Ash Park.

When George finished his secondary education, Elizabeth saw it fit to throw him a coming-of-age party. She was more than happy to show off her son and to demonstrate, to any single women present, the power and passion of a solo parent. She wanted to showcase her own success and triumph.

Elizabeth did not ask for her son's opinion; she simply informed him that the party would be held at Ash Park, and she would be delighted to present him to the world.

On the big day, Elizabeth dressed in royal blue and greeted her guests with pride. Her beautiful face lit up as she watched her son, grown, good-looking, and successful. Among the guests, the Standish family attended, and two young women were introduced to George—Elaine and Regina.

The night flew by with lively conversation and dancing. The food was excellent, the beverages plentiful, and champagne flowed. Major speeches were interspersed with laughter and jokes about George's time at secondary school. Now a fully-fledged twenty-year-old gentleman, George was the legitimate heir to the Bligh fortune and all that came with it.

It was a beautiful night, remembered by all. The newspapers reported it the next day, with pictures of George, the lively setting, the food, and the companionship. George fell deeply in love with Elaine Standish.

For all intents and purposes, he sought to learn more about Elaine and her family. They were wealthy and prominent within Australian society. Her debutante ball would soon take place the following year, and naturally, the Blighs were invited, much to their delight.

George might have been in love with Elaine, but there was much to achieve. He ensured that Ash Park ran smoothly. He oversaw the cattle industry, kept records updated, and introduced modern equipment to make work easier for his employees. He expanded business through exports and established a better-equipped farm for milk and cheese production. He loved it. His ideas were progressing.

Everything seemed to work perfectly around him. He reveled in his status and often visited Elaine and her family, to the delight of his mother, Grand Elizabeth. The Standish family admired the Blighs. When Elaine's debutante ball finally arrived, George, as a most elegant gentleman, could not hide his excitement. That same night, he proposed to her, and Elaine happily accepted.

Summer came and went, and their engagement took place in the midst of autumn. On a mild, sombre autumn afternoon, everyone of nobility and who was who, attended the engagement party at Ash Park. Elizabeth Bligh would not have it any other way. It was Ash Park or nothing.

Guests were happy to comply, enjoying the precious and expensive offerings of the Bligh household.

Meanwhile, watching the proceedings was the young and beautiful Regina Margaret Standish. Younger than her sister, she observed Elaine becoming engaged to one of the most eligible bachelors in Australia. The sapphire ring dazzled as George placed it on Elaine's left hand. Regina looked around and noticed the joy on everyone's faces.

Her older sister was beautiful, with long dark hair and crystal-clear blue eyes, much like Regina's own. When Regina saw herself in a mirror, one could easily mistake her for Elaine. Same face, same eyes, same contours, same skin tone, same hair colour, same beauty. One day, Regina would be as tall and as impressive as Elaine. But Elaine was marrying into the Bligh family, where George was not only handsome but rich. In prominent Australian society, he was known as the cattle baron. Regina thought him too suave and soft to manage horses, let alone cattle, in a harsh environment demanding blood, sweat, and tears.

She was invited to Ash Park countless times, along with her parents, attending many official Bligh events, including formal balls in Sydney Town Hall. She loved Ash Park and admired how fortunate her sister was. Perhaps one day she would marry someone like George. Whether it was the idea of marrying someone like him or George himself, it was hard to tell. Regina could be complicated and confusing.

While these celebrations were ongoing, Regina became Elizabeth Bligh's close companion, spending time talking, laughing, and sharing jokes, showing her more social, outgoing, and vibrant side.

During this time, a pair of light blue eyes followed her. Richard admired what he saw. He knew that Regina, young, fresh, and beautiful, would respond to his attention. She was ripe for the plucking. Richard, a young, handsome, suntanned Aussie with beach-blonde hair and striking features, introduced himself to Regina as the plain and simple "Dickie Boy." Once their eyes met, they recognised each other's character and saw how they could use each other for mutual advancement. Their smiles said it all.

George and Elaine's faces appeared in the newspapers the morning following the engagement party. The black-and-white pictures showed off the beautiful sapphire ring capturing everything that had transpired the evening before, including the notable guests who officially attended the event.

Their wedding date was still to be set, but it would be announced in the newspapers. In the meantime, Elaine and George continued their merry-go-round of social engagements. Wherever they went, whatever they attended, the press followed. She was classy, beautiful, and intelligent, and she was truly George's pride. He would swell with love and pride whenever he took her out or spent time with her. His love for Elaine knew no bounds.

Elaine now needed to visit the modiste in central Sydney to choose her wedding dress, satin shoes, veil, and tiara, and to rehearse for the event. Her little sister, Regina, would accompany her as a bridesmaid, wearing a petal-length gown. They collected shoes, flowers, and everything required for the bridal preparations.

Knowing how hot summer could be, the Blighs decided on a spring wedding. The venue would again be the luscious green grounds of the famous Ash Park, Elizabeth's pride and joy. The matriarch swelled with pride. Her little boy had come so far. Now, a man in his early twenties, he is getting married. Elizabeth's eyes welled up with tears, and her daughter Caro wiped them away with her own tissue. She too cried, for the event was emotional, profound, and beautiful.

The bride entered the chapel, radiant and lovely, and her brother George waited for her at the altar. The beautiful bridesmaid, Reggie, observed the proceedings closely. Richard Bennett, George Bligh's best man, was fully entertained by the whole affair. Elaine was the dream of every lady, and the dress she had chosen suited her perfectly.

The wedding reception was a blast. Balloons and Chinese lanterns adorned the grounds. A band played, and food and beverages were plentiful and highly exquisite. Elizabeth spared nothing for her son's wedding, and once again, the press covered it with great enthusiasm.

They went on their honeymoon, and when they returned, their happiness was evident to all. Within a year of their wedding, Elaine announced that she was pregnant, and the joy was ecstatic.

Regina became a constant visitor to Ash Park. Now that her sister Elaine was expecting, she had every reason to be there, repeatedly enjoying the majestic Ash Park manor, the sprawling grounds, and the breathtaking surroundings. She loved everything about it, especially riding horses and galloping whenever she wished.

She often wondered how lucky her sister Elaine was and how handsome George was. And once again, the question surfaced: was she in love with Ash Park, or was she in love with George Bligh, or perhaps both?

Chapter 05:
Sir Richard Bennett. The Smooth Operator.

The Blighs… a family that was always in the news… either for one thing or another… and the good deeds that they'd done… they'd attended charities… they'd donated money… they were always seen as very much a part of highly elite Australian society… they were considered to be Australian royalty. But much has been written about them, such as:

Louis Bligh was always outstanding in his demeanour… his always primed and properly dressed status made him cut a very dashing figure. By his side, as usual, was his beautiful petite wife, with her long curly honey-blonde hair all done in a beautiful decorative fashion that was very trendy at the time and held with sparkling combs. Dressed in the fashion of the day, she also cut a very interesting figure, one who knew her failings when it came to the fashion stakes. Of course, husband and wife had never committed a faux pas… they were always elegant, sophisticated, conducting themselves to the extremes. Except for what happened in the background, which nobody bothered to check or confirm, their other sad tastes. The Blighs were not classified as nouveau riche; they were deeply steeped in tradition, with fortunes inherited from good Bligh families. As per inheritance, they very much kept their make-believe lives to themselves… or so we all thought… or they thought.

With them came the Swansons, close friends of the Blighs. Lady Swanson was forever injecting Elizabeth Bligh with information, whether good or bad. She had come into a huge fortune when she married into the Swansons. However, they were not really the idyllic family they were supposed to be. The press were always catching Sir Swanson with his pants down. The press's love–hate fascination with crucifying him kept going on. If it wasn't one thing that Sir Henry Swanson did, it would have been something else. At the time they were the laughing stock of the Aussie elite involving themselves with the other elites, being laughed or not.

Throughout it all stood a man who watched and smiled, finding the whole thing amusing, highly entertaining. More to it, watching the lovely Elizabeth Bligh strut her cool demeanour and scoff at him… his own amusement was becoming highly abhorrent.

Bennett was the quintessential Australian Peter Pan of youth… and who could ever deny this? Yet one could also have said that he was a bit of a bum.

Suntanned, with sandy blonde hair, sparkling blue eyes, medium height… who could ignore a man like him, possessing such a feverish shape and form? He was the ultimate Aussie boy, and he loved the ocean, surfing, camping… and time and again, one would find him relaxing and resting his laurels on the plain sandy beach of Bondi in summer. That was his home, the beach, endlessly surfing, boozing, smoking cigars, and always with any number of women, all decked in their beautiful summer swimming frocks. Otherwise, he'd be revving his "super" Harley Davidson, all clad in black leather, boots, helmet, and goggles, trailblazing all throughout Sydney's CBD and entering his rich and powerful media mogul father's office, **Bennett's Press** (later to be renamed), newspapers in tow, setting the girls' hearts aflutter. Dickie Boy, as he was known, was at his best a flirt, a playboy, and at his worst… a heartbreaker, and for some, the black sheep of the Bennett family, or even a bum.

Each time he appeared in the newspapers, oddly enough, they were about one thing or another. The papers sang either his praises or lambasted him. More often than not, they could never ignore him. The news painted him the bad boy… which he…

enjoyed being the quintessential Peter Pan of youth, the forever sandy-haired, suntanned, blue-eyed beach boy. For starters, he didn't get along with his parents. He did what he wanted, either excelled in doing so or was thrown into the rubbish bin for overdoing it and doing it the wrong way, which brings us to the same topic: he was irresponsible, irreverent, and had never done an honest day's work, nor did he see the reason for doing so.

Like his ten or twenty years-younger rival, George Bligh, he was born into a pretty wealthy and fortunate family. Richard was the youngest of the Bennett family and, as such, was lucky enough to belatedly inherit what his older siblings could have easily afforded.

Dickie Boy was not born with a silver spoon in his mouth; by the time he was born, the silver spoons had already served their purpose. He never had that kind of luxurious taste. As a matter of fact, he grew up more in the oceans than trailblazing around the Australian countryside. He returned home only to change his clothes, then flew off again. He couldn't stand being under the same roof or going through the same shenanigans the family always did. His elderly mother had to plead with him to attend official events, dinners, family parties, preside over formals and balls. But he took his time. Unlike the Blighs, he stood out like a green or black thumb, much to the distress of the more consolidated and traditional Bennett family. He had two older brothers who went through the highs and lows of structure, the laws, rules, and regulations drummed into them from the beginning… and his father had a terrible temper. Dicko was fed with a golden spoon.

Richard Bennett and the Second World War

Dicko was born under a fortunate star. Some are born struggling even to fit into this sometimes cold, cruel, and reticent world. Others are born into powerful and glorious families, with desires of going overboard… with investments nationally and internationally. Others are left alone to fend for themselves. Still, there would be others whose ultimate escapism would be a factor for a broader life, going to extremes in adventures and proving their own worth, while others lived a very oppressive, lonely, sad existence, lacking love, tender, caring love, which in many unprecedented cases was missing. Yet some of these rare people are happy with their lot. For the rich, poor, or in between, we mostly accept our own destinies, our fates, however hard, however difficult, good, bad, or fun. One needs to face the fact that life can never be perfect, and somehow we can never be completely happy and content with whatever is thrown at us. Procrastinating about it will never make us realise the actual goodies we all have.

Richard was born the youngest and least important in the Bennett family. His older siblings took centre stage. They were the new Bennetts who would carry the family further into a new era. They were in the mid-term of a new war descending around the world. The First World War had gone, and the Second was looming. One could smell it, feel it. The man leading Germany was a lunatic with dreams of a white, united world, preaching a new creed where Asians and Black people were nonexistent. He called himself the Kaiser (Caesar), loved to be hailed with the right arm extended, and demanded his citizens follow his beliefs. Jews, he claimed, did not belong in this world.

He created *Mein Kampf*, his account of struggles, dry and belittling, and rose to Chancellor, gathering and training the youth military army, spreading Nazi ideology, brainwashing citizens, and holding fiery, hypnotic speeches. The threat of war was imminent, though no one knew when it would start. Hitler was a fascist with unfounded strategies. He slowly collected males to help him conquer the world, from the Orient, the Japanese, to the Occident. Germans would occupy; Italians would follow, hence the Axis Treaty. But the Japanese told Hitler that what they did in the Orient was their business and had nothing to do with him or Mussolini. Hitler and Mussolini had reserves of money for whatever purposes they wished. Naturally, this brought the worst impending happenings worldwide. It no longer remained just the Axis of three, it became the whole world.

NOTE FOR FILE

(Australia got involved at a later stage. Macau was neutral, as was Portugal. All the same, it was inevitable… the Second World War would explode in many ways… with the VE as the Allies and the US finally entering after the bombing of Pearl Harbour on 7th December 1941. As the war with the Japanese didn't seem to stop, the Atomic Bomb *Enola Gay: Little Boy* was created and dropped on Hiroshima on 6th August 1945, followed by the second on 9th August in Nagasaki.)

Richo. The BENNETT heir.

After the Axis Treaty, The first casualties began with the early invasion of Poland and the imprisonment of the Jews. Meanwhile, in Europe the

Germans, along with their wartime allies the Italians, started their invasions. On the other side of the Oriental world, the Japanese under Emperor Hirohito invaded all of Asia. Their infrastructure established a base in Province of Nanking when they settled there in 1935.

Meanwhile, the price of petrol went up, and President Roosevelt of the USA staying out of the war. At this time, in need and in aid, one would prefer to sit, watch, and observe. Joe Kennedy Senior, who wanted Americans to join the war. was asked by Roosevelt back to the USA, but the Kennedys had two sons serving as well and also a daughter. Over here in Australia, the Bennetts also had two sons. Richard Bennett's older brothers joined the Australian Army to serve for King and Country.

Before their departure, their enthusiasm were electrifying. But between the sad tears of Richard's mother and the heartfelt speech of his father to their two sons, Dicko's older brothers… the dinner, as usual, was a casual affair in the Bennett household, enjoying the fare, the drinks, the family company, and light banter. Music played as usual. Somehow, this happened in most households… dinner seemed to be the centre of any family's structure, while Sunday lunches were a family treat after mass. Were a respectable and sacred odyssey,

Bennett's siblings

It seemed the night went on forever. The Bennett family didn't want to let go of their two older sons… but they at least had little Richard to console themselves. Richo would stay behind and maybe serve in the army locally. Young was hardly suited for the horrid conflicts and bloodshed. Richo, as the whole family could see, was not cut out for the heavy artillery. All the major responsibilities laid on the first two siblings.

As the night passed and the crack of dawn brought its first rays, the Bennetts happened to mention the new Dr Jack Duncan, Elizabeth Bligh's adopted son, who was also serving while distressingly and abruptly leaving socialite Caroline Bligh's debutante ball. The night was awash with so many problems. Even though the Bennetts had to admit that the party was elegant, beautifully planned and organised, Caroline spoiled everything by falling ill and being rushed to the ER at Inverness Hospital.

Dickie Boy smiled broadly. He saw Jack, with his own eyes, going all gah-gah over the Australian socialite, the refreshingly young Caroline Bligh. He thought of her as beautiful, comely, dark, exotic… and what was with the Bligh girls? They were all beautiful, a treat coming from Elizabeth herself. He also noticed the youngest, Little Lizzie. She was light and flighty… one moment here, the next nowhere to be seen… yet another Bligh creature, so different from Mother Elizabeth and sister Caroline. On the other hand, another flirtatious, young, bewitching girl caught his eye: the delightful Regina with those flashing blue eyes of hers, and…..man can she flirt. He knew her very well then.

The following day, as early as six in the morning, proudly wearing their Aus Armies' uniforms, both brothers hugged Dicko's parents tightly, their mother convulsing in huge, teary goodbyes. The father choked back tears but felt so proud of both of them. The three brothers for once, hugged together in a tight embrace. Now only Richo remained with the parents, serving the army locally. Army regulations now dictated that brothers could not serve simultaneously in the same office, but the two older siblings were inseparable. Where one went, the other followed. Richo missed out, with always being with them, being born the youngest and in a different era for his parents were expecting a little girl, but Richo was born..He simply sat behind a desk and aided and abetted when needed. Young as he was, he continued to love what he did best, surfing, surfing, and more surfing. Besides, it cost nothing… the ocean was free, as was camping.

Others fought a hard war anywhere on earth, and casualties were terrible. Richo couldn't care less. He surfed wildly, revved his Harley, and left the worries to his parents. Dicko lived life wild and free, boozing big, smoking big, dazzling girls always hanging on his arm. Now this is living. The crumbs he got from the army were made up by the pocket money his parents gave him. He didn't have to work, and why should he? He needed to serve his country… but for the life of him, he could never understand how people could live on such meagre means while risking their lives.

Sir Richard Bennett and Elizabeth Bligh

Richard continued with his wild, pure, and puritanical ways… free and totally raunchy. Fast, furious, to the extremes, one might have thought he was living his last days.

One day Dicko was told that the whole Bennett family was invited to a debutante ball. Her name was Elizabeth, and she was a sight for sore eyes. For once, he decided to change out of his swimming decks, removed his leather-clad black outfits, kept his parents company, and magically transformed from a sloppy, die-hard surfing guy to a handsome, debonair gentleman, looking suave and genteel in his de rigueur black-and-white tuxedo. Not all the time did Dicko grease his hair à la rock-and-roll style, but my, oh my… this little frog now was the prince that maybe Elizabeth Bligh would kiss at her grandeur debutante ball, her coming of age. He broke a few hearts… but not Elizabeth's.

She looked ravishing, an unique beauty. One by one, the girls and the guests were introduced to the loud Aus elite society, with flashings of cameras and the bright lights of the glamorous chandeliers hanging down from the tall ceilings, with tables being decorated with crystals glasses shimmering and the guests all perfect in their expensive clothes and jewelleries, and lo and behold, there was stick-in-the-mud Louis Bligh taking her in, walking her through the hall all decked in glitz and gold, dancing seriously boringly, tall and stiff, while poor little Elizabeth, smaller and daintier, a breath of fresh air, twirled around the extravagantly decorated hall as the waltz played its suave, breathy tune. Elizabeth conceded to dance with Dickie Boy a couple of times, but her heart was fully with Louis Bligh, who waltzed her through the night and, metaphorically, to the end of the world if it were needed.

Elizabeth

But being Richard Bennett… Elizabeth could wait. Meanwhile, the war raged. Even though Australia was involved, allies were working hard to fight off the Germans invasion. In Asia, Singapore was the first to fall and the Japanese took over.

They also dominated Hong Kong, where they totally ruled, abused, and subjugated, imprisoning anyone English or with a British passport. Only in Macau, under the Portuguese flag, was there safety under the Red Cross. No harm came to citizens or new refugees, who, each night along with the Macanese, Portuguese, and Chinese, held parties, dancing away the worries and fears with food, drink being the supper. People from Shanghai, China, and other nationalities arrived. To outsiders, it seemed as if great celebrations were held nightly, rather than a raging, bloodied war. The Jews were decimated by the Germans. Hatred and hostility spread in Europe, but the more the Germans killed, the more the Jews persevered. Other nationalities also stood up, being counted.

The Portuguese Consul in France, alone helped more than thirty thousand Jews escape with his motto being..I would rather be God's true friend than to be man's thousands friends. He and his family were ostracised and kicked out from their own mansions and palaces in Portugal. The family went through the hardest but they were compensated at a later date. For that in Israel they named a street in his great honour.

In Australia, the influx of refugees increased rapidly, doubling within months increasing the serious shortage of everything: food, housing, water, clothing. As always, the children suffered the most, followed by the elderly. The government was stretched to its limits. In this way, a moderate Italian family entered the lives of everyone in Inverness. They were the newly arrived Polettis. Their arrival heralded a new era. The winds of change were seriously blowing, whether people liked it or not. But …. As usual…nothing was and would complete. Australia now was in the early stages of by and large an international commune.

The audacious Japanese, now completely took control over Asia, They became bolder…irrational…overly domineering and overly confident.

Therefore, on 7th December 1941, they took Pearl Harbour by surprise and bombed the naval base without mercy, fear, or foe.

The war in the Pacific exploded into action. It went on for another three years with losses on either side. Then someone developed the atomic bomb. *Little Boy* or *Enola Gay* showed its explosive presence, with the USA using it on 6th August 1945 in Hiroshima, and another on 9th August 1945 in Nagasaki. This put an end to the Japanese Empire's dreams of owning all of Asia and the Pacific. Herewith in Darwin, Australia the bombing was executed on 19th February 1941.

The VE forces went on liberating other territories. After landing on 6th June 1944, D-Day, the Allies fought with their might, ardour, hard work, pain, and sorrow… many never returned to their loved ones. But it did pay off.

By September 1945, the peace treaty was signed, the Sino Japanese in Macau, and all things were supposed to return to normal… or did they?

One day, Dickie Boy was summoned home for dinner. It was the beginning of Spring. The war was over and he was preparing to go to the beach. Against all odds, even though the parents' summoning came at the wrong time, he shrugged it off and after dressing up went, against his better judgement, muttering here and there, cursing, with no inkling of what was going on. His Harley and Davison could be heard miles away, as he arrived and parked his motorbike in the family garage. Then he removed his helmet and cladded in his daily black leather suit with boots and all entered his own mansion.

The house and himself felt cold. The employees carried on with their duties by bringing in the food to be served at the table. The atmosphere felt heavy and oppressive. The glinting lights shimmered on the silverware set on the table. Everything seemed the same, yet different. His parents were waiting for him in the dining room. The only ones missing were his two older brothers. His mother, as usual, was pristinely dressed with taste and elegance. His father was the same, wearing a white starched shirt, sleeves halfway up, and grey slacks.

He greeted both of them by kissing him mum and then hugging his dad. Still he felt like an outsider. The windows were opened, and the breeze blew softly. The aroma of the food assailed his nostrils. The wine were being filled into the glasses. The butler smiled and nodded at him.

Food was served in a deeply morose atmosphere. No one spoke, they seemed like robots. Every movement appeared staged. The silence was terrible, one could cut the air with a knife. Every now and then, his mother brought out her handkerchief to dry her tears. Dicko thought she missed his two older brothers dearly. Then, to his horror, his sparkling blue eyes noticed the black dress his mother wore. She was in mourning. His father lost his unanimous valiant spirit. He sunk in his seat.

Bennett and the brothers

His father continued eating in reverent silence, serving one portion after another. When he finished, he brought the serviette to his lips, wiped them, and slowly stared at Richo. Dry and emotionless, he stated that both of Dicko's brothers were dead, then choked, sipped his wine, and fell silent. His mother remained quiet throughout dinner. Outside, the sun's red spots glowed, lighting the house, while the chandeliers danced merrily. The servants cleared the table and served coffee and sweets. This time, they stayed in the dining room for coffee. Dickie Boy lit two cigars, one for his father and one for himself.

"I want you to come to the office tomorrow," his father thundered dryly. Then he rose from his chair, pensively looked out the window, turned, and faced him, the hard way… or perhaps his own pitiful way.

"It's time. You've pulled your socks up, my boy… it's time you earned some responsibilities and your own quids." He gritted his teeth; his face was drained of colour, his grey hair permanent. He choked to speak, then left the dining room. His mother's face was swollen with tears. Dickie Boy didn't know what to do… he didn't know how to soften the blow. Seeing her body shaking and hearing her uncontrollable sobs, he embraced his mother. Both cried together. Once upon a time, a little boy had to grow up very fast… and faster indeed. That was then.

The following morning was a new day. Richo did not wear his uniform. He rode his bike, clad in black leather and boots. His love for revving up his Harley Davidson and his surfing days as a bum were now over.

When he arrived at Bennett's Press, the secretary already knew of his appointment with Dickie's father. She closed the door behind him. Matter-of-factly, he sat down, crossed his right leg over the other, and lit a cigar.

Richo's new beginnings as the BENNETT

His father looked long and hard at him behind the desk. For all the things Dicko or Richo had done or created, one fact remained: he was his son. Senior and Junior shared the same teasing blue eyes and the same grin. One was older, with grey hair pulled back into a small bun, a grey mustache, wrinkled skin, and pale from ageing. He would have been handsome once, but old age was catching up. The younger version was muscular, with long, straight, blonde hair, deeply suntanned, and a clean-shaven face. Both were the same height… both were Bennetts. But that was where the likeness ended. Young Bennett was no puppy.

Bennett Senior, with trembling hands, poured himself a drink. It had been a distressing ordeal. Now he addressed his youngest son, still faltering every now and then. He was no longer the tough, disciplined father; his eyes were moistened, and he openly cried. It was a long, terrible morning. By the time his father finished all instructions and advice regarding the business, Bennett got to know his father better. Once finished, Dickie Boy left the building. Two weeks later, he was discharged from the Australian Army and returned home, to the Bennett mansion.

Young Bennett

Like it or not, he was needed around the house. Like it or not, he was the new entrepreneur. The funerals of the two Bennett boys were held. They were honoured with medals, their epitaphs reading: "For the love of their country… they will not grow old. Lest we forget."

Richard Bennett didn't like it, but someone had to run his father's press. The women looked ripe for the pickings; girls were falling in love rapidly with the new young media mogul. But his work was never done. Outwardly, he became obscenely dapper and wealthy, shining like a new star in Sydney's social scene, which none could deny and to which Bennett, resignedly accepted the new role.

He had served his country well. As he returned home in his chauffeured limousine, he reflected on his army days. The memories were good, bad, and dangerous, but Bennett glammed it up, spiced it up, and lived through it all. He had become a legend in the Aus Army.

Bennett Junior proved his father wrong. Initially, his father doubted Dicko could handle the business. But he fell easily into his role as the new boss, staying well informed on company matters, which raised his father's attentive eyebrow. His father warned him: "One wrong move, my boy, and you'll be in the oven being roasted." He was instructed to avoid office romances, antics, and blunders, sighs…another thing he was being assigned to. He did resigned to it again.

His memoirs, now home, reflected on the good times in the army, learning to speak and write German, and decoding cryptic messages. Dicko became a spy, but he was not solo in the process. The game was ripe.

Dickie Boy. The Heir Apparent

Dickie Boy was a quick learner, though it was a different kind of challenge. Learning his father's business, he did. The suntanned, blonde-haired, blue-eyed true-blue beach boy, the Peter Pan of Never Never Land, was no more.

Now, instead of black leather outfits and boots, and spending time in the ocean, he wore expensive suits. Instead of a helmet, much to his regret, he wore hats; instead of goggles, he wore the latest Ray-Ban pilot sunglasses. The man was "smoking," still puffing his cigars, drinking hard, and continuing his merry-go-round with beautiful women outside of his office hours. That of course was a blessing in disguise. His father breathed a sigh of relief.

He then learned the true meaning of being a Bennett. Everyone was at his beck and call. They grovelled in a servile and ubiquitous manner at his feet. They treated him like a god. He was respected; his word was law. His instructions were the new rules and regulations. Whatever he wanted or desired was just for the taking. He discovered that power exuded everything, status, privileges. He loved it.

One Sunday, after lunch following church services, his father muttered that Dickie Boy should be getting married. He looked back at his father and retorted, "Give me time to really enjoy this new status. I am still getting used to it," savouring his brandy and smoking his cigar. His parents noticed that young Bennett loved being rich.

Now he needed to compose himself, learn the trades and tricks of the press, and understand the media business. In doing so, he learned that being the commanding chief of a press brought news to him fast and furious, as easily as drinking. Narrowing his eyes with complete abandon, he discovered the job offered access to private, top-level information. It wasn't long before he got to know who was who in official circles. Furthermore, he learnt some of the perks that came with the role. His father was friends with the commissioner and well-connected in government and social circles worldwide. This provided excellent opportunities for both the business and the public.

His father was knighted by the King, so Sir Richard Bennett was born. Now, Sir Richard Bennett Junior emerged, father and son everywhere together, living the high life where everything could be bought, or would be in the near future. The espionage work would also come in handy. Dicko was everything he could ever be… except for Elizabeth.

The Peter Pan of Never Never Land now belonged to a world of wealth, privilege, and power. Clad in his new expensive suits, his hair heavily greased in the style of the times, Sir Richard Bennett Junior was slowly emerging.

Sir Richard Bennett Emerges

What a difference from yesterday's Richo to today. Trading his old days for a new, vibrant, handsome, and ideal man, many in the elite social gatherings were highly impressed. These days, he spent time exercising. His years surfing and riding made him fitter, so he installed a new swimming pool and a small gym. Nostalgically, he remembered those days of freedom, now ended, but he found new joys in his present life or better in his present job.

He began to meditate and reflect on his life. The old days were no longer accessible. He needed to develop his character, appraise his personality, and modify his ways. He was now Sir Richard Bennett, surveying the state of his affairs. Through the deaths of his two older brothers, he had inherited the entire fortune. Living in his palace, ruling his kingdom, he was adamant about maintaining the status quo.

Life had to be taken seriously. The man who loved freedom became harder, disciplined, calculatingly cold, and driven. He loved his power, his wealth, and his reign began, especially after his father suffered a fatal heart attack followed by the strokes, compounded by the grief of losing his two older sons.

After the funeral, light refreshments were served. They gathered at the office for the reading of the will. His mother would remain in the manor, with a summer house for her retirement. Dickie Boy now inherited everything. His father had wanted his youngest son to continue the press and media legacy. Sir Richard Bennett was now the Emperor, the King of his own kingdom.

Bennett and "THE GLOBE"

What his mother saw in her son, the new Sir Richard Bennett, frightened her to the core. Long gone were those sparkling full of fun blue eyes. They were profound, serious. Only his mouth stretched to smile but his eyes remained cold, penetrating and evasive.

But not all were ready to bow to him.

He soon discovered that there were exceptions to every rule. Not everyone shook, rattled, and rolled. He realised this when his love and hatred towards the Blighs ran hot and cold. He wanted them to bow to him, but he also loved Elizabeth.

Elizabeth, the beauty he thought he deserved, was by then betrothed. Both he and his mother received the invitation to Elizabeth's wedding to the honourable Louis Bligh at Ashpark County. She was emerging as the new Mrs Louis Bligh. Elizabeth rejected and ignored him. Despite initial attempts to woo her, they failed. He was attending her wedding to a man he found dull and unremarkable.

That was his first mistake. Women like Elizabeth did not wait. They were wooed with everything, the very best.

On the day of the wedding, at the time, he couldn't hide his subtle hatred for the couple. She looked heavenly in a regal 1920s-style white dress. Her long, thick golden tresses were covered under a headband and long veil, magnifying her virginal beauty. She bewitched him. He realised how much he loved her… and how she had broken his heart.

He looked around the vast palatial place, needing air. He raised his eyes to the heavens as he sipped his champagne and understood the whole sordid situation. The Ashpark of broken dreams made him feel sick, as if punched in the stomach. Then he returned to the event.

His attention shifted to Louis Bligh. Somehow, the man seemed out of place, performing in a rehearsed manner. Dickie Boy smiled to himself, thinking the wedding was a farce and that Elizabeth had received her comeuppance. He felt deeply entranced in thoughts of revenge.

His mother, tired and emotionally drained from three deaths in a short period, came to him, wanting to return home. He abided. They left after wishing the newlyweds happiness. Inside, Richo was seething, angry, poisoned. Now he thoroughly hated Elizabeth and the Blighs. If anything presented he would not stop but go ahead in revenging on them. But that would come at the proper moment.

Bennett's New Project: "THE GLOBE"

The next morning, he returned to his duties. His father was dead, leaving a huge legacy. Everyone was on deck. He increased the typing pool to thirty girls, with a secretary excelling in shorthand and administration. He augmented his empire and raised her wages. His methods were straightforward, money.

More journalists were hired, and the newspapers published daily editions to attract clientele. The papers sold like hotcakes. The Great Depression hit Australia hard, but Sir Richard Bennett, the wealthy media mogul, revelled in his vengeance and in the love-hate relationship with the Blighs. Boy, how long ago was that. Those long years of war and depression have left their indents marking the time and the memories linger by.

When Elizabeth Bligh was expecting her first child, it was announced in his newspapers to the delight of Louis Bligh. Another pregnancy followed, a little girl named Caroline. Dicko and his mother were invited to both baptisms.

Years later, he heard Elizabeth was pregnant with her third child and had adopted a little boy. He raised his thick eyebrows, his skin cracking, now sporting a moustache. He was still fit and healthy. He replaced the BENNETT PRESS sign with a new one: "THE GLOBE." It shimmered high above the building, symbolising everything.

The Globe excelled, and Bennett beamed in ecstatic exaltation over juicy news and elaborate scandals. His reporters were performing magnificently with the aid of the informants and political spies.

He continued navigating the social circles and integrated the Blighs, attending Government Houses and the Lodge. Young Bennett was mesmerised by the luxury and privilege, but Ashpark remained a sad, morose place with dark secrets. His predictions there would later prove true.

As Georgie Bligh grew, Louis Bligh suffered an accident. At the funeral, all attended except Little Lizzie, whom he kept in check with the Blighs.

When Elizabeth threw an emancipation party for her older son George, he attended. He was getting used to being around the Blighs, now without Louis. He still wanted Elizabeth.

He was also reunited with a stunning lady: Regina, the youngest sister of Elaine Bligh. A model-like, a ravenous beauty, she immediately caught his eye. Shamelessly, Regina and Richo became a terrific couple. Under his tutelage, she thrived, an eager, highly spirited young woman, perfect for him and so alike.

Chapter 06: Between Two Worlds.

James Arthur Bligh... **THE HEIR PRESUMPTIVE TO THE BLIGH'S DYNASTY.**

He was tall, dark and handsome. He was chivalrous, charismatic. He had a soft-spoken voice. He was talented. He sang beautifully. He was everything that any woman wanted and more. His dark wavy hair shone against the dire sun as his blue eyes roamed around the vast place at Camelot's Kingdom. He reigned as the Prince until later on when he ascended to the "throne" as the heir presumptive to the Bligh's inheritance and the vast fortune, such as the land sprawling in front of him.

Being the son of **THE BLIGH'S CATTLE BARON**, the one and only George Bligh, was not an easy task to accomplish, and neither was it being the stuffy but stalwart grandson of the BLIGH'S indomitable grandmother Elizabeth, the matriarch of **CAMELOT'S KINGDOM**. For some, she was the Queen… for others, Camelot Kingdom was the making and the breaking of anyone… it was also called the Camelot of Broken Dreams. How much did it break.

Many women would have swooned all over him, batting their long or faked eyelashes, as on those days they were the trend, trying to seduce him with their sinuous bodies, tight dresses and rock-around-the-clock skirts… or wearing those tight, sinewy dresses or pencil-slim skirts… that highlighted the designing of their beautiful womanly silhouettes… those twisting and turning… with the help of those sexy high heels… and the perfect picture was complete. And guess what, besides that, James Bligh was also filthy rich… affluent… wealthy… and with him carried the colossal responsibility of being the BLIGH. The surname spelt everything, connecting the huge status, the power that so much belonged and exuded from the BLIGHS… a long legacy… woooops… Dynasty, to be more precise. Whisper… whisper… whisper, James Arthur Bligh was the heir presumptive to the Bligh's EMPIRE. And the Bligh alone were the Australian Royalty, by and large.

Ahhhhhhh… is such a dream, being born into such wealth… wealthy, power and status… but James Bligh was more than that. Besides being wealthy, James was very good looking… handsome to the extremes… gallant… and his Grandmah's favourite grandson until another sibling was added to the Bligh's family. James loved it. He loved his own sister like anything, even when both of them were poles apart. The Bligh family was complete, at the time, with mum Elaine, dad George, himself James, and his little cute-as-a-button sister Anna. In the shadows behind his complete family saga was the famous and indomitable grandmother Elizabeth, plus more.

Born and raised in the utmost privileged society, James was privy to the world outside… and its salacious surroundings. He never knew why some people would stare at the huge imperial **CAMELOT'S** building and structure… sighing… as their eyes completely wondered what it would be like… to really live in the stately mansion… one which could tell various romantic stories… one could envisage the lining up of knights in shining armour, rescuing those beautiful damsels in distress… falling thus in love… with appetising adventures to soothe the soul… to actually liven up the melancholic spirits, more… more… more… being someone like JAMES BLIGH… the cavalier… the sunshine and the knight… the prince. How could one fail to see the tall and distinguished young man… towering over the others… being commanding and dominating… or per se, was he?

More to it. In case no one noticed little James had an official notable name…no…no…and no…not James…but Arthur as in Arthur Pendragon, king of the Camelot kingdom.

Every morning it was easy to catch a glimpse of the tall and handsome rider mixing with the other workers inside Camelot, going through all the hard work, wearing nothing except for the casual workers' colourless trousers, sometimes with a t-shirt all soaked in his own sweat, with his upper torso totally dampened by his own extreme perspiration, revealing thus his well-toned upper torso muscles, with James going around fetching and carrying hay to and fro into the horses' barn or simply helping out, per se sitting tall in his saddle, riding in his own domain as he rounded the cattle. He had to work hard for the upkeep of his own kingdom and his own self privileges. It was on a daily timetable, rising early and retiring early to rest, being fed by the best and kept in the good company of his granny, sometimes with his dad and, for the time being, with his little sister, sometimes Dr Jack Duncan keeping them company, which sometimes he took advantage of, spending overnight and departing the following morning to **INVERNESS HOSPITAL**, where now he was the extended GP.

James undertook his boarding school elementary and secondary, never the brightest student. He longed to return home to his domain… his own kingdom, where he, as usual, would rise early, saddle his horse, galloping against the wind, the rain, the sun… whenever it suited him, enjoying everything, including swimming totally naked in his own streams… nature and water brought him nothing but rest… he loved his own prized horse… but his love life was dubious. He did not feel the common and natural attention towards any females… and he was brought up by all females in his own home… he found out that many of the females could be highly troublesome… but that males could be really bitches, as he'd seen them up close. And personal.

Like his father George, he was very much a man with their principles and an humble attitude, as his father was very empathetic towards the plights of everyone… including his sister, aunty Caro, and never once had he mentioned anything about or against her, and he suspected there were extras in this huge house, but unlike his father, he grew up without his mum, with such a traumatic past, as his mother died in the Japanese bombing in Darwin… still no one ever found out her reasons as to why she was there in the first place, that, of course, was his primary loss, a shock, he would never see his beloved mother ever again. Then his father mourned her death terribly, trying to find his own peace by keeping himself away from the house, and his absences were duly noted, as James, at the time, badly needed a male's strong, mature influence around the house to guide him, except for Roy, who was an all-Australian tough guy, but he also had his troubles too.

Then he had his grandmamah, the indomitable matriarch Grand Elizabeth, who took him on board along with his little sister Anna. The pain and sorrow were so deep that George, by himself, tried his best to heal alone… in his own world, eliminating almost everything connected to the house, including his own family… the loss of a woman or lady like Elaine finally broke George into pieces, she was everything he had always wanted, having also the blessings of his own mother. HEARTBREAKING.

Being Elaine, also the mother to his older son James. Both father and son seemed to need time and space to recover… anyone does psychologically. The husband mourning for his wife and the son for his own mother… sad… but George stayed out of his son's life, period. He was never there for his son, never.

But James Arthur Bligh, of course, would be the apple of his own paternal grandmother's eyes. If she had a soft spot for him… it would literally be shown, in the way she saw fit in doing it. Therefore, he was brought up very close to his grandmum and solo… in a world you could maybe call Solitary Confinement, not a prison. But living alone with his little sister Anna Elaine, she was named after his own mother. He was James Arthur… one with the romantic ideas would have known that he was named after King Arthur, the King of Camelot and the Knights of his Round Table. It was fitful, for himself and his kingdom the Camelot.

But in the near future, he would procure his own Guinevere… his birthmark corresponded to this kind of birth mapping. When you looked around him, besides his grandmother, the Camelot Castle was surrounded only by maids, cooks, male employees abounding on a daily basis, working on the land, the cattle, keeping up the whole maintenance of Ashpark. The first impressions were that Camelot was loud, boisterous, alive, colourful… and to a certain extent really gregarious… but that was on the outside. In the vast green carpet of the rolling lively lawns, the murals, and the peaking of the delicate flowers blooming, the monumental sprawling mansion that many called **CAMELOT'S KINGDOM** was a sight to be reckoned with. But living inside amidst all the splendour, richness… with maids running around… life was so different that whoever lived inside would actually wonder what it would be like to live outside and vice versa.

As James would later say to his own father… "Living in those circumstances was asphyxiating, claustrophobic… I feel like being strangled…" words to these effects. But then again, on reflection, his ex-wife Olivia said the same thing when told to return to Camelot by direct orders of George, her father-in-law, the Camelot of Broken Dreams or Ashpark of Broken Dreams. Is Camelot jinxed, cursed?

The Bligh family reunion came by when George, once in a while, returned from his frequent absences, which took great emphasis for one reason or another, but not enough for James, who was growing fast, making him rely on whoever he saw fit and easy to accommodate… in this case, some of his maids' sisters and also the other males who actually kept him company at his all-private school for boys. With Oxford… later on.

Alas… for his all-too-consuming and dominant grandmamah… James was perfect. The song "You must have been a beautiful baby" haunts as the lyrics… can really enthral and play all over one's mind, with James growing up to be really the highly ostentatious ADONIS. Belonging to the **BLIGH'S DYNASTY** was not an easy fit, with the fun of constantly teasing his little sister Anna. Then there was nothing else to do except for his own enjoyment, trying to find fun and amusement whenever he saw fit elsewhere. Who would really say no to this immensely handsome, but private man? Or so we think he might have been. But was he really? James was so lonely, sad, and highly sensitive towards his surroundings that his time at home was his undoing. He found solace elsewhere.

During his own adolescence, James took several trips down his own lane, all outside, all within the walls and limits of what Camelot's surroundings were all about, needing still to really evaluate everything besides himself and his own family… his own self-discovery. To one other forbidden world… onto the other side of his own world whilst living permanently in this world. By the time he found it, whether he wanted to or not, he was already living between two worlds. Now, which one was which… that was the question.

James Bligh… yes… the distinctive heir presumptive to the Bligh's Empire, was indulged since he was born, growing up in this distinctive… majestic… "palace" casting shadows… stern reminders of forbidden fruits covering the darkest of secrets that were kept hidden at all costs, but dealing with tradition and culture. Life was a triple deal that was highly important, which was tied, as usual, in a cold and freezing environment… or per –se. but all was not lost. As a matter of fact… no one would dare to think of the inevitable… what could possibly go wrong and be wrong… with such a statuesque house, boasting such high standards and privileges… to accommodate… and to enjoy so much and the living… Who could actually doubt it, in particular, the name BLIGH.

For the outsiders looking in, for the employees going about their businesses, and the others with their affairs, James Bligh was the sole inheritor of this colossal place… it was named the **CAMELOT**, or Ashpark of Broken Dreams… such romantic ideals gives birth to a mystical kingdom where James would be the next King Arthur. James turned his nose down unfitfully to that kind of richness… he would rather be free… on his own… doing his own thing.

Many years later, his father George tells James' half-brother, young little David: "Even the stars and the clouds, Dad?" as innocent little David asks his elderly father George about the future. George points out to him: "Son, one day all of these will be yours to own," as he shows little David the power of the Bligh's Empire and George's own wisdom, but more to it, showing David what it meant to be a Bligh, with entrancing and mesmerising views that promised a king's ransom in David's prospects of a wonderful and spectacular future… filled with so much promise, dreams, with firm results. "Indeed, indeed…" would be the words belonging to busybody darling of Inverness, Doris, at the time, "Indeed, indeed… a mighty… gigantic place… with the land and the horizon mingling together…" It could only have spelt BLIGHS.

The Bligh's power and resilience was vast and prominent, as evidenced in the large, undisputed mansion, property, land, wealth, investments, the horses and their stables, the barns, the employees. And so it must have been with his older son James in mind, by naming James with Arthur, so fitful for a mystical and magnificent future in a place like this, colossal to a point. When George, who might have presumably said the same words and done the same… or did George?

Being born a Bligh meant having everything… James was under so much deprivation from the love of what a mother's real love could give… Like any boy who missed the male company at home, his own father's… the things both of them could have done together, such as going on excursions, fishing, camping, swimming, mountain climbing, boating journeys… they were eligible for any dreams that could be accomplished by most kids, be they male or female. It was called bonding… but poor James… he never had it so bad.

…His grandmother was still far and distant… she didn't have any feelings… so where would James lick his wounds in the dire straits that he was in? He hurt… he cried. He needed to find solace in some soft and tender arms, the love lacking inside the mansion.

NB:

Reference: Elaine, James' mother, died during the Japanese Bombing in Darwin on 19th Feb 1941. James grew up in a land of so much magic… but the commanding LOVE never manifested…

CAMELOT'S KINGDOM… a fairytale.

Flighty. Fickle-hearted… as one bitterly disappointed Henry Fox labelled James. Dr Henry Fox had his own troubles in fitting in when he grew up, but James lived almost in an "institution" of self-doing or making, trying now too hard to make up for the past, living in a type of institution unequivocally where hardly anyone was disposed to help him into his morals and establishing ways… as a man.

Male and a Bligh, only the outsiders, Dr Jack, Briggs, the Polettis… the Bennetts, yes, the Bennetts, who in each and every turn were an obstacle, as each day was a new revelation with so much more to be highly contented… losing count of them… then there was his beloved aunty Reggie… one could always smile when one mentioned her. Sassy, young, refreshing… beautiful… an icon of fashion and making a name for herself in the elite Australian society… the bad in a good way personality. Everyone who knew her knew her to be a socialite. Brash, colourful, dedicated and "happily married" to Charles, who served as an ambassador to the Australian Government. But did anyone know that she was also a spy, a conniving theatrical "bitch," and also a gold-digger? No… no one knew these details until later on.

Then there was another colourful lady… his aunty Caroline… ohhhhh… the stories he could tell… she was the "bad person" mentioned at home. Then again, there was another one… Little Lizzie… he learnt about her when his own bright and sunny "sister" went beyond anything but building and creating the big painting that was now well positioned in the parlour. He had never heard of her, as no one spoke about her… she was a legend in her own right, the cooks, the maids, even the chauffeur knew about her… Briggs was the one who deeply shrugged his shoulders, shook his head… but always resentful against his own grandmamah Elizabeth, burying his mind into his own business. Briggs never elaborated anything, and now that this is being mentioned, apparently James thought, it seemed that all of them had something or rather to say and to be done… they all had been victims of one thing or the other… were they all?

Submitted to the curse, jinxed, or was it normal to deal and live a life in this way? James, for all his riches and wealth, never understood the law of life. It was an immense vale of tears. Pain, sorrow and suffering but he never lived through it all.

Whilst his father buried his life in a world of contracts, selling the cattle overseas, renewing the licence yearly… having by law registered the basis of their cattle business… (please note: I have not as yet received anything that refers to 18th Century Australia's law and legislation about buying and selling or import/export of Australian cattle… I have written to them… but insofar nothing except some excuses due to COVID-19.)

James' initiation into his preparatory studies at home, a natural norm that happened to the children of wealthy people, was mild. When he went on to primary school, as per usual, instead of being an extremely potentially high achiever, which he was not, those years went by without flinching anyone's notice. Before long, James was attending all-private privileged boys' secondary school. Boarding school was nothing but hell for James, just like with his aunty Caro.

If he had a sordid upbringing at home, James Bligh was well known for his failings where sports, recreation and athleticism were concerned. He was not a competent and aptly student, suffering many detentions for lacking one thing or another, getting the teachers really upset with his failings. Not that he was a dumb student… but he was really a person who did not simply fit into the more open and exuberant boisterous male-dominant society, the type inclined to the real macho, alpha-male syndrome. He lived in another world, entirely his own. But he couldn't fail to see, and even though he fought his own homosexual tendencies so hard, alone. But so deceptively desolate for his own deep male attraction… the guys' physiques… good looks and handsomeness. But they were ALPHAS, and seldom a day went by without female company and loving it.

The boys at the all-exclusive secondary privy where James tried hard, and badly, to fit in, mixing and being one of the raucous, noisy, loud rough boys, and to a degree making it into their teams… intentionally or unintentionally to be a part of them and making himself highly useful, but no one knows if he failed to make it or the boys did not accept him at all. But now, more than ever, he thought that being at home would be a far better world and a private well-proposed choice. He hated boarding. Boarding schools nauseated him. He was never going to be the ALPHA male. Of course, there was something in it that James refused totally to even then admit, even though he had already unconsciously admitted.

Many a time, whilst other boys had wet dreams and fell prey to the damsels in distress, bragging about their sexual and adventurous conquests or prowess, highly captivating stories, the ALPHAS showing off their supreme dalliances with several girls, getting more sexual experiences with adult women, where their "virginities" were lost, recounting their prolific sexual activities for the fun of it all… James, however, found them sad, vicious and abhorrent. He was unable to bring himself to really fall for a female, let alone do what must be done to a naked female body. But James was gallant enough to proceed and join his boys' team, and finally a victory… he too also lost his "virginity"… was never ecstatic about it. Actually, it gave him nightmares and terror dreams where he would wet his bed. Thankfully, it was at home in his grand mansion.

Returning home was a safe sanction for James. He could now be himself. But home for him was not where the heart was… James Bligh felt empty… emotionally deprived and numb… ineffective… Camelot of Broken Dreams was that realm… in which he felt totally annihilated… far removed… distant… he never experienced depression, but he felt lost… despondent… now at home, he also felt a tightness in his chest… he was totally lost in his own translation. He also found it totally sickening taking a dire look at himself. He felt like an outsider gazing from outside in.

The voice of his eternally benign grandmother brought him into reality. Usually, she would send the car to pick him up either from Inverness train station, or directly from school… Lying to his grandmother, he gladly hugged her, telling her how good it felt to be home.

…James was the missing Prince Arthur PENDRAGON, and Elizabeth never hid the fact that she adored her grandson. There was a lack of male influence. James, deservedly, was meant to be the ruler. Along with him came his little sister, the ebullient, noisy, happy-go-lucky, effervescent, colourful, full of gossip about Inverness and its surrounds, she was the one with I HAVE and HAVE NOT stories to tell. Her light green dress made so much noise with the inlaid petticoats, rushing and flushing over here and there, with her blonde hair tied in pigtails with light green ribbons, exacerbated by her huge soulful dark brown eyes covering so many questions, doubts, curiosity, flamed by her gushing, chiding, quipping, joking, laughing, measuring, admiring, concentrating on her older handsome ADONIS brother, she couldn't stop quipping, screaming, dancing, jumping, doing the rounds of rock-around-the-clock, singing, and totally brimming with full spirit, like the happy-go-lucky little girl who had just gotten her own prize… He also noticed how much his little Anna Elaine was growing up.

Elaine being the Queen, the mother to Sir Lancelot du Lac, Lancelot, who was involved in the trisme love mythical story, married Elaine, daughter of King Pelleas, then fathered a son, Sir Galahad, following the steps of his legendary father Lancelot, the first knight in the royal court of King Arthur and the Round Table. King Pelleas was the keeper of the Holy Grail, and in this mythical Camelot realm over in Inverness, it matched up with the fairytale. Missing were a witch… and that witch came through aunty Reggie… she of so many tales, travels, adventures.

James noticed how beautiful Little Anna was growing into, the high cheekbones showed how strong her Bligh genes were. Her presumably matter-of-fact and happy-go-lucky personality was his good luck charm. She was full-on with everything, who was who and who was not. Anna Elaine Bligh was all sunshine and goodwill. Again, James smiled remembering the words of "indeed, indeed" as he mentally reflected on his overwhelmingly refreshing little sister Anna. Even more, he laughed incredulously if his grandmum was there to watch the flighty, flying, hovering, skittish, whimsical, capricious, lightly butterfly, constantly warping in and out over here and there with no shoes. Queen Elizabeth, his grandmum, would have a fit… whilst Anna continued creating loads of stories, controversies… fun and fun. Ah yes. Anna was a dreamer. Her wish was to be an author.

The Polettis turned up with their usual vegetable baskets filled to the brim in their red truck, with Mama Poletti going about cleaning the household. The maids all giggled at their young master's presence, with James being the centre stage, inquiring of Amy if they needed more help around their three-bedroom cottage, but there was no mentioning of her brother Harry. Amy was so glad that finally James was home, he was such a man's man, handsome, gentle, and so soft, a real ingénue… wait till Harry returns, as she couldn't wait to tell her brother. All seemed to revolve around James Bligh… good, better and the best… but that was his final retreat… who wouldn't love to be in the place they'd called home?

After all, he was **JAMES BLIGH, THE HEIR PRESUMPTIVE TO CAMELOT'S KINGDOM.** The similarities would end here… he was

PRINCE ARTHUR PENDRAGON, the dragon being his grandmother.

Elizabeth continued with her own "merry" ways, ruling **CAMELOT'S KINGDOM**… with some of her selective friends that she indulged herself with carefully, using them as she saw fit… if they actually suited her. Her frequent visitors were far and few. First: Dr Jack Duncan. Second: Roy Briggs. Third: The Polettis. Fourth: Mrs Doris Collins. Fifth: Sir Richard Bennett. Sixth: the beautiful and elegant aunty Regina. Seventh: the flamboyant but fun-loving suffragette Lady Swanson. Eighth: the BLIGHS' lawyers. And towards the end: Mrs Pang all the way from Macau… if you could call them Elizabeth's friends. But they were, and they wouldn't have it any other way. One would have to admit… traditionally wise, the Camelot matriarch kept herself not only highly regarded but colourfully entertained. After all, James' grandmother was the heart and soul of the Australian rich, privileged society… and she was prime in her fun and fair liaisons.

What? Elizabeth, in her socially rich circle, should have had plenty of friends. When Caro wrote about *BEWARE OF THE FEMALE... (FATALE)*… who did not have any friends…courtesy of her family's good friend, Sir Richard Bemmett. Unknowingly Caro was actually writing about her own mother tooa reflection deep and controversial… Elizabeth Bligh.

But Elizabeth's humbleness and friendliness went far beyond the constrictions of Camelot's Kingdom… then again, one too many times, as James observed in his own reflections when he finally admitted who and what he was… he came to realise that Camelot's Kingdom was not that simple. Ashpark, for the more lucid people, was indeed a place of broken dreams… with dreams that could be accomplished but not Until then, he disputed his future… he was, by all intents and purposes, the male BLIGH… but more appropriately… marriage and his own line of Bligh succession. Now he realised that that was an impossible dream or could?

Elizabeth, on her own, would not have a bar to do with anyone else that could intrude so much into her private family's affairs, and now that you are speaking about it, her own life. Now you know why she has few friends.

The Blighs were not a simple registration in black-and-white ink… it had lots of ink impressions, and the Blighs had different images and designs of themselves… but that was only an supposition, with supposedly images and their own interpretations of themselves which were to cover the more serious sides of themselves or the same thing, gathered implicitly by the others… of course, to each and everyone its own. No one could accurately pinpoint what the Blighs were in real life, or even describe them in social circles. By social circles, they meant the gossipy status in the after-hours in pubs, dinings and Sunday barbecues, socially.

George healed by focusing on his work, but James was growing in his own self-imposed solitary confinement… James was in a world of his own.

He was happy, jovial, impune in his cracking jokes, a hands-on man at work, helping in the fields, doing the accounts, taking brief and enjoyable trips to the tailor's shops to have his more formal and serious suits, all cut well and outstanding. Both ways he was an APOLLO of such good looks and looked good on both accounts.

Camelot's own exciting and exalted prince of hearts, James Bligh, loved being home. His little sister Anna, as most young sisters go, idolised their older brothers, enjoying quality time lunching and dining with their grandmother and, of course, spending time on horseback riding, swimming, around their own turf, taking the usual trips to the local movies, dancing during evenings… not returning home until the wee hours of the morning or not returning at all.

It was to be expected for teens like him and anyone else. A matter of time when the teenage boys go about their own hormonal adventures. Now that was what one would call self-discovery.

As the heir presumptive, he actually needed to learn everything about the whole set of Camelot's business… an enforced labour making him feel vacuus and steaming, with attacks of anxiety, which, ironically, would be the same sour words that his enigmatic grandmother would use against the more fallible Anna, being herself the self-proclaimed reluctant fundamentalist… rather, all of this talk made James empty, innocuous and sooo vacuus… his "steaming" would be reserved for a better fit… he was drowning alone in the midst of such gorgeous paintings… of flowers, richness… all embroidered in silver and gold… he himself also being sewn in the vast well-crafted embroidery, which he himself was also crafted into. Would he look good, though?

Little James, the Arthur Pendragon of Camelot Kingdom, tall, strapping, good-looking young man with curly black hair shining under Camelot's hot sun, cut a most distinctive figure in the dry land of Ashpark, gleaming and shining with good health and vitality, sporting a refreshing suntan. And the pros were that he possessed a terrific athletic body, long legs. James Bligh rode tall in the saddle, his imposing figure cutting through Camelot's scenery, charming, respectful, adequately well-educated ALPHA male, with the women giggling all the while, covering their faces, batting their eyelashes at him, charmingly smiling soulfully at him, requisites afforded to all women including his first wife… leaving James totally confused… for women were the last thing on his mind but, according to his grandmamah, worth trying.

Poor little rich boy growing up… trapped in his own wealth, prestige and status… and as his aunty Reggie would one day say to aunty Caro about him (poor James… so sensitive…). Aunty Reggie… yes… aunty Reggie saw through James right from the beginning… suspicions that regrettably became true and, at the time, a real shame for the Blighs. History was repeating itself, much to the detriment of Elizabeth Bligh, but the evidence came through Amy herself when innocently she revealed and confirmed Reggie's suspicions… his own father George accusing him of "lagging behind" and that he had "thrown away all that was his" in so many short angry words. James' reaction was that "I can't go on living in that, asphyxiating…" That was the process of him feeling so inadequate in a place that was meant to be called home… Camelot KINGDOM or Ashpark, later to be regarded as the place of broken dreams.

James' happiness was not returning home, not to his own palatial Camelot, but to some of his friends. His love for his male counterparts started off really early, but home at Camelot only exacerbated his feelings of inadequacy, he resorted to his own excuses in not joining those private friends of his… the latter were getting engaged, then married… again, a woke.

MARRIAGE was the pressure, making him even more paranoid, desperation now devised its own plans.

His grandmother, the indomitable Grand Elizabeth Bligh, threw an emancipation party with no hold barriers. It had been a while since Camelot had a decent party… such celebrations were far and few. Caro's "Debutante Ball" flashed by, in the back memories, no betrothals came through, no suitors, and no boyfriend… being marred with problems and troubles, not to mention scandal. To Elizabeth's disappointment… nothing… then the secret was revealed… about Caro. But now this was James coming of age, his own emancipation, with Elizabeth decreeing her own laws and regulations. Where this was concerned, nothing was new,

James' eighteenth birthday party, was based on such opulence, such extravagant, de-luxe emancipation, but it was only materialism: the show of power, wealth, privilege and James' good looks. The official guests, the A-list, turned up… again the sun shone even though it was Winter. Bands and music went about, with the guests enjoying the all-appetising but classic buffet a la carte… barrelling laughter, drinking, fun time… they all had a whale of a good, if not excellent, time.

There was, of course, the huge cake imploding and a beautiful half-dressed lady coming out from the cake… doing her bit and stuff, singing happy birthday, proceeding to the beat of the sounds and sinewy dancing of what one would have called a "strip teasing," with winners and grinners… exploding with loud and deafening hand claps amidst screams of joviality and goodwill. Naturally, the lady kept her clothes on, joining all of them by sipping champagne, tasting the yummy morsels, chit-chatting and immersing along with the other guests… swaying to the beat and dancing… until the right cake, where naked dolls were part of the cake and moulded into it… beautifying the cake in the shape of the number 18, with all the lights flashing about the vast and grande Ash Park, the evening drew into the night, with guests returning home to their homes, motels, some stayed behind crashing in the sleeping dreamy AshPark's quarters. A dream come true… NOT.

It was amusing; therefore, more excitement and applause followed. It was a sea of entertainment, goodwill, fun, and enjoyment ushered in a new, added era: an unforgettable evening that soon turned into a night of pleasurable amusement. Nothing was missed, and even the night seemed to dance under the sterling stars glaring down on CAMELOT'S KINGDOM.

The following day, the newspapers sang delightful praises of the event, with dazzling pictures of the "who's who", including the Prince of CAMELOT'S KINGDOM with George, Elizabeth, Anna, and the beautiful Aunt Reggie smiling. Reggie, as usual, sophisticated and elegantly dressed, enchanted everyone. Her perfume, *Fleur de Lyz*, lingered in the air, leaving traces of her presence. She sipped the delicious French champagne, sampled some of the more delectable morsels, smiled, and glammed it up, twisting and turning through the crowd as she saw fit. Her husband was unwell and couldn't join the Blighs. Her older son, her only child, was overseas enjoying the fruits of his wealth; he couldn't be bothered with the Blighs.

Once upon a time, all of this would have been frowned upon as tasteless, decadent entertainment. Events such as these carried high sexual content and connotations, some kind of sexual celebration not for the faint-hearted, but it always happened, as Society was promiscuous. Sex or no sex made all the difference, or none. Society, highly hypocritical, not only failed to frown upon it but also considered reading about it a token of high life's experiences, using the knowledge to censure anyone who stepped out of line, which happened often. Once, his grandmother would have been mortified… but Elizabeth, the matriarch, was moving with the times. She could tolerate a few modern things, though, tough as she was, she occasionally found herself reverting to the old system, which was indeed a hard task. Tradition was tradition, but even rules were meant to be broken.

With all of that in mind, any man would have felt proud of himself. James looked around, searching for someone who would support him, love him for who he was. His coming-out, his EMANCIPATION PARTY, was nothing more than a farcical state of their affairs. display, a social charade.

The Blighs did not represent him; it was not him. As he blew out the candles, his eyes searched for the one he most wanted, beneath the smiling and grinning faces, through the sea of cheers and goodwill, until he finally met the gaze of those who smiled from afar. His friend had not been invited, as he was not on par with the Blighs. He was the younger brother of the maid, Amy, who helped with fetching and serving during the banquet.

More's the pity. Perspiration beaded on his temples, and one of the ladies wiped them away with her perfumed handkerchief. He flashed a polite smile, thanking her for the effort. The faint perfume was overpowering, refreshing yet intrusive. He longed for the breath of his *amato*. He blew out all eighteen candles, smiled awkwardly, and, with trembling hands, cut the cake smoothly. The aroma of chestnut filled the air, it was chocolate with chestnut, and the creamy top was heavenly.

Cheers and applause were deafening. Champagne bottles popped open, and firecrackers exploded with a thousand noises, filling the now cooler air. As darkness deepened and the temperature dropped, the party grew louder. James was expected to choose a lady to spend the night with, a way to prove his virility.

The occasion was astonishingly and culturally ordained, steeped in tradition, historical lore, and ideals maintained over centuries. James was now meant to be one of the princes, a knight in shining armour, in this very CAMELOT'S KINGDOM, his feet planted firmly on the green velvety lawns. CAMELOT… the Great King Arthur.

Culturally, the raw symbols of a man's virility began with the softer peasants or wild ones, brutal to be exact, progressing through the tough

Vikings, Celts, Vandals, Iberians (Portuguese and Spanish), Moors, and even perhaps Orientals (Genghis Khan). All these males underwent similar EMANCIPATION rituals, legends, certainly, but rooted in traditional historical factors.

NOTE FOR FILE

EMANCIPATION denotes the freedom to conduct one's total liberation. It marks the transition from boyhood to manhood: the voice deepens, muscles develop, facial and body hair grow, skin becomes ruddier, and both mind and spirit expand. Childhood shackles are removed; permission is no longer required. The EMANCIPATION PARTY celebrates a boy now free to smoke, drink, and consummate his adulthood, historically with a virgin woman.

More than ever, James faced trials and tribulations….he felt like the retributions were coming slowly...tentatively.. Creating a whirlwind of dark double shadows...now more torments, nightmares…heartbreaking...a nail biting feeling that gnawed at his own flesh leaving scars in his already tortured mind, creating more doubts lowering his self-esteem and triggering panic attacks. Almost collapsing under the darkness and dizziness, he quickly recovered and composed himself, trying to enjoy the trysts, flow with the emancipation ritual, respond to the toasts, and grin through his grinding teeth as a dutiful birthday boy.

He left the following morning for a few days' rest and relaxation, returning to what he later complained to his father George was "oppressive, suffocating… asphyxiating." A place nefariously cold and austere, haunted by spiteful shadows. The prince expected of him had been reduced to simply… James.

That alone... was the start of his own trip descending into his hellish living... there were no words to describe his feelings. After the emancipation, sad as it was, disappointing as it was going to be, James came to realise his own sexual tendencies. That there would not be any changes in him… James Bligh was living **BETWEEN TWO WORLDS**… one he was born into… two, all of his own. **ALONE.** But of course, there were many others who shared the same downtrodden feeling, seeking out a solution, like him, they also suffered in great silence. But they did have an unsolicited place where they could meet, smoke and drink… enjoying their personal liberties and freedom… thus James was also introduced to the underground Gay Clubs.

Now it was his turn to take a trip into his own journey of self-discovery… he loved being with them. He actually slept with a few of them… made hard love… kissed. He and they enjoyed.

Trapped between two worlds. The right and the left. The black and the white. The sun and the moon. The Orient and the Occident. The North and the South. None were complete.

The Yin and the Yang… Now he appreciated exactly the way his palatial mansion shone on the good days and drabbed on so melancholically, looking immensely forbidden, powerless and a threat to the whole wide world or Inverness. This was exactly what he now felt like… but those were the opposing polarities… what happened if he had two left dancing feet and hankered for the same sex? He knew himself. For him he was both… the Yin but not the Yan. The sun with the sun. Two left feet. The North and the North… but he was sensitive, his feelings were more of a female than that of a male. He could understand and not understand, but he empathised…

Back at his forbidden world, each time he was home on holiday, at the time, the staff were all used to his boyish, gleefully and highly powered character and personality, he cracked jovial jokes, he had a heartfelt laughing, inviting the others to join him at everything, driving not only the staff but the admiring female fleet, both his grandmother and his little sister wild with laughter. With Anna completely in full admiration of her older brother, her chirpings, her joie de vivre, her ultimate candid look at the outer world, her full and lively uncontrollable enthusiasm towards life as it was. He wished that nothing would ever hurt his own little sister. James never suspected how rebellious his own little sister was… when his grandma called her the reluctant fundamentalist, he smiled… it would always happen to the female species of his Blighs family. She could be annoying, like a little bird chirping incessantly and flying here and there… but the Blighs alone couldn't and wouldn't be able to live without the chirping, the twittering that was his little sister.

Inwardly, feeling dreadfully, James was derailing himself… but living in his CAMELOT'S KINGDOM… he found himself happy to go and find whatever he could to occupy his mind… so he undertook every morning, like his aunty Petite Tante Lizzie, going out on his early morning rides, only returning at night time, as he now did it regularly on his holidays, relaxed, happy, his skin darkened considerably by the roasting sun, making him even more the stuff of a movie star.

That all the ladies thought a marvel. He was so endearingly handsome, what with his black glowing wavy hair suavely shining under the blazing sun and his blue eyes surveying his own land, his mouth cracking in that big grin of his… James sat tall in the saddle, would plough ahead for the day. Now he played a different song… one that only he could sing and danced to it. His emancipation night was gone and forgotten.

…turning 21 years of age, now more than ever, he was in control of his own domain now. He selected his own timetable to exactly suit his own working requirements… sending for his cooks to have his lunch brought to him as he would work and enjoy an early morning ride, swimming in the lake. Fresh air was what the doctor ordered, as he subjected himself under the roasting sun. The burning sunlight lightened up his curly hair, his skin deeply suntanned, and his rugged good looks streaming with devilish attraction. James was getting used to all that breathed life into his land. Now that he was home, relaxing more at nighttime, he frequented the pub, movies, some dancing events, joining in the fanfare of the fetes, bazaars where his grandmamah was always featuring, and with young Anna running around in her summery frocks, one moment giggling in sweet surprise at the beautiful toys and other things that Elizabeth and himself would buy her. Flittingly and flightingly, there was no stopping young little Anna, as she was like a young little deer, jumping up and running like there was no tomorrow, enjoying the Spring weather and dazzled by everything that was shown to her… enjoying the good briefing, the food… different from the Autumn and Winter bazaars, as they were different from the present one…

Incredibly, James found a way and went on with his sneaky activities to the gay club, secretly… without raising a single suspicion on him.

Now that he could go excitedly about the new journey that he was now undertaking to the other world, there are questions about him, as if he actually found the expected fulfilment, or was it just a flight of fancy???? With James, no one could be sure. He could ever be the capricious Bligh kiddo. He could also be relieving his moments of sadness, of loneliness, of such utter isolation where he could never communicate, relate to anyone, the traumatic years of a motherless and fatherless child, adding to his tale about the sad years in which his poor schooling attendance was also marred by deep disappointments, tedious involvements with the rough and the gutsy… James thought that one could be a man without being rough, violent, practically callous… cruel… demeaning… as he found that growing up outside the CAMELOT'S KINGDOM was actually a concrete jungle… where there existed males and females alike, savage animals, tearing at each other practically but uncalled for. But he was the male Bligh when he confronted Gino at his worst.

For a great many people, these couldn't have been a more appropriate and delectable time for a youngster to enjoy the beauties of his natural surroundings, with Camelot's Kingdom disposing of such disponible places where one could ride their own horses, have picnics, swim… and work on their own land. Here and there, one saw the excellent land being grazed by the animals and horses being carried in and out of their own stables in a newly working shop with its new normal but new timetable, Camelot's Kingdom employed more people, all in a plain bright day or a cast day… enjoying the tranquil views and the privacy… of what one owned… which is what anyone would have loved and appreciated all the more, desired, and had it within their means. James, the presumed heir, was the one moaning and groaning about his luck and fortune… The pressure weighed on his broad shoulders. They looked wide and strong, but in reality James was not the person to actually carry the load. He felt completely out of place.

Inside the grand Camelot of broken dreams, as it was called now, cooks and maids were all used to James' comings and goings and his daily timetable and demands. Gently, softly as they were, the food would be delivered in time as he laboured under the harsh elements of Mother Nature. Lucky for him, the storms had been very mild… with heavy but not swirling hurricane winds, and the rain would go down after a huge deluge, minus the terrible flooding. There were sometimes fires due to the harsh environment… with the dry land catching fire on its own, the rubbing of two branches, the reflection of a mirror belonging to a car, or lightning striking Camelot during heavy rain, starting a fire… It was a huge job running a castle like Camelot or the Ashpark.

James continued on his daily habitual routine. He rose early, worked hard for a while, then headed to the lake for a quick swim.

Ordering the staff to pack a picnic lunch… taking sole advantage of the world surrounding the mythical land of Camelot, anyone wise enough to seek out such picturesque surroundings, being real, with one's imagination running wild, into one's mind a vision, a picture being painted that one could easily put the multicoloured effects on the easel of one's canvas… the magical intricacies of the ink and pastels forming into a kaleidoscope of vivid and dramatic colours, mingling and statistically projecting them around the land, thus… the natural beauty of CAMELOT'S KINGDOM comes alive and kicking in the single stroke of a painter's easel… and, of course, also to soak the Vitamin D of the Camelot iridescent strong sun rays.

Hence, enjoying the tranquil landscape, with nature bestowing a calming and peaceful atmosphere, with the views soothing one's eyes, relaxing the physical constraints, with the palliative sing-song of the lake's main streams, finding all the time James and his "beau" enjoying themselves… both were definitely two handsome, good-looking boys… for the innocent observers, these two boys epitomised the happy, free, youthful days… with their new founding status. None at the time would have thought that they were anything more than "just friends."

Young Bligh, trying to find his stepping stone in a sea where there were only slippery rocks for him to hang onto. One needed to feel sorry for this young man, because for the keen observer, such as his grandmamah, Grand Elizabeth Bligh, the matriarch of CAMELOT'S KINGDOM…

Grand Elizabeth… her heart pounded… it was in its extremes… she did not miss a beat.

In a house where impositions on James were just women… with the secret soirees of James' gay club, which at any time or another he'd be lost, isolated, living the double-edged sword, he longed only for male companions. To his chagrin… it was time for his father to heal from the loss of his wife, who was then his own mother. True… James could also be so adamant and selfish. James, like any of the males trying to find a grip, had his own beau who at any time would come, visiting him and staying the night wherever he wanted. He was also thinking of moving to the cottage, with Elizabeth negating him…

Roy Briggs was still busy and at odds… the man had lost practically everything… little wonder if he did not lose his mind. James thought of Roy as a lonely man, but he admired him… the man was in a lost world of his own, the pain etched over his rugged face. But Roy was a real tough guy and he soldiered on.

Then he surveyed the Polettis family. They lost their first son and had barely a ten-year-old second son. The family built what they could to proficiently call **A PLACE TO CALL THEIR OWN HOME**… the family were also busy working in, out and around their own farm and their own house, trying hard to find something to cling onto. James admired the Polettis' great faith, they were Catholics… and accordingly so was his aunty, Little Lizzie, but he had never met her. At the time, when he was still young, getting acquainted with Mrs Poletti as she found herself then, pregnant… and she was soon due. Their second son, Gino, was slowly growing into his teen years… he was dark, with haunting dark eyes, massive curly hair, but scrawny and skinny. He hung about with his little sister, Anna. They both made such a different couple. Still, they were both kids with a future in their hands. She would find herself a suitable husband, and he would find his own Italian wife.

The Polettis were refugees, who fled during the Second World War, looking for a **PLACE TO CALL HOME**… James noted, as one could have come up with a HOME… for the Polettis… they needed to dig into their own roots, traditions, culture, language, folklore… a house which was their house… where they could come home and crash after a hard day's work… where hot food waited for them, taking their own vino, living their own lives… James shook his head in wonderment… he thought about the new DAEGO word for them… (little did James suspect that one day that little boy would not only come to be one of the Bligh family… Gino would tear and break the Blighs. His fury at them and being used by them… challenged Gino to his own modus operandi… his own form of REVENGE.)

"Revenge is best served cold." Sicilian proverb.

Mrs Pang would come and go. She was here to meet up with his family. But she dealt with real estate, ran her own restaurants and laundry services… a very wise, savvy lady. His own grandmamah loved the idea of having such a friend… and he also welcomed Pang's family.

There was that busybody lady, Doris. Always updated in everything, but always willing to help.

Where Jack was of concern, James still did not understand what, in effect, Jack was for the Blighs' family… didn't know why his grandmamah was so fond of him. Jack was just Jack. The man did not have a dollar to his name, and now he was the Blighs' personal doctor… Something was really wrong here… but James did not want to analyse anything… he had his own pressing problems… and those problems would soon surface, and soon enough. But was he prepared to face them… was he brave enough to endure what would come by? He sought refuge, unlike other males, in a house bereft of masculine or male companions… in the comics that he read when he was young, becoming infatuated by the blazing fire of those strong and pulsating males… with their robust and athletic, flexing muscles… James, who was more placid, more self-oriented then… being a bit like his father… harbouring strong principles… who followed the Bible and the Sunday sermons… was still highly unsure and insecure of himself… until Gino pointed it out to him at a later stage… coldly and cruelly pointing it all out… what James really was and is, and how much Gino despised him for that and that alone.

…and he would see fit how he would manage it… no one knew him better… but his childhood friend… but his friend had no class… no money. In fact… he had nothing… except for a good body, and good looks… his name? Oh yes… Harry Poulson… Amy's brother, the Blighs' maid.

Theirs was a friendship made in heaven… it started when both of them were still young, caught in a thunderstorm of their own beliefs, as both lacked the male influence at home. What started as innocent, with both escaping towards their own misfits… escapism… adventures… games… a world of their own, born of their own friendship around Inverness town and Camelot. They knew each other during their kindergarten years, and in later years, James undertook a private education, being free to go out with Harry when he was home on holidays, and that was how an innocent friendship developed… into a mutual and deep affection for these two males. Handsome, young, with thick dark hair, always together until one day it exploded into one of the warmest love-making…

Each time the sun shines, it brings a new day.

Were they born this way, a natural phenomenon, or was it pro-cuo to the detrimental factors surrounding James Bligh?

Please note:

There was a debate and discussion in the **SAVE A PLACE TO CALL HOME** group… where one of the members asked if being gay was actually born, descent (taking into consideration the liability that James Bligh's grandfather, Lewis George Bligh, was also gay), or simply influenced and forced… such as peer pressure… and I was meant to do the research by asking more questions and to record and register them into my book… this book… **BOOK 1. A PLACE TO CALL HOME, "The Forensics"** (characters and personalities… exposed), which was meant to be an innocent, realistic, fun account… no offence to anyone.

What began as just a few questions, so I could implement the members' questions and answers, me asking them for their authorisations so I could collectively connect all the dots and have them printed in my book, became a terrible ordeal, with someone being rude and "self-centred", ill-intentioned… even though many knew that I was writing this book, it had never occurred to anyone that I was actually doing research… (in **A PLACE TO CALL HOME**, even James asks Anna why she was asking all those questions about James' past boyfriends, as she was referring to Harry Poulson, and if those questions were some kind of assignment or project for Anna's research for her book…) and this is what we WRITERS (in my case PROLIFIC AND EDITORIAL WRITER/S) go in search of in order to write a book.

A WRITER needs to do research and compile it with references… but I am sorry, that this could not happen.

The debate ranged from late August 2019 and went until mid-September 2019. To this effect, the debate culminated in something, and it came through a person who was hateful enough, who actually spoilt everything for me and for you, loving readers. The post was removed due to the person's incoherent, nefarious, sickening, and ill-intentioned ramblings. She was also deleted from two groups.

Anyway, I would love to let you all know that gay, lesbians, transgenders, queens, eunuchs… and from some extended points of view, also (pedofilia)… Pedofilia still exists today, as many elderly males, or males in their late thirties or forties, marry young virginal brides still in their young and pubescent years. It is happening. It is their law, and it has been a terrible crime, thankfully outlawed here in Australia and in Macau. However, I am not writing about this.

These come as nothing new to any of us… History has documented great men and women who were gay… some flaunted their status and were never afraid to show their homosexualities, be they women or men… some others enjoyed dressing as the opposite sex… In that time, they were called "dressing rehearsal" for their exchanged genders.

Myth about being gay.

There is a myth that one day a slave Greek boy, who was as beautiful as anything, saw an apple and went to pick it up on the top of a tree which was standing inside a crystal lake… the boy climbed up and when he got the apple, he looked down to find a footing… but what he saw was staring back at him, his own reflection… and the more his eyes and his reflection crossed, the more transfixed he became, to the point of falling head over heels in love with his own reflection… but the slave boy never knew that it was his reflection, and not having his love respond to him, Narcissus became heartbroken and died of sadness, pain, and sorrow. So there we are… gays, lesbians, transgenders, queens, eunuchs… it happens all the time.

All of these have been happening since time began.

Most of them were slaves, and they did not know the rights from the wrongs. More often than not, their masters (as they were called at the time) and mistresses could be gay and had the slaves working for them as gay prostitutes… or serving their own masters and mistresses, as they were gay themselves. Gays and prostitutes are as old as time began.

One without the other would never have completed our own Universal History. It took everything to build this world, and both the sun shines and the moon sends her luminous silver rays to all of us residing on planet Earth.

References:

- White Slavery / Black Slavery: https://wikipedia.org/wiki/white_slavery
- https://www.apa.org/lgbt/resources/history
- Pederasty / pederasti: intimate sexual relationship between an older man and a younger male (the erasties)

Eunuchs: https://www.britannica.com/topic/eunuch

And, of course, the real pedophiles. At the time, marrying young girls or boys was part of living this kind of "other life."

But there is a difference between marrying a child bride and actually abusing a child before their pubescent years… but we are not discussing this here. We are just talking about child brides, and child / white / black slavery, and slavery in general.

We are discussing gays, lesbians, bisexuals, transgenders, queens… and if one reads the explanation of it all, which has existed since men and women walked on Earth, it becomes an acceptable option, and people will stop being so judgmental.

- Black slavery: https://simple.wikipedia.org/wiki/slavery

James kept on with his trysts with Harry… anxious to meet… and one would ask… one is so rich and the other so poor… a poor, ethnic, young, handsome boy… never mind their work ethics. His sister Amy worked for the Blighs.

Harry Poulson became the lost boy with nowhere to go, except for Sara and Roy helping him out.

It was a revelation. It was a new world they found themselves in… They loved it… They now had someone that belonged to one another in a world of their own, apart from the present one that caused their pain and suffering, but at the moment, their love sufficed. Their meetings were fleeting. Their lives intertwined… they would even travel to Sydney's gay bars when they were visiting or in town… they were always together, working together, riding together, they swam in the lakes together, they took lunch together, they kissed, made love, at the time they both adored each other, for them, this was love, so easy, so normal, both resting on their backs on the big rocks, resting in each other's arms, relaxing, watching and listening to the sounds of nature, the water in the lakes gurgling, with the leaves weaving and softly moaning, sometimes a bird would fly by in total sync, making perfect sense to both of them, at least.

Maybe for Harry… but James was a social butterfly… flying over here and there… posing to chit-chat with the flowers in bloom… and then would leave… one could not really trust James and his feelings… so fickle. But who could blame him, as he was heartbreakingly handsome and never seemed to fit anywhere, except in his own world. Harry, however, was another story. Living in poverty, he needed to work hard for a living. He was solid. He was also grounded.

Such serene times… peaceful… enjoying the cool, crystalline, clear, and concise water… and never a day went by when the cook would not pack off James' lunch on the double, sending someone to deliver it. The cook crowed so much about her food that it landed in Elizabeth's idle ears, about James' huge and voracious appetite… finding James always alone, ready to devour his huge lunch. The coffee thermos and lime water flasks were always empty.

The cook's crowing about her delicious fare… Elizabeth at first thought it highly amusing… At night time, true to the cook's words, James would also devour his own dinner, drink his own wine, and practically enthusiastically consume his own share of coffee and desserts… always relaxed and happy as all could see, sated, ecstatically satisfied, smilingly, but to Elizabeth's eagle eyes, some dark shadows enveloped James… dancing around in her mind, arousing suspicion about James. But at the time, Elizabeth allowed it to go on, thinking that someday her grandson would see sense and bring the girl home, which was a hard task to follow, as James was always absent. Elizabeth would inquire, but nothing came out from James himself. But one day, out of curiosity, Elizabeth decided on an impulse to deliver the lunch herself… the real reason, also, was that curiosity was catching up with her, to find out who the "mysterious" lady was keeping James so well occupied and his attention averted.

The night before had been high, with bitter winds and rain pelting the grounds of Camelot's Kingdom. Anna went about her own studies, and soon she was already in bed. James returned home, all soggy and wet, looking the worst for wear, going straight to dry off and shower himself… then he had a late supper… but by then Elizabeth had her sweets and tea, and was happily ensconced in her own comfortable bed, resting and sleeping, with fulfilling dreams of her own. In her dreams, she saw both of her grandchildren happily married, toasted with sparkling champagne. Her dreams would soon turn into hellish nightmares.

The following day, all in the residence woke up in full bright spirits. From the hellish night of strong winds and hail, the day turned out to be lovely. Elizabeth loved the new day and the sunshine. She could still smell the earth through the air, as the water seeped into it… she glanced around after her early breakfast, realising that the place was all hers.

Anna went out shopping to collect more ideas for her books and novels, and James departed as early as anything… the sun was shyly peeking out, and the gentleness of its light was slowly spreading around Inverness and, more to it, around Camelot's Kingdom… She had finished her early breakfast, went about her daily duties, checked into Anna's bedroom, and then went to change into her own riding gear, wearing the jodhpurs with her long shining boots, and a white shirt with her jacket, directing herself to the stables, asking for her own horse to be saddled, which was done.

Elizabeth was highly excited, elated… it had been a while since she had ridden a horse.

As the cook brought out the picnic basket, Elizabeth was already mounting the horse, making sure the basket was secure whilst attached. She asked the employees where James was, and the answer was that he might be at the lake somewhere. Elizabeth raised her eyebrows… at the lake? At this time of the day, when he was meant to be working? Nevertheless, it was a beautiful day, and Elizabeth always enjoyed these rides… going against the wind, enjoying the sunshine… until she reached the destination where James and Harry were.

What Elizabeth saw sent her into a spinning spell. The lunch was never delivered.

***

Dr Jack Duncan was sent for. Elizabeth Bligh, the grand matriarch of CAMELOT'S KINGDOM, suffered one of her many first heart attacks.

Three months after the heart attack, Elizabeth was hard at work finding a place for James.

Six months later, James Bligh found himself in London, staying with some of the Blighs' friends, and in doing so, his betrothal was announced to the lovely Olivia on the night of Olivia's debutante.

They did not call ELIZABETH BLIGH the Queen of Camelot… for nothing. It was high time James felt the razor-sharp edge of his grandmamah's spiteful nature… now she unleashed her full imperious power… and dared James to disobey.

James followed the rules and the instructions to a T.

When James returned home after being summoned urgently, he found the lunch basket still sitting on the dining table. He realised what had happened… but Jack was ignorant, and after sedating Elizabeth, he asked James about it. James shook his head. Jack insisted on knowing what had happened at lunchtime. Hungry, Jack opened the basket, with the food still intact and untouched, still sitting at the table, with the sandwiches still warm, the flasks of ice lemon tea untouched, and the vegetables still crunchy. Jack took a bite of each and drank the icy lemon tea; only the coffee thermos was warm instead of hot. Jack couldn't find any fault, and he carried on eating the remaining sandwiches.

He summoned the cook, who explained what had happened, but Jack was still puzzled, flabbergasted… the food was good, tasty, and still fresh. Then he looked at James, his eyes asking the reason behind Elizabeth's heart attack, while feeding himself with the remaining sandwiches. Jack said he would return later, but to let Elizabeth sleep in her own bedroom and not be disturbed. Jack left. George hurried home, only to be told that Elizabeth had suffered a heart attack, with Anna crying uncontrollably.

When Elizabeth recovered, she demanded a meeting and wanted to know about James and Harry.

James shook and trembled, begging for his grandmamah's mercy… actually prayed for it. He could be her first grandson… but for sure, it was time to shake it all up and down… and if he did not comply with what she so firmly demanded (it was a command…), then his inheritance and his residence at CAMELOT'S KINGDOM would be annulled and totally terminated.

Queen Elizabeth of CAMELOT'S KINGDOM showed James that he was actually the heir presumptive to the throne of CAMELOT'S KINGDOM, but that could be easily eradicated.

Dr Jack Duncan never knew what had happened then and was hugely surprised when he was told that James was in England to woo and marry a beautiful lady of ample wealth and dignity. Except that Jack was not invited, and it was only later that he found out what James was all about, and for what purpose.

No one would ever understand how tough, highly manipulative, and shrewd, despite her fragile and delicate frame, the new Mrs James Bligh was. The Blighs were in for another long and hard trip. One that would remind Elizabeth of herself, and she would duly admit it to Olivia, coming to actually admire Olivia's inner strength and suitability. Like Elizabeth, Livvy was also very unlucky in love. History was repeating itself.

But James was what he was. Even in London, he nurtured the affection of someone else. Besides Olivia, the young, beautiful, soft-spoken, versatile debutante, who saw the world, like her aunt-in-law Caro, through pink-coloured glasses, nothing mattered; she fell in love at first sight with handsome James Bligh. But, as we know, James had another "beau" whom he would come to love tenderly and affectionately… Olivia's own older brother, William.

Now we await the next… more dramatic scenes and adventures. By the way, I also dedicate these five editions to the LGBTQ community.

Chapter 07:
Roy Briggs

INVERNESS was a relatively new town to many people. It was a place where people kept close and almost lived in each other's pockets… everything was known by all who lived in that beautiful place where nothing ever changed. Time stood still. It was still well preserved, like pickles, jams and other elements kept in jars, sealed away from estate developers and the expansions that were now creeping in.

On one side of town, Inverness was surrounded by lush green grass, tall trees, and animals grazing peacefully, existing in quiet harmony. It was a calming and deceptively peaceful place. One could easily picture Inverness in their mind, a pretty, picturesque portrait, painted and brimming with lively colours, alive and kicking in such delights. It created a spontaneous sense of love and family atmosphere, cared for with natural tenderness… or so it seemed.

Occasionally, a car would go by. Others would pedal to and fro on their bikes, as it was the trend then, especially for women. Truckies went about their daily business, hauling cartloads of whatever needed moving, majorly anything and everything. By majorly, they would even transport pregnant women if such an emergency was needed. Inverness relied on its own, and trusted itself blindly.

After the First World War, things slowed considerably. The Inverness town folk worked as hard as they could to put bacon on the table. Life was not getting any easier. They rose early to tend to practically anything, as things were hard to get by. Still recovering from the war, the Roaring Twenties were settling in, and a new decade was turning up, though not without scars.

In Inverness, there were moments of happiness and celebration, whilst others were down in the dumps. It was still the local shop where one got what they actually wanted for a fine meal. Sandwiches were the easy way to eat and even easier to make, and they did not cost a fortune. Sometimes the town, with the local Church, would hold fetes, charity balls for

Christmas, masquerade balls for New Year's Eve, and large lunches for the disabled, the poor, and those who could not afford a proper New Year's lunch.

But wait… there was more.

Easter was an enchanting fun day, as the Church sold raffles, offered pony rides, and ran competitions mixed with food and drinks. The Church appealed greatly for the help of the Inverness community… and all of them contributed. The ladies were a force to be reckoned with, the true blue heart of Inverness, never shirking their responsibilities.

One of them were the **BRIGGS**.

The family was as rough as guts as anyone could be. In true blue style, they spoke in their broad Aussie accents and worked to the peaks and back.

Mrs Briggs was a bright, sunny person, always well dressed, very prim and proper. She cut a distinctive figure with her petit chapeau, her blonde hair always well secured into a bun with glittering combs holding it in place. Her face was beautifully made up: thin eyebrows painted dark brown, eyeliner and mascara only, moisturiser as the base, a light dust of powder, light blush on her cheekbones, and red lips, of course, as it was the trend.

Daddy Briggs was a laid-back man and easy on the eye. He was fit from all the hard work he did on his farm, his face leather-like from air, weather and sun. He still looked tough and enjoyed his own beer, and more so, he was proud as punch of his lovely and talented wife. Adding to his already inflated ego were his two handsome sons, always ready for anything the town required.

One only had to say the time, the date, the week or the month, once the "call of the wild" buzzed, the Briggs would march into town come rain, hail or damnation, as religious as they were, unless God alone didn't want them doing their good deeds. Cakes, party pies, sausages, sandwiches, stacks of them, all for sale to gather donations.

Apart from that, the Briggs' truck was used for whatever the Church wanted it used for and done. And even more... the town of Inverness could not survive without the Briggs.

The Briggs were not bludgers, with their motto being one for a penny and one for a pound. They gave as good as they got, plus more. Their mother and wife was a lady whose cooking, baking and catering were everything. Mrs Briggs was wise and smart. She made money on the side by catering. Any time there was a celebration, the Church contacted Mrs Briggs. Any time there was a fete, bazaar or fair, there she was, with all her fine gastronomy, the best anyone could taste in Inverness. Delivered on time, every single tasteful morsel would be gone in a fraction.

Their three-bedroom cottage was built solely on love and dreams. Being out of town kept the Briggs' life private and successful. Both parents wished their two boys would be brought up sound, safe and good, achieving with bright reviews.

The Briggs boys were strong, strappy and sturdy. Both were educated at the local primary and secondary schools. Naturally, both boys practised sports such as Aussie Rules football. Like any healthy boys with hormones, they enjoyed female company. Both learnt more from the outside world than inside the classroom. They excelled in carpentry, woodwork and mechanics, a huge plus for both of them.

They always represented their schools, learning multiple subjects in any shape and form, triumphant for them, as they could use these skills later when convenient.

The family worked hard and long. Dad Briggs ran a construction business and employed town folk. The Briggs' lives were not easy. For most, the Briggs were thought to be wealthy, financially good, but sometimes they struggled. Nothing deterred them.

They enjoyed cruises during summer trips, crossing Australia by driving their jeeps (not trucks) and caravans interstate.

The family enjoyed quality time together. Their extended family travelled far to visit them for anything, birthdays, the annual Debutante Balls, and sometimes Christmas and New Year celebrations.

Yet behind the warmth, behind the charity, behind the perfect Inverness smiles… something darker was quietly waiting its turn.

They were two Briggs brothers… always into every single mischief. Both were taken to the local circus, to the beaches, and into Sydney's CBD for weddings, christenings, and engagement celebrations, ideal weekends spent staying in local bed and breakfasts. To most, they looked like ordinary boys growing up under the wide Australian sky. Yet even then, there was something restless about them, something that never quite settled.

Meanwhile, back in Inverness… the hospital was abuzz with its annual Anzac Day celebration. A mass would be held, followed by a small parade to honour the Fallen Ones, *"Lest We Forget."* Afterwards, the fair at Inverness Hospital would take place, much to the delight of everyone, and very much including Mrs Briggs and her thorough fares.

There was pride in the air that day. There was reverence. There was also a solemn stillness beneath the music and chatter, as if the town itself remembered more than it ever spoke aloud.

A TRIBUTE.

FIRST WORLD WAR 1914–1918.

THE ANZACS.

HISTORICAL AUSTRALIAN BACKGROUND.

Short version…

(I am a FANATIC about world or universal history, and naturally I could not go by without writing a short version about our own AUSTRALIAN HISTORY, which I love recounting. Being a PROLIFIC WRITER, this gallant history of the MIGHTY DIGGERS, who fought brilliantly without fear or foe, sacrificing their lives for other families when they alone left their own families to do so, was very much in my timetable to write a short chapter about it and honour the FALLEN.

Today they are called the DIGGERS, the HONORARY NAMES to our own CHAMPIONS and HEROES. Please read on…)

(Notes: Even though I started to write this Book 1 (of Book 2 and Book 3) of *A Place to Call Home, "The Forensics"* back in 2014, with each chapter displaying their own life stories, my ideals about lives and personalities, emancipated by their characters and based on their backgrounds, were laid out in this book.

When I spoke to Bevan Lee, and with his authorisation for me to write about what I actually thought about the actors or stars who made *APTCH*, as Bevan put it, all writers write differently and place their own art and creations down. Therefore, my own theoretical ideals were established as the basis, and the framework was created.

Thus far, I have managed to create a field where one can imagine the characters. But again, all of us will have different opinions.)

The initial reception of the ANZACS as symbolising the birth of a NATION was followed by the concept that during the First World War, and in the decades that followed, the legend of the DIGGERS was heralded when the ALLIES decided to invade Turkey with the idea of fighting the OTTOMAN EMPIRE.

It was one of the biggest mistakes the Allies ever made, including the Australians and other nations who fought against the Ottomans. The campaign failed terribly.

GEOGRAPHY:

Gallipoli is located in the southern part of East Thrace in the European part of Turkey. It is surrounded by the Aegean Sea to the west and the Dardanelles Strait to the east. That is why it is called a peninsula, much like Macau, once a Portuguese colony in South-East Asia, now the "Las Vegas of the Orient."

The Gallipoli Campaign, later known as the Dardanelles Campaign, was initially seen as an important military operation. It was meant to be the place where the Allies would invade Turkey's side of Gallipoli, sending the message that it would be a casual affair and that the First World War would be shortened, bringing it to an early end.

Instead, it became something else entirely.

Gallipoli is now connected to modern times as a war that was a tragic wastage, where thousands of young, and not so young, perished.

It was a downfall and devastating campaign, still spoken about today, with questions lingering over why it was such a huge failed attempt.

However, whatever it is, we still honour the FALLEN... the LEGENDS... the HEROES... who championed their ideals and fought with bravery and courage. Even though it was a most lopsided event, today thousands of proud Australians pay their respects by honouring those who died fighting for King, Country, for us and for their families.

This is AUSTRALIA, a NATION'S DEMOCRACY with FREEDOM OF SPEECH, and I am proud to be one of them, one of you all.

I salute the FALLEN ONES by giving them the MILITARY SALUTE.

LEST WE FORGET.

Referrals to the Anzac Days in *A Place to Call Home*, Season Five, practically seek out our attention. It was smart of Bevan Lee to institute it as part of our glorious history, and it certainly remains a topic for anyone who wishes to debate or seek the ANZACS' history.

Herewith are the references:

Jack HAZLITT, WORLD WAR 1, DIGGER

Digital Resource Finder.

These references will knock the socks off you. They are thoroughly conclusive, covering the whole set of history with video references, video clips, and in-depth depictions of the First World War. They undoubtedly explain and reflect on the author's works.

Jack Hazlitt also served as a runner in the trenches. It will be pure suggestion, but he was the runner in Gallipoli's trenches, as was our Mark Lee. He too was a runner, as I mentioned above when he made the *Gallipoli* movie with Mel Gibson.

Mark Lee's role as Archy Hamilton, the rising sprinter who momentarily defers his wishes of being the best and joins the Australian Light Horse Men Division, remains iconic. (A movie in this category was also made.)

Please watch Mark Lee's interview on being on the set of *Gallipoli* and the great time he had. Please check this on YouTube:

"The Making of the Movie, Classic."

On **10 September 1982** (I watched this classic at the drive-ins with my ex… then), *The Lighthorsemen*, an excellent movie.

Set in 1917, when the British Forces were caught between the Turkish and German forces, right in the middle of these two armies in Palestine, the British were relying on the **Light Horsemen Regiment** to break the deadlock. The movie starred Jon Blake (RIP), Peter Phelps, Tony Bonner and Bill Kerr.

Gross revenue then: **AUD $1,620,000.00**.

Winner of the **AACTA Awards** for Best Original Music Source.

AACTA Award for Best Sound.

These are my own personal references. *Gallipoli* and *The Lighthorsemen* were two CLASSIC and EXCELLENT movies. I took notes and observed the Anzac Day traditions. Of course, I was also present during the Anzac parades.

I was so proud to be an Australian, a new Australian, anyhow. It is still an ongoing celebration, with Australians starting their day with the Dawn Service, where the Eternal Flame burns at the Shrine of Remembrance. But this year, 2020, due to COVID-19, it is still going on, though with fewer people attending the service.

My further reading tells me that the ANZACS are followed by the "concept", an ideal, an ideology, that during the First World War and in the decades that followed, even one hundred years later, the legend of the DIGGERS was born.

As two in one, they originated in the contextual form of a military figure, and the DIGGERS became one of the grand personal histories of those who fought, who bravely confronted everything. Some returned. Others did not.

Below is still a further reference to the magnificent series of *A Place to Call Home*, which explains the pride of a NEW NATION born and bred through sweat, blood and tears, now spoken loudly and vibrantly, totally venerated and revered.

For more information about **The Legend of the ANZACS (The DIGGERS)**:

WARTIME@awm.gov.au

Phone: 02 6243 4489

Fax: 02 6243 4325

For overseas: please add 61 (02).

Honouring the FALLEN, which at the time was called the “Great War”.

(Again, we refer to the DIGGER as a NATIONAL AUSTRALIAN MYTHOLOGY, the history of Australia.)

Further references:

https://www.theguardian.com/australian-news

Some of these tributes to the FALLEN come from assignments I worked on during my time at two universities. Later on, my daughter also wrote a short 5,000-word composition about the FALLEN, *Lest We Forget*, using much of my notes and photography during her schooling years at two Catholic secondary colleges.

Another reference is to our brilliant star, theatre and film director, and also a singer, born in 1958 in NSW, our own **Mark Lee**, aka Sir Richard Bennett in *A Place to Call Home*.

His movies include:

Gallipoli (1981) with Mel Gibson.

Vietnam with Nicole Kidman (1987).

Everlasting Secrets of the Family (1988).

It was highly fitting that Bevan Lee gave Mark the role of Sir Richard Bennett. For all intents and purposes, it was a brilliant move.

The Bet (2006).

And the more recent current ones…

A Place to Call Home series.

Channel 7.

Home and Away, playing the role of Rick Booth since 2019.

Clearly, Mark Lee and the rest of the cast who played their terrific and brilliant roles in *A Place to Call Home* were outstanding. They portrayed their characters with depth and conviction. One does not need to think too hard about where such fantabulous talent comes from.

"…and down with the tyrant…", during the election campaign in *A Place to Call Home*, Season Five.

They are now investigating Regina's "suicide", which is revealed as murder committed by Sir Richard Bennett's colleague, the "mole" in Inverness Hospital.

The question is: **WHO KILLED REGINA?**

(Reference: Book 2, *A Place to Call Home. "The Forensics."*

The Return of Little Lizzie.)

More will be elaborated and done in Book 2. Please don't miss it.

What a tremendous cast of professional stars we see, meet, and most of us have had the pleasure to connect with. We thank Bevan Lee for a thorough series that had us twisted in a frenzy, culminating in my writing this fun-time book.

Even though there were outside forces who tried everything to stop me, robbing me of the manuscript, creating their own sickening team and then trying to make do with it, as Sara Adams said to George:

"Not by force, not by power… but by spirit."

Exactly right.

Sadly, for this ANZAC DAY 2020, we are all in lockdown.

We cannot do anything to help us celebrate this terrific day.

We are proud to be Australians, even though I still speak with a pronounced Portuguese accent betraying my ancestry, being born and raised in Macau. That will not dampen my spirit.

My ANZAC TRIBUTE is done.

Now for Chapter 8… come along and join us all.

Roy turned up with his wife and his kids. He was happily married and happier still, head over heels with Mrs Roy Briggs and his two boys. He sparkled like a rough diamond.

There was a time when Roy was a young, naughty but handsome larrikin who would come and go as he pleased. His singing and guitar playing, his hip ways and teddy-boy style of the times, made him a familiar sight, along with his older brother Frank, with beautiful ladies hanging on his arms during his young and exciting days.

The girls were also a treat. They were young, vivacious, and looking for fun and diversion. For the two Briggs boys, the ladies came in every single shape, colour and frame.

The Briggs boys were Inverness's Fifties Everly Brothers, popular, centre stage, au centre de la scène. Both were enjoying life to the extreme, and why ever not?

Roy was the ultimate good-looking boy next door at the time. Roy and his older brother Frank enjoyed the youthful ride. At the mere mention of marriage, the boys would run for cover. But sooner or later, there would be a good catch for both of them.

But one day, his older brother went off to fight for King and Country… and it was the last time Roy ever saw his brother Frank.

That was what the First World War did to people around the world.

And if that was bad, the future and its wars would be far worse.

War is war.

There are no lines between.

Roy also went ahead and fought for King and Country. Lucky for him, Roy returned home, to his now ill parents. They lived with terrifying nightmares. Their health suffered tremendously, especially after the sudden and shocking news of the death of their older son.

It all began when Roy's father developed a dry cough, which many thought was just a mild case. Once, Roy's dad's appetite had been large, washing down the delicious morsels Mrs Briggs cooked with copious amounts of beer, enjoying meals with his two boys, cracking jokes over excellent fares.

Like his father, who joked about Roy's name being the last thing on his mind.

"What was I to do… the woman had me in a total trance. I was told by myself to marry her."

They all cracked up laughing over dinner with friends coming over for Sunday roast chicken, a special treat during those hard days.

Mrs Briggs would cook up a storm when the boys and her husband were home. The beautiful lady still found time to tidy the house, do the washing, cleaning and ironing.

In the meantime, she would go and help around the Church, catering to the churchgoers' tastes and adding more specialties for debutante balls when they were held.

If that was cumbersome, then think about the large numbers of people ordering Mrs Briggs' busy catering schedule, official dates that were called for, such as Christmas, New Year, Australia Day, Easter and school fairs. Mrs Briggs mostly did all of them without her two boys.

For Mrs Briggs, it was her own *bonheur* (happiness).

Both boys would go to school smart and clean, with their shirts and pants well ironed early in the morning, and would return home all black, dirty and scruffy. Both were unruly. They were always involved in scruffies, but they were always boys. Yet, whatever happened, the boys would never step out of line.

By now you would have guessed it… one could really imagine that they were as thick as thieves. Where one went, the other followed, with the good and the veracity of entertaining times they both would have enjoyed.

Now that they had part-time jobs working for their dad for extra pocket money, they would vanish during the weekends. In typical boys' style, they were larrikins, enjoying booze, driving and girls. The sticker on their trucks read:

"Have girls and booze, will travel."

Pronto.

Saturday nights, both of them would court their girls and take them to the local drive-ins.

Sunday mornings, with their parents and their on-and-off girls, the whole family would attend Sunday services, looking both the heart and soul of Inverness Town, properly dressed. Then they would help around the Church, consequently joining in the lunch that the churchgoers brought for all the parishioners, including the party pies and sausages that Mrs Briggs baked and set out on the tables.

Other times they would drive early to the Church and set up stalls for the fetes. The Briggs trucks would be there for all to see, with banners flowing about. Sometimes they would also sell their mum's food, then donate all the money to the Church.

For all of his rugged personality, Roy Briggs was traditional, cultural and a homebody. He loved his mum's food and enjoyed his father's lovely larrikin ways. His dad was always good fun, spinning a good yarn about the good times and the hard yakka, what Inverness was all about. In elderly Mr Briggs, it was always a good story.

The Briggs family were very much loved and respected. When hard work was concerned, the whole family rolled up their sleeves. They were all systems go, all the way and without pause.

Their personal, fun, their own lives went on…

but something on the horizon was brewing, and it was not a good sign.

Flowers in Bloom.

Ever since he was a kid, Roy and his brother Frank Jnr would watch and help their parents set up tables out and around the Church, more often than not.

During those days, the Church all around the world held the power, the vision, everything: money, power. The Vatican was well known to be the wealthiest and the most powerful. Therefore, during these uncertain times, people flocked to the Church for various reasons, mainly for being Christians, believers with their faiths, relying solely on the Bible and the sermons.

Being a Christian, a God-fearing community that believed in all the revelations and prophecies, including, of course, the Ten Commandments, the Seven Sins and the Seven Virtues, some people would ask a question and open the Bible for an answer. Others would do the same with the Psalms.

One would give everything just to believe in one single word that came from the Priest. Others enjoyed the services, taking the Holy Host, the wine and the blessings. The incense burned in the Church also helped by relaxing one's tired, worrisome and weary mind, spirit, body and heart. It was virtually a balm for everyone. Each time the parishioners attended, they prayed Psalm 23 for their own delivery and safety.

Inverness was beautiful, away from all the hustle and bustle of the more rousey, noisy but exciting Sydney and the other suburbs. Inverness remained aloof, in her own solitude. It gave the idea that there was no rush anywhere, any time. The town and its people would still be there for all, for the good, for the bad times to roll on.

Frank and his older brother would watch the ladies going about their business on a busy daily routine around the Church, with their own mates coming and going with one thing or another for that same reason.

Something good or bad happened in Inverness and there was, or always had been, something to chance, in particular the weather. Oh boy…

Mother Nature was fickle and terrorising when she lashed her earthy powers and showed who was boss.

That was the beginning of it all.

Then there was something terrible that happened during the full moons.

Talk about feminine or female all-too-powerful control all over the world… even more so when Earth consisted of three parts water and tiny bits of land. Some places, of course, had not been explored. But all the same, one respected the females around the world.

Roy noted that when his mother was busy and sometimes irritable, his dad always did things to mollify her and soothe matters. He would also cook, allowing his mum to rest for a day or two. His mother's work was never done, and he thoroughly admired and truly appreciated having a mother, his own mother.

Then he also noticed it was the same mostly all over the world.

On those days, the Church held all the power and would organise every year a Debutante Ball for charity purposes, for young girls in their youth and in goodwill, so they could marry into good families.

Note for file:

Debutante means "premiering", making the debut of one lady or ladies into more traditional and cultural societies.

Background, A Fragment of British and Australian History

Australia was, then and now, very much part of the United Kingdom, where the English language was written and spoken, by the same token, Australia being a Commonwealth nation.

Yet beneath that polite constitutional phrasing lay something heavier, more binding, something inherited, imposed, and never fully questioned.

A Brief History of the Commonwealth

Commonwealth is a traditional English word that, for us, denotes a political community founded for the common good. For some, it carries links to a more pronounced official term: *Republic*, *Democratic*

Republic. But it can only be one or the other… it is either *Republic* or *Democratic*.

The word *Commonwealth* could also simply mean *public welfare*, *general good*, or *advantage*. It dates back to the fifteenth century.

It could also mean, quite literally, *the Common and the Wealth.*

This analysis was one I first made when I wrote a composition back at university, when we were asked what *Commonwealth* meant to each of us individually.

For my own study, the noun itself seemed to spell out its significance. *Common* meaning *public*, or more significantly, to me, *Vox Populi*, the Latin term meaning *the voice of the people*.

And *Wealth* meaning the people's labour, production, and contribution: how the *Populi* paid their taxes, how governments extracted them, and how, in theory at least, that wealth was meant to benefit the *Populi* themselves.

And of course, being a *Democratic Republic*, one did not merely wish to be politically correct, one had to find ways to implement such legislation and law.

(University of Swinburne, Hawthorn… 1974–1976.)

Hence: how to establish the *Common* and its *Vox Populi's Wealth.*

Australia is a Commonwealth and is based on federal and state elections.

And yet, curiously, we are still not a Republic.

For that essay, I received an A+.

Not appropriate to mention here, but perhaps worth crowing about just once.

The study of what constitutes a Commonwealth stems largely from whether it is an independent country or community, especially a democratic one.

These are formed through an aggregation or grouping of states or other bodies into a union: a commonwealth of democratic, self-governing countries.

And in doing so, it arranges a community of shared interests, sometimes far-reaching, sometimes remote, sometimes deeply non-political:

(Commonwealth Government.

Commonwealth Welfare.

Commonwealth Christian Organisations.

Commonwealth Banks…)

Not forgetting, too, that there is an international association of Commonwealth countries consisting of the UK and states previously part of the British and Portuguese Empires and their dependencies.

Portugal and England are allies.

Here in Australia, we still follow Commonwealth laws and legislation. And while the Democratic Republic exists in principle, in reality it consists of men united by compacted agreements under one form of government, one system, and one law.

It is, essentially, and more appropriately, applied to governments.

(See: cefa.org.au/cef/why-are-we-called-commonwealth-australia)

Having written the foundational purposes of the Commonwealth and its laws and regulations, we now turn to something far more ceremonial, and far more revealing.

A Brief History of Debutante Balls

Each country holds its own debutante balls.

Each colony once did too.

In Macau, where I myself was one of the manner ladies involved, the School of Debutantes was established by the first Portuguese fleet that arrived in the sixteenth century.

Two institutions were founded:

the Fort, and the Military Club.

The Portuguese government then implemented the School of Debutantes. My mother became its director. She herself, along with her older sister, had once been among the ladies presented to elite society.

The ball was held every year in May, the month of Our Lady of Fatima, the month of Mother's Day, the month of feminine "orientation".

Girls were trained.

Conditioned.

Prepared.

They were introduced to society, and, quietly, to expectation.

Debutante balls were formally established when King George III held one in 1780 to celebrate Queen Charlotte's birthday.

Later, they became the annual Royal Ball.

Elite daughters were trained for years.

In Macau, two years.

Etiquette.

Protocols.

Charity appearances.

White gowns.

Jewellery.

Curtsies.

The ritual never changed.

During the reign of King George V and Queen Mary of Teck, their son Edward VIII ascended the throne.

And then, disastrously, abdicated.

For a woman.

Wallis Simpson.

A constitutional crisis followed.

His brother Albert became King George VI.

And from that fracture in royal tradition, something subtle shifted forever.

And somewhere between ceremony and power, tradition and secrecy, obedience and rebellion…

Roy Briggs learned exactly how to break the rules, and how to disappear behind them.

One of the Royals' debutante balls was held then at Buckingham Palace, where the young Prince Edward, as he was called, David, introduced his new girlfriend, Wallis Simpson. The chandeliers glittered, orchestras played in disciplined harmony, silk brushed against marble floors.

Both monarchs stared ahead in frozen expression, not merely composed, but rigid. The silence around them tightened like a drawn thread. At a later date Queen Mary was heard expressing her thoughts about what exactly she thought of Wallis Simpson's debutante frock: "absolutely horrid." That was what they had to say about it… and more words to this effect.

Those words did not evaporate. In such circles, they lingered. They attached themselves to reputations. They divided rooms.

However, on the positive side of this elegant and more sophisticated event, debutante balls were in fact a reason for the young ladies to be highly trained in a more elegant and sophisticated way in anything that could help them in the future, either by marrying into an elite family or, by the same token, should any one of them miss out on being married, as many times they turned down proposals. But beneath that polish was discipline, relentless, unyielding.

Their future would be sealed, as presumably they would know thus far how to conduct themselves, with class, their own fashion savvy, being elegant and effervescent, sophisticated, knowing the subjects to be debated, discussed ably, organising the pre and post effectively in setting up the tables, writing a specific menu à la carte, walking, giving speeches about their own charities… and why they were so attracted to them and attuned to it.

But training of this calibre does not come without scrutiny. Nor without pressure. Every misstep was remembered.

For the next two years in Macau, the discipline acquired to become a debutante was tough, with the girls who belonged to the Portuguese Feminine Youths knowing all the facts and fictions about it… sadly it finished in 1975… but in Australia, it was far more relaxed and more stress-free, continuing it all the way. Relaxed on the surface, perhaps, but still watchful.

Even though it was banished by Queen Elizabeth the Second, Debutante Balls (for a majority of people called COTILLION, French garden or country balls), Debutante Balls are by and large events that keep on developing and expanding. Traditions do not die easily. They evolve.

Over here in Melbourne, for starters, we do have them in Geelong and Ballarat and for ones residing in Melbourne, Victoria, Debutante Balls are held annually, and here is one of Studio One, Ballarat's Debutante Ball.

For the ones who are interested here it is.

Here is the information: https://studioarc.com.au/ballarat.debutante-balls/debutante

Jane 0431 32 7583.

Email debbal@studioarc.com.au

To register or sending please write on the EXPRESSIONS OF INTEREST and complete a form.

It required hard work… and one needed to really concentrate, focusing one's all. The girls were often in rehearsal mode and constantly trained on a daily basis for anything pertaining to them… Naturally there were therapies (something akin to assessments, tests… and so many things for a girl to accomplish) and needless to say on those days the poor mite was in excruciating pain under the more ancient traditional teachers who were supposedly the mentors or their "model" teachers.

Smiles were corrected. Shoulders adjusted. Voices lowered. Laughter softened. Tears unseen.

However, it was in this mode that Roy Briggs and his family attended for the amazing and spectacular main event of the year.

Roy, in his rebellious and "teddy" boy ways, for once turned up all dressed up in his tuxedo, feeling a tad uncomfortable with the crisply starched white shirt rubbing the man's neck the wrong way. He tugged at the collar more than once. But it was for one night only.

He shone like a centre-polished button… and his hair was the statement at the time, into the brazen years of his youth. Now we had the duo Fred Astaire and Ginger Rogers dancing and singing, plus the Andrews Sisters along, echoes of glamour drifting across the polished floorboards.

The Briggs family and the entire community of Inverness were doing everything right for the event of the year. Each time it was done, the tickets flew out the window the moment it was on sale. Now if one counts the girls and their families, extended ones, grandparents on both sides, aunties and uncles from both sides, and with the list going on… not forgetting friends, in my case even my own cousins, which kept multiplying as it went about… so now we are talking about the agglomeration of everything only to celebrate a very special day and for a special young lady.

By now you would be thinking how the tickets would be stretching… it was their little girl that was being shown to the elite, or not so society.

Wouldn't you attend?

The cocktail began in earnest. Glasses clinked sharply. The ladies again managed to really shine brightly… their gowns dominated the event, as they were doing their utmost to look like the beautiful lady at the ball. It might have been a debutante, but competition was high in every major and minor way… furthermore there was a prize for the lady who would be the star of the evening.

So again it was full speed ahead.

A "sisterhood":

(what one would have called the "Suffragettes", Aus History 1890s–1900s whereby legislation was passed by the Aus Government duly authorising women to have the rights to vote, and also for more pressing rights) were busy taking notes. Inevitably they made up the Debutante Ball Organising Committee Group of the Debutante Ball.

With these ladies, they would vote for the girls' perfect presentation. Their records. Their deeds. Their dresses. The hairdos. The headpieces. The gloves. The shoes. The lengths of their dresses. The collective maquillage. Their own characters. Personalities. And plus their own voices, which usually sounded like they wouldn't melt butter in their mouths.

These "Suffragettes" were busy taking notes, coming and going, always discussing, debating and comparing notes.

Watching.

The girls could arrange themselves and do their toilette… by beautifying even themselves, none of them could really afford to have a hair out. Due to the warm weather, the maquillage was to be minimal… they needed to always look refreshing, youthful, like flowers in blooming… delicate… fragile… emanating from them the pure honeysuckle scents, as one could imagine walking into a garden at dusk, being faced by a myriad of these flowers in their own major delicate colours…

Meanwhile the ladies of the Committee, working on the ball, needed to go about their own rehearsals and their own recitals. It was a thoroughly ladies' event and the ladies could not be overshadowed by anyone… each one had their own duties to carry on and to make the best out of it.

It was to be a successful and triumphant evening and no holds barred.

They had come such a long way…

There was no stopping now.

Not even if something, or someone, threatened to disturb the perfect presentation.

The girls were introduced, being called by their original names, stating who and what they were, what magnificent deeds they had performed, and what they would do after being the nominated one, or for that matter what life would be for them after finishing the evening. After the original lady was nominated as the Best Dressed, the nominations for Debutante of the Year would go on.

(Delays, sickness with the Spanish Flu, others suffering from PTSD, then the ending of World War One, which usually ushered in the Great Depression and money, as usual, was tight as there was much unemployment and people were getting only crummies, therefore the debutante girls, on their own, worked their butts off raising money to be donated to the Church… as usual. The Church tried all avenues for the Debutante Ball to go on without a hitch, but they were facing so many obstacles, obstructions… delays… lack of food and also beverages… driving everyone up the walls.

But on the other hand, business thrived one hundred per cent, as the girls' parents spared nothing for that unique event of high elite and privilege. Therefore Inverness, during the Debutante's time, came alive. Seamstresses were busy sewing the dresses selected by the girls. The shoemakers came alive and kicking. The bakery, the flower shops, the bands chosen to play for the night, the kitchenhands, the menu, the decorations, the gifts, everything was amalgamated into one as they formed the shape, the basis and the turning point of only one evening to be successful.)

One looked at the priest and understood how much he was going through. Seldom a day went by that, if not one person, another would tackle the question: When will the Flowers in Blooming take place?

Some of the parents were getting aggressive, furious even, that their daughters were still to be introduced… and no wonder.

When one looked at all the pros and cons, one could easily understand their frustrations. Times were really hard and not getting easier. A gown such as a Debutante's cost immensely, and the parents would not only save for their daughter/s but would actually pawn something of value just for their daughters' debutante. Now they were consistently at the priest's door demanding action. When the affirmative word finally came, for the parents it was a triumph.

So the posters and the banners were now being hung and the invitations for the occasion were on. Newsletters bearing the highly exciting news were sent all over Inverness and in particular to the secondary school. Nominations of the girls were received. The decorum training for them started for their everyday activities. The newspaper continuously printed and lauded the Debutante's Ball, and for the girls it was now or never.

Exciting times.

Each girl dreamt about that evening, the night of a thousand stars, their own. They also kept their fingers crossed… for the weather.

The newly elected council, as per usual, would be involved by trying to hold events, thus raising more money for the Ball. The Government was stretched to the limits, so they needed to manage their own Debutante Ball with their own costs and expenses in Inverness. The hospital was again holding one of their local fairs. Everyone contributed, either this or bust. The community, as usual, stood up and was counted.

Out of this abnormal chaos, comes Doris.

She of the beautiful, huge rounded yet soft dark brown eyes, fanned by long eyelashes… the perfect nose, the pinky pearl lips, and the well-formed, fragile face.

With those beautiful long dark tresses now all curled up in a perfect coil adorning her face, she moved bricks to have money donated, by her own parents, who would contribute.

They failed to mention that Doris, by and large, accumulated large amounts of money for the donations. When she reached a point where there was no more money to be collected, Doris gallantly broke her little piggy bank and offered her own money to be donated.

Needless to say that the effort of what kindness alone was being done, showed how much Doris in her simple mind alone created her new ways...could do. More than once she would apply herself dutifully to the aid, to the help of the others. The lady had class. Now prominence. Style and later grace.

No need to tell anyone that she became nominated Debutante of the Year for Inverness. But that was a year before. As per usual, not many were elated by the Debutante Committee's decision, but they failed to see the good and kindness that Doris did. Where Doris was concerned… there would always be cynicism about her.

She held her title in good stead with an engagement proposal and later her own wedding. She was not the type who chose a great deal. A faithful companion and a follower of the Bible, she thought that whatever God gave her was for her "bonheur" (happiness), which it was.

But for Roy, this was the night that the event would completely bamboozle him… and change the whole course of his life.

As always, he felt terribly uncomfortable in the starched, crisp white shirt, looking impeccable in his new black-and-white tuxedo. He was not very fond of wearing the long top Uncle Sam hat, but whatever his state of mind was, he was totally good-looking, debonair. Conducting himself as a perfect gentleman gave him the irrits, and he went around sampling the light nibbles with a beer in his right hand, also helping his mum who was busy handling the food. She distributed the food, placing it in trays to be served at the tables for the early starters, and also serving the girls who had been starving themselves the whole day as they were so busy with rehearsals.

The Menu à la Carte only served to make the guests even more hungry, the beautiful smell of the food emanating through the air, plus the glorious sunset, impressed all the guests. There was something about nature and the food spread out in the open air, with champagne flowing… what perfection could anyone ask for?

Roy was now well settled and sat along with the other guests, enjoying the best the event could give him.

He enjoyed the sterling composition of the music. He gazed around and tapped his right foot in sheer spirit of fun. His table, and the others, were impressively decorated and adorned with flowers, porcelain and crystal beautifying them. He loved it.

With the banners being smoothly swept by the gentle breeze, it was a beautiful evening.

Lucky for all of them, Inverness' springtime was at its best. For once Mother Nature was behaving herself and showed her magnificence with the beautiful sunset, sending her hues vibrantly around Inverness. Before the lights were switched on, Mother Nature dazzled the guests even more with her constant myriad of changing lights from one colour to another, and the guests went totally ga-ga admiring such an extravagant exposé of nature.

By now all the guests had arrived and were officially seated in their designated seats.

The stage, built for the occasion, was not yet lit as it was supposed to be, as the natural light had not subsided. But as the Maître de Cérémonies (MC) ascended the stairs and introduced himself, he completely sparkled in his tuxedo. His hair gleamed heavily against the soft lights.

"Hello and good evening, ladies and gentlemen, boys and girls." The guests clapped their hands.

"First, for those who are here for the first time, welcome to our beautiful and remote INVERNESS…" He stopped and took a breather. "Thank you for the privilege of having you all as our guests…" He paused again. "Before we go into the event that is being held, please allow yourselves to enjoy the beautiful, raw but natural sunset of our Inverness." They all nodded affirmatively.

Now the sunset was sending its beautiful rays around and all of Inverness was painted in garish hues, red, pink and orange colours spreading fun and celebratory signs, inviting for once the guests to wake up and take notice. It was indeed a calming and harmonious setting… some felt a peaceful but exciting sensation overwhelming them…

They felt so proud at that precise moment. All the delays that had harassed the function/event were forgiven, as now they had found their ways and their excuses, this now being an affordable explanation and the real deal. What could have been better than this kind of setting? No money could ever buy it… no money could even afford the idea of creating it. Thank goodness it was spring.

The Maître de Cérémonies continued on. He too was really feeling uncomfortable with the starched shirt but continued nonetheless, moving his neck from left to right constantly. By now you would have guessed it, the warmth of the night was making him sweat profusely.

"Now, we are going further. With your consent, I am now introducing the Debutantes who, as you already know, are as per usual beautiful as the flowers in bloom." His voice boomed. The scent of the honeysuckles spread and lingered ever so lightly as the windy breeze fanned over the guests.

"Miss…" There was clapping and the girl came out, walking the little bridge and showing herself to all. With her, a gentleman-in-waiting kept her company. She ascended the stairs with the help of the young man and approached the MC and the microphone. In her delicate voice she spoke about herself, what she was doing, how much money she had raised and what, in fact, she would be doing after her debut. They all clapped. She received her certificate and walked down the stairs on the other side where her male companion awaited her, then descended with him in tow, joining her family who were waiting at the table.

One of the Committee's ladies came over to the Briggs' table and whispered into Roy's mother's ear. The young gentleman who was meant to keep Millicent company had taken sick and, in so doing, she needed a beau to take her to the stage. Could young Roy do this as a favour for all of them?

Roy's mum whispered something into Roy's father's ear. The elderly gentleman turned around, looked Roy directly in the eyes and said, "Son, you are wanted. A lady needs a real man like you to take her to the stage." Briggs Senior smiled and winked. He was always full of fun and expected his son to play his role.

Roy looked at his father as he winked at him. Roy's face broke into that familiar larrikin smile, showing the crevices edged into his more manly face.

"Go, son… now is your time to strut yourself. Now behave yourself too… these ladies per se are still virgins…" His father winked and broadly smiled. He too had more crevices edged into his face, one could almost draw a map on it, but his spirit was young.

And there went Roy… one moment shaking his head, but what the heck. Now the sunset was going down… the lights were being switched on… seven debutantes had already gone through, sashaying in their beautiful gowns, all prim and proper, perfect… now casting their beautiful shadows as they directed themselves onto the stage. Each gown was breathtaking. The flowers on their heads, symbolising their freshness and youth, were a statement, but the thing was, how would you classify these young ladies when they were so beautiful, dutiful and hard-working?

Roy, ever since he was a minor along with his older brother, had loved to watch the girls strutting their stuff. It was spectacular and indeed an event that Roy always looked forward to. On the other hand, before this main event that was always playing inside his mind and ticking away, he and his brother had looked a treat at their own confirmations, followed by their own emancipations. One party for both of them, it was a celebration of the times, the passage of time, and look how good-looking and strapping both men had now turned out to be.

They wore their finery for the services, joining other boys and girls, and they all had a small celebration, again around the Church, with their families and of course the families of the others who had officially completed their Holy Communion and Confirmation. In their hands, their certificates were later framed for posterity and hung in their bedrooms.

However, their celebratory emancipation was a totally different kettle of fish, but enjoyable. When one gets emancipated, the males enjoy it roughly, wildly, and the parties go on for the whole night until the wee hours of the morning. It was akin to a male in medieval times who was knighted after long, strenuous training, undergoing and readying himself for a life in Court and at the service of the King.

By this emancipation in the early twentieth century, they were legally and officially independent males… in all shape and form. No serfdom and no king in Inverness to serve, but there were several ladies for them to serve and choose from.

That was for the Briggs' brothers. Then both brothers waited endlessly for the debutante ball. Each year, things grew far more sophisticated… far more expansive… and of course developed. Every year the ladies became far more interesting… as the ladies of Inverness grew up and were about the same age as theirs.

For once, both brothers would not mumble against anything, as it so happened that when the debutante balls were held, a number of inconsistencies could occur. Beginning with the fickle Mother Nature, whose mood swings could affect everything that was meant to be organised. We all know that when it comes to the power of destiny, any organiser of anything will tell you that, unfortunately, nothing will go according to plan.

So many times, over so many years, the debutante ball struggled to be held. Girls who were destitute had a hard time finding the money to buy the correct attire for their debutante balls. If they struggled to keep themselves fed and clothed, where would they find money for an expensive gown and the correct accoutrements to go with it? Shoes were expensive, gloves too, and the crown of flowers… cost an arm and a leg when acquired.

There were not many rich or wealthy people in Inverness. The Church was rewarded when they actually asked Grand Elizabeth Bligh to be the patron of their Debutante Ball. Of course, Elizabeth contributed with great fanfare, making large donations, her expressive way of helping. She also brought vegetables, fruits, and wines as extras to fulfil her current curriculum. For once, the Ashpark matriarch was not disappointed by the good deeds performed by Doris, but as usual, they overlooked Doris and instead nominated and elected Elizabeth Bligh after apologising to Doris Collins. Later, however, suffering from devastating blows, harassed by tensions, heart attacks, and high blood pressure, Grand Elizabeth Bligh then Goddard relieved herself from that position, and lovely Doris Collins stepped up and took over.

Being patron occasionally meant that Elizabeth also presided over meetings for the minority of the group that attended. She created the committee and, at first, did not want to share her status with anyone. In those days, women mattered very little, and positions were generally filled by males, therefore it was always going to be George Bligh who was attentive to such details. At the time, Doris and her mother always fulfilled whatever was needed, nominated or not, knitting intricate wools, crocheting, arranging flowers with Roy, carting large bouquets and boxes of gifts. Volunteer work was at best cooperative, at worst hard work. Roy struggled at times.

Roy met his present wife during one of these exciting events. Millicent looked like a princess when she descended the stairs after her name was called, and Roy was the one chaperoning her for the evening at the last minute. Millicent's "beau" had been sick and couldn't attend the event, which was entirely a blessing in disguise.

Millicent's dress was long and flowing. It looked like a Roman gown with gold embroidery. She wore her hair adorned with the "Corona Civica," or Civic Crown, encrusted into her soft, long flowing blonde hair. Yes, that was the correct name, a Roman or Greek princess. Unlike the other ladies, she wore Roman sandals to complete the whole picture. She wore two gold armbands and, instead of a pouch, Millicent carried a basket of flowers and other small feminine items she needed, tissues, gold compact powder, lipstick, perfume, comb, purse, and her own card.

By the time the nominations were finished and the girls sat at their tables with their parents, Millicent was happily grinning, showing her parents her certificate and personal gift. Roy was so enchanted he fell in love with Millicent right from the start.

As tradition went, that same night, not only did he dance the night away with Millicent, thunderstruck as he was, but he found himself asking Millicent for her hand in marriage. As per tradition, he rose from his seat, climbed the stairs to the stage, knocked on the microphone three times to gather the attention of all the guests, and declared in that very moment how THUNDERSTRUCK and in love he was with Millicent. If anyone was expecting it, it was a real surprise, but then again… where the Debutante Ball went, it would always be full steam ahead with surprises. A thunderous ovation followed, and so the engagement was announced.

Roy surprised himself… but when one is in love, one is trapped and nowhere else to go. He was walking on cloud nine and couldn't wait for the engagement to be held and the wedding.

Time and life in Inverness moved slowly for Roy.

When they married, he thought he could live with his bride at the cottage.

Millicent agreed. Both of them were hardly out of school. She was working part-time in the local library, and for the time being, neither could really afford to buy or rent anything, let alone a house. The money her parents had saved for Millicent became her dowry for the wedding and expenses.

Millicent did not want a huge engagement party. But it was okay for the wedding, after all, one married for keeps, or so they both thought.

So the engagement was held, and it was only a barbecue. The Briggs were close friends of the Blighs, therefore they were invited. It was typically an Australian affair, simple, loving. Roy's mother cooked a storm; the Blighs brought beverages and, of course, their engagement gifts. It was a small party, and it remained a small one. Maybe fifty of the closest friends attended, and fifty of the closest friends enjoyed a moment of what love could really be. George Bligh considered having Roy do a few jobs at Camelot for extra quids, and really, Roy had the best empresario, he was working for the Blighs. Even though Millicent was still new and only a friend of the Blighs, she was not thinking about Camelot at all. But Roy had a job there, and that alone served the purpose.

So… of all the people… the happy-go-lucky, roguish Teddy Boy of those times, Roy Briggs, was getting hitched… and so it happened. It was so hip.

He gave his heart to Millicent… now he was giving her his ring. They were officially engaged. The little white gold band, set with a small diamond, glimmered as everyone went "ahhh" and "ooohhhh." It had taken Roy six months to get it, with the help of his father and extras working for the Blighs.

Six months later they exchanged vows. Now she was the delectable Mrs Roy Briggs.

Millicent was ecstatic, and Roy? Well, only one could imagine.

But now, just as the highs came, the lows followed. Roy's parents were already seriously unwell. Their health was crumbling fast.

Every year, on the anniversary of Frank, their older brother, the home they all now resided in remained silent, cold and sad. It was indeed a sorrowful day. They would hold a small mass in his honour, followed by a modest lunch with the priest. That was natural, Roy understood. He was his older brother, the son of his parents, now a brother-in-law to Millicent and a darling uncle to his own sons. He felt the same pain, the same sadness… he was also the father of two boys. Roy had temerity.

After their annual Christmas and New Year's trip, where they usually enjoyed cruising down Australia's shores and spent time taking pictures and sampling the local gastronomy, his mother became seriously ill.

She went from one hospital to another in Inverness and was eventually diagnosed by a tall, dark and handsome young doctor, Dr Jack Duncan.

Dr Duncan took X-rays and samples. He wanted to delay the diagnosis, but he knew that one day he would have to inform the Briggs family of Mrs Briggs' state.

That day came. The family was thoroughly devastated. Mrs Briggs was suffering from cancer… nothing could be done… it had spread throughout her body, and she had only days to live.

This began a truly terrible ordeal for them all. Six months later, it was Roy's father who died of a broken heart and senility. It had been a struggle keeping and looking after him, but sadly, he lost his will to live.

Tragic times struck the Briggs family. Mrs Doris Collins helped where she could, and so did the Blighs. Due to their popularity, the Inverness community also stepped in to assist. Many times, they would see Roy Briggs, the tough guy, crying like a baby. Millicent remained silent… but one day she asked Roy to take care of his father's business. She didn't like Camelot.

Roy Briggs indeed wore his heart on his sleeve. Losing his brother was terrible… now losing his mother… the blows were almost too much. Three strikes in total… but seriously… what was going on in Millicent's mind? Yet she never told him.

Not everything was true blue… if anything, there were grey and black shadows curtailing every single moment of their lives, so much mustard colour integrated into it. The winds of change were forever blowing in every direction. Life was never meant to be easy… it was not meant to be that hard either. But that was just the beginning of all the trials and tribulations for Roy.

Before the 1950s arrived, he and the others would go through a journey of extremities, thoroughly trapped by the duties laid upon them, Roy's included.

Roy was happy for a few years, even though his brother remained in his thoughts, then his parents. They were a few good, whooping years as he watched his two boys growing into fine men, as he was… in the meantime, his wife was the love of his life.

Years later, during the Second World War, his two sons enlisted. To the sorrow of Roy and his wife, they never returned. He also lost his adored wife. As the saying goes, death comes in threes… how truthful. Still, Millicent never revealed her fear of Camelot, making all manner of excuses to avoid it. Roy never forced her… he respected her reasons, and therefore, he and Millicent missed a great deal of events at Camelot. More so after Roy's mother told Millicent the devastating news of how Little Lizzie had been left to fend for herself.

Roy became bitterly disappointed, wallowing in self-pity at home… in the same cottage where he had lived with all the Briggs family, including his wife and children.

It took a long time to heal… who in their right mind could really heal when so much was lost? Later, Roy, the happy-go-lucky, all-Aussie, true-blue rugged guy, was now a shadow of himself. His hair went grey overnight. His sun-beaten face bore the sufferings he had endured, visible even when he smiled.

Life continued with its ebbs and flows… one day cold, the next hot. His cosy cottage was now devoid of warmth… filled with pain and sorrow, stifled into a solitary mind. Alone… thinking deeply… bitter… with no guidance or order. Yet he insisted on living, revering the love of his wife, cherishing his two sons, claiming their memory forever. Roy Briggs. At that time, a little girl appeared who would come to mean so much to him.

Roy emerged daily, but was lost to the world for many years. Yet the Blighs never forgot him… he was always their friend and they would stand by him through thick and thin. He always wondered why Millicent had never liked Camelot.

His days as the natural, happy-go-lucky Roy returned with a little girl, tumbling long mahogany curls, slanted green eyes, high cheekbones, pale porcelain complexion, a delicate nose, and a sweet, expressive mouth speaking in her French accent. She opened his heart. He thought of her as the little girl his wife and he could have had. But his wife could only bear two… and the rest had complications.

The beautiful little doll was always there early in the morning, riding her horse and training for competitions. She was tenacious, hard-headed, and no matter what, she would get what she wanted through gutsy determination. It was a new beginning, as Roy enjoyed listening to the thunderous hooves, dominating the grounds and shaking the earth beneath him.

After all those terrible years, Roy was healing slowly. Little Lizzie was a breath of fresh air. She referred to Roy as “mon oncle.” But life had to go on… until one morning he woke to see that he had new neighbours, also full of life and excitement. They too had lost everything. Worse still… they had lost the country they were born into and now lived in a foreign, distant, and sometimes cold place. But now they were living in Inverness… and like the little porcelain doll who rode by every morning and would be a champion for the Blighs, as they called her Little Lizzie, came a calling. He would indulge with her in fancy, hot, piping scones and coffee. Woops, sorry, little Lizzie… she was a real welcoming angel.

The new arrivals were of Italian stock. They were nice people and spoke with deep southern accents… they might have been Calabrians or Sicilians. They had their own lingo, culture, and traditions, plus their wine and gastronomy. They were also Roman Catholics.

The future looked rosy… after such painful experiences. Roy's journey of self-discovery was only beginning. As they say, the good Lord is everywhere, and the good Lord works in mysterious ways. For Roy… he would eventually live on and reinvent himself.

The day Little Lizzie returned… would be a day of reckoning.

He sorely missed her. It took only one day for him to realise he needed to do something. He went away briefly… and when he returned, he thought it strange that Little Lizzie hadn't turned up for her early morning breakfast with him. Now he also missed the sound of her thunderous hooves… shaking the grounds… making the leaves fall… it was so raw and beautiful… so normal.

He looked around. The place was empty… silent. A deadpan stillness. Not even the breezy wisps murmured. There was no chirping of the birds, no buzzing of the insects they were nowhere to be seen. It was dead silent. He shivered. He didn't like it. Too calm… too… he felt another cold finger run down his spine. He felt cold. Roy thought he had a fever… but no… something was amiss. Where was Little Lizzie? Fear gnawed at him.

He waited a while, then went into the house, searching for his hat and gun. He climbed into his truck and drove into some rugged areas to check if anything bad had happened… but nothing. Then he made a short visit to the Polletis, wondering if they knew what had happened to the little girl. The Polletis refused to answer, with little Gino looking at him with teary eyes.

So he went to Camelot's Kingdom. As he stepped out of the truck, he saw Dr Duncan and asked him what was going on, why Little Lizzie wasn't home, and why no one seemed to know of her absence.

Dr Duncan shook his head, clamped his mouth shut, and shook his head again. As he placed his doctor's bag in his car, Roy bellowed…

"Mate… we're on the same level. Little Lizzie is very dear to me… why won't you tell me what's been happening? Where is she? I haven't seen her this morning… I didn't…" He stopped, staring hard at Jack.

"It's not like her… you do realise she loves her equestrian championships, and she was training for the next one. If she misses it… her daily training…"

Jack looked deeply into Roy's eyes and replied, "Okay… I'll level with you…" He glanced around, sighed, then said simply, "Little Lizzie is gone." And shook his head again.

Roy's face changed colour… contorted. The pain was palpable to both men.

"Gone? Gone? My God… what happened to her?" he demanded desperately.

Jack looked elsewhere and continued, "You know… how mother and daughters are." He rested his arm on his car, avoiding Roy's piercing eyes.

"Still… Awww God… what has she done to Little Lizzie?" Roy was crestfallen, heartbroken again. Tears welled in his eyes. The sourness and immense pain cut through him. He clutched his chest, trying to breathe.

"Christ…" Roy mumbled. "How many more will leave her before she learns what she's doing to her own kids?" He was referring to Grand Elizabeth Bligh, the Camelot matriarch, and her cruel treatment of her own children.

"It's not simple being a mother…" Jack tried to explain. "She suffers too." He looked at Roy, trying to make him understand.

"What on earth happened?" This time Roy's tears rolled down his cheeks. He reached for his handkerchief.

Jack was not one for gossip. He knew most gossip was the invention of idle minds, designed to trigger malice.

"The same story… all over again." He shut the car door. "They quarrelled last night. A terrible fight between mother and daughter…" He paused, then added, "You know how Elizabeth can be. She is hard and follows all the rules. Little Lizzie… well… Little Lizzie is just like her mother. It was a real calamity. Little Lizzie left in the middle of the night. I was here all night looking after Elizabeth, she felt faint and dizzy, with high blood pressure, and I fear it might trigger a stroke… we are all on tenterhooks… treading really lightly…" Jack had to warn Troy.

Roy's eyes were fogged, blinded by his own tears. Jack got into his car, telling Roy he would drop by for a cuppa or a beer one day. Roy nodded. Jack drove off.

For a while, Roy stayed behind… he felt empty, lost. He looked up at the sky and prayed Psalm 23 for the safe keeping of the little girl. He also noted Camelot's Kingdom… then his blood ran cold. Millicent never liked that place. He kept wondering why.

Returning home… still, there was no Little Lizzie.

It was another cold night. The breezes became biting winds. The drizzle turned heavy. Thunder screamed loud and boisterous, shaking the whole of his cottage.

He drove his truck into his own man-made garage. He shut the door. From afar, he could hear the long, imaginary hooves of Little Lizzie's pureblood, black as carbon… powerful and enigmatic… galloping at full speed… the thunderous hooves shaking the ground as usual. But he looked up… now he saw a foggy mist. The rain kept falling. By and large, the wind whistled, brushing his face and disheveling his short hair. The lightning began.

He lost his appetite. He looked at the cold pumpkin scones and, beside them, the cream on the oval crystal plate and the red strawberry jam. He had a quick shower, then sat on his porch. It was cold… dark… and he waited for the return of Little Lizzie. The lightning struck… the wind hollowed… the rain fell hard… the thunder roared… it was bitter.

He remembered Little Lizzie. He remembered going to her baptism. He remembered her on the grounds of Camelot's Kingdom, still crawling… still trying to find a place to stand.

But Little Lizzie would not give up.

Then she grew up… and when he lost his own family… she was there. That beautiful face, so radiant… that broad, inviting smile… those long, curly mahogany locks tumbling down, usually worn loose, showing how Little Lizzie loved them all free… a spirited filly… but more than that… how much she truly enjoyed life to its utmost extremes.

Even that was a prelude to so many things he had also cherished. Little Lizzie was the balm for all his losses and sufferings, and he treated her as if she were his own… except that she was a Bligh. Flashes of those early times when he was still married to his wife and had his two kids returned to him.

Now they were gone.

But Little Lizzie… where is she?

"The Return of Little Lizzie."

Chapter 08:
The Femme Fatalle

The Spy Who Resided In Australia.

Refreshing... sinuwe... sash sexy... eloquent... stylish... effervescent... modern... innovative... per se...

Classic.

Oozing self-assurance, confidence, intelligence, independence.

Whilst other women lagged obediently behind the velvet curtains of propriety, Regina Bligh stepped forward, unapologetic, into the new Twentieth Century. Regina was among the first ladies to seek independence by obtaining her driver's licence. And not merely for display, she drove. She commanded the wheel of her own luxurious, jazzy "chariot", steering through Sydney's prominent boulevards and narrow political corridors alike.

Engines roared beneath her gloved hands. Men stared. Women whispered.

She trailed the European cities and roads, Parisian cafés, Viennese salons, Roman courtyards, speaking different languages, shifting accents like silk scarves. Regina diversified herself in numerous networks, expanding ecumenical and advantageous politics and business ventures with strategic elegance. She understood alliances. She understood leverage. She understood that information was power, and power, when handled correctly, was survival.

She was always proper. Always diligent. Such an organiser of official events, gala dinners glistening in crystal and candlelight, high teas curated to perfection, garden parties orchestrated like theatre. Regina played the terrific hostess, that was her major talent. She exuded magic. Loved. Trusted. An indelible lady with formidable skills, that was her forte... that was the positive side.

But brilliance invites resentment.

On the negative side, she needed love. And love was denied.

She trusted, she was betrayed.

She gave, gave, giving always, seeking a way out of the invisible cage she felt tightening around her.

Helping her husband shine. Elevating him at every turn. Constructing his legacy whilst eroding her own. Yet at every single step she was jeopardised… hated… despised… used and abused, strategically sacrificed for selfish ambition.

Jealousy over her beauty fermented quietly in drawing rooms and behind lace fans. The very admiration that crowned her also isolated her. Anxiety crept in, subtle at first. Seeking approval. Seeking validation. Seeking reassurance from those who offered only calculation.

So disappointing. So unequivocally wronged.

By those she believed she could love with fiery abandon. Faithfully. Conclusively. Be one of them.

Poor Regina…

Such a troubled soul.

Such a sorrowful life.

Always misunderstood.

Regina was never meant to become what she ultimately evolved into.

Regina Bligh.

The Narcissist.

The Sociopath.

Finally, the Psychopath.

The misunderstanding and the misunderstood.

They misunderstood Reggie.

And she misunderstood them.

Until the night restraint fractured.

"You survived by opening your legs in the Nazi concentration camp."

She bellowed it, venomous, feral, unrestrained, throwing those deranged, calculated words at Sara Norrmannd. The insult did not merely wound, it dissected.

The room froze.

Champagne stilled in crystal flutes. The orchestra faltered. A single violin note dragged across silence.

Regina stood unmoved.

Regina was the spy.

And she became wealthy.

But wealth born of secrets always leaves fingerprints.

When Elaine, Regina's older sister, descended the white marbled platform of Sydney's Town Hall, the luxurious staircase gleaming beneath chandeliers, she did not simply walk.

She arrived.

Layers upon layers of petticoats whispered with each measured step. Her debutante gown, slightly garish, intentionally so, shimmered like frost beneath gaslight. Elaine looked like a vision.

Older. Wiser.

Elaine had never put a foot wrong.

Her hair was meticulously arranged, secured by exquisite diamond clips, long pearly ropes encircling the intricate coiffure. The soft make-up, beautifully applied, enhanced her gentle features without overpowering them. The jewellery was simple, but unmistakably expensive. Long white sleeves. Dainty satin ballet shoes, precisely as she wanted.

Beautiful Elaine glided through numerous glares in her sparkling white viscose gown, carrying her silky embroidered pouch, completing the bewitching tableau. Her captivating smile, bright, generous, almost saintly, drew sighs from every corner.

"Oooohhhhs…"

"Ahhhhhhs…"

She was voted Debutante of the Year.

Sydney's gallant, and mercilessly judgemental, elite society elevated Elaine as their Society Queen of Demeanour. A lady well versed in etiquette. In protocol. In restraint.

The pride and joy of her family.

No scandals. No controversy. No missteps.

Yet beneath the applause, envy simmered. Many wished to glide across that same polished floor. Wear that same gown. Capture the same suitors.

Jealousy does not applaud loudly, it waits quietly.

Elaine was vivacious, a seductress in her own measured world. A trend seeker. A lady who threaded softly into Australian society, sweetly and strategically. The debutante ball yielded wild attention. Prominent suitors attended the expensive affair, eager, calculating.

It was worth every cent.

The gamble paid off.

Elaine was now the official Australian socialite.

And attending that evening, the Blighs.

Australian royalty in land and cattle.

George Bligh was thoroughly enchanted. Elaine embodied everything love could blindly evoke. Tall. Dark. Handsome. The Bligh dynastic cattle baron heir rose to the occasion, publicly asking for Elaine's hand in marriage.

Applause thundered.

He proudly announced the engagement would be printed in the newspapers. Invitations forthcoming. Cameras flashed. Society sealed the union in gossip before ink touched paper.

The first to congratulate him, Sir Richard Bennett.

So… Little Reggie.

The younger sister.

The shadow at the edge of perfection.

Regina was captivated by the fairy-tale spectacle, but she was taken, utterly, by the tall, dark, handsome Bligh heir. George Bligh. Her soon-to-be brother-in-law.

Regina was clad in her own long, flowing gown, light, suave blue hues. When she walked, it followed her like a tide pulled by unseen gravity. Wealth ensured indulgence. Her parents spared no expense for their younger daughter, capricious, petulant, headstrong, wild, and undeniably beautiful.

Reggie was blooming.

And she knew it.

Her dark hair fell long and wavy, enhanced by delicate garlands. She meticulously painted her eyelids light blue. Rouge warmed her cheeks. Pink lipstick completed the youthful illusion. Short blue gloves adorned her hands.

Smiling, always smiling.

But watching.

Reggie observed everything. Every glance between suitors. Every whisper behind fans. Every flicker of rivalry. One day it would be her debutante ball, and tonight was reconnaissance.

Another flute of champagne.

She surveyed the “landscape”, decadent morsels, fragile alliances, concealed resentments.

Then —

Her eyes locked with sparkling blue ones.

Sir Richard Bennett.

He did not look away.

Highly amused. Intensely appraising. His admiration lingered too long to be innocent.

Little Reggie felt the charge, dangerous, intoxicating.

She could not wait for her turn.

She relished male attention, even at her age she had admirers by the truckloads. She gathered them effortlessly.

The women, however…

She could not stand them.

They were like her.

Ambitious. Competitive. Jealous. Uncomforting beneath politeness.

Reggie reasoned they were hardly worth worrying about.

But within that glittering ballroom, beneath chandeliers and silk and champagne, alliances were already forming.

Secrets were already circulating.

And someone, unseen, patient, was already watching Regina Bligh with forensic precision.

Because long before a crime is committed…

A motive is born.

She loved what she was experiencing, sipping champagne beneath the huge chandeliers, dancing luminous lights spreading strong gold and silver reflections across polished marble floors, amusingly Reggie admired how the taste was grand… imposing… magnificent… spelling privilege… luxury…

Each sip burned slightly, not unpleasantly, but like a promise. A promise of entry. A promise of belonging.

The orchestra swelled. Laughter echoed in crescendos. Silk brushed silk. Jewels flashed like coded signals across the ballroom.

Reggie approached her sister, embracing her and George, lingering perhaps a moment longer than necessary. Elaine glowed. George beamed. Cameras flashed again.

The next morning the newspapers and magazines screamed at the public, the headlines flamboyant, triumphant, society intoxicated with romance. The pictures showed blatantly the wealth of the successful night they had experienced. Crystal, gowns, polished smiles, perfection immortalised in ink.

But photographs never reveal what is simmering beneath.

Sir Richard Bennett… newly crowned with title now that his elderly father had passed… the "Smooth Operator"…

He looked… in awe…

Was it amazement…?

Was it bewilderment…?

Flabbergasted…?

Astonished…?

Or per se… speechless…?

Ah yes.

He was completely taken by the alluring dark-haired girl.

The world was Elaine's oyster, effortless, open, awaiting harvest.

A trait that little Reggie would learn to accomplish at a later stage… and in years to come… but not with innocence.

Reggie smiled back, acknowledging Bennett.

He nodded.

A silent exchange.

But whilst Elaine's smile was pure, honed with honesty, brimming with joy and de bonheur, dissolving into sheer delight, Reggie's smile was frantic… double-edged… a rehearsed mask.

Especially when she dealt with something that thoroughly displeased her.

And that moment came swiftly.

That was when Reggie's rivalry rose to the fore.

It had been there before.

Now it was boiling.

Not loudly.

Not publicly.

But intensely.

After the debutante ball, after the official engagement was announced, Regina and her parents were invited for a short stay at the Bligh's plush… ostentatious… grand and vast mansion.

The Bligh wealth was endless.

Endless in land. Endless in cattle. Endless in inherited prestige.

And for Regina, endless in comparison.

During her stay in Camelot of broken dreams…

Instead of enjoying everything at her disposal, the sprawling gardens, the marble corridors, the servants gliding silently like apparitions, all Reggie knew was rage.

Bitterness.

A continuous, seething undercurrent.

As a fiancée, Elaine was fussed upon. Adored. Consulted. Paraded.

Elaine would one day become the mistress —

Reggie shuddered.

But who knows…?

Planning her own future became highly relevant, especially when Elizabeth and Little Reggie formed what appeared to be an everlasting friendship.

They were the same.

Observant. Calculating. Composed.

Elizabeth loved Elaine's family, and young Reggie was part of it. Naturally, when Reggie turned on her charm, even the mosquitoes and the snakes would bow, paying homage to the queen of subtle deceit.

But as Regina once stated:

"We both are cut from the same cloth…"

So they would also bow in reverence to the matriarch, Grand Elizabeth Bligh.

For she too was mistress of deception.

A dynasty does not survive on politeness alone.

Regina came from an Australian elite wealthy family, yet to some… commoners of fortune.

Her parents made their wealth grazing cotton and cultivating coffee plantations on the north side of Queensland. Previously they had tried their luck establishing their own coffee plantations and wine collection, extending both into Sydney markets.

Yes, the winery, the coffee, the cotton.

A wide amalgamation of products that progressed steadily, strengthening finances, affording the family far more privileges… far more luxuries… elevating themselves into high society status with their own large pedigree, their own trademark.

And of course, their inflated volumes of personal egoistical promotion, society seeking out the "family célèbre", remaining friends for convenience.

That was easier said than done.

In a world of nouveau riche, wishes often remain merely manners of the heart. Hard to accomplish. Especially in Australia, so deeply British in tradition, where status flowed through title and inheritance.

Traditionally they did not buy, they inherited.

Elaine and Regina's family bought.

They created.

The Australian people worked. Survived. Built their own businesses. Their own lives.

The nouveau riche found it hard to swallow the hard line imposed upon them.

As Australia developed, wealthy families constructed their own rules… their own circles… their own guarded sects.

The nouveau riche could not cross the invisible line into their neighbours' ancestral drawing rooms.

They would never fully belong.

Not then.

Not easily.

But over the years, with influxes of immigrants and refugees, the rigid grip of traditional elite society began to loosen.

One such family who balanced both worlds —

The Blighs.

Australian Royalty.

Into this playground entered Regina's family.

They faced hard liners. Restrictions. Subtle exclusions.

They were not always included in the same repertoire of the rich, the high flyers, here and there perhaps, but never entirely.

Not fully embraced.

Into the foray entered the Bligh family, socially magnetic. Wealthy. Popular. Astute investors. Brilliant operators. Business entrepreneurs. Highly respected with thousands of aristocratic connections.

The Bligh prominence stretched long within the elite Australian community, alongside names such as the McArthurs.

Regina's family lagged slightly behind.

Yet her parents served as ambassadors… consuls… delegates.

"Nouveau Australian riche" or not, they performed their duties magnificently.

Their wisdom knew money could purchase many doors.

And by and large, they were liked.

But liked is not the same as accepted.

And Regina felt that difference like a bruise.

The completion of official tasks and ambitions brought compliance, even satisfaction.

Reggie's family had nothing to lose.

The perks were generous.

Official cars driven by professional chauffeurs. Welcomed by VIPs with royal reception. Paid accommodation. Paid staff. Security. Diplomatic privileges. Commonwealth duties that gave them extra "hmmmph"… collectively.

A good time.

Stylish wardrobes displayed unapologetically. Glitterati jewellery, expensive, dazzling, proudly paid for by the family themselves. A mere trickle of expenditure in comparison to what they could afford.

Famously trendy.

Especially when the parents boasted two beautiful daughters.

These VIP treatments were supposedly delightful, glamorous.

And by the same token, their honorary duties transported them to European countries… exotic Asian cities… representing Australia with pride and honour. Short stays. Long stays. Presence always noted.

After Commonwealth duties were executed and approved, accepted gradually into elite society, Elaine rose as the primary establishment of new socialite prominence.

Invitations increased.

VIP functions. Galas. Balls. Operas. Official receptions.

Meeting and greeting hosts, becoming hosts themselves.

Everything was game.

In a polite, yet eccentric, society ablaze with brazen gossip.

All were happy.

All were content.

Or…?

Because beneath chandeliers and diplomatic smiles, there were ledgers.

There were quiet conversations in corridors.

There were alliances being measured.

And somewhere, someone had begun observing Regina Bligh not as a wallflower…

But as a threat.

In the midst of all that elegance, sophistication, glamour, the pussyfooting around the intertwining politics, Little Reggie looked at a world of immense privileges, completely different from her present status. She was looking from the outside, following behind, observing, noting everything, spoiled by the new servants, butlers, at her family's beck and call. Elaine's little sister, by then a whopping eight years younger, and counting, was growing up steadfastly.

Reggie joined them at daytime official outings, walking in the sun-drenched avenues of Camelot, absorbing manners, gestures, alliances. But nighttime, nighttime was different. At night, Reggie remained behind, alone in her quarters, mollycoddled by stern nannies in a safe, cozy, comfortable place, tucked securely in bed until she was safely and soundly asleep.

Meanwhile, Elaine was treated as the regal princess, shining like, twinkling like, the prime star in the new society's splendour. She mingled with the official elites, wined and dined, danced the night away, all conducted before her own debut, exciting and highly romantic, an imaginary, conceptual world that Little Reggie was only allowed to glimpse. Impractical. Non-objective. Yet assertive… Reggie's ideal. Reggie's imagination running wild.

But by night's end, Reggie was tucked in her bed, dreaming quietly, or so she thought. She only knew of the glamour when she read the tabloids the following day… weeks and months passing in careful observation.

Now Elaine was getting hitched.

Now it was Reggie's time to shine.

Richard Bennett's sparkling eyes followed her every movement, even when they were staying in Camelot, he, as a special guest, observing. And as she met his gaze, she smiled back, smilingly lifted her champagne flute, tipped her head slightly in salutation, elated, like the cat who got the cream.

Sir Richard Bennett could never resist such a lovely temptation, especially when it came from such a delicious young lady. He wondered, silently, if she was still a virginal, plain coquette.

He smiled back, his sparkling blue eyes twinkling sinfully, like stars winking in the Camelot of Broken Dreams skies. His mouth cracked into that well-known smile. He lifted his champagne flute and tipped it in Reggie's direction.

Time stood still for a moment.

It was their time.

Ahhhh… and what a time they would have.

They both recognized in each other what they were, mirrored desires, reflected ambition, shared recklessness. At one time or another, they had both known that they would be more than friends, at the cost of everything.

Bennett already had plans for Reggie. She was game.

Daring. Defiant. Classy. Dangerous.

On the edge.

In the zig-zagged, perilous corridors of society, politics, and desire, Sir Richard Bennett recognized in Reggie her own desperation to be unique, to shine, stopping at nothing to prove herself.

The "contract" was on.

Both reflected, mirrored each other. One needed action. The other would provide it.

As the night sped on, the band played relentlessly. Guests danced. Drank. Laughed. Chattered. Joy mingled with intrigue, desire underlined with subtle calculation.

As the first light of dawn crept into the skies, the opulent household began to shimmer. Rays reflected on rolling lawns, manicured gardens, and moats glinting in green-gold splendor. Reggie felt a twinge of awkwardness, swaying in the winds of change, yet she accommodated herself comfortably, seduced by the soft, gentle lullabying of her own heartbeats, each thrum full of dreams and sinful desires.

If only they were dreams.

If only desires could remain so innocent.

Regina's desires? Her ambitions? They were never innocent. They were never simply dreams. They required stealth. Fast, hard work. Luminosity. Ingenuity. Perseverance.

Would Reggie achieve it all?

Of course she would. She had already planned everything.

But would it be accomplished? That remained to be seen.

The late thirties and early forties surged onward. From every corner of Inverness to Sydney's bustling streets, the boom of American music invaded, fusing with the new trendy fashion. Dancing. Hamburgers.

Coca-Cola. Chips. Drive-ins were already the rage, even reaching Queensland.

After the trendy 20s, the fabulous "mode a facile porter", easy-to-wear fashion heralded by Gabrielle Bonheur (Coco) Chanel, liberated women from oppressive corsets. Hair and fashion transformed, haute couture igniting a global fire of creativity.

Now the forties arrived with elaborated shoulder pads, and Australia's youth absorbed every trend.

Times were changing rapidly.

Elizabeth Bligh once sighed, "Exhausted by so many changes."

Little Reggie, however, was not exhausted. She was anticipating. Contemplating her own debutante ball.

Again, she joined her parents for another trip to the Camelot of Broken Dreams. The cheerful voices of the Andrews Sisters boomed through town.

It was a time of dancing. Singing. Cigars. Champagne flowing freely. High tea, conducted to perfection.

The Second World War? Too far away for her to care. Reggie lived in her own stylish, privileged world, insulated, coveted, untouchable.

She was growing up into a young lady every male fell in love with all too easily. Her first desire was coming true.

A coquette. A real flirt. Why not?

Women were like this. Males came from Mars. Females came from Venus. And in between… who cared?

Wolf whistles. Invitations, slowly… slowly… piling up.

Her beauty was "le centre épice."

Reggie's features developed, sharpened, pronounced. The elite Australian society noticed. Naturally.

Such beauty could not go unnoticed.

Elaine's little sister was growing into her own phenomenon. Now she had them eating from her hands, just like her big sister had.

Reggie became the *Modelle Australianne*, strutting the latest fashions, a trendsetter, a fashionista. Sliding smoothly with style, class, pizzazz.

Dickie boy, Sir Richard Bennett, invested in her. Not only for modelling, promoting her into one of Australia's top modelling agencies, but also into the espionage world.

Let's face it, Reggie fit the curriculum… to a T.

"Coco Chanel," Bennett whispered into Reggie's ear.

"Would be highly honoured with such a perfect model…"

Chomping on his cigar. Eyes glittering like diamond stars in the night sky.

Sipping his whiskey. Perfectly satisfied.

Reggie glowed.

His own recommendation. Categorically… effusively… a guarantor… Sir Richard Bennett… was securing, highly and expensively, his investment. Regina was his main element. Now more than ever… as he noticed that Reggie's older sister was married to the Blighs. Old Mah Bligh, as he called Elizabeth Bligh, was now firmly in Dicko's radar. The Blighs… now that old Mah Bligh was the new mother-in-law… the new grannie… but this lady here, sitting right in front of him, little Reggie, would soon be pulling in the finer strings of all themen in the world and in Australia.

Reggie had to fall hard for George Bligh…

Dickie boy was wondering if the woman was mad. He thought hard, considered carefully, and came to the conclusion, yes, Reggie was mad.

Dickie boy shook his head… his sun-beaten, weathered facial skin cracked into that morbid smile… now sporting a mustache, giving him even more of a sinister look… foreshadowing his mood… power… his own words forming in his mind: "treacherous"… but… wait… that could be the turning point. One for a penny, one for a pound… and that little beauty would be the one to help him do it.

George and Reggie… hmmmm… it had a good taste.

By the way, he needed a "mole" inside the Ashpark of Broken Dreams. Both his eyes narrowed into slits… yes…

George Bligh… hard to read. He could be highly decisive, but not impetuous… he was cool… slow and hard as… Bennett had a serious time reasoning, reading George, his feelings, his emotions… George always contemplated rights and wrongs. Yes… George was a man of principles. He would never dare to cross the lines. George would find it difficult to explain his own ruses to Mah Bligh… referring, as usual, to Elizabeth Bligh.

But the thing is… why did Bennett have this crucible status against the Blighs?

Yet Bennett knew that Old Mah Bligh was no saint. He had seen the dark, if not the darkest, side of hers. He badly needed the aid of Little Reggie. She would find the details he so desperately wanted… then…

Finally, her own debutante.

Her imaginations, wildly firing up her dreams, were now coming to the fore… and the look on George's face. The more she frequented Camelot of Broken Dreams, the deeper her infatuation grew… more dangerous… which was a good asset for Dickie boy. He loved it. It was a sickening obsession, one he would be using to his own advantage.

The good news was that Elaine gave birth to a baby boy.

Reggie couldn't hide her excitement… and loathing… it was disgusting to see how her own parents bent over backward to fit into the Blighs' lives, licking their shoes, making complete fools of themselves.

This was, primarily, one of the major lessons she learned: what it was to be a Bligh.

The Blighs radiated such power… such a formidable force… and she loved what she was seeing… felt… but… unless something happened to Elaine…

Now that a baby son was born, all the more reason the connection would be a forceful one… little James Arthur Bligh. Elaine, again, had done herself proud… she secured the "firm" strongly… she gave the Blighs another heir presumptive to the Blighs' dynastic power…

Damn… be damned… she cursed the day Elaine was born. Elaine was perfection itself. She handled everything meticulously well.

Reggie and her parents' presence were duly observed, to congratulate Elaine on the new arrival… to see their first grandchild… then to extend the Blighs' Reggie's debutante invitation.

They were now complete.

Reggie's debutante now came full circle.

The plans. The organisation. Her wishes, to rival her own sister, and that of Caro's.

She chose her own modiste. She also chose… choses her own beautiful gown… the shoes… her long white silvery gloves… and the suitable jewellery… awww… she was debating about flowers, the sac, or perhaps a beautiful basket…

Now she needed to engage with the other anomalies, such as the venue (hmmmmmm… must be unique, original), the menu (cocktail stuff… yahhhhhnnnn… the best), the band, the music… she was going to shine, with her own personal touches to be seen everywhere… softly… softly… softly… gently does it…

She chose the colours. She chose the tables' arrangements. Anything connected to her passion.

One needed to note: the lady had a terrific talent, brimming with creativity and artistic ideas. One needed to give Reggie credit for her excellent taste.

But there was one problem.

As per usual… whether "fate" was conspiring against Reggie, or she was at the wrong place at the wrong time, or simply the victim of bad timing… for all her best dealings and organisations per excellence, delighting herself in completing scheduled tasks personally… disappointment was never far behind.

Either Reggie lacked the talent of being predictable… or, per se, she was indeed out of luck.

The latter kept creeping up… yet Reggie ignored it all.

The Second World War was raging.

Reggie's own labour of love, the invitations, were sent out already. Replies were quick. But as one would have guessed… the outbreak of the Second World War brought hardships that would crash all of Reggie's wishes and dreams, with little Reggie waging her own war at home.

War meant rationed food…

So instead of the grand, lavish moment of Reggie beaming happily in her debutante ball gown… devastatingly, as it should have been, all was curtailed. Guest numbers shortened. Safety concerns, fear of raids, and money conserved in case of disaster, all conspired against her.

Regina's parents never saw it coming… in their marital lives as doting parents to both daughters. To their horror, to their shock, they witnessed Reggie, their precious little flower, going wild into uncontrollable rage.

The explosion terrified them…

The screams. The breakages of crystal…

This was the first lesson they learned of their daughter's extremities. Her face, twisted, contorted into that ugly, voracious hag… yet still, Reggie didn't notice.

The Second World War raged on. Food rationed. Young men conscripted.

Everything now was counted, recalculated.

Far from the huge guest list, dwindling to mere "fitties."

Canceled venues, both Inverness Hall and Sydney's Town Hall, shut. Sydney's Town Hall closed for the additional platforms added for Gladesville. Inverness Hall? Never existed for Little Reggie. She didn't want that poor, unclassic place.

For reference: Sydney Town Hall, Wikipedia

During the Second World War…

Brief History of Sydney's Town Hall, during the Second World War:

Sydney Town Hall (and, it was believed, all the Town Halls created in each and every state and city) were founded and established for the elite and the wealthy, those who shared top billing, handed the vital and official VIP status. Events and functions included majorly debutantes, gala dinners, and annual masquerade balls for Christmas or New Year.

At the time, these were official events where the elite and wealthy attended. That was then, when society's classes were rigidly divided. Now, it is far more relaxed. Town Halls across interstate cities now also host Seniors' Balls, alongside Debutante Balls and promotional activities, a far cry from the exclusivity of the past.

Debutante Balls were practically held all over the cities and towns, the responsibility of families, secondary schools, and various venues such as Masonic Lodges. In Macau, they were once thoroughly funded by the government. At the time, there was a Debutante School for girls; those attending Portuguese Government Schools were automatically enrolled, linked to the Portuguese Feminine Youth Orientation, not to be confused with German Youth Orientation, which was entirely different.

But at the time, merely the word **Debutante** was enough to gain the utmost respect, and financial surplus.

Debutantes were di rigueur, as mentioned, and nobody wanted to miss out, either on the invitation or the opportunity to be seen. The debutantes themselves wanted to be photographed with the elite, the wealthy, the powerful. Their images would appear in every newspaper, locally and in magazines.

Each year, debutante balls were famous for the money the Town Hall netted, but primarily, they were dreams come true. Young girls dreamt of wearing that once-in-a-lifetime princess white gown, the tiaras or crowns of flowers on their heads, the gloves, the shoes… all so effective, so glamorous. The young girls **de genre**, typically feminine and dreamy, exuded perfection. From beginning to end, everything was orchestrated to precision. Rewards of critics were expected, huge yet excellent, and the expenses doubled the returns, kching… kching… kching…

Reggie's disappointment was at its peak.

Unable to control her rage, silent upheavals began, the commencement of her psychotic behaviour and sociopathic indulgences. As a socialite, all too well known syndromes collided with copious drinking, inhaling the hard stuff, and smoking, creating hallucinations, delirious high delusions…

From George wanting and loving her, to the most despicable torments she inflicted upon herself…

Yet she also had Sir Richard Bennett, the operator, who smoothly, in his own guise, tormented Reggie, instilling hope while psychologically developing in her the mad wishes she wanted fulfilled. She suffered deeply, navigating pain that created inconsistencies and a lopsided view of an already fragile, mentally unbalanced mind.

Bennett added a touch of insecurity, jealousy, if Reggie did not already have an inflated ego from her beauty and raison d'être.

She, bursting with raw energy and sinuous beauty, never realised that in life, plans rarely go accordingly. She was living testimony, over and over.

Reggie existed in her sordid, morbid dreams, yearning for manifestations of her desires while Bennett, the smooth operator, repeatedly manipulated her. Her debut was thwarted by unspeakable problems and disappointments, marring her special occasion, everything she considered justifiably correct or incorrect.

Spoiling her debutante ball was a terrible thing. And while no one was to blame but Fate, her well-intentioned plans fell by the wayside. Elaine triumphed in the shadows, or so Regina imagined.

The Debutante Ball triggered side effects. Reggie fell prey to dark episodes, defective, wild, coercive. Her own anxiety, stress, insecurity… coupled with her constant attempt to supplant Elaine… Reggie was at loggerheads with anyone who opposed her, enhancing the sad state of affairs.

She always tried to compete with, outdo Elaine. Regina never forgot, never forgave. Elaine was absent to witness Regina's "triumph."

Regina, married to an ambassador, faced the harsh protocols, the rigid rulings, the etiquette, all feeding her bitterness, demoralising her further, enraging her spirit. Yes, her spirit was broken… or was it?

The sourest part: Elaine was dead when Reggie triumphed, so she could not gloat. Even alive, Elaine excelled, the good, the better, the best.

Reggie's dark mood was uncontrolled, shaking the very turf she walked on. She was never afraid to show her mettle, yet for Sir Richard, she displayed a double- or triple-edged sharpness. The third edge: a demented, insane streak. The only flaw: Reggie did not know it, and could not control it. She was falling apart. Deranged.

For her benevolent, loving parents, cute little Reggie, their beautiful younger daughter, was still innocent to the world. The poor little tike… so lost, so immersed in a cold world that could either take you or leave you, never suspecting the deep resentment, which festered into a huge hatred… creating havoc deep within Reggie's mind, against her own sister and the world at large.

Reggie was, at best, her own worst enemy.

That little tike was their beautiful daughter. Such a little bewitching tyke, a child model, holding star power in her youth. Her parents would steadfastly mould young, beautiful Reggie into the same stature as Elaine. Understandably, they felt sorry for their ostentatious young daughter.

What parents would not?

It was her debutante… Wouldn't anyone react the same?

Having so many things aborted… well… things could only be improvised, improved, made better.

Reggie's parents made excuses, allowances, indulging her every whim.

Reggie felt cheated, insanely jealous of Elaine, for what Elaine had. Little Reggie wanted more, George included. And the damned Camelot. The Ashpark of Broken Dreams.

Still, both parents failed to see this…

Trouble was… the more Reggie's resentment grew, the more Elaine's success blossomed.

Elaine seemed to live in a magical world, comfortable in her marriage, with her real, handsome little man, James, heir presumptive to the Blighs' dynasty. Elaine was now the Queen of Camelot, writing a new chapter in her life.

The picture of her older sister being loved, adored by her husband, her in-laws, her own parents… watching Elaine cradle her son lovingly in her arms… Surrounded by love, tenderness, care… Elaine was revered, adored, respected.

She was now the new Queen of Camelot's Broken Dreams.

It was odious, disdainful… Reggie wanted the same adulation, reverence, respect… to join the upper echelons of the more popular superstars. Broken dreams or not… how quaint for its prophecy.

Sitting on the Blighs' family porch, covered by tall shades, the undying rolling green mosses, the refreshing green grasses… the obscene respite wind teasingly caressed her rouged cheeks… Mocking her, laughing, inflaming her further…

Reggie was now, more than ever, hypnotised by the joy of the natural views, sweeping her heavily lidded eyes across the stately grounds, breathing in the soft earthy scent… taking in the grand, heavy atmosphere surrounding the majestic palace…

Regina thought of Elaine while smoking, young Reggie still consuming almost a packet a day. For Reggie, it was a stress reliever. Drinks… champagne was very much her *"presentee sa boisson préférée"*, and sometimes some kind of… errrhhh… sniffing… some kind of stuff… mind-blowing… relaxing… feeling good.

Reggie was daring, trying drugs to numb the cruel existence of the world, and her own pain.

Yes, unbelievably as it is… poor little Reggie… in great spiritual pain… only she did not yet know it. By the time she took notice of her mental and physical state, it would probably be too late.

But this lady was made of tough mettle. Never would she consider suicide.

She glanced at the past, through the soft and gentle sounds of a beckoning summer, the heat, the gentle breeze, the effortless buzzing of bees… playing soothingly around the manor.

Her tea was being served as she wondered how on earth she, Regina, was born so late in the years… What happened to her parents? Why the eight-year difference between herself and Elaine? Or maybe even more…

Reggie was now in Elaine's thorough domain, who never ever committed a "faux pas."

Elaine's Sweet 16th birthday celebration happened just around the time Margaret Mitchell, the American novelist, published the romantic and dramatic book *Gone with the Wind* in 1936.

By the time the *Gone with the Wind* movie premiered, Elaine had had her debutante, the film winning eight Academy Awards, Elaine getting engaged, married, and the proud mother of a baby Bligh, now the mother of another baby, a girl named Anna. Elaine had everything done properly and brilliantly. She had the Midas touch.

The dumbest thing on earth that could have happened was, of course, the Second World War. Yet *Gone with the Wind*'s movie still netted millions of dollars and collected more awards than anything else. Was it an omen?

But with Regina… there was no *Gone with the Wind*. Nothing so romantic ever happened to her. More to it, she watched the movie and reasoned… here was this young, beautiful, heartless heroine, who married three times and yet was still in love with her own cousin, Ashley. George Bligh was no Ashley, more to it, he was not in any way Reggie's cousin. But George Bligh was her brother-in-law.

As her older sister's life was perfect, being Elaine, purportedly the new "Queen" of this Camelot of Broken Dreams, Reggie's pure hatred had reached its climax. Reggie's fogged mind, exacerbated by the drugs fuelling her fantasies, made it impossible to decipher fact from fiction.

Reggie did everything dramatically, smoking and drinking heavily, but that was not the only thing she did… read on…

The clock chimed, revealing the time for dinner. Apart from George and Elaine, with the household bustling around, Reggie was the only one alone, sitting with her parents absent. The maid brought Reggie a tray of food and settled it on the table. Reggie was having dinner by herself.

Darkness now supervised the place. The cicadas could already be heard. The dryness of the earth seemed to penetrate the nostrils, and the light perfume of the roses, magnolias, and cypresses blooming nearby exalted one's mind.

Regarding the maid:

"Please," said Regina, "could you bring me a bottle of French Champagne… with the crystals… and serve me the caviar with the crackers, thank you."

The maid nodded, returning with a bottle of French Champagne, popping the cork, and filling the flute. She then placed the tray of Russian caviar and crackers on the table, removing the previous tray.

Now Reggie sampled the caviar. Imagine that, outside her own world, with food being rationed and horrors surrounding her. These were the food of the gods, and she was the goddess.

"What are we celebrating, Miss Reggie?" dared to ask the maid.

"Ohhhh… sweets…" Reggie replied nonchalantly after a sigh, lighting another cigarette, lifting the champagne flute, and drinking it in one long pull.

"Life is indeed a celebratory thing," she added.

The maid shrugged, and Reggie wilfully asked, "Have you had your debutante, ever?"

The maid replied, "Yes… it was the thing, and still is…"

"Was it expensive?" Reggie asked again, drawing deeply on her lit cigarette, exhaling slowly.

"My gown was. Very expensive. My mother had to pay close to fifteen pounds for the whole gown…"

Reggie scooped the crackers and smoothed the Russian caviar onto them. She ate with gusto. "Mmm…" she murmured, deliriously delighted. "Delicious."

"Where was the ball held?" Reggie asked again, relaxing into the maid's company after swallowing both morsels.

"At the Inverness Primary School Hall. Previously it was held on the Chapel grounds, or somewhere around there," the maid related. "Depending on the weather," she finished.

"And the food and drinks, how did they come by those?" Reggie asked now, curiously, smiling sweetly, the champagne flute poised in her right hand.

"Oh…" the maid replied, "…the Inverness community gathers together and makes it an annual affair. Most worthy of the occasion, that is."

"How much does the Church pay or charge for these kinds of events?" Reggie asked again, curiosity sharpening as she drank the champagne, closing her eyes in thorough pleasure.

"Oh… I wouldn't know, Miss Reggie," the maid answered apologetically. "The Church holds the event. Mrs Doris Collins and the late Mrs Briggs would collate and organise the food and drinks. Mrs Doris Collins usually holds fetes to collect money for events, especially for the Debutante. It's the main one. The event is important. We cannot wait for the young girls and their respective young men walking them down, and we so hope for the engagements to be officially announced on the night…"

The maid was highly enthused, almost breathless in recounting it all.

"Our own Mrs Elizabeth Bligh also helps with large donations, usually donating, from the start, one thousand pounds for the event. Mrs Bligh loves these kinds of functions. She donates huge boxes of vegetables she buys from the Polettis, there are many contributions —" she paused for breath, then continued, "Now that the new Mrs Bligh has arrived and joined in, the Church has gained even more donations with the extra contributions…"

The maid chimed happily.

Reggie's curiosity froze.

At the mention of Elaine's name, her composure faltered, just for a second. Reggie smiled crudely, waving her hand dismissively, dismissing the maid entirely.

Reggie remembered Caro's stylish, trendy, utterly *de rigueur* debutante. It had been held here, exactly in this sacrosanct place. Flashes pierced her mind. It had been a privileged and expensive affair, breathtaking in its splendour.

But it had produced the wrong effects.

Grand Elizabeth Bligh wanted nothing but the best for her eldest, though wayward, daughter, Caro. It was an event highly anticipated. Magical. Enchanting. A fairy tale made flesh.

The elite gathered. Lively decorations loomed overhead. Champagne flowed endlessly, Reggie's favourite drink. The food sprawled across immense, talkative tables: tempting morsels, delicate nibbles, knick-knacks of indulgence. Crystal glittered. Silver and gold twinkled, casting fractured colours across polished floors. It shimmered with feminine subtleties.

It was gallantly magical, but not a fantasy.

The centrepiece was a towering tiered cake, finely decorated with Chantilly lace, Caroline's name encrusted upon it.

Food came and went, hot and cold, including Reggie's cherished caviar and crackers. She allowed her imagination to run wild, tasting everything, indulging, dreaming the dangerous and effective thought of one day living permanently in this sacrosanct place.

Later, her own daughter and sons, Sissi, Robbie, Be, and Frederic, would discover, to their disbelief, that Camelot, Ashpark of Broken Dreams, harboured darkness. The gossip did not call it sacrosanct, forbidden, austere, for nothing. There were reasons. There were always reasons.

The vision of her older, beautiful sister Elaine passed through her mind. Elaine was always one step ahead, reigning as she saw fit, capable and assured. It was an enviable position.

Then she heard George entering the porch, asking if his little sister-in-law was being well looked after.

As usual, Reggie replied demurely, with that lethal smile.

She nodded.

She looked at her brother-in-law.

And from that moment, the die was cast.

Little Reggie fell hopelessly in love with George Bligh.

In truth, she had loved him since the moment she set eyes on him at her sister's sixteenth birthday, and beyond.

Queen Elizabeth Bligh returned home from that busybody Lady Swanson, accompanied by both of her parents.

Reggie shivered, but it had been delicious fun leading that Swanson pervert on.

She remembered recounting, with relish, to Sir Richard Bennett how clumsy and fumbling Swanson had been. That had been truly amusing. She smiled inwardly.

Bennett knew Reggie was a useful mole. Now she was his dangerous spy. He had introduced her to espionage, to secrets, to leverage.

In Sydney, with Sir Henry Swanson, Reggie divulged official information, to Bennett's delight, feeding his sordid double life… and fuelling her own.

Swanson and Reggie. Was he fortunate, or was she recklessly mad?

As Elizabeth Bligh would one day confirm: "But Sara, she is mad…"

Promiscuity was her middle name. Her sexual prowess was too scandalous to be spoken of openly. Swanson never knew what truly struck him until he was required to pay her a handsome sum, one thousand pounds and counting.

He served her purposes well. As long as he paid for her exquisite services, and her silence, the arrangement endured. Unbeknownst to all, Reggie was Swanson's mistress. Money flowed into her eager hands.

Now, back to the present.

Ah yes. Reggie promised herself that one day she would reside here. Rule here. Just like Elaine's mother-in-law. Just like her sister. Three Mrs Blighs. An excellent prospect.

She coolly drowned two bottles of champagne. The caviar was endless. She toyed with the notion that she could, and would, become Mrs George Bligh.

She never realised how prophetic that thought would become.

Nor did she see the shadows gathering.

Perhaps they would have children of their own in this property, this estate heavy with secrets, with darkness that lurked dangerously beneath polished floors.

Poor Reggie.

Blinded to everything, including her own peril.

She would learn, at great cost, why it was called Ashpark of Broken Dreams.

Meanwhile, more pressing matters intruded.

Her own debutante.

Now more than ever, the final, disappointing truth.

She was not merely heartbroken, she was crestfallen. Bitterly devastated.

Her parents regretfully informed her that her debutante would be held on a cruise, the best venue they could manage.

Food and beverages would be served continuously, at least no one would go hungry. A band would play through the night. Everything was included in the prestige package. The bookings were confirmed.

Reggie agreed.

The debutante, held aboard "THE DAHLIA" cruiser, was pleasurable, even a touch ingenious. Exquisite, in its own modest way. It captured her attention.

But they had no other choice.

It was romantic. Adventurous. Exciting. Not lavish, not truly, but it would suffice.

Reggie's proclivity was born.

As stated before, fate was never on Regina's side. Even the Fates themselves seemed to conspire against her.

And this, though she did not yet know it, was only the beginning.

On the day her debutante ball was held, it rained.

Fog swallowed the harbour. The sky was grey, bruised with dark blue, menacing clouds. Wild winds shook the cruiser, and mounting waves slammed the ship high and low, as though testing its resolve. The hull groaned. The decks trembled.

Reggie should have been happy, half the invited guests attended despite the weather. The band played dutifully. The food and drinks were the best the ship could offer. To any observer, it was a jolly, lively occasion. From time to time, performances entertained the guests; if not, the smaller party amused themselves with jokes tossed lightly across the tables.

Apparently, it was enjoyable.

The cruiser was decorated as lavishly as possible under the circumstances, ribbons, florals, polished brass, all arranged to appear triumphant against the storm.

But the storm did not care.

Flashback to the early days.

Reggie's utter desolation at knowing the Blighs would not attend. George would never see how devastatingly beautiful little Reggie looked that night, a princess fashioned in white. Though, truth be told, it would never have affected him. He was entirely in love with Elaine. Happily married. Final.

The Blighs' absence ignited something corrosive in Reggie.

Her gown was all white, billowing to the floor, the neckline closed with tiny buttons flaring delicately at the throat, tight sleeves embracing her arms. Little diamonds were pinned into her wavy dark brown hair. She crossed the floor holding her flowers tucked into a small basket. Her make-up was applied heavier than usual due to the lounge's harsh lights. Her lips were painted red, bold, deliberate, claiming the night.

She was exquisite. Meticulous. Every detail perfected.

But before that night, days earlier, there had been the rage.

Ferocious. Demoniacal. A tirade so savage and brutal it frightened even her parents. Reggie only calmed once she drank herself into oblivion. They allowed her to sleep it off until the appointed hour of the debutante. Thankfully, the worst of the destruction happened days prior. Still, objects were broken. Shattered. Replaced at their expense.

"Debbie nerves," her parents explained stiffly to the captain, paying for damages with forced smiles.

The captain himself escorted Reggie onto the floor as her first cavalier of the evening.

There were no beaus. None. Not even Bennett, delayed by other business.

And the Blighs' telegram? Hidden.

The mounting bills, the venue, accommodation, damages, breakages, rose like a tide her parents could scarcely manage. They were proud of their daughter's accomplishments, yes. But they were also terrified.

What kind of demon had their sunflower daughter become?

That night, when society expected a proposal, perhaps even several, none came.

None.

Reggie felt the humiliation like a blade. Aggrieved. Exposed. Embarrassed. The sting of rejection fed something unstable within her.

Hatred began to breathe.

Someone would pay for this.

But who?

She sifted through her debutante gifts. The Blighs had not attended, yet they had sent a precious, expensive present. Their excuse: James was teething. Anna had a fever.

The following morning was crisp, bitterly cold. The sky was heavy and black. One moment showers lashed the decks; the next, hard hailstones struck like thrown gravel. The ship pitched violently as waves battered its sides. Lightning fractured the sky, illuminating the docks and Sydney's CBD in stark, unnatural flashes. Thunder exploded with tremendous force.

Inside, guests gathered for breakfast. The sharp ocean breeze cut through every opened door. Reggie remained indoors, reluctantly entertaining with polished conversation, reflecting on the night before, her night.

For the guests, it had been delightful.

For Reggie, it had been a quiet catastrophe.

Sir Richard Bennett joined them at the breakfast table. He read her instantly. The humiliation. The disappointment. The fury simmering beneath porcelain composure.

No one complained. Only Reggie's silence spoke.

She wore a beautiful pink dress that suited her. Blue shadow circled her eyes; rouge coloured her cheeks. But her face looked drawn. She had not slept. Embers still burned behind her gaze.

She stared at him, those sapphire-blue eyes locking onto Dickie boy's equally bright, calculating stare. Now cool. Now observant.

They were friends.

Too close for comfort.

Their friendship ran deep into darker shores.

Bennett, the cunning fox, always knew timing, and women. His wife lay in bed, seasick. Gleefully radiant, he recognised opportunity.

From breakfast through lunch, they spoke almost exclusively to one another, oblivious to the rest. One moment laughing, the next whispering. Their conversation deepened, illicit, strategic, and carried through dinner… perhaps beyond.

The remainder of the trip passed without incident. Nothing outwardly dramatic. No visible scandal.

Yet newspapers and magazines carried Reggie's image, framed against the brewing Cold War tensions of the era. What may have felt insipid to her was enough to attract attention. The photographers did not fail to capture Regina had done herself an immense favour.

Now she was the sweet taste of success in New South Wales.

She was the SUNFLOWER, radiant, poised, luminous with star quality. Sophisticated. Fashion-forward. Her dress now sat above the ankle and below the knee, layered with frills and flounced petticoats.

"Come on… I am yours for the taking… marry me."

It was unspoken, but clear.

Beaus flocked to her. Some were genuinely besotted.

With Sir Richard Bennett's *The Globe* behind her, the wealthy media mogul grooming her carefully, Reggie became more than a debutante. She became an asset. A mole. A spy.

She had the criteria, beauty, intelligence, daring, and Bennett knew she would deliver.

Their affair resumed with reckless intensity. She lived it shamelessly, determined not to sit idle, not to be dismissed. She would act. She would manoeuvre. The proof was there.

She wondered how Elaine received the news. How the Blighs reacted in private.

Dickie boy, a man with women by the dozen, loved Regina in his own dangerous way.

Again, they met in Sir Richard's hotel, *The Australian.*

Like two ferocious animals, they tore at one another's clothes. They bit. They snarled. Their lovemaking was wild, raw, intense. Fast. Furious. Unrestrained.

It was thrilling. It was dangerous.

They were left sore, exhausted, breathless after hours, days, of indulgence.

She was insatiable. He was virile, athletic still despite his age, a marvel, really.

But for Reggie, nothing was ever enough.

Both would sit huddled together in their bed, after their endless, energetic and hard love-making… sipping champagne, smoking, tasting "lobster thermidor",a delicious French dish,and sniffing the socially fashionable, high-status drug. It was de luxe. Then you wonder why Reggie's mind was so fogged up.

"I can get them anytime…" boasted Sir Richard Bennett. "Sniffing it too… they were not only exhausted, ultimately sated, but unable to move. But there was far more detrimental stuff to concentrate on or focus on…"

"There is something I want you to do," Regina would laugh herself silly. "It is warranted for me to do it," she clucked… then wimpishly added, "By the way, Dickie boy… how on earth did you marry her? The woman has no spirit. She is so… clamped… dismissal…" Bennett kept his counsel.

He knew he had lit a dangerous fire in Reggie… he winced gleefully in the sole knowledge when he told his secretary to "give me the good oil on young Reggie." Sir Richard Bennett loved all the grimy, wild, dirty, sinful, evil "oil" on Reggie's magnificent performance in bed and outside of it. But then again, he was the one who introduced wild Reggie to this kind of social and espionage life, as she would for sure rival the colourful Caro Bligh,but Caro was never, ever a spy, although wild and promiscuous. On the one side, he had wild Reggie to be happy with… as he read the tabloids, seeing how perfect this irrational woman was… yes, you have read it right… **IRRATIONAL** was the word. Reggie, in all her glory, smiling bountifully, posing for the pictures, clad in that beautiful all-Australian gown… alone… those eyes… that perfect face… that perfect makeup… hiding the truth,deranged, psychotic, delusional.

Elaine was now gone, and George had two kids. No wonder the Debutante Ball failed… white was never a distinguished colour for the over-sexed and nymphomaniac Regina. Only Sir Richard Bennett knew Reggie personally, warts and all, every nook and cranny of her body too well,and one day, Sir Richard Bennett promised himself… Reggie would not only be something he would keep for his own pleasure, but one day she would do him right. Sir Richard Bennett smiled, lighting his cigar, contemplating the vast Sydney CBD… and until this date, he had lived his life according to his principles… misconstrued… lopsided… unbalanced… rooted in evil… but these were the remnants of his ways.

Elaine Bligh was now dead and buried. Sir Richard Bennett couldn't hide his delight, as he definitely had a "job" for his beautiful Reggie. But as usual, it would take a bit of time. Miraculously, it came in the shape and form of Camelot of Broken Dreams' doomed matriarch, Grand Elizabeth

Bligh. For Bennett, that was a token of good fortune. Now time was pressing, and he direly needed Reggie's help, as the doomed and damned matriarch Elizabeth Bligh, of Ashpark,the broken, gloomy place,no matter how much he drummed into Reggie's ears, she would never listen. Good… better for his high self-esteem, with rumours assailing him about a certain Jewish lady.

At his command, Reggie was instructed to attend the annual Christmas Ball, where he would personally introduce her to a young man who was a bit dull, rich, and held a very high position. His name was Charles Standish, and that was all she needed to know. Charles suited mostly Sir Richard Bennett's ideal. Reggie would spy for Richard, letting him know the ins and outs of the more "bourgeoisie",the different classes between the rich, the poor, and the middle. On those days, the differences in class were far and few between. Being the ambassador, she would have covered practically everything politically, and much, much more… Reggie accomplished them, with Bennett expecting no less of her. On the other hand, Swanson abandoned his wife and son out of shame but ran away with his other mistress. But Bennett was now fully informed on everything he needed to know.

As she celebrated her wedding, returning from her nuptials, she was only informed of the funeral, marring her own happiness all over again,the news coming from Bennett that Elaine had been killed in a Japanese bombing in Darwin. Being the wife of an Ambassador meant so much for her. Charles was delighted, and more so now that Reggie was pregnant… Reggie was flat out.

For Regina's parents, they could not thank the heavens enough. Finally, Reggie had found a good and decent husband, and they no longer needed to worry about their wayward daughter. But they were thoroughly heartbroken when Elaine died.

Charles was tall, dark, and handsome. He was rich, enjoying the good investments, his status, and privileges,plus whatever else life could give him and his family. As he continuously rose in power and popularity, so did his vast estates and accomplishments. Whilst people didn't call George Bligh, the Cattle Baron, inheriting the Bligh dynasty for nothing,

Charles was his own man, with his own cattle,which was the way of life at the time. Regina played the role of a happily married lady, giving Charles an heir too,little Frederick,meanwhile reporting to Bennett everything she knew. She had no qualms in betraying her own husband, the father of her own son, continuing with her sexual perfidy,highly enjoyable sex with Bennett. He knew how to satisfy a woman… she was that woman.

Reggie was the symbol of positivity and security,by and large how the suffragettes were… strong, independent, articulate, poised, elegant, sophisticated. As we speak and write, one conjures the legend of a femme fatale,one that, instead of working for herself, was wild and famous for her daring. The female spies, with their own feminine wiles, soft-spoken voice, lovely skin, and beauty, endeared themselves to anyone by playing the damsel in distress, as high-ranking officers would often fall for these women and reveal confidential information. Under the bed sheets, enjoying the ultimate with champagne and caviar. Many women brought skills and personality to carry out these highly classified duties… she was the Jane Bond of the species. James Bond, the British spy, only came into play in the 1960s with Sean Connery on the lead, and other female spies followed. The espionage network started long before Regina was born, and James Bond's movies would later herald it.

Reggie was conversant, knowing the subjects, the inside and outside of any politics (well, she had to, as her husband was the Ambassador). No topic was taboo,current affairs, international politics, fashion trends, movies… she knew all, and personal matters too. Each time she revealed something to Bennett, it almost immediately appeared in his newspapers.

Now an Australian, all vivid within a myriad of colourful social circles, Reggie was seen everywhere clutching her husband Charles. Charles, on the other hand, glowed with pride and anticipation. She was so popular that she was once interviewed, questioned about her younger years as a model. Reggie had the capacity and intelligence all wrapped up within her well-educated schooling years, which were remarkably strong, and this proved beneficial. As expected, she became very much a world traveller and a most welcome, inviting social presence that everyone wanted to befriend, including Sir Richard Bennett, who would send her on many assignments per se.

Reggie would rather live her entire life alone, with fewer friends, than allow others to usurp her top status. No one could compete with her. She did not need any more competition. Her waging war against her own older sister was enough for her to delete and abstain from having female friends, either she would grow jealous of them, or they would grow jealous of her. Usually, it was them against her. Not many could truly attain Reggie's high status, let alone become her friend. She trusted none of them, per se. It was a cold war waged by women, and where they came from there were never limitations to it. It happens. Reggie knew JEALOUSY, for she was deeply jealous of her own sister.

Now that her older sister was dead, one wondered whether Reggie would pursue George all the same as when she had been thoroughly infatuated with him. Fate, this time, helped her.

Regina was often misunderstood. The word narcissist would frequently surface. Being beautiful did not temper her animal instincts. Regina's beauty and grace were tools to enhance her status, if she knew the correct and wise way to use them. Beautiful women become accustomed to what is bestowed upon them, and the extras, admiration, flattery, undue fawning, reverence.

However, George Bligh was immune to Reggie's will, grace and beauty. He did not concur with her at all. As she once told him, "I am insulted, you are ignoring me… for a book," or words to that effect, when George was deeply absorbed in Leon Uris' *Exodus*. That was after the death of her husband.

How was Reggie going to pursue George now that she was married and had just delivered a baby boy, if Charles were alive?

It begs the question.

No… this is not baffling at all. If you know Reggie's style, you are inclined to answer it. What if she had him? What would have happened?

That George never loved her but married her, used her skills and knowledge for his own betterment, through Reggie's beauty and talent, a force to be reckoned with, then ignored her entirely, leaving her subject to abuse. He was the one who gave her morphine to numb the pain… and she became addicted to it.

Was Reggie so blindly obsessed with her "infatuation" for George Bligh that she failed to notice Charles could have made her happy? So he died. Rumour mongers believe it to be more sinister. The innuendo was that he swallowed some kind of poison administered by his own beautiful, smiling assassin wife.

"Regina had truckloads of males entertaining her," so claimed Lady Prudence Swanson, the fast, effective, fun-loving, always elegant and self-possessed social companion of Elizabeth Bligh. In reality, a rumour monger. A busybody. One who knew the social news inside and out, yet ignored the fact that Regina had once been her own husband, Sir Henry Swanson's, highly maintained mistress, paid in hard dividends.

It happens.

Blinded by one love, forgetting the present one.

Or was Lady Swanson seeking revenge on the delectable Mrs Regina Bligh?

Or was Regina falling under George's spell, like Scarlett with Ashley?

Or was George merely another passing fancy for Reggie, someone to use and discard once she tired of him?

However… we must analyse further. And here is more.

Why was she always comparing herself with Elaine? By comparison, why did George fall deeply in love with Elaine and not take into account Regina's beauty, her stronger sexual allure? He felt nothing for Regina. Period.

Therefore, there was nothing between them. Right?

The answers may lead us to both agree and disagree.

Regina was, perhaps, a sociopath and a psychopath. Spoilt and revered by her parents while growing up, ideology around a child can shift, and that can have profound consequences. These can constitute severe psychological traits, a sickness that slowly overtakes one's thoughts and demeanour, turning positivity into negativity. Sufferers have their own inner conversations, but with whom? How does one reach a stage where they are consumed by their own thinking? Is someone speaking to them? If so, who? Or is it imaginary, compounding in the mind, dividing the person into two, three, or more personalities?

It is known that some individuals assume numerous personalities, sometimes as many as seventeen, often due to abusive childhoods.

By and large, such fragmentation stems from abuse. Regina was indeed used and abused, despised and hated by the Bligh family and by Sir Richard Bennett. Yet she was doted upon by her own parents.

Could she have contracted some form of venereal disease, given the number of her sexual partners? Venereal diseases can spell death for some. Apart from being used by Sir Richard Bennett, Reggie was also the second child, and second children often resent the older sibling.

Witnessing Reggie's modus operandi, one moment she is all smiles, batting her eyelashes… smooth as a slender deer… submissive… well poised… brilliant… self-assured, confident. She is social… effervescently savvy… that's how we might have warmed ourselves to her… which is why, despite her own travesties, we still admire such a beautiful lady like Reggie, who would use everything to get her way. She blackmailed Dr Henry Fox. She alone destroyed Sir Henry Swanson's life. She brought many incidents upon herself and to the social life.

The dark side to Reggie, a well-informed spy, a wise informant that Sir Richard Bennett trained her to be. Please note, being an informant (working undercover) is different from actually being a SPY. These could very easily have contributed to her downfall, but I doubted it, not forgetting that Australia had been through two World Wars. Anyone like Reggie, acting as a spy, and the setting of ASH PARK in CAMDEN, came through as the ideal place for espionage, palatial, remote, distant, far away from all Sydney's suburbs… a respectable garrison that no one would suspect. Where Regina was concerned, the adventurous side of her would compel her to do it… in the mainstream, she would have been the tantalising seducer, a la Australian MATA HARI, or the AUSTRALIAN ROSE, against the more delicate and oriental TOKYO ROSE. Maybe this could be the start-up for all of her inferiority complex, making her see double and hate her older sister Elaine as she measured herself against her detrimental status, wanting to be the better one.

After the introduction of the “tonic”, the morphine drug that Reggie takes, which turns her into a volatile, irrational, deluded, violent, angry person, (actually, for the record, she was already that irrational person), it was all brought to the fore when she actually takes the morphine liquid, coupled with her chain-smoking, hard drinking, and dejection in all forms and shapes.

Let’s analyse what, in fact, is a sociopath (later, a psychopath).

A sociopath is a person with a major personality disorder. It usually manifests itself in extreme “anti-social” attitudes and behaviour.

This kind of syndrome is synonymous with words such as: “madwoman/man, deranged, maniac, lunatic, psychotic (psychopath), loony, fruitcake, basket case, nutty.”

To recognise these traits in one person’s character or personality is quite tricky… for in the case of Regina Bligh, “sociopaths” like her are smart enough to disguise their own faults and their “anti-social” behaviour. They are very sneaky, having created by themselves a world of imaginary double personalities, or perhaps even more. On one side they are charismatic, kind, seeking ways for a better world, highly conversant, knowledgeable… and on the other, creating havoc and misdemeanour, lacking conscience and empathy.

But there is more. It can be genetic or environmental… however, it could also stem from a sociopath’s self-involvement with their own peers, influenced by peer pressure… which often occurs all the time.

In Regina’s case, she could be psychotic, and her behaviour resembles that of Dr Jekyll and Mr Hyde. A sociopath, bordering on psychopath. There are no two ways about it.

With all intents and purposes, this lady was suffering from everything called a sociopath, turning her virtually into the psycho she became, due to so much use and abuse… despising and being despised (the contempt the Blighs had for her, then the hatred infused into her by the rivalry with her older sister and later Sara Adams).

We also have referred to venereal disease as a possible cause of her inconsistent behaviour.

With so many sexual partners, Regina could have suffered from syphilis or gonorrhoea, among other elements tormenting and persisting in her uncontrollable mind. For the record, these are the symptoms venereal diseases can inflict: arthritic disease (not necessarily in all cases; globally, people suffer from arthritis or rheumatism, but it is always wise to check), pelvic inflammatory disease, ectopic pregnancy, infertility, cervical cancer, and serious infections transmissible from mother to infant.

They could also render a man impotent, as with gonorrhoea, causing erection failure and flaked skin. In women, syphilis (more evident during the Vietnam War as "Vietnam Rose") could induce madness. These diseases are sexually transmitted.

Symptoms of syphilis can include a persistent cough (acute or chronic), frequent watery stools, fever… and in stage three, the sufferer can go MAD, among other effects.

Reference: Venereal Diseases, Syphilis: www.everyday.health.com/syphilis.myths.facts

One sole suggestion was that Regina was actually suffering from **LIMERENCE**, a state of mind forming a romantic attraction to another person, typically including obsessive thoughts and fantasies with a desire to form or maintain a relationship, or to be the object of love and have one's feelings reciprocated.

LIMERENCE can also be defined as an involuntary state of intense romantic desire (Wikipedia).

I would ask our readers: How many of us relate to mad Regina and her psychotic and sociopathic delusions? How many of us would hate or kill a rival simply to secure the object of our affection, or out of jealousy?

We all live in a dangerous world. While Regina believed she could actually gain George Bligh's love, it only served George to use her for his own ends, a radical position, the election campaign advised by the all-too-smooth operator Sir Richard Bennett, so George could further his career as a married man, with a lovely wife in Regina, completing the family picture.

We cannot forget that it was Elizabeth Bligh who brought poor Regina in, so she could remove Sara Adams, a good excuse for Reggie's mind: everything was fair in love and war. She might as well take full advantage.

However, Regina would never have committed suicide.

This book is about "The Forensics," and there is nothing in the series to suggest that Regina, a firebrand, would be foolish enough to kill herself. The autopsy lacked many elements, failing to prove whose skin was collected from Regina's nails. By the same token, questions have arisen about the entire autopsy conducted by Sister Adams, Dr Duncan, and Dr Fox, none of whom had the authority to do it.

"We shall need to move. This place is no longer safe for all of us Blighs... it brings so many painful memories..." says Master David Bligh. "When Uncle Jack recovers from the shot and returns home, we will be living in the other mansion." David Bligh, Bligh's Cattle Baron.

Sara and George Bligh's son, David, was openly branded as the "Blighs' BASTARD."

More will be revealed in **BOOK 3. A PLACE TO CALL HOME: 'The Forensics', The Bennetts vs the Blighs**, with the following to whet your appetite:

Regina's marriage to George Bligh will mark the start of the **Court Case in NSW**, brought on by the Bennetts. It involves the following:

- The highly "mysterious" death of Regina Bligh.

- Regina's four children, the eldest by her first husband Charles, the twins by George Bligh, and the fourth by Sir Richard Bennett.

Court case references:

- Regina Bligh's admittance, three years into the mentally insane asylum **while being married to George Bligh**. A most comprehensive and detailed report about Regina's state of mind at the time, and what actually drove her completely mad.
- ((George Bligh's mistress, whom he kept at the mansion, as pointed out by Anna Bligh when Caro was instructing Anna on how to conduct herself at AshPark. Anna highlighted George keeping his mistress in the cottage, James, his own lover Henry, all living under the same roof at AshPark. Anna's words were instrumental in showing how Regina was driven entirely mad.))
- Regina's own psychiatric doctor, who treated her in the asylum… at this stage, we cannot reveal all details. Regina Bligh's sad story will be unfolding in court. (The treatment was well established, but under no circumstances will the austere absences of the Blighs be ignored… inquiring about Regina. The only one concerned was Richard Bennett.)

Chapter 09:
Dr Jack Duncan. The Lost Boy

"Sergeant," commanded Mrs Elizabeth Bligh, facing the copper head on. "Remind me again why you did not go to war?"

The cop stuttered. "I couldn't. I had to stay home and look after my mother," he replied uneasily.

Elizabeth Bligh sarcastically smiled, confronting the copper. "Oh, I know your mother. She and I served together in the Corps." Elizabeth continued, "She certainly was more than capable of looking after herself," or words to this effect during her confrontation with the Inverness Police Sergeant. The Inverness Sergeant could not run away faster than a speeding bullet.

Dr Jack Duncan was highly impressed. Whenever he was in dire straits, lovingly and tenderly the indomitable Queen of Camelot's Kingdom, Elizabeth Bligh, would come charging in his defence. Jack admired the lady a great deal. His appreciation for her was immense. She was his adopted mother, but sometimes he wondered if there were more to this tale.

Before she sits down, she states drily, "I have made a promise to your mother that I would look after you, and I intend to see it done." She firmly confirms her motherly responsibilities.

As Dr Duncan's affection, his love and admiration continued to grow, mind you, his adopted new mother, or so, could also be highly unreasonable: precariously stubborn, cold, hard and also undemonstrative. Yet Dr Duncan saw both sides of the grand Elizabeth Bligh, knowing her only too well, as he usually would breathe a sigh of relief that she was on his side and vice versa. Elizabeth Bligh was a beacon of pride when he himself, Jack Duncan, took off and served in the army, the Australian Army.

The truth of this analysis was that Elizabeth Bligh was a most private person. She was brought up to never show her feelings and emotions.

Jack hardly saw her being receptive with open arms, hugging anyone, but more so, over the years he had never witnessed her crying, not even at the funeral of her late husband, not even when Carolyn left home, not even when Little Lizzie disappeared. The woman was made of steel. What in reality was she?

Elizabeth was the epitome of her own confidence. She was a tough lady by all means: implacable, insidious, rigid. She had set herself high above anyone else, and her reserve and the dictatorial conditions that were inflicted on people silly enough to step on her toes, the ones that wanted to actually instil their own superiority into the world of this lady, who could be ruthless and a stickler for all the rules and regulations. But she was also human.

As a matter of fact, not even when she suffered a heart attack, one of her many, did Jack need to be by her side in a major emergency, to which he still finds it strange, for he had not been updated about what really triggered it in the first place.

But today she was full of confidence and happy, and of course when she was in this mood, he thought he would go with the flow. He would never want to get on the wrong side of the grand Elizabeth. Spoiling the day was not in his agenda.

Both of them seldom had a disagreement, but there was a time that he did put his foot down, and that was when Elizabeth precipitately could not stand, one way or another, the new lady by the name of Sara Adams. For no apparent reason, Elizabeth took a profound dislike towards the blonde-haired, blue-eyed woman. Elizabeth found nothing but anything that she could have made creating obstacles, problems and making Sara's life completely horrendous and miserable. The two women started on the wrong side of the tracks.

It was his hide which was on the line. Now, come to think of it, Elizabeth had always been there for him, been at his beck and call, worried for him as she was also actually worried for her kids. Still, young Little Lizzie, the Blighs' younger daughter, was nowhere to be found. Carolyn was now home after exiling herself for more than ten years.

George's wife Elaine had died a few years back. Elizabeth was looking after George's two kids from their childhood until now. Both of them had reached their adulthood: James and Anna.

He glanced at Elizabeth and thought how quaint that Elizabeth had gone through so much and still remained so strong. A woman was far stronger than a man, any man. Jack thought lightly, but then he would never oppose Elizabeth Bligh.

Jack reflected on how he was surrounded by beautiful, strong, energetic and independent women, and by the same token, miserable, unhappy, scheming and manipulative ones. He himself was also tangled in the same web as they all were. His thoughts were of Sara, Anna and Caro.

Elizabeth left Jack behind in his office at the Inverness Hospital. It was largely a calming day. Outside, the sun shone softly and the strong lights shimmered around the hospital and Inverness. Someone outside was playing music. As per usual, Mrs Doris Collins was around, visiting and praying with the patients. The nurses as usual were running around, going about their duties, fulfilling them, facing any single problem however hard they could be.

This same day, when the sun shone so softly and everybody seemed to be happy going about their own lives, brought back the memories of something like this happening, the same day when he alone was attending school and was left alone in the classroom completing his homework.

The Blighs' car turned up to pick him up, taking him to Camelot's Kingdom. Jack had been inside the mansion with his own late mum a short time ago, when he met the young and beautiful Elizabeth Bligh. Now again he was facing her and her own family. Jack felt enthusiastic but felt out of place, too confused to be highly impressed with what he saw or felt. He hardly noticed its opulences, the garish decorations, the imposing structure, but for him it was highly frightening because it was a strange house bereft of warmth. Camelot's Kingdom's fame and fortune was such that when Jack was in school, his mates used to talk about the "huge house" that existed, and somehow how much one would have loved to go and live there or even take a good look per se.

Jack shrugged his shoulders. He had never boasted. Besides, it was none of anyone's business.

Meeting with the family then was no easy deal. George was something new. He was nice and kind, but he had his own set of friends and he went to a different school. Caroline was also there at the time. She was almost about his age. He thought of her as being cute and approachable. She was warm and funny. He thought the world of her. Then there was the youngest darling of them all, with all curls tumbling down and with a red ribbon tied to her hair, wearing a white dress with countless petticoats. He smiled at Little Lizzie. Wasn't the little tike adorable? Then there was the older Mr Bligh, seated beside grand Elizabeth. Her warmth and smiles were sort of a kind of enforcement. Now he was meeting all of them, becoming thus a part of the Blighs' family. Now he completely revered Mrs Elizabeth Bligh.

Elizabeth got Jack to go to his own boarding school. She carefully organised that where George went, Jack would go somewhere else, not at the same school. Caro was also enrolled in an all-private girls' college. Little Lizzie was still learning to walk. They were all far and uncomfortable, living in boarding schools, coming home for Easter, Winter and the long Christmas break. He was a keen student and was the lead in the class. He was also popular with everybody, but Jack was born a loner. He preferred his own company to being with the other boarders. When he could, which was seldom, he would join them too. He took part in sports and recreational activities, but like all the boarders, they were also bereft, sad and longing for home.

Jack was a lost boy and a lonely soul. He had no home to return to. Elizabeth showed him that his presence was very highly welcoming, but that he would be better living on his own as all of her kids did, minus Little Lizzie. Therefore, he returned to his own one-bedroom flat nearby. Other times, when he actually finished his schooling, he would apply to be a doctor and would take residence in the Inverness Hospital. He lived alone but was always invited to attend major and minor events at

Camelot's, where slowly he was falling in love with the beautiful dark-haired Caroline. When mother and daughter took the trip to Paris, France for three months, they were at the time his loneliest and saddest time. But when she returned, they stole time together and were so passionately in love that they made love everywhere, even in the stables at Ashpark, with Jack leaving in the earliest hours of the morning. He knew about Caro and how much she had failed in school, but he never told her off or anything. Love was blind. But it was a shock for him when he returned barely alive, or totally alive but with a real impediment.

His own. But the infernal shock was to learn that Caro was not living either at home or in Sydney, and Little Lizzie was nowhere in sight.

Jack's friendship with George was that of a brotherly one. He too was facing a terrible dilemma. Now that Caro and Little Lizzie were nowhere to be seen, he was happy only to attend some of the functions and lavish events. For him, Jack thought that it was embarrassing for himself to actually go to the wide mansion. He was only enamoured and missed dearly Caroline. At times, he knew that he was an outsider, and such frivolities and grandeur were indeed frightening for a country lad like him. But now with his professionalism and working as the doctor in the Inverness Hospital, he was allowed to come and go, which he was getting used to, the grand mansion with its opulence and riches, which only spelt grand and vast privileges. The only thing that was missing was the title. The Blighs were the Australian royalty. That was the first time he looked around himself and saw the maids, servants, the cooks, the chauffeur, the extra employees at the Blighs' demanding beck and call. Something was always needed to be done. None of them served to impress Jack, even though Jack would hear what many now spoke about the Blighs. It seemed that the Blighs were larger than life. But now he was part of this family, still being him, Jack would always miss one's parents. But the bitter taste of it all was that his parents were now gone, and the Blighs were his adopted parents, with adopted brother and sisters. (But his dad was still alive and kicking and watching over his own son, happy that he was doing well.)

With a sigh, as he was looking through the window to an outside world, he knew then and there that it might have been a new life, a new brand status. But one like him now needed to adapt to this new kind of life. He opened the drawer and brought out the syringe. It was time for his injection. It seemed that he was always evolving: first his parents, then the schooling, then the boarding school, then the internship, then the conscription. Each time he became a man, not necessarily human.

He sat down and again gazed emptily around the office. He adapted alright, because he sensed that it would be far easier to do so than to rebel against them. It was now their way. His ways would come back later on. Meanwhile, to his ways of life, he needed to like and love Camelot like his own. How fate would turn on him and make him perfectly moulded and loving Camelot would for sure make him think twice. One day, not too far away, Dr Duncan would come to love this magnificent, vast and grand place, that he would be humiliated, embarrassed and shamed. But pain came with everything, and he knew pain, deep pain.

But fight for it he would.

And then they perhaps would all come to love and reside in this palatial place. He shook his head. There was something about this place that until he got used to it gave him shivers. At first he didn't like it at all. Jack kept reflecting on it. It seems now that all that was there was now here, but there was still hard work to be done, redone, worked, reworked. More to it, one begs the question of who would accomplish them. Everything was changing at a terribly fast pace. One moment they were here and the next somewhere else. New stuff and gizmos were coming to the hospital, a modern era, easier. Only time would tell.

Right now, the warrant was very much a reality. The detectives turned up impeccably dressed, with their hats on. They showed him and the nurse the badge and read Jack's rights, then they actually placed the handcuffs on him, leading him out and into their Inverness Police car.

The summons read:

At such a time and date, a young woman was dead, having been operated on by Dr Jack Duncan.

The charges were an abortion cover-up.

That was the first of many charges indicted on Dr Jack Duncan.

Then they read the second charge.

Again a third charge.

A fourth one.

Apparently there were plenty of endless charges to his name alone.

And unfortunately they were adding to his name and poor status. Now he was also a drunk.

He was now and definitely the defendant.

And the prosecution stands.

As it states, "that something must have happened and it has happened, more likely with all the evidence confirming it, it did happen."

So what else was there? The Inverness Police Sergeant shook his head and avoided eye contact. Then, after writing in his registration book at the police station, another policeman emerged who took the fingerprinting of Jack's. Then Jack's pictures from left, right and centre, checking for scars, moles, birthmarks, anything that would identify him in the near future.

Then he also asked Jack if he had anything else that could be of relevance, anything, any deficiency or abnormality in his body condition.

Jack looked at him for a long time, choking back tears. Until such date, Dr Duncan was still a most wanted man. Dr Jack Duncan was now in gaol, awaiting trial. In the Inverness Police Station, by reputation all the coppers could be hard and tough, but they were pretty good to him at the moment. But then again, they knew Dr Jack Duncan and also Mrs Elizabeth Bligh.

The main doors crashed open as Caro burst in screaming, fighting off the other cops as they tried hard to control her by holding her. Caro was in hysterics, screaming, "Noooooo, you're making a mistake!" She was now beating the doors to the cells. She was in a dour, sorry state. She was let in.

In came Dr Henry Fox, trying to calm Caro down. Anna came into the police station, all pale, shaking, trembling and also crying. They were also trying to restrain Anna. She was defending her own father and trying to get into the cell.

Roy, demanding to know what was going on, also turned up. He was aghast to witness what was happening.

"We are all immediate family over here," Roy urgently stated, before the sergeant and officer in charge reluctantly answered as it was asked of them.

"What are the freaking charges?" He bellowed. Dr Fox calmly injected Caro, who not only was in hysterics but was in a terrible state of mind. She was totally dishevelled, her face completely swollen from crying and screaming. She seemed to have aged. Caro only stopped and calmed herself down after being sedated by Dr Fox. The ambulance came through and took her away.

Caro was now sleeping, totally sedated, and taken into one of the wards at the hospital, much to the horrifying news delivered to Mrs Collins, who at that moment had her basket full of herbs for the tonic. Her eyes glowed when she heard the bad news.

Dr Fox and the rest demanded to know what was going on.

Sergeant Bill Ways, on the shift, was very apologetic. "Sorry, mate, this is happening, but they are all beneath my control," as he brought in a tray with coffee, milk, sugar and sandwiches.

"Who's charging me?" Asked Jack, pretty indisposed by now.

Sergeant Bill Ways again spoke. "I hope the conditions are good here, and I hate to say this, Dr Duncan, but please be comfortable." At that he left, closing the doors to the cells behind him.

Jack, now recovering from his shock, started to actually try to make heads and tails of it all, speaking now with Roy, who acquired permission to also be inside the cell with Jack. He shook his head. "Surely there is a mistake?"

Then he asked Jack how he could help. As they were talking, Dr Fox turned up, announcing that his meeting was brief, for he was needed in hospital and Caro was in the hospital sedated. He released a sigh of relief.

"Who is doing all of these?" Jack shook his head and replied, "I have no idea."

Anna, coming through, crying, was screaming and was fighting all the way in. "Pappa, pappa!" She threw herself into Jack's arms and sobbed.

Jack was also in tears. Both father and daughter hugged and both of them cried bitterly, painfully.

"Pappa, who actually did this and why?" Anna continuously asked, choking on her own tears.

Jack shook his head. For the time being, he knew nothing.

Roy stated, "Blimey if I am more than ever going to find out who did this." He promised.

It was then that Elizabeth Bligh turned up. As usual, haughty, dominating, for some even unbearable. Sergeant Bill Ways looked at her and breathed a sigh, rolling his eyes up. It was a muggy day, and he was feeling the heat on both sides. He knew a great deal about her and her dominant personality.

As usual, she was not running or even puffing. She was calm, self-contained, confident, projecting a tranquil sense of atmosphere. She kept her cold demeanour, but clearly she was hurting, worried and also seething.

"Now, what seems to be the inappropriate problem? What is happening?" She demanded. Extraordinarily, Elizabeth was highly controlling her nerves. They all feared for her health. Another heart attack and she would probably be gone.

Grand Elizabeth was allowed and taken into the cell where she faced Jack and Roy, with Anna throwing herself into her arms and sobbing uncontrollably.

Elizabeth found a place to sit down, reasoning, trying to find some understanding, some explanation for it all. Honestly, she was totally confused.

Roy stated, "No one knows what is happening. Jack here has been charged, but no one is saying about what."

"If there are no charges, they cannot keep him here," Elizabeth adamantly reinforced her words. "He cannot be here, charged on things that he does not know of," she haughtily stated.

Anna returned. "The warrant had been issued, and these are the charges." Anna read them one by one until the end.

There were at least more than four charges, adding on to it.

One of the reports clearly stated that Dr Jack Duncan was also an alcoholic.

In another folder were pictures in black and white of Dr Jack Duncan completely drunk, sprawled shamelessly and openly in the dry green grass of Inverness. Notices of his self-indulgences, nights and days of alcohol bingeing, with empty bottles surrounding him.

The pictures told the story: notices painting Dr Duncan terribly, a popular Inverness doctor married to the local beauty Caroline Bligh, dramatic, morbid. It was embarrassing to say the least for Dr Jack Duncan.

Dr Jack Duncan's fate was sealed in that terrible musty, damp four-square, stinking cell where the yellowish paint of the walls showed him misery. The bars in the windows only proved how life could be divided from the cell and the outside. The sun was going down. The place was getting dark with sinister shadows playing alongside Dr Duncan and growing colder. He did not want to sleep on that bed that thoroughly smelled of urine and looked dirty. All he remembered was Elizabeth speaking, his daughter crying, and then he felt his own tears and the deep pain gripping him. Now he was alone in a terrible stinking cell. He did not want to eat anything. He wanted his own freedom.

Back at Camelot, Dr Fox, Roy, Anna and Elizabeth were going through the file and the folder.

Anna added, "Only these, and the affidavit." Elizabeth sat down on the porch, the maids scurrying around to make their mistress comfortable, as Anna filled the crystal glass with water and handed it to her grandmother. "They are all court orders, summons." She stated matter-of-factly. Her eyes still red from crying, with Dr Fox enveloping her with one of his many hugs. Roy shook his head. Inevitably, he suspected the person that had indicted Dr Jack Duncan.

"Have we called George to let him know what is happening?" Elizabeth was gritting her teeth by now, clearly getting highly irritated, feeling too the oppressive heat.

A long silence. "Well, does he know or not? Has anyone contacted him or not?"

Again a long silence.

Harry Poulson said, as usual very calm and composed, "We need to think this through well. There must be something wrong. We need to go down to the root of it all."

Anna replied, "You see, it is more than four charges." Then she again said, "And counting." Then she showed the black and white pictures of Jack. The sergeant said that they were these. Harry picked the folder up and went through them. "He wants all of these back and returned to him. He told us that for our sakes we did not see the photos."

"We did not see the photos," Elizabeth queried. "Why not?"

"They are using these photos against Papa in court," Anna replied.

"A meeting at home tomorrow morning after we see Caro," Elizabeth informed them all.

For Jack Duncan, the handsome gentleman of Inverness Hospital, he knew the way Elizabeth Bligh conducted her own business, to say the least, indeed very professionally. By now she would be thinking about something, either positive or negative. After they had left, Jack asked the constable if it was possible for him to be washed and cleansed. He also asked if there was going to be any bail, now to the Sergeant who came into the cell.

The Sergeant replied, "Listen, Jack. I do sympathise with you, but you know yourself that these charges are really serious. It will all be up to the judge and the jury. But I am only following their orders. If it was up to me..." He sighed, again rolling his eyes up. His face was puffed up and red as a tomato with the heat, as sweat was filling his rugged bearded face. "I might be a man of the law, but unfortunately there are things that we cannot undo, such as these." He held the folder with all the jurisdiction stamps and signatures. "Their autographs," the Sergeant stated drily.

"My advice to you is to get a good barrister, someone who is a QC." Then he said, "Could I get you something? After you washed, you are expected to be in court tomorrow morning at 10.00am. Sleep well after your supper, eh mate?"

With this, the Sergeant guided Jack to the bathroom, then brought him the pyjamas and the towels.

"At least let me know who's pressing the charges." Again Jack asked, now that he was thoroughly cleaned.

The man of the law, Sergeant Bill Ways, replied, "I am calling your family to bring your stuff for tomorrow. Please, no more questions. I cannot answer." He left.

Two hours later, Anna and Livvy turned up and handed over the clothes to the police station. After more talking and tears of sorrow, they left. Anna continuously cried. She was broken-hearted. Her mother was in the hospital, totally sedated. Livvy offered to look after little Elaine. Lady Swanson turned up with Livvy's husband Andrew. He was pale, knowing already what was happening. For all of them, it was a terrible day that had started so well in the beginning.

At home in Camelot's, the next day, after visiting Caro who was consequently sedated, they all returned home. All, and by all, even the Swansons. Dr Jack Duncan did go to court, and the family needed to get his bail.

Elizabeth again held court. The phone call from George came through. George Bligh did not understand what was happening.

Elizabeth sat down in the dining room. She was being served with the rest of them too. It was dinner time. Once that was done, it was time to discuss. But discuss what?

The day started off mild. The breeze was warm. The air was humid but not heavy. The "Summer Place" song was being played. It was soft, suave and gentle. The damp air smelled of aftershave, his own. Outside, the green leaves and the flowers were blooming beautifully, making the day garrulous, coloured, and the sun for once was shining hard as if protecting Jack.

As the day progressed, it became hotter, far more humid, slow and lazy. The radio in the police station kept on blaring with the incoming and outgoing of day-to-day activities, even though it was pretty slow, with people coming and going, with the officers turning up for their shifts. Slowly but surely it was becoming abuzz with so much activity. It was not going to get better.

Now that the fifties had finished and the sixties settled in, there was an explosion of everything and anything connected to the psychedelic time, where drugs were now more prominent, causing hallucinations, with drugs such as LSD. And so it was how the sixties came into the lives of the more simple, sleepy Inverness citizens. It was a time for rebelling.

The fashion trend was a new thing, going along with the invasion of the British Rockers, heralding thus a new generation which came thorough and fast. Universally, the Fab Four were an instant success, and with them came the Shadows, Ventures and one that replaced Elvis: Cliff Richard, as the British Rocker. (The Big Cat from Britain, whilst Elvis was the Big Cat from the USA, but the King of the Wide World.)

The new decade generated independence for all women. Vanessa Redgrave burnt her bra and made a statement that no longer did a woman depend on a man. Women could do anything they wanted. On the British throne sat a woman, Queen Elizabeth the Second, daughter of King George VI and the Queen Mother, Queen Elizabeth the Dowager. Elizabeth Bligh, in her own terms and conditions, always referred to her.

President JFK rose to power for his own charisma, good looks and energy.

Not to mention wealth. Accordingly, President Kennedy was really intelligent, but ahhh, he was a bad speller and no one could read his handwriting. Now that alone speaks volumes of himself and the nice and bright family that they were and came from.

Australia was recovering now from the Great Depression. They had another problem: Japan's cattle trading, as they wanted to be the best in the beef commerce worldwide. They were fighting off the Australian industry as the best beef in the world, which in reality they were, but highly expensive. Japan was becoming steadfastly one of the most modern cities or countries, becoming thus the second worldwide.

The dairy milk was getting by. In Macau, Australian milk and also butter were famous for their brand, so the new era started well in many directions, except that Dr Duncan was now being charged.

Questions: Did Elizabeth Bligh take care of Jack because:

A. Elizabeth Bligh felt guilty? Because Elizabeth enjoyed a relationship with Jack's dad, or was it far more sinister? Could this be the reason behind her faith and devotion for Jack?

B. Getting rid of Jack's dad as a pretence to cover up her folly. So Elizabeth covers her own guilt by taking care of Jack? Sounds good? Elizabeth's implying all the time that she is looking after Jack due to the promise she made to Jack's mother sounds indeed incredulous. Right? What happens if Jack was Elizabeth's own flesh and blood? Only Elizabeth couldn't afford to have Jack, considering how cruel and nefarious those times were. If so, wouldn't Jack and Caro be half-brother and sister, and Anna their incestuous fruit?

(Please note: Take a good look at the vicious circumstances that were surrounding Rose. She was forced to get rid of her baby son, and she followed her "son" into the Blighs' lives only to be kept near him. But disappointingly, little "Georgie" had nothing to do with Rosie, but all the same she kept her man, Gino. Now read on.)

So what more of the family's secrets were being kept by the Blighs that were not divulged?

It was Christmas after all, and Elizabeth could have forgiven Jack's dad for being a bit wee indulging. Jack's dad could have been a bit overwhelming, simply because it was a festive time, with Elizabeth being solo, alone with her three kids. Her husband was nowhere to be seen, which again begs another question. Christmas time is when everybody becomes "drunk" with goodwill: friends and families, gifts, food and drinks. How long did Elizabeth and Jack's dad have this kind of relationship? Elizabeth might have been cold and distant, but wouldn't these be a part of her denial? Being haughty with her nose stuck in the air, so one would believe. How hard was it for any males to approach her? Per se, I do not think so. Elizabeth was starving for love and affection, and for a keen eye like Jack's father, who at the time was teaching, he might have been alerted to that. Not saying that Jack's mother was ugly, far from it. But where love and attraction are together, a man can be the world's intellectual, but they are still human only. And Jack's dad and Elizabeth were only human. Elizabeth had only her kids. Sadly, not even her kids were insufferable. They all suffered from post-traumatic stress disorder. She had seen too many things, and they were playing havoc.

Elizabeth could be highly unforgiving. She gave Jack's dad three months' severance pay with a good reference letter. As Elizabeth is so famous and in accordance with the times, noting that Elizabeth extended her unforgiveness to Amy (Harry Poulson's sister and the Blighs' maid), continuing in her path of righteousness, which was highly destructive. The same Elizabeth's rules were applied against Rose. Karma retaliated as fate played a hard, devastating blow when Anna lost Gino. Too late she realised that. Elizabeth always failed to see that she could be her own and her worst enemy. That was her own self-defence trajectory where all the rules and regulations, seen and unseen, were all about. Hers only.

Now it gets better. Jack's dad would hear the sad news about his own son Jack Junior.

Duncan Senior follows the dramas consistently, reading the major and minor reports about his own son.

Duncan Senior was indeed a proud dad. A couple of times and from a distance, he would see his son driving in and out of the Inverness Hospital. Jack was the younger version of his own older and elderly dad. It meant so much for him to learn that his own beautiful, caring wife had lost her life. He grieved. He went over the bend. He drank. He was in a foggy place, pretty much like his own son. But his son had one reason. He, however, had his other reasons. He left his wife alone in this hard and capricious world. He never intended to contact them due to his shame.

Duncan Senior was a dashing young man. He cut a handsome figure. He was tall, dark and, of course, handsome, just like his junior.

It had been a long time, those long, depressive, dark, lonely years. He left everything: his own beautiful wife, his young and innocent, chubby little boy, fighting his own demons. Those years of self-pity and self-guilt ate at him, turning him virtually into an old man. The massive dark hair that once proudly was his crown of pride now lacked lustre, grey and thinning badly, even to the point that he was going thoroughly bald. Suffering badly from rheumatoid arthritis, preventing him from walking without a limp, having a cane to help him. His back arched badly even when he tried hard to stand up. His tall frame was bristling, weak and fragile. Each step was painful. His face was riddled with dry patches of red and white skin. What was meant to be once upon a time a really handsome man was now the exhausted personality who had terribly lived a life of disappointments and failed accomplishments, and who had nothing to be proud of, even at owning anything. He certainly did not owe and owned Jack. Elizabeth was for the second time a widow. Duncan Senior, a shadow of himself, couldn't care less.

Driving his own broken truck, one that he had for years, now driving into Inverness town with the sole direction of going into the police station, time stopped. He took a backstep at the "golden times" of his early years, as he remembered the good times he had then as a teacher. His family and him would spend time going to fetes, bazaars, anything that was fun and inviting. There was always a reason for the family to enjoy. But as luck would have it, he was fated to meet with the delectable petite frame and delicate Elizabeth Bligh.

She was a breath of fresh air, completely at ease, working happily under the sun that brought up that delicate and beautiful face, the Australian rose's skin, pale and natural. She wore light lipstick, and her cheeks were flushed red. Her hair was caught up in a French chignon with loose tendrils, as she was so decoratively and so elegantly dressed in those early twenties de rigueur dresses. She was holding her little bag and the chapeau, and behind her her older daughter Caro and the youngest daughter Little Lizzie, buying intricacies and fancies that so much became the ladies' accoutrements. Both daughters were noisy bumblebees, buzzing about frantically, trying to buy everything as most little girls and girls would do. On the other side was their older son George. He was contemplating buying a few books, trying to choose one.

He was totally mesmerised by the delicate beauty, the eyes, the mouth. More to it, he was totally bewitched. Imagine his delight when he found out that she was the Elizabeth Bligh, the actual Mrs Lewis Bligh, who was nowhere to be seen.

To say that Duncan Senior was totally enamoured of this little beauty would have been an understatement. He fell hopelessly in love with her, lock, stock and barrel.

After that, Elizabeth and him did share a few of the good times. As much as she was a stickler for any rules, she did respond to his "over-familiarity." But after such a long interlude, he was totally lost when she fully rejected him, hook, line and sinker. Well, women.

The question was, was it him, or was it Elizabeth who coldly and bluntly used him for her own selfish endings? He had heard a great deal about how unscrupulous and cruel Elizabeth Bligh could be. Now that Elizabeth had found the thrills and spills, plus the fulfilments of her own desires, love was denied by a cruel and distant man who played tricks on her, the father of her own three kids. Elizabeth came into her own of self-consciousness as her own marriage disintegrated. If her adultery was found out, Lewis, the man of the house, would not have put up with Elizabeth's idiosyncrasies and would not have hesitated in throwing her out onto the streets of Inverness, brandishing her as the scarlet woman, curtailing her motherly love by not allowing her to see her children. Elizabeth might have been a wanton woman then, but she would always be a good mother, even if she deviated and had other sexual escapades. Let's face it, she was human after all, and the way one sees it, she had the rights to find fulfilment, seeking love and comfort elsewhere. But Jack's dad was actually hired and employed by the Blighs. Both their attractions were mutual.

Imagine the mistress of Camelot's Kingdom finding solace and love with a mere teacher.

He had figured that where Elizabeth was, he could have never been matching against her if she chose materialism over fulfilment. That was a prerogative and her own ideology, her main frame of mind, where wealth, status and power meant everything to her. He could have never afforded such a blatantly extravagant life of luxury, privileges and powerful status maintenance, the lot. He was an impoverished bloke who had to borrow everything to become a teacher. But that was not what Elizabeth was thinking about. On her side, she had three kids to think about.

Even out of his depth, questions going by, observing every single detail, clicking up and picking up the fragments and putting them into the fitting puzzle, something that was so inconspicuously a firm reminder that it could never have lasted, which in reality could have never been happening, but did happen. He shamefully disappeared out of the Inverness town. The pain was terrible. He found solace in the alcohol that he drank so hard, going downhill. Depression sank in. He had a deep hatred of filth, a compulsion about himself, but he kept tabs with the

Inverness current affairs on a daily basis. Over time he read about Elizabeth and the Blighs in the newspapers, all sizzling and glittering in some magazines, all fashion and entertainment in the others. He read with pride when his son became a doctor, and even more when he enlisted. Memories flooded back onto that long hot summer afternoon where the nightmare started, the CWA then Inverness. He should have never been there in the first place, but like all of the good Inverness citizens, he was with his wife and son.

Elizabeth Bligh, intentionally or unintentionally, destroyed and ruined their lives. His wife died.

What is happening to his son now? Things completely changed when they moved into the vast surroundings of Camelot's Kingdom. He was interviewed and given the job and a cottage to live in with his wife and son. It was meant to be a dream come true. But it was not.

Questions would be arising when Duncan Senior returns to Inverness, seeking out his own son.

Duncan Senior comes to realise that whatever Elizabeth Bligh did to him and his family, at least she looked after Jack. She treated Jack as her own. Was it out of guilt? Or was it something far more sinister?

Now that he was more sober, time was on his side. Duncan Senior was allowing himself plenty of time for extras, contemplation and deep reflection. There was so much to ask, but would there be any answers? What in fact was Elizabeth? Was she really an enigma to be understood, or was she a legend that was born out of coldness and chiselled ivory? How and why would Elizabeth take such extreme measures in having and keeping Jack at all times, but by the same token keeping him, Duncan Senior, outside the reserved fences? She was indeed a perplexing type of person. Complex? Confusing? Well.

As he was driving the long stretch of the Inverness Road into the town, he passed through lots of places that brought him lively reminders. He also heard that his son did not bow to all the things that grand Elizabeth Bligh wanted and wished. There was some kind of personality clashing between Elizabeth and Jack which did take precedence. Looking into it, it was revealed that Jack took a tough stance against a furthermore authoritative, forbidden and tough persona in Elizabeth, and fought for Sara Adams to stay and work in the Inverness Hospital. Upon hearing these things from the other nurses at the hospital and about the loathing that Elizabeth had for the blonde, blue-eyed nurse, he smiled inwardly, stopped his truck on the side of the road, rolled out a cigarette and smoked. Outside, the rolling hills of green grasses went on and on and on. The sky was peppered with white clouds and the wind was gentle. The cattle grazed peacefully. His thoughts were of how a divine place like this could live up to any other expectations, such as perfectionism. Or was it?

He did not have the radio on, but he had his smokes and was enjoying his drag. He inhaled and exhaled. Ahhhhh, it felt good. Right now he was all tensed up, with such rigor mortis running through his mind. Yes, rigor mortis. One dead man walking. But he still had his blood running hot through his body, and no, he was not a vampire or even a zombie.

For once, someone like his son would dare to take on the Blighs. It was a tough assignment.

He smiled again, relaxing his head against the rest of his seat. "What would it take for him to go out and enjoy the benefits of nature?" He again reached for his pocket and took the pouch and rolled another ciggy. It was too good to worry about anything. When he finished talking to his own son, he might venture into the pub and have some drinks. He badly needed a drink now. He had dried up and cleaned up his act.

Where was he when he was so rudely interrupted? Ah yes, full marks for his daring son. His own son did it his own way. He nodded. He was having a small talk with himself and enjoying it thoroughly all the way. His son took on Elizabeth Bligh, and moreover, he now had the total respect of the dowager, Queen Elizabeth Bligh of Camelot's Kingdom. On the other hand, his own son, like himself, fell under the bewitching beauty of Elizabeth's older daughter Caroline. Duncan Senior was highly impressed. Jack married Caro. Now that says something about his own son. He wondered how Elizabeth felt. From the rumour mongers, he heard that she married a bloke by the name of Douglas Goddard, who himself had two sons. As luck would have it, he died. He was wondering if Elizabeth was jinxed. With Douglas, who was conned to marry into the Blighs' family with everything that the Blighs had and still have. But whatever the circumstances, one could have never stopped her from being an adulterous person, someone who married for high maintenance, and with everything that came with the Blighs' dynasty, she of course took them as her rights. Goddard was well known for his own capricious ways. He lived in the lap of luxury and could fancy himself ordering the most extravagant and expensive French champagne. And Elizabeth married him? Now, that's the full story about a social climber as Elizabeth was, he bitterly concluded.

As Jack grew up, looking like his dad more and more, to the point that both of them were almost the same in height, expressions and other personality traits, Elizabeth's shadows lingered coldly and freezingly. Or were there any other motives? With Elizabeth Bligh, one could always find more secrets in the family's vaults. What could possibly be there?

On a more fragile moment, sensitive and obligingly feeling conscious about it all, one will always remember Elizabeth Bligh's ways of talking to Olivia Bligh. It was by far a most sensible and emotional moment where and when Elizabeth showed and confirmed her own status.

Elizabeth Bligh, the commanding Queen of Camelot's Kingdom, literally told the beautiful Livvy, Olivia Bligh's Elizabeth's own side of her bitterly disappointing side of life, how she was also tricked into this kind of marriage. "When I see you, I see myself." "Never underestimate yourself. You're more capable than you could ever think," or words to this effect.

But Jack Duncan Senior did not know at the time that Lewis Bligh was gay, nor was he about to find out. Neither would he find the time to learn that James, Elizabeth's older grandson, was also gay. Chances are he would never find out about any of them.

He had seen the blue-eyed blonde nurse. He had also seen them in the bazaar often, with young David running around. The little tike had so much energy. He reminded himself of Caro and Little Lizzie.

Note for file: When Elizabeth had a close and affectionate talk with Olivia, these were her own words: that she saw in Olivia the tough little girl's simple determination in a far-away foreign country, as it was now being established over here in Sydney, Australia. How Olivia really measured up to everyone's expectations. Whilst that was happening, Olivia had shown her own tributes when she faced up to her own trials, hanging in there. Elizabeth Bligh had a torturous married life the same way Olivia did, and was rewarded for it. Livvy really stood her own ground. She was now a Bligh in every single word of it. But Elizabeth's three kids all belonged to Lewis Bligh, whereas little Georgie did not. He was not a Bligh at all.

Here's the big comparison between the two of them. Olivia Bligh had an adulterous affair with Lloyd, the family's portrait painter. (Please read Book 2, A Place to Call Home, "The Forensics." It is pretty much covered in there. The title is "Lloyd's Return.")

Elizabeth Bligh had an affair with Jack Duncan's dad.

Both might have been the l'affaire du coeur. It stopped when one or the other side saw how futile it could be. Lloyd ran for cover. He could have never been responsible for a Bligh's bastard and spoilt London's Ivory Tower Princess Olivia. And Elizabeth's, as we do not need to go into that anymore, for the comparisons are almost the same.

Olivia replaced her dead baby. Olivia claimed at the time that she did it for love, her "love" for James Bligh, which was then another story. Please note that this is covered in Book 1, A Place to Call Home, "The Forensics," Olivia Bligh, Chapter 12, The Ivory Tower's Princess. Based on A Place to Call Home's popular Australian TV series.

Bringing them to the fore, the Elizabeth Blighs', her own tell-tale signs where Jack Duncan was all about. In reality, if so, Caro's and Jack's marriage would be incestuous. But it is now revealed. The suspense is now cleared about Caro and Jack, as both are not blood related.

Questions: How did Elizabeth Bligh manage to pay for all of Jack's enrolments, short trips to and from outside Camelot's, without revealing herself to be the indisputable matriarch of Camelot's Kingdom?

Furthermore, one would not fail to wonder how on earth Elizabeth managed to fill in the respective forms. However, were the private schools in cahoots with her? And by then, wouldn't anyone actually raise an eyebrow and questions? In those days, secrets and confidentiality could easily make one lose their tongue at the end of their own career, with scandals erupting and shaming a good family's name. Anytime, any era, a good piece of dirty information would be spread like hellfire. Elizabeth could never have afforded this, so how did she manage to keep it low and without one single word of shame that would have caused so much embarrassment and humiliation?

Testing the waters, even the schools where Jack boarded would have asked what Jack was to Elizabeth and the Blighs' family. Jack and the Blighs were never blood related, as was certified by his own birth certificate. The names of both of his parents were there and the date of their marriage. Then whatever happened to Jack's mother and three. Where was Jack's dad?

Résumé:

Like Olivia, Elizabeth was tricked into marrying into the Blighs' family.

All the Blighs' women were wanton women. Elizabeth Bligh had a liaison, therefore both were the wanton women, as James Bligh referred to his own wife Olivia when he found out that she was being adulterous. Then there was Caro. She lived a colourful, capricious and scandalous dilettante life, with numerous lovers, to which Sir Richard Bennett called her "a slut, a whore, a tramp," names that are hard to swallow, but it was the name that society imprinted on them. Yet there were plenty of them circulating around in the main corridors of the elite.

Anna became completely sardonic, laughable, a cynical, chain smoker and a heavy drinker.

Then another Bligh woman comes up trumps with her liaisons du coeur with other males, including Sir Richard Bennett and the so dreaded and fearsome Constabulary Sergeant Taylor, that aided and abetted Regina and died at the end in the hands of the lunatic Regina Bligh. Regina, for all intents and purposes, was a classic lady, with so much going for her, espionage included.

Unlike, or like, Olivia, Elizabeth did not switch a dead Bligh's baby to a "mysterious" live baby. But Jack could have been the one. But it was not.

The Blighs' women, none of them were pushovers, but delectably determined women who wanted to live their own lives the way they saw fit. Is this a sin, do you think? Aren't we all entitled to some of our freedom and happiness?

What of Sara Adams? "You survived the war by spreading your legs. You're a whore," screamed Regina Bligh to Sara Adams. Another Bligh woman. They were all in the same boat, always rocking to the upper extremes of the ocean surfaces. "Checkmates, I think," Regina Blighs.

Did Jack's late mother know about the affair, and if so, is Jack her real son, or was she entrusted to look after him so her husband's affair with Elizabeth was kept a secret? Does that ring true?

But just in case that it was not, and she did not, to what purpose and ending would Jack's mother take Jack Duncan to Elizabeth Bligh's, asking Elizabeth to actually vouch for Jack and look after Jack? Why? Why? Why?

Was Jack's mother emotionally blackmailing Elizabeth, knowing about the affair? Would that be the sordid reason where stress actually caused the cancer striking Jack's mother? As stress and anxiety, caused by the liaison, gossiping and shamefully knowing about it, which over the years aggravated and deepened, sending Jack's mother to an early grave?

Jack Duncan. A man in the wilderness. A popular person in Inverness.

Young once but handsome, good looking, intense, faithful and loyal to the core. To everyone that knew him in Inverness, he was popular and even loved, happily married to Caroline Bligh. Together they had a daughter, the beautiful and colourful society butterfly Anna. However, was Jack Duncan a mollycoddled man, living in the lap of luxury, having his ways the way he saw fit? Or to use more exact terms and conditions, was Jack Duncan someone who took extreme measures to go as far as to stand on his own? Jack could easily be a weak man.

For one, he was deeply entrenched in his own mysterious past. Indeed, a man deeply in pain had the rights to live it up to his own, for he had worked extremely hard to achieve everything, again with the help of Elizabeth Bligh.

We have already seen him facing "execution style" shots from our own Elizabeth Bligh where Sara Adams was of concern, and in due course both of them became good friends with Sara Adams.

"It is getting harder for me to find the exact reasons for me to extricate and explain them," he warned Sara Adams, when he saw for himself that Elizabeth Bligh would not let it go, one way or another. His mother died when he was very young.

But what if Jack Duncan finds out that actually Elizabeth Bligh was, and from the mouth of his own father, that both of them enjoyed a very close tryst, when and how she saw it fit. But for some unknown reason that only Elizabeth thought about, she saw Jack's father packing and leaving, and his own mother consumed with her own guilt and shame, dying. And now she had passed.

Now Jack's father is returning. It was highly time that Jack and his father were reunited.

Now it was highly time for a thorough confrontation, and more to it, compensation. Was Dad's father going to revenge and also blackmail the Blighs on how grand Elizabeth used him and sent him packing? Also, would Jack Duncan, who once went against the mighty Elizabeth Bligh, would this time revel, creating a thorough revolution against Elizabeth that virtually would send her to an early grave, just like his own mother did?

Or would Jack look into another direction, seeking a peaceful time, harbouring no antipathy toward the Blighs' family? Living now in love and harmony, continually harvesting the best for his life and family, coming down to terms and conditions to actually spend unprecedented time with his beautiful little princess, his own granddaughter, whilst moving forward with his own father. For what has happened, that was then, in the past. Now, in the early sixties, they could only move forward. His wife was a Bligh. His daughter was also a Bligh.

Jack Duncan, for all intents and purposes, was also a Bligh. Not by blood, but with everything that counted by. Jack proudly reasoned with it.

Jack figured out that everyone makes mistakes, and Jack was not going to dwell on it. Or, like his own daughter Anna, would he turn into another cynical, bitter and highly disappointed person and go the length of targeting Elizabeth Bligh? No. Jack was still wallowing in his own self-pity.

He was desperate. Everyone knew that he was actually half a man, as cruelly Sir Richard Bennett stated, "The Japs cut it off him." But he was still a man, poisoned and bitterly disappointed, and also going through the highs and lows of what really happened in the Japanese concentration camps. His father would later find out. On his own deathbed.

He was suffering severely and acutely from the PTSD overview. At the time, it was not known how much this affected the sufferers. His mind was totally framed by all the disgusting, terrible and appalling treatment that all of them suffered at the hands of the Japanese, where flashes of the torment, torture, starvation and beatings flooded him.

But now a new revelation and a new journey were coming through. Whether they would all ride it well and happily into the sunset or not remains to be seen.

The day Duncan Senior met his own son, the reunion was by far dramatic.

They both stared at each other's mirrored reflection, one an older version and the other still young and handsome. One was recovering inside the Camelot's place, the other having a terrible time climbing up the stairs into the safe haven of the house.

As both of them stared at each other, facing one another, they still couldn't believe it. It was hurting. Still. As Duncan Senior, both knew the deepest pain that both went through.

The bitter, painful, terrible moments flooded Jack's mind. The pain was indeed deep, cutting so much so that he landed in hospital suffering from panic and anxiety attacks.

During his treatment and recovery, poor Jack's mind went through all the levels of deeper anxiety, disappointment, sorrow, desolation and sadness. The memories induced pain. There was no respite in it. It went all the way, those memories, those times, flooding back like a real storm breaking all the barriers. No wonder Jack was in such a mess.

Once upon a time, Camelot's Kingdom had now a queen. The king is dead, long live the queen.

She was the ever Queen Elizabeth Bligh, the matriarch. Now she was the whole effervescent, mesmerisingly legendary, far and distant dowager, grand Elizabeth Bligh.

Apparently, living inside the gilded cage was meant to be good. One always thinks what money can do and buy. Jack was sought after. The Blighs' car came to collect him from school.

Jack came to reside for a short time with the Blighs.

His old man left without so much as a word. No one suspected anything. There shouldn't be anything to be suspicious of. Or was there? Now he was back, older and sicker. It reminded Jack of his mother, who was sick and bedridden with cancer. Those times when Jack felt so safe and sound, living with both of his parents at the cottage. Life was simple, fun, and they wanted for nothing.

When his parents originally met, his beloved mother was already suffering from the female maladies. Each month the temperature elevated, coming through her, attacking her with terrible headaches, bloatedness and sexual problems. Today, these terrible symptoms are diagnosed as premenstrual tension. In older, ancient times, these gave cause to what we call "hysteria," and the women were treated as mental cases, with no cures whatsoever. Being afflicted by all of these symptoms was no easy task, yet she badly suffered from asthma. Hardly a day went by when his mother could ever be alleviated from any or all of these terrible symptoms. Jack also noted that if it was not one thing, detrimentally, it had to be another thing.

She was also advised to get married before, at the time, because of "hysteria" that was going around the world. Most mental institutions could not really afford to take any more in, and Jack's beautiful mother married then a handsome man who was to be his father.

Once being married, her own dreams and wishes were to have a child, her own flesh and blood. But even these were also a struggle, as she kept on trying but not succeeding. However, his mother did laundry for a Chinese lady, and over time she would go into Inverness to collect clothes to be washed at home, being paid for the ones she had already done. One day, she told one of the ladies who also, like her, did laundry on the side to have some more money for their families. Jack's mother sighed at the sight of those young children that she did not have the pleasure of having. One lady heard her complaints and introduced her to this Chinese herbal medicinal small shop, which she went into. The shop smelled of fresh camphor. It was small but with loads of glasses with all the dry elements that his mother could not decipher. Jack's mother was shown into a small office, and the gentleman, all dressed in silky black garb with his long braided hair tied in a long coil, smiled, welcoming her to sit down, taking her left wrist and pressing down, checking for the pulse.

"I can't conceive," she stated. The Chinese man nodded. Then after a while he smiled back and guided her into the main room. There he took a number of exotic elements, mainly herbs, mixing them all, weighed them, then he wrapped them up and gave Jack's mother instructions on how to use them, three times a day until it finishes.

He told her that the first six packets were remedial herbal teas that would help her control her premenstrual tension, and it would also help her in getting pregnant. For the supply of six weeks, he charged her one shilling.

Reference:

The Chinese community in Australia grew and grew. They had been in Australia after the Portuguese discovered Australia five hundred years ago. With the lands given and distributed by the British Crown, Australia was meant to be called the New World. However, whatever the name, foreigners all over the world turned up in droves, including the Chinese.

The Chinese were highly productive, cultured and traditional. In the beginning, their community was small in number and they very much kept to themselves. They were also grand in their social status. They had their own restaurants and clubs. They also created their own secretive martial arts schools where only the Chinese knew about it and practised it. But they also helped the community in healing them of any maladies.

Reference:

The Chinese arrived in Melbourne, Australia during the Gold Rush. (My daughter did an assignment about this subject, and even more with the new Australians in the Sovereign Hill, Ballarat in 1999. At the time, I took her to watch the fabulous Eureka Stockade, and we went through all the major tours inside Sovereign Hill's Eureka Stockade's celebrations. We had a thrilling time. With the arrival of the Red Coats, the period years, both ladies and gentlemen dressing up, the ladies looked beautiful and the gentlemen were so smoooooking handsome. We also rode in stagecoaches. The few days granted to us during the November month, with the weather being beautiful, gave us all a whale of a great time, including the food, which was terrific. Everything was perfect, with the following guidelines of a spectacular Eureka display of modern technology.)

At 8:00pm we were solely entertained by the spectacular Eureka Stockade performance. It was electrifying and highly interesting. It went for two hours, and my daughter and I loved it.

https://www.victoria.goldrush
https://en.wikipedia.org/wiki/Victorian_gold_rush 1852. Address: Bradshaw St., Ballarat, VIC. (03) 5332 1107.

At the time, Melbourne was a major boomtown during the Gold Rush.

Melbourne City became the centre of our colony, with rail networks radiating to the more regional towns and also ports.

It would take one to travel to Melbourne either by coach (horse-drawn carriages) and boats, about two weeks' time to arrive at Melbourne's docks.

Today you can still find gold in Sovereign Hill and to really enjoy the variety of entertainment. One can also dress up and have their pictures taken.

Meanwhile in New South Wales, the Chinese arrived when one Chinese gentleman wrote home detailing about the gold rush and employment. Three thousand Chinese bought their passages and arrived in the Port of Sydney for employment contracts to work in the New South Wales countryside.

Read: Chinese Settlement in NSW. www.environment.nsw.gov.au/resources/heritage. Years: 1848 to 1853. Excellent history.

The Chinese have always been exemplary where their science and technology history have emancipated over the years. Being born and raised in Macau gave me a thorough insight into their modern lives and their own culture, traditions and medicinal technologies, with acupuncture being one of the many maladies that they can cure.

Even though they kept very much to themselves, the Chinese established their own tearooms, dining halls and, to a degree, also established opium forums, interestingly more for therapeutic treatment than for anything else.

To the early Chinese that arrived in both Sydney and Melbourne, also had escort dens for the rich and powerful mandarins' descent. But more to it, a place could not be Chinese without their temples and also herbal teas that were brewed in those special containers to keep the benefit of it all for someone who, like Jack's mother, needed it. On the other hand, the benefits of cupping and also the needle therapy, which are currently called acupuncture, a therapy that is still being used and one of the top martial artists in China, so-called Wong Fei Hong, used for the great benefits of his students who trained with him at his own Chinese martial arts school.

Wong Fei Hung was born in Foshan (this is the cité célèbre for all the martial arts and martial artists establishing their schools). Having said that, Wong Fei Hung was born on 9 July 1847 and died on 17 April 1925. He was a master in Hung Ga martial arts, a physician and also a folk hero. I have seen and watched many of his legendary movies starring the terrific Kwan Tak Hing, who usually played opposite the legendary Shek Kin, another professional Hong Kong martial arts persona. Of course, he was the good guy. Shek Kin was the bad guy (he played the bad guy opposite Bruce Lee in the 1972 Enter the Dragon movie). Master Wong was professional in using the therapy of acupuncture, but he also invented the Dit Da, which was used for traumatology therapy. The ones that I used on myself were all in oil and rubbed onto the place where it hurt.

Acupuncture, then and now, is still used in helping to decrease pain and promote tissue recovery, including helping one's body to release pain-moderating chemicals, which for our own knowledge and record, as we all know, are called endorphins and enkephalins.

And in doing so, it signals and helps one's body to increase blood flow to the surrounding tissues, wherefore the nutrients are brought forward, including oxygen, hormones and chemicals, to help increase the blood to flow freely, to alleviate the pressure on the wound or the area that is hurting. It also applies to the trauma induced by the needle, which of course would be helping to stimulate one's body's immune system, whereby promoting healing.

www.naturomedica.com.blog/news/acupuncture/rec.t_

Jack's mother was the beneficial recipient of all of these treatments, but more to it, there was nothing wrong with her fertility problems, which was indeed a good sign.

She used the money to cure herself and drank the herbal brew when Jack's dad was not home.

The acupuncture treatment helped to alleviate her terrible headaches and also the tensions that gripped her body. Within months she was smiling, as the pain was easing, and she found herself pregnant. She was walking on cloud nine, and so was Jack's father.

Jack's mother eased on her loads of washing and ironing clothes, as was advised by the Chinese herbalist. Once every week, Jack's mother would go to the Chinese medicinal shop to report on her weekly pregnancy. Then she gave birth to her son, their son, and he was named Jack. For a time, the family lived well and happily.

The two-bedroom cottage was brimming with sunshine, love and so much tenderness and caring. Jack, being the only son, was naturally the apple of his parents' eyes.

As the family now had another mouth to feed, Jack's father accepted another job as the teacher in Inverness, which was pretty close to the surroundings of Camelot's Kingdom, which Jack's father could afford more money for. And so, once they were all well established in the little fairy-tale cottage, all was well. At first it was a dream come true. Jack's mother enjoyed her domestic home duties, tending to the garden too. They were living the dream.

The three of them were happy, comfortable and they got used to the gentle side of living in Inverness. Life was affordable, as his mother continued with the weekly laundry. Every Saturday morning the three would saddle up the horses to their cart, upload it with whatever they could, spending quality family time together, with weekend family picnics. Other times they would spend the day at the lake, the famous lake that most people went to, or by then attending fetes, bazaars, some of the most famous debutante balls, and Christmas and Easter festivities.

But his mother now had another kind of malady. She now suffered from vertigo, which usually caused her terrible dizziness and vomiting. Then his mother's acute pain with her bending over. Of course she would go to the Chinese Medicine Shop, telling them about her discomfort. She was so sick of being sick. One day, the shop owner spoke to her specifically about her health. It was a sad state of affairs, as Jack's mother's health problems were deeply pronounced. But even though the shopkeeper could not give her any other indication or any other cure, he sadly advised her that for her own good, her diagnostics would be better off and cleared if she sought more advanced technology, which would reveal what was affecting her. Then they could seek further guidance to cure her.

But Jack also noted the changes in his father too.

Jack's father was now more tired, more solo, more himself. He was always irritable. He was always away, and when he was home he was always distant, far off, living in his own world. Jack's mother was always working in and out of the house and would always take young Jack with her for shopping trips and also leaving and collecting laundry. His dad seemed to be happy at times, as he was a doting father to his own son Jack. But as time went by, Jack's father dismissed even having anything to do with his mother. He saw his mum crying a few times, but he thought that it was because of the physical pain that she was going through. Each day that went by, she was getting paler, and her hair was not only thinning but also falling in thick chunks. Jack noticed a funny smell emanating from his mother, even though she would always be perfumed and well dressed, running errands. Now, instead of a firm family solidarity, it seemed that his family was breaking up, in particular his father, who found fault in everything. Then he completely stopped going out with mother and son.

Jack was too young to understand the changes in his father. As his father drifted away, sometimes sitting in front of the chimney, contemplating the logs that were burning, he seldom joined them. But when it suited him, he prayed and shared with them at dinner times. At times, he would not bother to return home at night time, but if he did, sometimes he was drunk. Jack's mother had a few rows with Jack's father. By now, anyone would have known that the constant fights between mother and father were now added to his mum's ordeals, adding more pressure to her fragile health. The problems of her health were getting deeper, but only as a strong warrior did Jack's mother soldier on. Nothing was far more important than her place where she called home, as she was cooking her son's favourite egg and bacon pie, with the veggies collected from her own beloved and tended garden, with chips, drunk with warm milk, sharing the fare with her own treasured son and her husband. Oh, did she really love them. On that one evening when dusk had fallen, they were preparing for dinner as Jack's mother retrieved the piping hot egg and bacon pie, along with the chips all sizzling and hot, as she set them on the table. It was that evening that his mother confronted his dad. "What on earth is going on with you?" "Why are you so distant?" Suspiciously, she asked, "Is it another woman?" She remembered how he could not take his eyes off the young Elizabeth Bligh, and more now that he was working for the Blighs as the new teacher in Inverness.

He retorted, "Don't be silly," drily.

"What on earth then, what is going on?" she asked again in that weak voice of hers.

"Can't you see, I do have loads on my mind? I am overflowing with work." He made excuses, then stopped, then continued, "Up to my neck." And then he excused himself. All of these questions only served to irritate him, and most of the time he sweated in his own anxiety's confusing statements. His mind was causing him tricks, maybe even nightmares.

Working overtime in the school. Sometimes his mother would bring him lunch, and when she did find the time and reasonable hours to kill, his mother would see his father talking to the young Elizabeth Bligh. So she would leave the food on his desk and wait for his return for dinner. She would draw the bath for him, have his clothes all fresh and cleaned for the next day. Breakfast was always ready. His father would return home for all of these. Still he was never happy, and to further up any reasonings of why he was behaving in such a poor way, coupling now with his poor sleep which was never restful, he would wake up with nightmares, screaming at night time, waking up the whole household, all bathed in heavy sweat, as if the devil himself was pursuing him.

Little Jack was growing up. He was the apple of his mother's eye. He kept her company everywhere they went. She would spoil him by taking him to Sydney's CBD and staying there for a few days, now that she had extra money to dispose of. Then returning home before school commenced. Those were such cosy and warm days of mother and son's love, closeness and short life's expenditures. It actually meant everything to little Jack. They were all that meant so much for him and for his mother's. If Jack was not that young, he would understand the nature of these small and cosy trips. His mother was trying very hard to spend huge quality times with her own darling son.

Jack's mother fiercely kept on going with her own work by bringing home loads of laundry baskets. She saved enough money for both of them to go on some small trips here and there, sometimes interstate. As a kid like any other kid, Jack loved Sydney, the mini trips to the docks, with his mother taking him on small cruises with all the goodies surrounding the best of the city's CBD. Now they would stay in a bed and breakfast, be it in Sydney or interstate, enjoying some short shopping trips and some souvenirs here and there. There were a few pictures, and they were treasured troves to both of them. They were simple but so endearing days of so much love and closeness. The tears were rolling down Jack's face. He could clearly remember those beautiful days of perfection with his mother, but he looked at his dad now, wondering what had happened to him then.

When he looked at his mother, she would glow with love and happiness too, always indulging in her own son. The sky was the limit where a mother's love was.

Whatever his mother was suffering, no one took any notice. But the dark circles around her eyes were now deepening. She covered her head as the hair fell in thick chunks. Both her eyes looked hollowed and her cheeks were highly prominent.

She kept on working hard. His father was the new teacher in Inverness and nowhere to be seen. Things were not getting better. If anything, they were getting bad and sour. Jack wondered in fact how fate could be so cruel. He felt the closeness to his own mum. It never occurred to him that one day his mother would not be there for him.

Remembering the freezing atmosphere of that sad state of affairs that were happening inside his home, his mother was always active. He remembered how tough she was, hard going, that she was suffering from anything she never said anything, no complaints. But he had seen her doubling in pain. He had seen her in bitter, painful tears. At a later stage, he, as a doctor, would come to understand that his mother was a frail, sensitive and sickly woman. As they were now further aggravating her health, his own dad was not improving at all, with his own narcissistic ways. Now he came to understand that he actually never knew his father, but of his mother, plenty of fond memories that now were besieging him.

He looked forward to the small short trips into Sydney's CBD and the stay-overs. It was now with Christmas approaching. Jack's mother took Jack for Christmas shopping. It was a whirlwind, fun affair. He enjoyed it thoroughly. The whole city and town were all decked in the best of Christmas atmosphere and ambience. She saved enough to buy the small hand clock for his father, and for him, he could choose anything. Jack was reliving his own life.

She took him to the newly opened Luna Park. Mother and son were having the time of their lives. When they returned home to Inverness, to their picture-perfect cottage with the Christmas decorations, however, his father just packed up and left. Jack remembered that terrible Christmas. It was no fun.

After the new year, after their extended school holidays, he noticed his mother crying in desperation, begging for an answer to her own prayers. Then one sunny morning, Jack's mother packed him off and both of them went to Camelot's Kingdom, where they actually met with the soon-to-be Queen Elizabeth of Camelot.

It was his first time inside Camelot. He was vastly impressed by the huge estate. It seemed endless. His mother, as usual, was well dressed, wearing a hat, a parasol and her handbag. She walked fast and quick, and now they were in the presence of the grand lady of the manor.

Like his own mum, she was gracious, beautiful, warm and intelligent. Elizabeth Bligh, the Camelot's Queen, was affectionate and welcoming. His mother thought that Jack was very lucky, highly fortunate to have met such a wonderful lady at her most relaxed mood.

After a brief, empty discussion, with his mother really feeling panicky and anxious, his mother told Elizabeth Bligh that she had done her utmost, and now it was all up to little Jack and whatever care that Elizabeth would see fit and justifiably apply and do for him.

His mother left. Now he was the adopted son of the Blighs.

Soon he found out what sterner stuff was when one like him was connected to Camelot's Kingdom and the matriarch. Elizabeth Bligh was tough, redundant, deeply emotional. Most of the time she was cold, distant and unresponsive on the one side. But the life ahead of Jack's as the adopted son of the Blighs was a long and distant road onwards, filled with so many holes, pebbles and rocks, with Elizabeth Bligh always maintaining her tough, resolute, standoffish status quo. He thoroughly admired the essence of this resilience in a woman, and he thought, "Pity is the person who tangled with her." She was dynamic and formidable. Jack Duncan found out the hard way whilst he was growing up.

Elizabeth Bligh laid down the rules and regulations. She gave tall orders. Her own expectations were that her rules and whatever she said and did were followed through and thorough, with reliance and purpose. Of course, the same criteria was applicable by not allowing the world to see the more intimate, private affairs of her own family. The privacy of the Blighs was indeed a most kept one. Now that he was meant to be their "son," Jack was soon sent out of Camelot's Kingdom to a far-away boarding school.

He enjoyed their breakfasts in an informal way when he would stay in Camelot. There was always a strong and dedicated family ambience. He was introduced to their own faith, the Church of England. But somehow, his little sister was a devout Catholic and attended a Catholic all-girls private college, and spoke French at home, driving Elizabeth up the wall. But for all intents and purposes, she was named after her own mother, and they called her Little Lizzie. Little Lizzie was practically non-existent. One moment she was there, the next Jack could not even ask for her whereabouts. The Blighs continued with their lives, their own purposes, living high and mighty with their own standards, their powerful positions, wealth, status, pedigrees, privileges and, of course, their own private lives.

It was hard to demolish that cold, sturdy, strong fence. Elizabeth did not want him around, as she had better things to worry about now: the latest sad story with her husband's death.

One day, in no uncertain terms, she told him how he was a smart lad and that she expected the best from him, in that decisive voice of hers. And when she was, she would fix her blue eyes intently on him. He felt like a bird being closed in. With that speech when she spoke to him during the end of the Christmas break, the following morning Jack was whisked away to the new secondary all-private school for boys. During holidays, he would spend quality family time with the Blighs. Elizabeth could not afford to have a stranger living inside her private house. Jack was invited for the coming of age of George Bligh's. He was also invited to Elaine's debutante. He was then introduced to the Australian gentle elite society. One needed to know that young Jack was growing up stealthily fast, popular, very much wanted and desired by the female gentry.

Needless to say, as a normal boy with hormones flaring up, he did have a few girlfriends. As time went on, he looked bright and sunny. With that sheepish grin of his, he went to all of the events, the engagement, the wedding. It was really fit for a king, with Elizabeth Bligh never once showing anyone who would be the rightful heir to the whole of the Blighs' Empire. Oh, one day, much to all of the Blighs' pride, Jack was now graduating from the medical school with flying colours. There, he was again smiling that sheepish smile.

Dynasty.

But Jack's heart belonged to a beautiful, dark, long-haired lady. She was everything to him. She was very happy-go-lucky, colourful, daring, bad and good at the same time. She always had jokes and cracked up in the most natural laughter. He slowly fell in love with her. To his delight, she responded.

He looked forward to returning home to Caro. He could not wait for the christening of young James. He thoroughly missed Caro for the three months on her trip to Paris with Elizabeth for the making of her debutante ball's gown.

When that day happened, Caroline's own debutante, she looked like a vision on that day. Then, as life would have it, he was conscripted to fight in the Second World War, to fight for King and country, breaking Caro's heart.

Elizabeth was thoroughly devastated. The next he heard was that Caro had a big falling-out with Elizabeth and left. First was Little Lizzie departing.

At the time, Elaine was pregnant, giving birth to her second child. They named her Anna.

Then the sad news came. The Japanese bombed Darwin, with Elaine being killed.

It made George go practically nuts, and Jack knew the feeling. He was now in the thick of the war. For all intents and purposes, Jack was missing home. Before he left, he had graduated from the medical school and was the new refresher at the Inverness Hospital. Now sadly, he was a prisoner of war. Jack was now in the Japanese concentration camp. But there were shocking news, one that he could not believe, that war could be so mean and cruel.

Now in the hospital, suffering from so many maladies, it brought back to him the sad memories of his own mother. Presently he looked and still could not believe it himself.

Now his dad was with him.

He also was being charged. The court was waiting for him on four accounts.

When Elizabeth saw Jack's father, she went pale and speechless.

There was a very tense reunion between his father and his adopted mother. It had been such a long time. Both were in their advanced state of age, but their love was still there, much to the chagrin of Jack's. Which was the main thing? His father or his court case? Jack shook his head. Life could be so ironic, uncanny and unreal.

But let's see what his father is going to do to help his own son.

But don't hold your breath. When his father finds out the truth about the Blighs, which I don't think he will.

They will all be coming through in Book 2, A Place to Call Home, "The Forensics," Jack Duncan, The Return of Jack Duncan Senior. Please check it out. See you there.

Jack was now alone.

In his cell.

The place was cold and dark, with only the outside bright light streaming in.

Even though he was now on trial.

Chapter 10: Sara Adams: Florence Nightingale.

1. Sara Adams. Florence Nightingale. Camelot of broken dreams.

"So he said to me: 'This is the Word of the Lord of Zerubbabel. Not by might, nor by power. By my own Spirit. Says the Lord Almighty.'" Zachariah 4:6.

"Un endroit pour appeler la maison." "A Place to Call Home." "Um lugar para chamar de lar." "A Place to Call Home."

When Sir Richard Bennett wanted to exact revenge on the Blighs, the man was so inventive that he would not leave any stone unturned until he found his goal.

And the new Mrs Sara Bligh, the new mistress of Camelot's Kingdom, was one of them.

Married and happily living as the new Mrs George Bligh, the blonde, blue-eyed lady was very much in the comfort zone of her home.

Now that she is the mother of such a beautiful little boy, David, with extras by having a husband such as the tall, dark and handsome gentleman, a man that would stick to his principles. The way he stuck by and solidly supported his new wife was not only a simple statement, but Bennett thought that George Robert Bligh went a bit too far, allowing a Jew to overtake Camelot. Then he smiled. They don't call it Camelot of broken dreams for nothing.

These two little lovebirds knew what love was all about. He loved his own Elaine in his way, and Sara fought tooth and nail for her René. Now both of them were complete. It was fate that they should have met. And as much as they had fought their tendencies of forbidden love due to Elizabeth Bligh's loathing of Sara, which also became a thorough obsession for her, despising Gino Poletti (please read The Polettis, Book 2, A Place to Call Home, "The Forensics," to further understand the story), it would be a fact that George would realise how much it was going to cost him in losing his beloved Sara, plus the fact that his beloved one was actually carrying his child. He, George, the "innocent, kind, soft Georgie" as his younger sister Caro completely described him, as he was meant to be, was decisive and in control. He fought everything against all the rigidity, the thorough prejudicial behaviour and the sordid past of Sara Adams, and of course he and Sara, both of them, won. Victory at its best. Or is it?

Sara Adams. What exactly do we know of her?

She is beautiful. Hard to say that this beautiful blonde-haired and blue-eyed lady was then a Jew. According to the Führer (Sie betrachtet ihn als ihren), "they all looked at him for leadership." (Führer in English means the leader, head, commander, chief, the driver and so on.) Most Jews were all dark with dark eyes, dark curly or straight hair. But the warrior lady, as our main Sara was, was not, therefore one gets a bit confused over here.

Hitler strived for a world of white people, blonde-haired and blue-eyed perfection. Hitler created the system of the Aryan, and the world would become all white, blonde and blue-eyed people. Still, there gets to be more confusion where this "Führer" is. If his policy and wishes were what he wanted them to be, with the world all white, populated and segregated under his only Republican and fascist ways of oppression and dictatorship, where every single person obeyed without questioning, bowing over to all of his wishes, as Hitler mainly wanted all to be white, then how on earth did he make a pact with Hirohito, Emperor of Japan, to divide the world into two? Europe would all be German and Asia all Oriental. This is another reason why we know that Hitler was a nutcase. He was deluded and a megalomaniac, in which he believed that he was born to achieve greatness. But in doing so, he needed to annihilate the Jewish population. Why are the Jewish so much sought after and persecuted? But that will come later. This chapter is dedicated to Sara Adams, or Sara Bligh, the new Queen of Camelot.

Historical Background:

The Holocaust. The Jewish Genocide.

Auschwitz and Ravensbrück.

27 January 2020. In loving memory of those who died innocently at the hands of the Germans during the Second World War.

This is the year that we as a whole, as humanitarians, remind ourselves of the state of the Holocaust, the real genocide, where millions of Jews were killed in the most despicable, atrociously inhumane murder, paedophilia, rapes, and still counting. Please refer to Book 1, A Place to Call Home, Chapter 12, Hitler's Furies, Gestapo SS Third Reich Lieutenant Cara de Rhe, for further information where our own Sara is concerned. Furthermore, my Books 1, 2, 3, 4 and 5, A Place to Call Home, "The Forensics," thoroughly portray our heroine named Sara Adams. She, being Jewish, practised all the sabbaticals, did the prayers, read the Psalms, applying the Jewish Creed.

Sara's portrayal of being a Jewish lady, following all the doctrines and beliefs, showing us how strong her own faith was towards Judaism, celebrating the Sabbatical days and the practice of bathing herself in the lake or anywhere during the Jewish feasts or celebrations. It was "fait accompli," as Sara never shrank from her spiritual and praying duties, with the sacred "Shalom Sabbat" being celebrated, inviting the likes of grand Elizabeth Bligh to enjoy and assist what in reality was the thorough involvement of the others who were totally foreign to the Jewish morals, prayers and traditions. I love and thoroughly adore the Jewish indoctrination of the Judaism religion, reminding ourselves that Israel is a country chosen by God and can never fail no matter what. Not by power, not by might, but by the full Spirit of our own Lord, it is done. Zachariah 4:6. This is the Word of God. The Lord be praised.

Sara returns home from years of exile from Sydney, Australia.

It is the beginning of the early fifties. Many things have changed, politics wise. Life as it was, and finally after years of hardship, Bridget Adams finds herself as the new Jewish lady and also a new job as a nurse and sister of the ocean liner. Sara is absolutely elated in taking such steps. She was trying to forget the existence of her previous years, which were turbulent, foggy and hard. She prayed constantly and thanked the good Lord for her own existence. To be here now on the ocean liner as a nurse and sister was indeed a miracle.

Even though Sara (new Jewish name) was all clean, cut and thoroughly pristine and affable, the socially interactive Sara hid a terrible secret which haunted her in dreams and on a few days in and out came into her in terrible flashes.

She recalled the whippings. She recalled the flashes. They were in black and white, cruelly and callously striking her like a thunderbolt of unhappy reminders. She almost stopped breathing, therefore needing to calm herself down.

She worked hard and saved hard to return back home to Sydney. So far, it was the best solution, so she could both rest and relax.

Hitler's demoniacal manifesto called Mein Kampf told of his own struggles, why and how he changed his own deficit, his most abnormal ways of thinking. His manifesto comes in a trilogy of his own making, where Hitler's theories of his own "avant-garde" (vanguard) come into play. One can read and analyse it. The man was an absolute psycho.

Hitler's percussive ways of establishing his superpower also related into making young groups of lieutenants, wherefore they would learn at an early age how to fight and honour their Germany, their country. So he created the German Youth orientation, where and when kids and young males and females were trained to honour the thorough German ideology and their main frame of using and killing philosophically by their own decree, which is then an official order carried out by the law. And by honouring their own country, it is thus far that fanaticism is born. However, we the Portuguese had the same thing, where males and females of youth orientation were of concern. I was the Commander in Chief for the Portuguese Feminine Youth Orientation, beginning kindergarten, 1961–1973 (then), where we the girls (speaking for ourselves) under the Portuguese Youth Decrees (Administration) were all inducted into this kind of solidarity. But the training was domestic: crafts, embroideries, cooking and reaching the platform of debutante balls, which were all subsidised by the government.

Having said that, we are now referring to the Tripartite Pact, also known as the Axis, which was signed by Germany, Italy and Japan on 27 September 1940. Three of them, Hitler, Mussolini and Hirohito, signed what was then called the Pact of Steel (more like the Pact of Evil, Madness and Mayhem), formed, signed in secret and established in Tokyo by the three leaders, where it was originally stated, designed and separated Europe from Asia, with Japan occupying all of Asia without the interferences of any Europeans. As Hirohito solely targeted his own invasion throughout China, beginning with Nanjing, where their headquarters were originally established in 1935, consequently invading China by 1937.

But except for Macau, the Japanese were not able to possess it entirely, due to Macau being a Portuguese colony. Therefore, it was completely neutral, flying the Red Cross. But over this sad plan, did you all see this? The great contradiction that Hitler made? Here is this nutcase of a guy, creating and signing a pact, then contentedly telling himself and his countrymen that he was organising the new coming of the Aryans, where all the population in the near future would be blonde, blue-eyed and white… what about the Japanese? And the Italians? On one side, they were all Asians, and on the other, most of the Italians were dark. Therefore, how would Hitler's madness accomplish the integration of all white people?

However, with the Japanese bombing of Pearl Harbour on 7 December 1941, the Americans retaliated. In *Tora! Tora! Tora!*, we see the five generals who would take on the might and power of Emperor Hirohito, the definition of war in the Pacific. Pearl Harbour, with the USA at a later stage through the launching of the atomic bomb ((((The Little Boy)))) into Hiroshima and Nagasaki (((Hiroshima 06 Aug 1945 – Nagasaki 09 Aug 1945))), stabilised the war after the final implementation and backing of the Allies on 6 June 1944, led by General Eisenhower, who put once and for all an end to the ludicrous attacks.

For the next two months, as the Japanese became more daring, more confident in themselves with their imperial victories all over Asia and the Pacific, the Japanese targeted Australia.

Initially, as per history and Australia's geographical position, the Japanese tried to quietly start their invasion by basing themselves in the North, just as they had their base in China's Nanking. But the geography of the Australian land was so hard, dry and vast, the climate being terrible, with constant irrational attacks of elements, creating so much conflict with the harsh and extreme conditions of the weather. One moment they would face the harsh sun burning their skin, the next, the low extremities freezing, with the constant threat of cyclones and daily changes affecting their physical status. There was no place to hide personally or physically, without a working plan to base their own headquarters. Facing these facts, it remained an open and shut case without an optional status to help the Japanese methods of operation during the war, which were secrecy, hideouts, and sudden raids, but without the camouflage that so much covered and protected them. Thus, they decided to resort to another way of attacking Australia.

...Two minutes before ten o'clock on 19 February 1942, 188 bomb air carriers with 54 land-based carriers, organised by Admiral Chuchi Naggamo (1817), who was instrumental in the same plot of the air raid on Pearl Harbour, devised the same plot to attack Darwin, twice on the same day, killing 249 Allied servicemen and destroying the naval and shipping ports, the same way as they did at Pearl Harbour in 1941.

The Japanese were ruthless, fearless. Then more bombs whistled down on 3 March 1942, before crashing, as the Japanese continued their merciless accounts, now attacking Australia, and this time Western Australia's Broome, again killing innocent people going about their habitual normal days.

It was in this way that Elaine Bligh died during the Japanese bombing in Darwin, with George Robert Bligh becoming a widower, and his two kids, James and Anna, becoming motherless. Such devastation, it was a blow to the Bligh family.

Sara was now the *Weibliche Führungskraft blockieren*, as the block leader in the concentration camp. Nothing much had changed, but for her toilings, the Hitlers' Furies decided to give her another position. Sara Adams was suffering the loss of her husband, Renee Normand, who was also arrested and sent to Dachau, as Sara was sent, as we already know, to Ravensbrück Concentration Camp, where human suffering, ostracism, and cruelty awaited her even more.

In the beginning, as mentioned before, they tried to crack her up, but her faith in her religion defied their conventions. So they put her through hard and heavy duties: fetching and carrying frozen water, cleaning everything from the break of dawn until late at night. Sara was allowed some freedom, such as washing in the toilet blocks in freezing temperatures, and at times was allowed to have her own room, as selected by the more avaricious and contemptuous Hitlers' Furies, who had better plans for her in the near future. The room was completely devoid of anything, so she had to sleep on the cold, hard floor with her coat for cover. She wore flimsy, torn rags and, as usual, was barefoot. Outside, the weather was freezing, with temperatures reaching well below zero. Others died as they were required to work their "shifts" during the night; some would never return. Food was just cold, frozen water, with nothing more added, and sometimes the Furies would add salt and pepper "for the thorough good taste of it all," saying, "Hmmm, köstlich" ((hmmmm delicious)), laughing. Another Fury would ask, "Das gut?" ((Is it good?)) and the one sampling the cold, frozen water with salt and pepper would say, "Das wird mein Menu sein" ((this shall be my menu…)) and she would go on, laughingly reaching her own table and eating her hot food of schnitzel with mashed potatoes and veggies, with hot bread and coffee und Malke… saying, "Ich beneide dich… ihr Essen ist so besonders" ((I envy you, your food is so special…)). They would tuck into their hot food while Sara would be reduced to drinking her cold soup, water only.

One of them, who had recently returned from her short vacation where she spent "quality" time with her husband, none other than the fat, unbalanced SS Gestapo Third Reich Cara de Rhe, was known as either the Viper or the Whipping Witch. "Heil!" she cried… Sara looked at her as she towered over Sara, who was brushing the hard, cold stone floor…

"Stand up, du grubber wench…" first she would command in her rough, accented broken English, "Steh auf, du gaudete wench…" (((stand up, you grubbered wench…))) - "Du stinkst, du bist eine Hure – Jüdin frau!" she would scream whilst pressing her heavy shoes on the hands of Sara… (((you stink – you are a whore – Jewish wench.)))

Her blue eyes would chip as she became brazen with such heated seizures of her separation from her husband. It had only been two weeks… and not even he wanted to leave, or so she thought. Her hair was now darker, longer, but well kept and tidied in a bun at the back of her head. She wore her cap and her crisp, well-ironed uniform, with her polished black shoes to the hilt. She wanted to shine, but she was highly miserable, even with all the comfort surrounding her, with the whip in her hand. Warm and cosy, Cara felt alone, solo, and so angry and frustrated.

The other Fury came into the concentration quarters… her softer voice calmed Cara: "Weitergehen… warum schreist du? Werden Sie verrückt?" (((what is going on – why are you shouting – are you nuts?))) the other queried, approaching both of them. "Mädchen, was machst du? Warum trittst du ihr die Hände? Hör auf," she commanded, horrified. (((Girl, what are you doing – why are you stepping on her hands… STOP IT.)))

Cara wouldn't let it go. "Sie ist eine Hure – sie verdient die schlimmste Strafe." (((She's a whore; she deserves the worst punishment.)))

"Sie wurde genug bestraft, um losgelassen zu werden," (((she has been punished enough – LET GO))) the other Fury kept pulling her legs.

"Sie hat nicht den ganzen Tag gegessen…" the other Fury was really imploring Cara to let go.

"Sie kann sterben," Cara tearfully cried out… she was full of bitterness, sour emotion, and she was taking it out on the prisoners. Sara was her target.

"NEIN," voiced the other Fury harder, "als ihr Vorgesetzter – bestelle ich Ihnen zu gehen…"

(((NO – I am your superior, I ORDER you now))) the other Fury commanded. "JETZT" (((NOW.)))

Cara lifted her heavy boot angrily, seething. "Was ist sie für dich?" confronting the other Fury… asking… (((What is she to you?)))

"Ein menschliches Wesen – GESEN," sick of her replies, the other Fury retorted and ordered.

(((A human being – GO.)))

With that, Cara left, tears running down her cheeks… her whip remained on the table. Someone was going to suffer from this… Cara thought as she left the concentration quarters.

The Frau Olga, the Fury, spoke to Sara then, advising her to: "Bleib besser aus Schwierigkeiten heraus und bleibe noch außerhalb ihrer Sichtweite – gehen Sie auf ihr Zimmer, wird das Essen für Sie nehmen – NEIN – isst essen bitte."

Softly now, the Fury spoke gently to Sara: (((Stay out of trouble, Sara Fraulein, better still stay out of her sight))) – she waited for Sara to slowly get up, continuing: (((go to your room; we will take food to you)))

As Sara looked at her now, standing face to face, the Fury said: (((NO – it is real food.))) Sara looked at her… as her hands were bleeding, the Fury spoke in English: "You will heal, and so will your hands…" Here she handed over a white, clean towel and pointed to the bedroom… which Sara obediently went into. Outside, the snow fell endlessly… there was nothing in sight… one could not even see the line dividing earth and sky. The temperature was below zero… she heard the faint cry of someone coughing… someone begging for water or food. They were all starving, and it was so freezing cold… Sara's legs were completely purple, and her feet frostbitten… she felt old and was in a great deal of pain… From her dark, barren room, she sat down, shivering in the cold, and crying. Her hands were now swollen and painful – underneath the heavy coat, she was totally naked, and that was her only comfort. Nothing else… Sleepily, she contemplated the stark difference from her dark, dank room to the blinding, searing, stark white outside, wondering how it was to die just like this… and she fell asleep, seated on the cold, steely ground with no comfort at all.

The Fury, as promised, returned: "Wach auf – Fräulein, Ihr Essen ist hier – übersetzen," as she touched Sara's lifeless body. Horrified, she cried out, "Mein Gott, du brennst vor Fieber – MEIN GOTT, FRÄULEIN, du brennst VOR FIEBER, NEIN – OH NEIN – nicht noch ein Tod. HILFE – ich brauche HILFE!" She started to scream for help… no one was going to die in her care. The food tray was put aside. (((WAKE UP, FRAULEIN – your food is here – MY GOD – Fraulein, you are burning with fever – Oh no – not another death – HELP – I need help.)))

Sara was taken to the medical centre for observation and care… she was so lucky… but not that lucky.

Cara watched Sara being taken to the medical centre as the other Fury made a report about Sara's condition. Then Cara went to check the documents relating to Sara's health… it stated that Sara was in dire starvation, and in the extremities of freezing cold. She had also come down with the flu. When the other Fury entered the medical centre, they both stared hard at one another.

They all stood to attention. KOMMANDANT FURY FRAU Olga Schneider came into the medical centre.

"Sie, Sara, geht irgendwohin," she spoke to Cara directly. "Sara bleibt hier." (((She, Sara, is not going anywhere – she is staying here.)))

"Was auch immer, so lange ich nicht verantwortlich bin," roughly the Fury said… (((Whatever, so long as I am not responsible.)))

Cara smiled. The receptionist, who was typing another file, looked up at Cara. She knew Cara and also knew Frau Fury Olga.

"Ich habe eine zündende Idee," Cara cried out, laughingly, her red-painted lips opening into a large emphatic grin; the make-up on her face creasing. (((I have gotten a brilliant idea.)))

Fury Frau Olga replied, "Sie krank sind," disgusted. (((You are sick.)))

"Wir sind alle krank," she retorted. (((We are all sick.)))

Frau Olga seethed. Staring at Cara, she almost spat. "Du bist geistig krank – VERRÜCKT." (((You are mentally sick – insane.)))

They both stared at each other. Olga was a simple woman – she abhorred all of these terrible things… it gave her nightmares. Cara lowered her eyelids and looked at the receptionist, who pretended she was ignorant of everything.

"Sie geht ins Bordell, wo sie sich aufwärmen und ficken kann." She leaves for the brothel – she gets warmed and fucked there. Cara enjoyed this shocking treatment.

Calmly, Frau Fury Olga voiced: "Wenn sie lebt, um dorthin zu gehen," (((if she lives and if she doesn't die))) "und wenn sie nicht stirbt…"

Losing her patience with Cara, Frau Fury Olga stepped up: "LASSEN SIE HIER nichts zu tun." (((LEAVE… you have nothing to do here.)))

With that hateful look, Cara's blue eyes searched Olga's eyes. Olga's equally blue eyes were stormy and cold… Cara turned her back to Frau Olga, opening the door to the outside, slamming it noisily behind her.

Frau Olga thought about Cara and said: "Cara sollte in eine geisteskranke Anstalt eingewiesen werden," then addressed the receptionist. (((Cara should be committed into a mentally insane asylum.)))

"Sie hat hier nichts zu tun. Wenn Cara wieder auftaucht, rufen Sie mich sofort an…" warned Frau Fury Olga. (((She has nothing to do here – if Cara turns up again, call me immediately.)))

Frau Fury Olga's voice indicated complete command. With that, she walked out of the medical centre.

Sara was recovering slowly under the command of Hitler's Fury SS Third Reich Commandant Olga Schneider… on a daily basis, she would check Sara's health, continuing to pursue her wellbeing. Meanwhile, Cara took a few days off to visit her other Fury friends and her own husband in the Auschwitz Station Headquarters.

She was glad to be reunited with her husband, and that was when she continued with her cruel plan. In bed with her husband, she asked how the brothel business was going. He told her to worry less about their business… it was their account, and she should focus on being a faithful, loyal and disciplined Fury. She was being paid high Reichsmark, and her duties were officially there. She tried to convince her husband about the blonde Jewish girl, Sara Adams.

He turned his back on her, cozily and comfortably sneaking under the covers and slept, much to Cara's dismay. But Cara was not done yet.

The following day, as her husband was sent out to carry on other official duties, Cara ventured into the main station to speak to one of the SS officers. She told them about a blonde, blue-eyed Jewish girl who was always falling behind in her duties, always sick, and not cooperating as she was supposed to be the "Blockleiter," going on and on about one and the other.

"Wie wäre es mit Kommandant Frau Olga Schneider?" asked the officer in charge at the Auschwitz Station. "Kommandant Frau Olga Schneider – sie ist eine versierte Offizierin," the officer coldly announced, staring hard at Cara. "Was ist Sie auch tut Sie gegen Sara?" (((What about Sara / her superior, Commandant Frau Olga Schneider? She is a very accomplished officer.)))

"Deshalb bin ich hier…" Cara was desperate – apparently no one listened. (((That is why I am here.)))

"Dem Bericht zufolge war Sara fast tot," the officer continued without any feeling – his words were hard. (((According to the report – Sara was almost dead.)))

"NEIN – nein – nein – Sara fälscht nur – Du brauchst Frauen wie sie!" Cara cried out desperately. (((No – no – no… Sara was faking it.))) She desperately wanted the officer in front of her to listen. She wanted badly to punish Sara, but the officer remained unmoved in his position… hard, unmoving, with his jaws completely locked and his handsome face changing colour constantly. He remained cool, hard, and unconvinced; his light corn-blue eyes just shone. He was not going to do anything otherwise.

Then, changing her tactics, she softly said, "Wenn Sara sich erholt hat, kommt und holt sie ab." (((When Sara recovers, come and see me…)))

Now the officer got up, standing straight as any officer of Hitler's regime would have done. Coldly, he said, "Wann sie genesen ist – warum, du bist der einzige, der sich über Sara beschwert…" His eyes glowed as he stood there imperiously, not taking down her words. "…so lange ist Sara unter Kommandant Frau Olga Schneider – alles ist gut, wir verlassen uns stark auf ihre Berichte." He was busy, and Cara's going about filled him with more anxiety as he needed to complete all the reports. (((You're the only one complaining against Sara – so long as Sara is under Commandant Olga Schneider, we rely heavily on her reports.)))

Then the impossible happened…

The officer's eyes glowed in anger as he stood erect in front of Cara. Then he clicked his heels and cried out, "HEIL HITLER'S FURY – FRAU CARA DE RHE…" At that, he extended his arm in front of her, palm down… he was done with her, and for good.

Cara stayed at the Auschwitz Station for a few more days with her husband. Then she made a report that was signed by her husband.

Before leaving the station, she handed the letter to one of the officers going into the German Administration Office, commanding the officer through her husband's name to deliver it urgently and ensure it was executed immediately. Cara might only have been SS Third Reich Lieutenant de Rhe and Frau Olga Schneider her Kommandant, but her husband, a De Rhe, was the Gestapo posthumous Kommandant.

Two months later, Sara Adams, against everything, was sent to the cruel German concentration brothel assigned to her virtuoso duties – as the Germans' sex slave.

Cara demanded pictures of Sara's status… but Cara again would lose in this detrimental, poor judgement. By sending Sara to the German brothel, which was the heart and soul of the Germans inside their station, she was sending Sara into the arms of the Germans' soldiers – and specifically into her own husband's arms. Gestapo SS Third Reich Kommandant De Rhe was very much taken by Sara.

When Cara received the pictures and saw her own husband doing what he was meant to be doing to her as his wife…

The Allies were achieving victory all over the world. Meanwhile, a Portuguese consul in Bordeaux would stand up to help anyone wishing to escape Hitler's madness.

Aristides de Sousa Mendonça was the Portuguese Consul for Bordeaux, and he lived by his own stigma and philosophical motto: "I RATHER

STAND WITH GOD AGAINST MEN THAN STAND WITH MEN AGAINST GOD." Aristides de Sousa Mendes do Amaral e Abrantes, born on 19 July 1885 – 3 April 1954 (died at age 69), was GCC.OL. in France, Bordeaux.

Aristides and his family were punished by the Portuguese dictator António de Oliveira Salazar, who tried all avenues to keep Portugal and its provinces completely neutral. Aristides' actions went clearly against his policies, rules, and regulations. The government removed Aristides as Consul for Bordeaux, destituted him and his family, throwing them into the streets, and stripped him of all titles and high status previously awarded.

His family suffered penury and starvation, and for a while lived on the streets. By 1954, Aristides – well known as the "beautiful angel" – died penniless, but his children and others mounted a great supporting base, honouring him. He is now recognised worldwide and awarded great honours. (It is said that Aristides rescued thirty thousand innocent people – some hidden in monasteries, others in convents – whilst the original twelve thousand sailed through with visas, and then others followed suit. Aristides was even offered two bags of pure gold from one man who was more than happy to get his visa.)

Meanwhile, Sara continued her sad and sorry state of affairs. She did not get to Bordeaux in time to secure a visa to return anywhere.

Now in her new status, she worked in the brothel. Kommandant Frau Olga Schneider was still reeling and highly suspicious about the requisite form and the letter commanding Sara's transfer to the German brothel.

By then, while her inquiries were ongoing, the German concentration camp where she was, was receiving more Jewish prisoners – the influx was terrible, as on a daily basis prisoners, not necessarily Jews, were dying in terrible numbers, making it hard for Olga to take proper account of them.

As Cara continuously received updates about Sara, and now with Sara actually being De Rhe's Gestapo favourite "hure," Cara became even sicker, going totally insane. She now regarded Frau Olga as her enemy –

not a rival, nothing else – just her enemy, because Cara reasoned that if they had kept Sara in Ravensbrück, her man would have never met Sara.

One night, when Kommandant Frau Olga Schneider was leaving the administration station after sending updates and reports, Cara lay in waiting, pointed a gun, and shot Olga, who died immediately.

Sara felt a great relief when the British and American armies stormed the German station at Auschwitz, liberating and saving many. Unfortunately, not many survived, as many succumbed to all kinds of diseases – dysentery, influenza, syphilis, lice eating them alive.

NOTE: From 1942, German camps were heavily infected by epidemics. Sachsenhausen, the medical camp in Bergen-Belsen, conducted terrible experiments on prisoners. Meanwhile, in Auschwitz from 1942–1943, there were terrible cases of typhoid, typhus, tuberculosis, malaria, pellagra (causing skin discolouration due to niacin deficiency), severe nerve dysfunction, mental symptoms, dysentery, and diarrhoea. Due to lack of hygiene, fresh clothes, and sanitation, prisoners had their heads shaved, much to the delight of the Germans – both Furies and male officers. Camps were riddled with lice, fleas, and rats, which attacked the living daily.

Cara was morbidly in love with castrating the males after her sexual encounters with them. She was not called the Whipping Witch for nothing – for the male prisoners, she was well known as a hard and cruel dominatrix, who loved to crack her whip on the backs of male prisoners who served her well. Along with her came these Furies.

Many of her contemporaries, Hitler's Furies, bore the ugliest names in conviction of the German concentration camp, such as: Erna Petri, Pauline Kneisser, Irma Grease (the Beautiful Beast), Lisel Williams, Vera Wohlauf, Johanna Altvater ("Fraulein Hanna"), Josefina Block. Their sublime non-improvisation of what was "kinder, küche und kirche – children, kitchen and church" – yet these women killed children without batting an eyelid… such cohesive actions. May they roast in hell.

Sara was imprisoned when she could have easily left the borders and enjoyed freedom on the safe side of the ocean. But now, even after being rescued amidst that sexual debauchery, she was still being treated cruelly.

As Cara's records and the immigration officials had registered, Sara Adams was Jewish and also a Communist – a Red, as Sergeant Taylor stated to both George Bligh and Mrs Doris Collins, who signed the petition. Much to the amusement of Dr Jack Duncan, when he was still at Inverness Hospital, all were getting ready to go to Ashpark and greet Prime Minister Menzies for dinner. Regina Bligh, the all-altruistic elegant Regina Bligh, dazzled everyone in a beautiful red dress. Now that is one for the money, two for the show… and GO GO GO. It was a magnificent evening, except that Bennett got stabbed – revenge of the mighty Elizabeth Bligh. Then you wonder why Bennett hates the Blighs.

But Sara Adams, in being saved, spent the next few months in hospital relieving the pain and sorrow, the torture and torment inflicted upon her by the sadistic Furies…

These are the sad and horrible faces of these cruel women. Their names are here for one to remember their factual, terrible deeds, repeated by adding their names to the list of those who terrorised, terrified, mistreated, starved, raped, whipped, and shot at prisoners in Ravensbrück's German Concentration Camp. But make no mistake – they were everywhere, as the respected, dutiful wives of high-ranking Gestapo and SS Third Reich officers. The list of their subservient wives goes on, but for your perusal, these will suffice:

- Irma Grese – The Beautiful Beast
- Ilee Kash – The Real Face of Horror
- Louise Dang
- Marina Rashkova
- Hermine Braunsteiner
- Dorothea Binz
- Marina Mikhailovna Reskob
- Diego Braghi

- Nashda Popova
- Maria Mandel
- Herta Ehlert
- Juana Boorman
- Herta Bothe
- Ilse Koch – the Bitch of Buchenwald
- Sophia Scholt
- Helena Kramer
- Erna Petri
- Annaliese Kohlmann and Elisabeth Volkenrath

Later, when they were judged for the genocidal crimes they committed against children, the elderly, and other prisoners, Erna Petri coldly shot six innocent young boys.

Ilse Koch – the Bitch of Buchenwald – was born Margaret Ilse Kühler in Dresden, Germany, on 22 September 1906, and was the wife of Karl Otto Koch, commandant of the Nazi concentration camp Buchenwald-Majdanek. In 1947, Ilse became one of the first prominent Nazis tried by the US military. When asked why they committed such cruel and antagonistic acts, they all proudly responded that they did so for their Führer, whom they admired completely, blindly serving Hitler. Survivor accounts of Ilse's actions, known as the Bitch of Buchenwald, were terrifying and left no stone unturned. Most of these Hitler's followers were executed, and Ilse Koch died on 1 September 1967, leaving behind two children.

Justice for the victims of Hitler's concentration camps came later, but it was achieved.

"Mrs George Bligh," stated one of the maids, "there are two gentlemen asking to see you."

Sara was going through some of the household accounts, sitting behind her desk, momentarily enjoying the sweet fruits of the day. The music played softly and gently, like a breeze blowing through the lounge, lightly touching her cheeks. Her hair was now shorter. Increasingly, Sara was getting older, more lines creasing her face. Her blonde hair had turned grey, and she had gained considerable weight, now walking with difficulty.

Sara was swayed by the suave summer breeze – so calming, so peaceful. She replayed the song again. Today felt just like a summer's day. She couldn't stop replaying it over and over again. The interior of the house, intermingling with nature, lulled her into a soft but false sense of security – and why not? The day was perfect.

It was very gentle, sweet, and pleasant… except for the running about of her "cheeky monkeys," making noise. David was growing up fast; he could be naughty and cheeky, but he was her little boy, and he would always remain so in her heart. The breeze carried the gentle aroma of roses and lavender. Nothing could spoil her peaceful state.

Regina was now gone – dead by other means. Dickie Boy – it had been a long while since anyone had heard of him. Even mentioning his name now sent cold shivers down Sara's spine, exactly what she felt at that moment. Suddenly, the day seemed to turn dark…

Those two men came into the lounge where Sara was.

Sara was unmovable, speechless. The two men were dressed in suits and still wearing hats. They were gentle but tough-looking as they introduced themselves and flashed their Commonwealth Immigration badges.

"Mrs Sara Normand? Could you kindly follow us to the Immigration Office, please?"

The maids stood by, unsure what to do.

Another tragedy was about to befall the Blighs.

"Please, Mrs Normand, could you follow us?" the officer repeated, gently.

"Why? What is happening?"

"I am Mrs Sara Bligh," she firmly stated, rising from her desk and confronting the officers.

"We are from the Australian Immigration Office. You will find out soon what it is all about if you come with us," one of the officers explained.

Sara, wearing her light blue kimono, asked both of them to wait, offering tea. Within minutes, Sara joined the men.

From the Immigration Office, Sara was able to call George's office, and his secretary told him that Sara was on the line. She was desperate and breathless, her face showing the emotional stress she was enduring.

George knew something was wrong. It was the middle of the day; they usually did not call each other because their timetables were already full and their daily activities were normal, with no problems unless an emergency arose.

Listening to his wife's emotional voice, unable to understand her incoherent words, he hoped nothing terrible had happened to their son David. But it was the Immigration Office.

George felt dizzy for a moment. He prayed that no harm would come to his family.

It was only last month, when Jack was convicted on criminal charges; now it was his wife.

George covered his head with both hands, trying to make sense of it all. George's mind was racing, going through all the possibilities and impossibilities. The phone calls came through every fifteen minutes. By now, Sara was in a state of hysteria, begging to be released.

"What release?" he inquired, and asked to speak with whosoever was there besides Sara.

A lady with a smooth voice came through and told George, "Sir, this is the Australian Immigration. We have to see you."

"Why would you want to see me about this? You have already taken my wife. What has she done wrong now?" he said impatiently.

"Sir, it is best that you come over. We cannot speak and discuss anything over the phone. When you arrive, I shall be waiting for you. My name is Linda. Linda Gray. I shall be waiting for you." After this, she hung up.

"Your husband is on his way," Mrs Linda Gray softly and smoothly spoke to a very agitated Mrs George Bligh. She was offered tea.

"Everything is going to be fine. Nothing to worry about," the Immigration Authority lady spoke again. Or is it?

Ooo0ooo

Sir Richard Bennett could not rest ever when it became known to him that the Blighs were living it big time and in a very happy environment. The Blighs were sailing smoothly into a new era, a decade's beautiful atmosphere. It seemed that yesterday and the past were all gone… except dust. But even dust can tell something: keep digging, and the dirt will come out, in small little pieces in the beginning… but slowly and slowly, the pattern turns up, and towards the end of it, the puzzle is complete and done.

Sir Richard's hatred for the Blighs knew no bounds. If the Blighs thought that they had beaten him and were living the high life celebrating Sir Richard's demise, the Blighs were very much mistaken.

One could really imagine Sir Richard Bennett watching through his company's window and puffing his cigars. When one looks at him, one sees the satisfaction as he smiles to no one but himself. For some, his deluded ways in hurting the Blighs were endless.

Presently, as he oversaw everything with those sparkling blue eyes behind the near-sighted glasses, he could never negate the pleasure. For now, Sir Richard Bennett held all the aces.

But more was yet to come. He smiled happily, and now that lunch was being served, he tucked into it unceremoniously. Revenge is best served on a cold dish.

When Elizabeth Bligh met Sara on the ship bound for Sydney, Sara, with her blonde looks and veiled blue eyes, stood tall, walking with a direct purpose, neat and tidy. One could always be assured of her non-complacency, virtuous but confident personality.

She was easy to get along with. She performed her duties with great aplomb, and she was also dedicated to them.

But scratch that confident, bravado surface, and we find that Sara was anything but confident and self-assertive, a little more to it: damaged goods.

Growing up in Sydney's suburbs, little Bridget was like any other child: cute, maybe spoilt, and the youngest of the family.

Like anyone else, the family lived as most Australians did. But Bridget was also a Catholic, and her family followed their creed and faith as they saw fit. They were a most traditional and very tightly knit family.

Sundays, as per usual, were the family's traditional day. Little Bridget would look like a perfect Dresden doll, all dressed prim and proper, attending mass with her parents, brother David, and, of course, Aunt Peg. More often than not, Sundays were a family time together. After the services, they would have a picnic at the local park, enjoying the scenic views of Sydney Harbour Bridge, built in 1932, so-called the "Coathanger," which was an ecumenical feat as well as an engineering triumph, and soon to enjoy its fame as tourists would visit. As for Sara, her family was more than happy to take snaps, enjoy their feasts, and delight in the simplicity of life. They were, by far, simply family trysts, of course noting the disposition of the weather too. During winter, once mass was finished, the family would buy fish and chips and sit in front of the TV to watch whatever was on.

Aunt Peg, the sister of Sara's mother, would help Sara leave for other countries for further adventures, as Sara's mother wanted her to become a nun. Aunt Peg was always there for Sara, who was by now thought of as her daughter. Even with Sara's conversion to Judaism, Israel's main religion, Aunt Peg loved her dearly.

For beautiful Aunt Peg, Bridget, or Sara, no matter what her beloved niece would call herself, was her flesh and blood, the daughter she had always wanted, and she would do anything for her niece. Life also came with tragedies. As David passed away from the Spanish flu, Aunt Peg reflected on those days over a cup of tea and biscuits, when life was simple, loving, and tender. But unfortunately, all good things come to an end. First, her own parents passed. Then the First World War came. The Titanic sank. The Roaring Twenties arrived, even though money and jobs were tough to come by, with unemployment at its peak.

It was a great time. It brought Aunt Peg to tears, thinking about those great but simple days. Where had they all gone?

One moment, Aunt Peg remembered the beauty and the solid family foundation, with dinners at home and family outings. The next, the family was divided; one by one, they disappeared from their lives.

No one knew young Bridget's whereabouts. But at home, two deaths within a few months made her sister collapse in one of her own sad and terrible moments.

The trials and tribulations put her through a hard wringer. She was completely diminished, crestfallen, and completely out of this world. Sara's mother was bedridden. Aunt Peg treated and took great care of her sister. Every day, the two sisters prayed for the safekeeping and safe return of their "daughter."

Finally, their prayers were answered. They both received a letter telling them that Sara was alive and kicking, returning home to the family. She was good. She was a nurse. And guess what? She told her mother and her aunt that she was now a Jew. She had converted to Judaism, and her new name was Sara, after Aunt Peg wrote to her. Sara was happy to return home to both of them, to their old traditional ways, to sample the good food she had missed so much, and to her adored mother and Aunt Peg, who was now besieged by herself with the excellent news. Happy in her own modest, humble ways, they were a normal Australian family, now reduced to practically one quarter of what it used to be. Life was never going to be the same.

But Sara, now an adult, beautiful Jewish woman, thoroughly undermined her mother by marrying overseas and renouncing her Catholic faith.

No matter the love, tenderness, and absolute family closeness, Sara Adams was never going to be the same. She went out into the wide world with romantic dreams, wide-eyed, innocent, longing for adventure. Sara spoke different languages and knew her geography well. She was a widow. Things that happened within those years, the close, very close encounters of any kind, left her damaged. Sara was damaged goods.

One day, Sara would tell Aunt Peg the horrors she herself went through, the so confident, altruistic, strong, and defiant personality in thorough contrast with what she suffered at the hands of the Nazis, shocking anyone.

She was a POW in Ravensbrück, the largest women's concentration camp, built by Reichsführer SS Heinrich Luitpold Himmler (07.10.1900–23.05.1945), who held one of the highest positions during the Second World War as Chief of SS and a brilliant architect. He made Ravensbrück the German concentration camp for women (Frauenlager), located in a swamp near the village of Ravensbrück, 50 miles (80 km) north of Berlin. Originally, it was used to train 3,500 female SS members, who later became known as Hitler's Furies. As stated above, the women's Furies were female SS paramilitary corps members.

Young Sara's adventurous spirit came crashing, one day, God willingly, she would tell Aunt Peg this side of her sad, tortured story… and the babies wrenched from her and killed.

Starting the revolutions in 1936 resulted in the widespread implementation of anarchism into a more libertarian-socialist-ecumenical model, eliminating the social influence of the Catholic Church and spreading the revolution internationally to neighbouring regions.

The goals: elimination of all institutions of state power; more worker control of industrial production; establishment of a libertarian-socialist economy; elimination of social influence from the Catholic Church; and international spread of revolution to neighbouring regions.

Methods: workplace collectivisation and political assassination.

Resulting in suppression, or suppressed action, after a ten-month period.

As Sara explained to little Leah, treating Leah to her early recovery, she brought Leah Marilyn Monroe's posters, revealing thus far the strong women of history.

At the time, another lady was surging to overwhelming power, until then unseen: Evita Perón (07 May 1919–26 Jul 1952) and her Descamisados. She was loved by the people but resented by the upper crust of Argentina's military personnel. When Evita was diagnosed with cancer, the military painted on the walls: "VIVA LA CÁNCER." The world's history is filled with powerful women, and this one made her mark. She was a warrior, as our Sara Normand was.

After all, young Sara was like all of us… ladies now, but beforehand we were young, wide-eyed, highly spirited, daring, adventurous, romantic. Being a youngster, developing at a fast rate, a day could be just a day: slow and long, colder and darker; or faster, shorter, hotter, and lighter. Summer, winter, spring, or fall, time could be of the essence, and the clock kept on ticking. Music and its sounds, the fashion revelry of the time, all contributed to our own development, self-expansion. Like any young girl, in her mind she was taken to far exotic destinations. Sara departed, never thinking that her mother would be in spiritual and physical pain after the death of her brother and father. Like a ragdoll, Sara, now suffering from PTSD, had the flashes of those days firmly setting into her mind.

But the good Lord worked, and would always work, in mysterious circumstances. He, the Almighty, definitely had plans for Sara, George, and the remaining ones.

However, with all this in mind, the thing that no one saw coming was the love affair between Sara and George. From my point of view, I thought that the Lord really worked in mysterious ways: as one door closed, with the war finishing and Sara returning to a place to call home, and having her first husband dead, the world now opened wide, beckoning Sara to a new, entirely different social world, one that Sara was never used to.

To the horrible detriment of Elizabeth Bligh, everything that Sara did was clear and concise, even though there was plenty of obscurity surrounding it. This prompted Dr Jack Duncan to tell Sara in no uncertain terms that "I am running out of excuses and explanations on your behalf," as Elizabeth, through Mrs Doris Collins, saw Sara bathing in the nude, daytime, which, when confronted directly to the grand Elizabeth Bligh, Sara had a good excuse for every single instance. Elizabeth, who was looking for ways to get rid of Sara once and for all, became totally speechless.

"Find anything…," Elizabeth irritably said, and then paused. "To Regina… anything that will rid all of us of her presence." Elizabeth Bligh's directive was heard and obeyed.

As George once told Sara, "I don't know. My mother is a tough lady." To which Sara answered firmly but lovingly, "I am tougher." He shook his head. He could not, and would not, believe that Sara could be that tough, or even tougher than his own mother. There you have it: two Bligh women and one Camelot.

"Not by might, nor by power, but by my own spirit." Zechariah 4:6. An excellent omen, and such good will, much like Aristides Sousa Mendes' motto: "I'd rather stand with God and against mankind than stand with mankind against God."

This is also one reason I am bringing it up. What happens when two psychos face one another, clashing explosively? Like Sara and Regina did.

Per se, Richard James Bennett the Third, son of Regina Margaret Bligh and Sir Richard Bennett, aka Be.

I am thinking of a conspiracy of all sorts, or of any kind: homicide, murder, and mayhem. But never, ever suicide. The verdict will not come out until Book 3: *A Place to Call Home.*

Now Sara was the new mistress of Camelot's Kingdom. She had already changed the accounts for the kitchen's expenses. She also, like Elizabeth, would learn to deal with and grasp the hard ropes of living in Camelot's Kingdom. For Sara, it was a new beginning. Her life would be the same as previous ones, and as the manor, or the palace, suggests, the dramatic and the tragic duality would always play havoc in their lives.

Would Sara herself be able to sustain all of this, or whatever impediments were and are coming her way?

It had started. She was now being escorted out of Australia. More charges were expected to come by.

Sir Richard Bennett and his small family were rejoicing with him: Be, Sissi, and Robbie.

Note: *Holocaust* is derived from Greek. The Nazis used it as they would cremate the bodies of the dead, or maybe alive.

Chapter 11: Olivia Bligh: The Princess in the Ivory Tower

The Brackleys of England. Olivia. The Royal Bubble. The perfect English rose.

"The Church teaches that a baby is a gift of God. Don't judge, and you won't be judged," Aunt Peg said to her favourite niece, Sara Adams, or Bridget Adams, as Aunt Peg used to call her.

"With her," referring to Elizabeth Bligh, "is a family totally dominated by her iron will. Without her, just look at Olivia Bligh." As she stared adoringly at her husband but defyingly demanded questions of James' servitude to his grandmother, the grand matriarch Elizabeth Bligh, the Camelot's Kingdom Queen, Olivia found that Camelot was a place for broken dreams.

Miss Olivia Brackley. Mrs Olivia Bligh.

Dark-haired, with big dark, soulful, and gentle expressive eyes, perfect English complexion, dimples, a soft smile, soft-spoken, medium-built, medium-height. Little Livvy came into the Blighs' lives as the beautiful, wide-eyed, impressive bride-to-be. Plus more: she had the perfect catch, the tall, dark, and handsome cattle baron James Bligh, the highly privileged, wealthy heir to the Bligh dynasty. Australia beckoned her with exquisite invitations, breath taking views, and a new land.

Yes… she sighed dreamily… yes, as she cuckolded herself and smilingly fell asleep. Outside, the moon hovered, and the twinkling stars blinked on… yes, blink or blinkers on. That was Livvy, the Ivory Tower Princess.

She, who grew up in a forbidden, privileged, ostentatious world, with aristocratic wealth, abundance, and opulence. Princess little Livvy had the world at her feet, leading a precious, magical life. But as on those days, where scandals could break anything socially standing, her parents made sure that while she was such a doll-like princess, little Livvy lived in her own world of grown-ups, highly privy from the start, meaning she was being hidden from the horrific and cruel world outside.

Being the youngest, little Livvy's parents took higher control, doing everything to prevent their cute little daughter from encountering all the modern, perverse, and seedy sides of London's dark streets. Little Livvy was brought up in a tighter, anti-social but comfortable environment, which to a certain degree pleased her and her parents, shying away from the dangerous, poverty-stricken streets of London.

Even though modernisation came with taps where water could be switched on and off and hot water that could be used, things were still going pretty slowly. It had to be. They were also suffering and recovering from the Great Depression and the First and Second World Wars. Outside her windows, whilst Princess Livvy slept peacefully and heavenly, people were dying of practically everything, such as dire sickness and hunger. The place was assailed with so much tragedy: annoyances, deaths, daily robberies, prostitution, with young ones working for the mysterious dimber dambers at every single corner of the avenues. And if that wasn't bad enough, London was awakening to the late news of the Jack the Ripper murders.

Princess Little Livvy would be growing up with nannies and would also attend royal functions and events. They were all in the state and the day-to-day curriculum of a young aristocratic lady. She also had royal connections to the British Royal family.

Even though Little Livvy was a fine horseback rider, she would look beyond it, as presently the cars and the farthings replaced the more popular horse-driven carriages and horses. Petrol, being introduced since 1864, was now a regular thing in the market. Electricity was taking place instead of candles, and for many it was a real blessing, as the Great Fire of London still played havoc in their minds. The Londoners would do anything to avoid such a tragic incident.

Britain by then had been through a wringer of wars in and out of the United Kingdom.

When Queen Victoria ascended to the British throne on 20 June 1837, the American Civil War was already raging. The Grey Coats, or the Confederates, believed that the British would come to their aid due to the British aristocracy who were also rich in plantations of coffee and cotton. But that did not happen. However, during the years that young Little Livvy was born and married into the Bligh family, Britain had fought many battles in Africa: a couple of Boer Wars (First Boer War 1880–1881 and the Second Boer War 1899–1902), not to mention the Zulu War in 1879. During Queen Victoria's reign, London, as above mentioned, was besieged by fear due to the Jack the Ripper killings in 1888, but there was another murderous case implementing its ugly head in the USA, but the perpetrator, H. H. Holmes, was found.

Livvy's family was afraid for many other reasons. There was also the plague that in one blow killed so many of the Britons. This and many others were the major reasons why Livvy was being kept in her ivory tower, the royal bubble, when she was brought into this world.

Then the First World War raged from 1914–1918, under the rule of King George V, before the ascension to the throne of King George VI, the father of the present Queen Elizabeth II (not forgetting the abdication of King Edward VIII for his love of Mrs Wallis Simpson, an American divorcee). Mad and tyrant Hitler started the Second World War, with many being conscripted to fight for King and Country. The war raged.

Little Livvy grew up in a world of "make-believe": a world of her own family's richness making it a real bewitchment, classy, floral, elegant, growing into her the semblances of romance and high integrity. She was the damsel in distress. Sometimes her dreams or fantasies blurred so that she couldn't see the difference.

Naturally, during her young and adolescent years, Little Livvy would have been to great movie entertainment, with her going into her own dreamy world, seducing her fragile mind into a prelude of would-be knights in shining armour climbing the tallest mountains, fighting for the maiden in distress in any shape and form and no matter at what cost. That could have been the start of Little Livvy's dream of a knight in shining armour, Little Livvy being the maiden in distress, and the ideal man. Love is such sweet sorrow.

Those nightly events attending the royal balls along with her equally royal family, keeping them company, enjoying and sitting at the same table with the newly ascended to the royal British throne, awing and ahhhing at the over-the-top fashion pedigree, the scintillating crowns, the elegant structure, the over-organised simple ways of decorating a table from A to Z, then all the glimmer and glamour of those seductive jewelleries which one wears audaciously for the evenings.

Being aristocratic to one of the last lines of the British Empire (no, there are no titles), Livvy, her parents and family would always be invited and would attend the parties. Errr, events: high tea, balls, galas, theatres, garden parties, the royal cotillions. Nightclubs in bustling London or out of town were regarded as a big no.

Little Livvy's parents made sure that Little Livvy was ultra-comfortable and surrounded by the best of everything, but also kept an eye on Little Livvy, opposing and not allowing Little Livvy to go on far outings with her friends. At home she played canasta, was allowed to organise the simple affairs for eventful afternoons, card playing, bridge and so forth, with cocktails and nibbles being de rigueur before the actual family's dinner time, which would be composed of a far bigger group going through the preliminary protocols completely with refinement and great control. And you have guessed it, all dressed up in their own finery, from the gentlemen's tuxedos to the ladies' ball gowns, as it never ceased to stop being the fashion then and still is.

She also attended some outlandish barbecues, garden parties in a more suitable open environment, and the royal cotillion. Livvy loved everything in her grandiose stature, which meant that she could sit down, absorbing everything in her more natural views and opinions.

Maybe it was a prelude to her less fanfare life in the Aussie land, or a new way for her to try and live a new life. Being kept in a royal capsule all of her life, now out in the open, enjoying the freedom, was breathtakingly delicious. You are right, she was trying her life out.

Living and loving the freedom of coming and going, exchanging views and opinions with so many people that once in her lifetime she would meet, converse with, drink and be merry with, these were for her nubile character new and comforting. With that in mind, young Little Livvy had her own comeuppance. Sooner or later she would be married to someone, needing to create her own organisation properly, while at the moment things were being organised by her own family. Even her modiste per se came to her. Her ways of being trained and learning the social protocol were another beneficial prospect, but one questions what for when being as rich as she was, having assistants, maids, secretaries to attend to her and to make everything happen without any questions, without even bothering to lift a finger. But Little Livvy was far from being such a doll-like personality. Still kept from going out like any ordinary person for shopping, meeting with her friends on social outings, the world was such a terrible place that one felt really insecure. Certainly Little Livvy was as confident as she was, but apparently not. The newspapers always registered in black and white the latest robbery, murders, homicides, suicides. A day didn't go by without any of this bleak news, plus more. The fog that covered London made it highly dangerous and spooky, adding more to its freaking stories.

Times were hard. Everybody was walking on eggshells, caused by a number of elements, excluding kidnappings and rapes. Lacking in economy, people were desperate enough to do anything preposterous and silly, adding to the sick shadow of the madman Jack the Ripper and the Whitechapel murders, still hanging around with murders very much playing the essential fodder and the second fiddle in their minds. But life had to go on, returning slowly to the modern world. The Second World War left its terrible mark on everyone, especially in London where it was bombed, including Buckingham Palace. As if it was not enough from all the living nightmares, pestilence went into overdrive. Deaths, whether forcible or not, made their rounds. Livvy was kept sound and safe. When these desperate things happened, the family booked a passage to another exotic world or country for months where all would be kept securely tucked away, returning home to London when all was right. Again Livvy was kept happily with everything at her beck and call, and more so with the modiste again calling on young Livvy with rolls of materials to even more enchant the princess in the ivory tower, whose wide dark eyes would stare in total wonder at those beautiful silks, satins, velvets, embroidered materials with patterns and designs too, so Livvy could choose her own material and then fashion them into her own dresses. She was spoilt with different styles and models. Naturally, now when you think that one needs to dress up for breakfast, lunch, afternoon tea, dinner, and sometimes supper, one got the picture that the woman's wardrobe was never enough, not for the likes of Olivia. Counting on the grand ball gowns, evening wear, riding outfits, and a few notes only for winter, there was so much to cater for and to accomplish the look, in which lovely Livvy would also choose carefully the pearls to accomplish, de rigueur, her attire. She followed the trendy fashion of the more reliant times. The fashion, with embellishments to her coiffure, would be added with the help of the maids. The pearls were then a further statement of her wealth and pomposity.

Pearls started during the Roman Empire and during the reign of Queen Elizabeth I, who alone had a collection of pearls. Pearls have been linked to royalty, be it here in the European countries or any other countries, but more specifically in the Orient. The Chinese and Japanese Empresses always imbued their own hairdos with lavish and beautiful pearl and gold and white gold combs. The same could have been said of India and also Persia.

Moreover, in China back in the early twenties going to the fifties, the Chinese made a beautiful pomade of pearl cream that cost an arm and a leg. My mother was the happy recipient of this beautiful cream.

The jewellery made of pearls was beautifully crafted and came in rings, bracelets, earrings and necklaces, either to be sold separately or by the same token as a set. The trend went for ages and in some cultures continues with its legacy. Pearls are revered still, a statement at any time. Even Queen Mary, the grandmother of our present Queen, would wear layers and layers of this beautiful gem around her neck, them being her favourite. Queen Elizabeth the Queen Mother also wore her pearls on outings. But then again, they are also well entrenched in the likes of

Jacqueline Bouvier Kennedy, Rosemary Kennedy, Coco Chanel, and some of the "goddesses of the silver screen" in Hollywood wore them too.

Pearls gave the ladies a certain "hmmmph" and also pizzazz, for it did add that special touch.

But in a more traditional British or English way, a young lady could be called the "Sloane Ranger", where they would wear a grey or black skirt (or even Scottish skirt), any coloured or plain white shirt and a light cardigan. They would usually wear a string of pearls. Their hair would always be neat and tidy, they would at all times wear stockings, with either black or brown thick medium leather heels, what we also called the librarian look: young nannies, maids and many other things. At the time when Little Livvy was born, scores of the beautiful "Sloane Rangers" plagued the whole of Britain as the trend continued more often than not; the ladies also came from the rich and the aristocratic families. This alone completed the picture of a very young and respectable "Sloane Ranger."

In my family, my maternal grandmother wore pearl strands and rings all the time. She gifted me one of her many pearl bracelets when I was only six years old, and when my daughter had her debutante, she was the recipient of a beautiful manufactured but expensive set of those beautiful settings and sets.

Pearls. Pearls mean purity, loyalty, and to some extent even virginity. Its folklore is also connected to the sea and the ocean with many mermaids' tales.

Debutante balls in Macau ended in 1975. But each one received a set consisting of a necklace, earrings, ring and bracelet pearl setting. The set that I received then belongs to my daughter now. It is light, feminine and very much a trend to be followed, an affordable add-on to our more complicated living lifestyle. Of course it also helps where you buy them.

For our own Livvy, the Princess in the Ivory Tower, leading such a magical life, everything was connected, everything seemed such a fairy tale, and her dream of meeting her knight in shining armour was coming true. So it would have never come to us and hers as a surprise when young Livvy was introduced to the all-Australian Cattle Baron, tall, dark and handsome in some way, rugged and laid-back in the shape and form of James Bligh.

Oh my. At the cocktail welcoming party her family held in honour of this young, interesting man, the good news was that James was staying with Livvy's family, which stood in James's good stead for the next twelve months. He was on a year off, a period to roam around the world seeking more buyers for his cattle business. Therefore, expanding the Bligh business would very much take him over to Japan for the export of the Bligh beef industry, as in years to come Japan's beef would become the best and also the most expensive.

Presently, handsome James was happy being kept in the good company with her older and wiser brother William. Both of them were so good together: rugged and handsome, well dressed, with one being blonde and the other being dark, both were well presented. They both seemed to have so much in common. They'd spend time locked inside the study room or the mansion's library, analysing, checking on their business, debating, playing bridge. Both were pleasant, both were thrilled to pieces to be together. It looked like William had a new brother and vice versa.

Everything was normal back then in the English Estate of Livvy's. Now it was time for Livvy to be prepared for her coming of age.

James's parents and the mighty Blighs were invited. The delight showed in Elizabeth's face when the Debutante Ball was held in Buckingham Palace at the time, with the present King and Queen hosting it in an official attendance.

It was indeed a magical dream come true, and not even Walt Disney could have written a better fairy tale. Actually not many authors could have written anything akin to it. But for Livvy, she could hardly believe in her own good luck and fortune.

It was going to be a most exciting evening. The Blighs turned up in full swing, the Camelot's Kingdom of Inverness "Queen" Elizabeth Bligh, observing the beautiful wide-eyed, dimple-smiling Olivia. Everything went perfectly. It was an awesome night.

Elizabeth Bligh was very much taken by Little Livvy. Something about the fragility of Olivia as she spoke intelligently, showing that she was not only a pretty face, sweetly, gently and softly. Olivia had style and followed the more trendy fashion of yesterday's. Olivia was also obedient, shy and also very traditional, cute and always ready to smile. Elizabeth observed and took notes. But most of all, Olivia could also be reserved. Olivia was exactly what Elizabeth Bligh wanted. But, being then and still Elizabeth Bligh, she wanted more "intelligence" on Little Livvy's life and per se revealing any secrets that would never ever cause any scandals to the more updated and modern Blighs of Australia. Elizabeth Bligh took no chances, but soon she would learn another tough lesson.

Elizabeth couldn't stand the chance of being done by, still suffering from the shocks which led to her traumas and suspicious nature due to her own ex. Presently with James, who was also gay intermittently, she took no chances, with Livvy being so demure, but looks could be very deceiving. Predictably, Elizabeth Bligh saw in Livvy her own self, where she would duly realise that Livvy mirrored herself, and therefore they were in the same dilemma.

At the time, so assured of her own comeuppance, it never occurred to Elizabeth that if Livvy ever got the goods about the Blighs' secret, what profound effect would actually deeply affect Livvy and the Bligh family. But then again, knowing how Elizabeth's manipulative personality was, by now knitting another net but full of holes, so that Little Livvy would fall into it, one would think that once Livvy was married to James, then a Bligh, living in Australia alone, then who would she turn to or would help her? Nice plan.

Elizabeth Bligh never thought about the safety of someone else's daughter, only the Blighs' reputation, covering the truth by hiding the huge scandal at all cost. As Livvy would have said, "You would do everything for the Blighs," with her voice rising in anger, trembling with the deceit she encountered.

This was the day Little Livvy was going to shine. As Elizabeth would be Livvy's next grandmother-in-law, Elizabeth brought with her the set of jewellery for her granddaughter-in-law, and tonight at the deb, her grandson would propose to Little Livvy. The beautiful intricate light blue box bearing the B's insignia was really a beautiful token, a rightful gift for a bride-to-be. Once opened, it would reveal an antique set consisting of white gold, sapphire, diamond earrings, bracelet, necklace with the engagement ring, which would be the start of everything that Little Livvy wanted and what exactly Elizabeth Bligh of the Camelot's Kingdom mostly wanted and desired. It would serve to be Little Livvy's new beginning and a new life.

For the time being and Livvy's coming of age, she has already earned the first good things rewarding, and in the near future, if and when Little Livvy would know how to conduct herself as a Bligh. And by now Elizabeth was busy fitting into her own ball gown. By the time she finished, she summoned her grandson James and gave him the ring in the small box as mentioned above. It was his engagement, and the extra set was the Blighs' engagement present for the new bride. It was a Bligh heirloom, priceless.

"No one would deny the beauty of this..." She looked deeply into her own grandson's eyes.

"And no one needs to know, but what bride would not be dazzled by this set of gems?"

The coach arrived. The Blighs went into theirs with a sullen and long-faced James. Next to him, brimming with excitement, was young adventurous Anna, ready to take notes for her novels, and the Bligh family.

Anna was full of excitement. She was cooing, giggling, smiling and so happy. She looked a delight, dressed in that lavender gown in conjunction with the white pearls adorning her long hair and the white glimmering wrapper that was hugging her. George sat opposite his own daughter and really marvelled at the way Anna's facial expressions changed remarkably all the time as she chirped and chimed about attending the Debutante Ball at the Buckingham Palace, enjoying firsthand the meeting with the royals, curtseying in front of the King and the Queen of England.

George as usual looked his best, all dressed up in his black tuxedo, white starched shirt, with a carnation on his lapel and still with his tall hat in his hand. As usual he looked really suave, somewhat a real gentleman. His hair was swept to the back and his face did not show one hint of his ageing.

Opposite him sat his stern mother, the beautiful but distant, however well ornate, Elizabeth Bligh. Dressed in a beautiful light blue ball gown, long with a straight skirt, its colour varied from the top being light blue and the skirt a shade of darker blue. She had the stole around herself. The nights in London could be cold. She wore her hair and ornamented it with diamond combs. Elizabeth looked like a million dollars.

Of course, James Bligh. Tall, dark and handsome, towering over his grandmother and his little sister. He indeed looked hip, a real dish, dapper. His dark wavy hair glinted under the harsh chandeliers' lights. Dressed up in the same fashioned tuxedo with George's being black, James's being blue-grey in colour, and the blue rose on his lapel said everything.

Handsome, hip and so stylish, his good looks were the dream of every single female, and young Livvy thought that she was the luckiest girl alive.

All the Blighs were now in their horse-drawn carriage being driven through the loud and noisy London streets, with Anna thinking that she was going to a Cinderella ball. Everything was so neat, mesmerisingly smashing, with the males smokingly handsome, whilst the Blighs were overwhelmingly seduced by all the glitterati and the glamour enveloping all of them and whomsoever was coming to the same venue.

As the night approached, London turned on her best, and the Blighs were totally mesmerised, overwhelmed by everything. There was no need to speak or talk. It was climactic to say the least. More carriages were arriving; the elite, the VIPs, the officials privileged enough to share a night like this, of who was who, were alighting from them, and their high status was there as plain as delight, so the Blighs were testimony to it all. It was an affair that was overwhelming, but one needed to blink a couple of times so that they knew that what they were seeing was not someone's surmises of blanked blubber. These were the real diamonds, exquisite and highly ostentatious. Each one boasted the best in everything. If there was a competition, no one knew who would be the winner.

Outside Buckingham Palace was one sighting surrounding the inviting and forbidden Palace, but inside it paled in great comparison with what was the immense luxury facing them all: what with the golden painted intricate furniture, the mirrors assembling on both sides, the statues, the jewellery encrusted, the huge paintings of portraits telling a different story of time, place, imposing their beauty and contrasts on the guests, making the guests gasp for the great opulent reception standing before them. All the intricacies, la belle épitome, the royal grandeur, conveying on them all. The waiters wore their puffing white wigs, red coats with their golden buttons shimmering, the white pantyhose and those black shoes, swerving around with the trays with all the drinking crystals thereof. Before the guests were shown into the titillating dining room, splendoured, showing off the wealth that could only come with royalty, the guests were more than happy, joshing, talking, exchanging everything on the evening, acquiring the best places in the house, adding to more fascination. Surrealism was setting in as they were all walking on cloud nine. Thank God the Blighs were living for the moment, as this would have been the last time anyone would attend a Royal Debutante. Then for their appraisal, the King and his beautiful Queen Consort arrived solemnly, greeting all, and all curtseying to them both.

Anna was grinning from ear to ear, cooing, being completely dazzled by the whole radiant environment, the so-called sophisticated atmosphere. As a woman checking on the British guys whom she thought highly proper, well composed and so arrogantly handsome in their suits and demeanour, they were breaking her heart, much to the amusement of grand Elizabeth Bligh, hoping for the second time that now her granddaughter would be the one to walk down the aisle with a prominent gentleman with ties to the royalty. She thought of Caro, then of Little

Lizzie. With Caro, her debutante ball was a failure. With Little Lizzie, Elizabeth choked on her own tears. Where could Little Lizzie be now?

Olivia looked like a vision, dressed up in her cool flowing white pristine debutante dress. She wore Juliet's embroidered cap on her head, as her dark long curly hair swirled down her back. The soft and gentle white dress changed the colours from gold to silver as she walked up the stage glowing under the strong chandeliers' lights, which seemed to be dancing along with Olivia, bringing on the sparkling diamonds attached to her cap. The dress looked like it flowed gently and softly, had long sleeves ending with the satiny white half-heel shoes with a bow, wearing white gloves, and the pearl-embroidered white sac, thus completing the whole wardrobe. The lady herself was happily gliding down with her all-too-willing smile. Her eyes, now lightly painted with dark long strokes, showed the delight in them. Her beautiful English rose complexion was now lightly enhanced by a shade of pink, her lips were painted hot pink, shimmering, adding more beauty under the strong lights of the chandeliers as all eyes from the guests followed Little Livvy as she glowed in great anticipation. Sadly though, beautiful young Little Livvy did not get the title of Debutante of the Year, but her Debutante night excelled, much to the pride of her own family and the Blighs. Elizabeth watched in awe and was happy she arranged a good marriage.

When her name was called and she exaltedly was introduced to the King and the Queen Consort, Little Livvy curtsied to both of them, as someone introduced her as their protégée, now going to the arms of her new beau James Bligh, now in tow. Remarkably, it was an unforgettable evening. She was now engaged to the most eligible handsome Apollo man, and he was all the way from Australia. She fell head over heels in love with James, lock, stock and barrel.

The following day her photo was in the newspapers singing Livvy's praises of a perfect debutante lady, promoting by announcing her official engagement, which would happen within six months.

Livvy gushed, chided with little cries, chuffed at everything. The gifts kept on coming, but when she saw the Blighs' gift, it took her breath. What a beautiful and delightful gift, with James pointing out that it was the Bligh heirloom. Then she glanced at the diamond sapphire ring now on her left finger of her left hand. She sighed. She now had everything, and her wedding date couldn't come quick enough.

As it was, it did. It took its time, but finally now she was the newcomer and also Mrs James Bligh. What's more, she also had a terrific sister-in-law and a good father-in-law. Now they were going home to sunny and loving Australia. Little Livvy could not wait to start afresh her new life in Camelot's Kingdom. Such enthusiasm. Elizabeth watched how flustered and excited Little Livvy was, reminding Elizabeth of her own dire circumstances, with Livvy arduously repeating and emphasising how her handsome beau bent on one knee and asked her to marry him. Livvy thought of naught except the all remarkable things that would happen, as they both would chivalrously do and go through, with James whisking her away to the land of their own dreams, which now was happening as she languorously stretched herself like the cat who got the cream, with her husband by her side, thus completing their dreams as husband and wife, happily ever after. You see, they have just consummated their passion.

The flashes came to her mind intermittently, remembering everything that happened in that colossal evening at Buckingham Palace. The diamond sapphire ring sparkling now on the left hand, Elizabeth, George and Anna beamed with excitement, joining James and Livvy in their cruising boat. Little Livvy was completely ecstatically elated, anxiously. She couldn't stop chiming about, young, sweet, a real tribute to her both parents when they joined her along with her older brother William, with James smiling forcibly with his eyes, constantly seeking someone else, thoughts somewhere else. His eyes and William's crisscrossed, meeting for a dire but bitter moment. William's eyes were moist.

Little Livvy was the young female version of her older brother William, reminding James of William and the hard and miserable moments of life. One moment she was reaching the heights. Now she was hitting her lowest ebb. Her new husband was cold and distant. What went wrong?

On the day that James and Livvy were preparing to move out of Camelot to reside in the Sydney CBD, alone in their bedroom, husband and wife faced one another. “You are sure about this?” asks Livvy. James nodded smilingly as he completed his wardrobe.

“Let’s not get cold feet about this...” replied James as he tries to right his tie.

While he completes his wardrobe and the maids take the luggage down to the car, Little Livvy goes to the lounge.

“I’ve come to say goodbye.” As Little Livvy knocks at the lounge’s door and says it to Elizabeth Bligh drily and without a single emotion. She looked so serious.

“I’d hoped you would.” Elizabeth tentatively responds, lifting her head to face Livvy.

“You do understand why we’re leaving?” Emotionless Livvy asks again.

“Because you’d find living with me intolerable.” Elizabeth replies, stating it firmly and looking back at Livvy. It was such a downturn, such sadness and sorrow.

“It is what it is,” said young and innocent Livvy, but firmly. The two women were really highly outstanding in their efforts as they both were fighting an inward war. “I am what I am.”

Livvy takes a breather and continues, “and you are not able to be what you are.” She reaffirms what she is stating. Both ladies are firm in their opinions of each other.

“I would like my great-grandchild to be born here.” It was a statement as Elizabeth confirmed her own status.

“Then we would return for that.” Livvy replies, agreeing to Elizabeth’s proposal.

“Thank you. I hope one day things are different,” concludes Elizabeth, relieved. One never knew Livvy’s next movement.

“I see so much of myself in you...” Elizabeth completely admits herself to Little Livvy.

Livvy helps Elizabeth to be lifted from the sofa and intertwines their arms together. Both were smiling.

"So do I." The thought really frightens Livvy as she looks at Elizabeth. Now she is doubtful. The black colour of her bitter eyes lifts and softens, and her mouth opens in a smile.

"I thought I'd married James to someone too weak to be a threat..." She pauses a bit to catch a breath, then walks out hand in hand with Livvy and continues, "but I'd married James to someone with strength that yet may save him." Elizabeth finally admits and concedes.

Elizabeth wanted her ways and done perfectly. Nothing was going to spoil her grandson's day, nor the Blighs' one too during their stay in London.

She kept a tight eye on her wayward grandson, continually watching his demeanour, his behaviour to the point that she actually rented a mansion until the wedding took place. She trusted her grandson to do whatever she, Elizabeth, wanted and directed. It was her way, and she wanted this way.

For young Livvy, things could not go fast enough. The wedding was traditional in every single way. Nothing was spared, commencing with the beautiful wedding white gown, the Juliet headpiece, the gloves, the embroidered shoes, the flowers, but to complete the high status, the glittering tiara, an heirloom not borrowed, but it would be William's wife who would then grace it later on when she ascended to their own throne. It was so beautiful, so abundant, so elaborate what was bestowed on young Little Livvy. Something blue was the bouquet for her flower arrangement, something borrowed was the diamond bracelet that she was adorning with a small leaf of their own institution, something new were her wedding gown, the Juliet's cap, gloves and the shoes. Little Livvy remained faithful to that memory. Traditionally her wedding flowers were gladiolas, proving thus her virginity.

Surreal, going through her wedding gifts after going through her engagement gifts. She almost fainted. For many years she was a wallflower. Now she was walking tall as a sunflower.

Now, on her way to sunny Australia, she was the perfect Australian to name the Common-Wealth, the "Epacris impressa", being the flower officially proclaimed as the Australian State Flower Emblem. That was exactly what our own Little Livvy was. However, like the flower, Little Livvy was the newcomer, but unlike the flower which was proclaimed, Little Livvy needed to fight for her sanity and place. Mrs James Bligh. Elation was the keyword. Excited, radiant and an exuberant bride. Elizabeth was growing tired and listless. Australia was calling them home where she could remain the Queen of her own kingdom. All of this good news and such affabilities were driving her to distraction. Elizabeth knew that more was yet to come. She predicted.

It was too much of a good thing for obvious reasons. She started to resent this kind of intrusion. The Blighs would be safe and well protected behind the strong and steel walls of Camelot Kingdom's tough and hard gates. But it was making her suffer from some kind of complexity. With so much ongoing, Elizabeth, the dynamic lady, was now suffering from a complex traumatic exclusion. Detrimentally, she felt not at ease. She wanted to be at her place to call home where again she could rule the roost and also be at her best, comfortably and free to live their own lives. Elizabeth observed. Now she was talking free, carefree, enthusiastic, revelling in her own new role as the new Mrs B. Olivia Bligh was happiness intended, but James now was another man. Her new golden gilded cage was firmly imbued in the heavy clinking, noisy, hard gates. Little Livvy, the Ivory Tower Princess's new residence, Camelot's Kingdom, was everything that she pictured, well endowed with Australia's breathtaking sunrises, sunsets, rugged cattle stock, kerkscham, as the Scots named it. Even though Livvy thought that they were away from the celebratory centres, shopping district, she predicted that unlike in England, all these extra trips into the city would come at a time when she mostly needed. Momentarily Livvy had shivers running down her spine. She closed her eyes and made countless wishes.

But (where for a time she would be confined and believing that she was the reason for her husband's freezing feelings), but the moment she realised that she was a prisoner, the dread made her hate living inside Camelot. Like her new grandmother-in-law, the formidable Elizabeth, young Livvy would think in the same line, both being so deceived and lied to. As both women were made of different stock, the patina was long and arduous in the same sphere. She was Mrs James Bligh, the new heiress to the Blighs' Dynasty. She felt sick. This was the real kosher. The patina was being repeated. Livvy was apprehensively disappointed. Again it was a woke, nonetheless.

The new beginnings at the Camelot's Kingdom was not heralding good.

With the social distancing of her own husband James Bligh, refuting all of her welcoming and carnal joy, constantly irritated, spoiling everything for her, as Livvy was also getting acquainted to the new surroundings at Camelot's Kingdom, along with her came the fluttering of her stomach. She thought it was her nerves, feeling sick, nauseated, longing for her parents in a new foreign country.

At home in Camelot, Elizabeth Bligh threw a dinner party to welcome her new granddaughter-in-law, so enthused, glowing, so chuffed, elated, finally a breath of fresh air and a decent young lady of upper-crust English society, living in the Camelot's Kingdom of broken dreams, so rightfully named. For once, her wayward grandson James did the correct thing. Now Elizabeth took a breather. The Blighs' good name was saved for now.

Livvy and Anna were two close friends, spending time shopping, with the Blighs always finding themselves with the goodwill and lots of good belly laughter, with young Anna confiding in Livvy her aspirations in one day becoming a famous writer, whilst living it up by sightseeing and visiting the whole city of London, with Livvy, a real dreamer, a dreamer could get together as Anna, being a writer, would be able to embellish anything to Anna's favour. Gladly, Livvy loved her new sister-in-law who was unlike her in so many ways, yet so much like her in so many ways, impervious to everything. After all, both of them were just like any other girls: young, affable, dreamy, extravagant, privileged, loud and petulant. They were both two sunflowers, elementary, physically and socially. But Anna was still to go through her deb.

But now herewith in the Camelot's Kingdom, a monstrously gigantic place, for some it could have been the Shangri-La, the Xanadu. Livvy felt alone and lonely. Little Livvy now exaggeratedly ignored the raw beauty of Camelot's Kingdom. Nothing good could come from all of these extravagant, wide and multitude of layers and layers of whatever was covering it. Later she would come to learn that it was called Camelot of Broken Dreams. So true. It was breaking her dreams, curtailing her more detailed wishes. Camelot was set in the middle of nowhere, so remote, alone, rooted in its deep deadset ways. She saw it for what it was now: stern, hard, impetuously dire, cold, steely, frozen in its time. But at the time, she marvelled at the building rising imperiously, being majestically magnetic and inviting, but now she felt something akin to the long-haired maiden that was kept a prisoner in the high tower, always watching out into the wide world, whilst the outsiders, the onlookers, passers-by, watched in awe, looking, wondering what it would be like living inside the Camelot's Kingdom of broken dreams, shades, dark secrets and all. For them, the outsiders, there would not be a woke, not even the kosher that usually came from the patina that one is used to precurse.

Camelot's well-structured building seemed to be unique, overtaking all of Inverness.

Spotted in the middle of rolling hills, tall trees, the grass and the immense but beautiful foliage where one could only see it up close and on a personal level, an ideal for anyone to feast their eyes on the kingdom. Livvy was all too happy to call it her new place to call home, to a degree. The maids thought of Livvy's predominant cut-glass English accent really "perfumed" with lavender and laces, ohhh, roses. The maids thought that their new mistress was nice and elegant. Livvy's life would be normal, but James's lovemaking remained loveless, lacking in passion, as if he was only conducting a major duty when he made love to her. Once finished, he would go off to sleep or not sleep at all. More often than ever, he'd fill his crystal with brandy, comfortably sitting in the big armchair, watching the night turning into day, deeply into his own thoughts, seemingly living a life of regrets, looking so downtrodden, so out of it. What could be plaguing him? James was colic.

Poor Little Livvy. She longed for fire, passion, animal lust, hard love with soft love intermingled into one. No pulling back, imagining herself tearing to shreds the clothes of her lovers and expecting the same. She fantasised about Harry Poulson's good looks, his steely hard body with the strong muscled arms encircling her, pinning her down under his hard body, making rough passionate love.

Her sexual feelings were shameless. These were in the early stages of Livvy finding out that James was homosexual and then Harry Poulson was too.

Her memories were all fogged. Now she was begging the fulfilment of the unbridled passion, desire, fire, raw.

The trip over from London to Sydney was marred by so much pain, a disastrous influx of so many disappointments. Since that trip, living with James was a living nightmare.

James was the razor blades snapping at her, and on the night that they had a guest in Sister Sara Adams, who James forbade her to speak or ask the lady any questions, with Olivia being really speechless, dumbfounded, but more to it, completely flabbergasted about the whole situation. James, did he perchance have two personalities, like his Aunty Reggie? She certainly had two personalities: Dr Jekyll and Sister Hyde, or was it Aunty Hyde?

Whatever happened to that so gregarious, so "joie de vivre", outgoing, social man who Livvy thought of James as a real "alpha" male, happy to sing a few notes? Anna, who was having trouble with Elizabeth with her treatment of Sara, now Anna. Her father-in-law George seemed to be absent of late when she heard him arguing with her grandmother-in-law. Anna was nowhere to be seen. Livvy would ride her horse early in the morning. But the days grew dreary, longer and sadder. There was no place to go and to escape.

She could feel it as tense as anything. The dining room could be so eerily freezing, cold, and one could cut it with a knife, the heavy tension, the thorough oppression. They had their hot debates, terrible discussions, and nothing was in the correct and tall order. Livvy was beginning to confirm about too many secrets to hide, and it was hardly a palace. But if it was not a palace, then what would it be?

A place so imbued in tragedy, disappointments, darkness, and Livvy was no pushover. The walls had ears.

Over time, as everybody knew it, James came to stay with them, and the rest is just plain history, or is it?

While he stayed with her family, Little Livvy was still attending the all-privy and expensive school where at the time she was also boarding. She has never had any problems being at school, but unlike James, she loved returning home to where she, like anyone else, would call a place to call home. She could then let her long dark tresses free and to put her feet high, manner of speaking, but this was no boarding school.

She felt so lonely, alone and empty.

Ironically, Nat King Cole's song came through the radio in the background with the romantic words sounding like "When I fall in love, it will be forever..." Right then and there, his smooth voice softly caressing the words as he kept on spelling and vowing about a love that would be forever being played. She swayed to the beautiful lyrics of the song. Now his voice became stronger and raw-timbred as the everlasting Nat King Cole sounded as gentle as a crooner should, but if there was such a beautiful but simple love, why in love it proved to be so complicated, asphyxiating, complex, distracting, morbid. Livvy felt sick.

The maid brought her breakfast and had already run the bath for her. The dress was chosen and the shoes all set up for her daily wear. The maids grew to like Livvy, and now they knew about her daily habits. Where on earth is James? James was naught, nowhere to be seen, and she refused the food. She didn't have any appetite.

She was bedridden with faint and dizzy spells. Then came that fatal day at the bazaar. She was expecting. Being confined meant that she had to stay home to the dreaded palace of broken dreams. Now it so happened that Elizabeth Bligh was being really romantic and wanted to find a good marriageable gentleman to her youngest granddaughter, the beautiful Anna Bligh, actually Livvy's sister-in-law. Or was it the Swansons?

Livvy observed Elizabeth, then came with the conclusion that Elizabeth would always be herself: cunning, crafty, wily, thinking about another society's wedding where the elite joined and gathered. Livvy stared at herself in the mirror. She was still sickeningly pale.

The Swansons were good friends of the Blighs' family. The elderly political Sir Henry Swanson was prone to all kinds of major scandals, a seeker of illicit sex. His name was always in the newspapers, much to the delight of Sir Richard Bennett, but shame on his own family. The Swansons came to stay for a weekend. Livvy was confined to her own bedroom. To her deep desolation, the real deal was confirmed when she saw the picture that told her everything. It almost totally derailed her, totally her dreams and convictions. My God, they were sinful, evil monsters. But neither George nor Anna knew about it.

"You are a Bligh now. Continue to be the happy bride." Livvy looked at her grandmother-in-law and almost spat at Elizabeth.

"You knew it all along, and you allowed me to marry him. How can you be so cold and distant to the point of agreeing something like that?" She audaciously ventured her own frustrations, anger and disappointment on Elizabeth.

"You will be totally rewarded." Elizabeth maintained her stance but now regarded Livvy coldly.

"You will be a Bligh. You will keep up with appearances as the young and beautiful Mrs James Bligh." Elizabeth stated calmly but also refusing to move. After all, she was Elizabeth Bligh, and what may come, she was still the head and reigned the Queen of Camelot. Therefore, Livvy would need to bow to her wishes. "I know it is too hard to ask, but consider all the privileges, the status..." she said.

"Oh, I don't believe you. I really don't believe you." Awww, the pain, the unreasoning, the desperation. She cried out, totally baffled, her voice shaking. The pain. Livvy, to Elizabeth's surprise, was a strong, thoroughly independent lady, with or without her parents, whether it'd be here or over there. It did not make any difference.

The news of her pregnancy prevailed. It was a Bligh. Now they had another heir to their dynasty. She cursed Elizabeth Bligh with all of her being. She looked at the mirror. The person in there looked back at her again. It was by now two different people. Then she realised she was the bird kept in the 24ct golden gilded cage. She screamed, then she fainted.

No one saw it coming, much less Elizabeth Bligh.

Livvy, it turned out to be, had an acid tongue. But more to it, she could ever be aggressive, and all that suppressed anger was coming to the fore. She was on the warpath.

And the fire was coming all the way from her nostrils and both ears. The war was raging on and on. Camelot Kingdom was burning, burning.

Livvy confronted Elizabeth in the lounge room for the umpteenth time. All was quiet. Too quiet. Still.

Elizabeth Bligh knew beforehand what Livvy was going to say. Livvy's portent demeanour spelt it right out.

"I can live with my conscience," Livvy stated crudely. "But can you?"

"You knew it all along..." Livvy bitterly accused Elizabeth. "And you let it all happen, taking me, a lamb, to be slaughtered." Livvy's voice was hard but shaky, trembling. She said, "I will never forgive you, never." Then she burst out into tears, walking away from the room.

Livvy refused to have anything to do with Elizabeth. She kept herself locked inside her bedroom, really feeling sorry for herself, crying buckets before she went to sleep and looking outside her window. For Livvy, looking out, then it hit her. This dreamy place was the Camelot of broken dreams. Now she was totally desolated, even desperate, disoriented, crumbled, with thoroughly shameful secrets. What more secrets could there be revealed? What was the position and status of Elizabeth Bligh in all of these: fake, two-faced, fraud? It was murderous.

More so, whatever happened to Little Lizzie? Why? Why was she the chosen one, and why? What was she supposed to be done, have done, do and shall be doing?

Livvy found out that George only had knowledge of it when he was being blackmailed. The whole world now was dark, black and worrisome. Sadly, Little Livvy now sank into a deep terrible depression, and apart from the baby who she gave birth to, she lived for nothing.

Days turned into nights, only finding comfort when she was alone. She was not going home. She was trying hard to find the solution to her own problem: stay there, bringing up her own baby. She would have been so happy, as her own parents were also thrilled to pieces with her pregnancy. They too were going to be grandparents. She cried in silence. She fought her own depression. She stopped eating. She stopped drinking any beverages, any water. She only wanted to be alone. She only wanted to go back to where she used to be, to her own fancy-free, footloose, fun days, when then everything was so precious. In her longing days, her dreams were of being with her parents' ancestral home, with her parents tending and lovingly caring for her and her child. She cried, yelling for her mum. She thought of her own father who was so much like her: strong and intelligent, doting on her son. Her older brother was like her mum. She was everything like her father, even her dark looks, but no one told her that her strength came from her father. He was strong, like she was now, but more to it, even though she thought that she looked like her father, William too was the carbon copy of her father, and Livvy followed suit. She was mortified.

A knock at the door. She heard it faintly, thinking that it was the maid. Livvy asked her to come in. Standing in front of her now, coming through her bedroom's door, was none other than the grand Elizabeth Bligh, the matriarch, all ruler of Camelot's Kingdom of broken dreams, desolation, a poisonous place to be. Not now, Elizabeth, the one that caused all of this. Elizabeth sympathised with Livvy. Once again, inside the bedroom, the curtains were all drawn in. It was dark, stenchy inside the bedroom. The sickness smell permeated the whole room. The bucket was changed constantly on a daily basis. Elizabeth could hardly see, but she managed, directing herself to pull the curtains open.

"Leave the curtains as it is." Livvy told Elizabeth drily. "You are not going to see me in this sorrowful state that I am in."

Elizabeth ignored Livvy, pulling the curtains wide and apart. It was a nice sunny day outside. Now that the windows were opened, the fresh air swirled into the big beautiful bedroom as if it was already expecting it. Little Livvy covered her face and hid herself under the covers, starting to sob all over again.

Now Elizabeth took in the surroundings. It was terrible. The trays of food were still there, and Livvy's clothes and garments were all laid and scattered all over the floor. Opening the windows, allowing the fresh air flowing, delivered the place from all of that toxic plasma and bad odour.

The terrible stench permeated around the bedroom, choking Elizabeth. She coughed. Once she felt comfortable and was able to breathe, Elizabeth sat down on the bed next to Livvy by uncovering her face, facing her full on.

"Come on, Livvy, please, please. We Blighs' women do not behave like this." Elizabeth calmly spoke and smoothly. "Livvy, come on, talk to me," she said again, trying to rouse Livvy. "Please." Livvy begged, "Go away. We certainly do not need to talk about anything. What has been said has been said and done."

"No, not one or another yet." Elizabeth soothingly said it. "Please snap out of it. I know that is shockingly terrible, but you are now a Bligh."

Livvy uncovered her face. She was dirty, scruffy, and her eyes were swollen from so much crying with crusts still on them, an obvious sign that she had not washed her face and herself for days on end.

Elizabeth spoke again, this time in a very motherly tone. "Livvy, if it makes you see and feel better, all will be alright," she said. "James is seeking treatment." Elizabeth said it again. "James has agreed to it."

"As if something like this has a cure." Livvy reproached Elizabeth.

"We can only hope. But he is going into hospital soon. Please, Livvy." Soothingly Elizabeth said, "We all need to regroup and continue with our lives in the mainstream. We are all Bligh. We all stay together even if we disagree."

"For your own sake and purpose." Livvy bitterly stated.

"Nothing has been done on purpose. You were in love with James..." Elizabeth paused and then sighed. "James was in love with you. Your parents agreed with the betrothal."

"They did not know the truth..." Livvy replied.

"No one does..." Drily, Elizabeth replied. "I am still saying he is getting the treatment. He shall be cured." With that, Elizabeth got up and slowly but softly walked towards the door.

Then she reminded Livvy, "I have done my part as a Bligh. Now is your turn to do your part as a Bligh." Then Elizabeth shut the door behind her.

At dinner time, Livvy showed up for dinner with the family, all scrubbed, clean, freshly dressed, as her bedroom was being spring-cleaned, a hard task. Livvy slept for a time in Anna's bedroom. Anna then slept in Caro's bedroom. Caro was still in the early stages of dealing with her own mother Elizabeth and was staying at the cottage, one of the many afforded by the Blighs' small little luxuries.

This time Dr Jack Duncan joined them. That same night, Elizabeth had another heart attack.

Two weeks into that, a Mrs Regina Standish turned up. She strutted her stuff into the mansion, all sophistication, elegance, knowledgeable, intelligence, confidence, beautiful. Livvy knew something odd or suspected about Reggie. During the time that Livvy was recovering and her mother-in-law was in the hospital, Livvy was herself. Any excuse would do for her to be roaming free as a bird from Camelot broken dreams. She understood then, sadly, to being a bird from the golden gilded cage: oppression, doubts, desperation. She was a Bligh. She should do everything for the Bligh. Her baby was a Bligh. Her baby would be the heir to the Cattle, being the Baron of it all, and then there was the Camelot of broken dreams. She hugged herself and silently cried. She implored God to have pity on her.

Then again she met with Andrew Swanson. He was typical, an Australian boy, to an extent in being really handsome, clean and cut, without a hair out of his place. His family was besieged by scandals, embarrassments, all caused by his own wayward father. One guesses that there is always going to be black sheep of the families all over the world, and to each their own "fun" and rebelliousness, depending how it fits into the society's history. Half of the time it doesn't, as Caro's didn't. He was always there to sustain, back up and fully support his beautiful, elegant but oh so funny mum, Lady Prudence Swanson. As for some, she was a shop with all the gossip; for the others, a good charity worker. And Andrew learnt a great deal from his all-exaggerated mum.

Now Andrew was another smooth-talking operator, but his businesses were to do with the Blighs directly. As the "Lothario", as Elizabeth then said it, but Andrew suffered no fools, except that the Blighs were having him on, being them friends of his parents. That really hurt.

The only son of the Swansons' family, having the green card to do whatever he wanted. His power came fully from the strength and magnitude of his parents' wealth. But he was also handsome, not in the rugged way, but more towards suave, sensitive, with the elegance and the Swansons' sophistication. What he couldn't do with his strong physique, he would do with his brains. More's the pity, because if only he used them to be kind, instituting the rights, the truth, displaying some sense of propriety, but when it comes to the Blighs, well, it's anyone's guess. The Swansons family was popular, well known to Regina and Bennett around town. Any idea of Elizabeth Bligh matchmaking Andrew to Anna was a thorough folly. Both of the families never learnt, but for Livvy, that at a later stage would become a blessing in disguise when she found out how much both of them were meant for one another. It took both of them such strains, both of their rollercoaster lives, for both them to crisscross again and to understand how much they were meant for each other. A woke.

Now she was in one of many of her own dire predicaments. What predicaments? Her baby Bligh died right inside her womb. She had two things to do: get rid of the baby and restart all over again, or well, the baby died. And like Gino telling Anna, "If it's not one thing, it's another. A baby dies and you buy another baby. Your family is sick..." That alone suffices what Livvy was doing: perturbed, losing her mind, took another way, disregarding the principles of lives with the Blighs, but then again thinking that she was a Bligh, she could do everything.

Swanson, like many others, would use this to fix Anna Bligh. Thankfully, he married lovely Livvy at the end, helping the Blighs onto other adventures and thorough journeys. One of them would be David's good friend in a not-far-distant future. He would father a daughter, Livvy's blonde-haired look-alike, Samantha Swanson.

At a later stage, she would claim it to be for love, but cruelly, she would tell James then, when she fell hard for Ellis Lloyd (Lloyd to be exact) that little Georgie was not a Bligh with the sole purpose in getting a divorce. Livvy has been so undermined, understated that no one believed what she could possibly do, and did she did anyway, with the power of the Blighs in the background, therefore letting us know the real reasons for it, which meant that she was as clever, astute and could also be like Elizabeth Bligh: manipulative, cruel and despotic, as she announced to James without fear or foe that little Georgie was never a Bligh. It was shocking, but James now learnt about his wife. A new era and a new Bligh were heralding, with Livvy's plans being magnificently executed, so happy, elated, that it never occurred to her that it would never work, as Lloyd was only an adventurer, not a man with a habitual income with staying power to be at home, domestic male. He couldn't run fast enough and away from the Blighs. The responsibility that he needed to have and supply Livvy with love and backing up went into the air, vanished. Livvy's supply of countless male companions were just starting.

Whilst Elizabeth recovered, and at her behest, beautiful Aunty Reggie, the so elegant George's sister-in-law, the Blighs' household with Anna and her amour fou, along with Caro, Jack, George and Sara, simply couldn't help themselves to their own romantic dalliances. They all seemed to be schoolkids who threw big parties behind their parents, in this case Elizabeth Bligh.

George was out of town. Rumours had it that he had a new "paramour" and was busy visiting her. Livvy was told by Anna that it was that blonde and blue-eyed nurse that the Blighs met during their trip home. The source was that Elizabeth loathed her so much, going the length, negating and being thoroughly toxic about Sara during dinner. How distasteful, with Elizabeth going on a bender against Sara, who states that "One can hardly mention the woman's name and all decency flies out the window," as mentioned. Caro, the Blighs' black sheep of the family, returned home, but she needed to look beyond that. Elizabeth was terrible, but with her came two: Reggie and later on Anna, whose mouth destroyed her own marriage, when out of the blue Anna told Gino that James was homosexual, which had nothing to do with him. She was now a Poletti.

In the Camelot's Kingdom of broken dreams, except for Little Lizzie Bligh, who was still lagging behind, she was still to morph but with suspicions, and the reasons for so much misunderstanding, pain going through Camelot's Kingdom of broken dreams were solely caused by one solo person. Livvy shook her head as she stared at the black and white picture showing the whole Blighs' family, pointing it out to James as he kept silent whilst Livvy went all the way against Elizabeth. It was about time that Elizabeth tasted the sweet taste of her own medicine. Still, the Blighs' family was not complete until Little Lizzie returned. The lively huge painting was all set and done in the parlour, one beautiful portrait that Anna now took pride and joy to exhibit, much to the pain and sorrow of Elizabeth's. She would cry often when she looked at the lively painting, with rumours that it was Elizabeth who drove her own little girl away. Roy was testimony to all of this bitter drama. He was unable to modify anything but to have some harsh words for Elizabeth, which he did: harsh but a woke. The patina was done and there was no kosher.

Presently, things look good. Many of the things were fitting into the puzzle. For one, Elizabeth now had Reggie to keep her company. That was a plus. Anna's love for Gino was going high on the Blighs' agenda. George was engaged to Sara Adams, Caro was home and Dr Jack Duncan too. More to it, James was home with her and their baby. Aunt Caro brought colour and warmth everywhere she went. The Blighs' atmosphere changed overnight: amicable and cosy, from that cold, freezing and austere ambience.

Andrew Swanson was hovering around, and his grandma's ring was given to the church then. Now happily married to Livvy and surrounded by two kids, Little Georgie and Little Samantha.

Aunt Reggie seemed to be always dressed to the nines, even though she was going no places. She was so different from Aunt Caro, who seemed to be at ease now back at home in Camelot, both lending their hands on everything regarding whatever was going on around Camelot. George Bligh was totally blissed in knowing that his "lethal" and "wayward" but colourful sister was back. Caro was the modern lady, moving with the times and often wore pants. Right now she wore a French beret, dark brown pants and a silk top.

Introducing Ellis Lloyd to the family: the family's painter, drawer, whatever and the thorough downfall of Livvy, now well known as the wanton woman.

Clad in black leather, riding a motorcycle and entering Camelot noisily. For some, he might have been a real stranger, funny and out of sorts, one that grand Elizabeth and her own would have never approved, let alone having him come into the manor. But, all things considered, Caro was the one who was the modern one, her own boss, blending the rules, having her own ways.

Reggie was holding a poker card night for a good family friend in Sir Richard Bennett. He was gross. He was open-minded. He was "braggadocio" and perverted. Of course he had to be. With money and power, he could easily have anything, and with him was the glamorous puss Aunt Reggie. She was busy organising the party: beverages, finger food, with everybody being kept on their toes.

It was scheduled that Livvy would be doing her first portrait.

And Livvy found herself in the thick of all she wanted and desired. The hard love.

The family portrait painter/photographer or whatever it could be. Lloyd was as easily a sleazebag as easily as he was fitting into Livvy's wild fantasies, living off the goodwill of good-natured people. Being this way, he worked here and there for a few dollars. His job was drawing in black crayons initially, painted in watercolours, by doing their portraits. Many women fell for him. However, these many women were not married. Lloyd had no qualms in living and using them. In this business, Lloyd could have never afforded his own studio. Therefore, Lloyd made do by creating his mobile business with the ample abundances of the lonely, sad and emptied women with rich allowances that afforded him. By his many women's employers, paid, maintained separately in a self-contained cottage where he could work the way he saw fit and show off his sexual prowess. Mrs Olivia Bligh was living thoroughly her own sexual fantasies.

In Livvy, Lloyd absorbed the knowledge of what he could see, had the benefit of seeing a lonely lost woman, not a wife. He noticed her longings and emptiness. Lloyd was not only a keen observer, but he always knew when women like Livvy were thoroughly sexually disconnected and love frustrated. One look at Livvy and he knew that she was starving for love. He could tell. Livvy was nothing but perpetually a little pet, asking for love, being patted on her head, badly needing, craving love. Now he was talking, with Livvy intently listening, completely devoted to Lloyd.

He only had to initiate it, and she exploded into tiny fractions of pleasure. It was her fantasy coming true. Before, she would have dreams of Harry Poulson tearing at her clothes, making hard crude love to her. Now her fantasies were blissfully happening, like wildfire, rampant, the real thing, as Lloyd tore her clothes, breaking thus the strand of pearls that she was wearing.

Her memories were all foggy but terribly hot: furnace, grilling, sizzling. Unfortunately again for Livvy, they were just that, surmises of blanked blubber, all covered in white snow with the snow keeping on falling until no traces were left for one to find the trail.

With Lloyd, this was all real: body, flesh, two bodies finally meeting. It was unexpected and all the more reason for her to love it. No consensus. No limitations. The sky was the limit. So the sexual encounters continued on with raw, animalistic, untameable, the so-called deconstructive erroneous ways of Lloyd's lovemaking: wild, setting Livvy on fire, brutal, with no strings attached, but he never hurt her physically. If anything, he encouraged her all the way. She followed suit. Damages be gone.

Livvy was now in her best element. She was experiencing everything that was a world of dubious reality. Finally, those electric pleasures, the fine ideal of the man that could so easily fit into her own wild dreams. Naturally, her deep pleasures, that Livvy never knew or even suspected for one moment that Lloyd, such a simple man, was using all the betterment of a wise man, a seducer who knew how to wound and attach to him a woman that was inconsistent, fragile, easy to be led on. Of course, typically of an airhead, he read Livvy like the professional painter that he was. Lloyd created masterpieces with his strokes or just a pencil lining or underlining, the same way he was a genius, and he knew how a starving for love, affectionless and sexually frustrated Livvy was, that Livvy neglected to see the kind of male that Lloyd was. Livvy was totally blinded with everything. She was wearing blinkers.

Lloyd usually simply preyed on the vulnerability of any woman's fragility, incomprehension, and deadset Olivia was in his basket. But in the latter years to come, how many other rich and neglected women of her kind, vulnerable and lonely women of her ilk fell for Lloyd's sexual praying mantis? He delivered the net, then he would slowly and gently wrap them into his own chrysalis, feeding them continually with everything he was capable of.

Lloyd learnt early the hows and the ways to manoeuvre himself into these poor, rich and spoilt little girls. Nothing was too good, but he was the best. He has done that before many times, and now he was hell-bent to make this irrational airhead, loveless, uncoordinated, self-righteous ladies of pleasure, except that he was the one pleasuring them. Naturally, he agreed to do the lively family portraits of the Blighs and anyone else too. He took one look at Livvy, Anna and the more mature Reggie, and his mind went blank with pleasure and money. Of course, Livvy was deluded to a point, but that did not mean that Lloyd himself could not stop having fun with these poor little rich lost girls and Livvy. Oh my, she was the real sucker. In later years, Lloyd would be on a flight back home due to his ingenuity of amalgamating work and pleasure, but the ladies in London would go on preferring more of the "alpha" males' pursuit, but that alone did not make him flee home again. His life was hanging on a thread: leave or be killed.

Way home from British England, having done more of what he was meant to, with his funds now being depleted, it reaches a time when one's youth and also good looks, plus pleasure living, would come to an end. When that happened, fleeing home to Sydney, with the husbands of his "paramours" chasing after him, with the last coins he had, he was sound and safe back home. Now he needed money. Livvy was now in a decent relationship with this Andrew guy, and Caro didn't want a bar to do with him.

However, Lloyd was desperate for money. As the saying goes, "Extreme times called for extreme measures," and Ellis Lloyd Parkins was down to his last penny. Okay, he only had five dollars for his existence. He has practically pawned everything: his bike, sorely missing it. Now he begged for someone to fund his extravagances, but he did not have anything to actually put up or advertise. But someone would, but...?

Lloyd screened the lot. There was a picture of the Blighs. He read about the multimillion empire that the Blighs were rolling in, and he thought long and hard.

Anything, and there were some scores to be settled. Lloyd had his resources. Money would be delivered into his own hands. He smiled when he envisioned the face of James Bligh when he would ring to personally talk to him about James's "sins". Supposedly, they were all aired and printed in huge black letters in any newspapers. Oh wow, what would the Blighs do to hide this kind of "scandal"? And all of sudden, the cash machines started to ring in his ears. It was so good, his ideas of blackmailing, that he was blatantly appalled by his new ideas and strategies.

He didn't think that it would work out. The Blighs were a tough lot, and Lloyd knew the price he would pay for blackmail. He has been there and done that. His timing was bad. However, now that he was in Sydney, how far would his bad luck run?

When their relationship ended, Livvy never knew how lucky she was. Throughout it all, James Bligh, the man that she betrayed (for no reasons of his own, except her own, due to lack of love, sex and lust), stood by Livvy through thick and thin, even when they'd discovered how treacherous, faked, terribly vindictive Livvy was for having another baby replacing the dead one (a baby dies, you buy another, your family is sick, says a drunk Gino against Anna), but they would stand behind Livvy all the way. She sees them as the Blighs with pure venom and poison. Poor Little Livvy, and she would never learn.

Livvy would soon find out that her discrepancies would come again to haunt her. She would be paying her own high dividends, with things would sink the Blighs and also the Swansons.

Matthew Goddard, the son of Douglas Goddard, was with the Blighs, insinuating himself slowly and surreptitiously into the Blighs' sacred sanctum.

But he would soon find out that that young tormented, tortured Livvy was not going to be judged and manipulated. His words were: "You Bligh women, it's your way or the highway," insinuating marginally his bitter feelings about how he felt with the Blighs' women, admitting thus his own defeat, talking to Elizabeth Bligh. Little Livvy might have been an airhead, but Matthew was a bitter man, a sour one, who was lost in his own deep sea of many misconceptions, many untruths, all made and built by him continuously to create havoc and also harming the all self-confidence of Little Livvy.

At this stage, he had all the credentials to take revenge on the Blighs. Matthew would be delighted to do so. He would not even blink at the pleasure.

Little Livvy was having her early breakfast along with Lady Swanston, Andrew and now a strong grown-up, strappy dark-haired boy, George, who was tending to the blonde cute little Samantha.

The maids announced that two policemen wished to see Mrs Olivia Swanston and Andrew Swanston.

Both received summons to attend the Supreme Court.

Both were summoned. Lady Swanston was given to hysterics too. Everyone that was Bligh or Blighs-related shook, rattled and rolled. They all were dancing to the same tune, a tune that had been played for years, then it stopped, and now the same tune was played all over again.

But louder, spectacular, and all eyes were on them. The Blighs.

The past comes over to haunt Little Livvy and her dubious wanton life as the righteous Mrs James Bligh, and if for her was bad enough, then for the Blighs it would prove a terrible ordeal.

But Livvy could count on Lloyd for once. The Blighs can breathe a sigh of relief.

BOOK 2. A PLACE TO CALL HOME. "The Forensics." The trial. THE BLIGHS VS_______________? If you can see the clues, then you are a smart lady and gentleman, but if not, more shall be revealed in the further A PLACE TO CALL HOME's editions. Only on sale.

Chapter 12:
Hitler's Furies

Sir Richard Bennett was having his businesses branching all over Sydney.

His Empire by now was expanding, developing. His own hotels were now branching all over Sydney's CBD and also interstate. Testimonies of his own business acumen.

He was now a mega-billionaire three times and over. He was called the mogul. First he was the media mogul. Now his business acumen correlated with his name.

Once he was just the average bloke. Now he was the Emperor of everything.

The Australian people with Dicko boy rejoiced at the ending of the war.

Today, he declared himself to be on holiday. All hard work and no play made Jack a dull boy, and he was after all a Bennett. It was time for rest and relaxation.

The two beautiful Thai girls provided the relaxing massage. They might have had dainty hands, but their firm grips on his muscles were strong. Dicko grimaced. He badly needed this kind of therapy. There was never a time when his small luxuries could provide for him: cocktails and delightful Thai dishes. His savvy blue eyes sparkled with thorough glee. His moustache tweaked. His grinning from ear to ear showed the status he was in.

The Beatles' heartbreaking but full of woes "A Hard Day's Night" kept on playing. One moment it was one vivacious song, and the other some other woeful songs of the sixties.

The majordomo came into his "paradisiacal room", as Sir Richard called it, exotically laden with Far Eastern decorations. He felt supreme. These days he'd prefer to rule from his all-powerful mansion, enjoying what his privileged money could afford him. He was wealthy. The surroundings magnified his own status. Bennett thought of them as mere material and collectables, with some being souvenirs, others on a whim, others as gifts, the way he collected his women per se. These happened to be his own trophies. His children were now all grown up, attending universities, taking their own degrees, his pride and joy. Alone where he was gave him time to reflect, meditate, but he also loved being in his office.

The majordomo cleared his throat and, matter-of-factly, stiff and completely in his black and white suit, announced that Bennett had a visit. Bennett's face changed the colour, and the irritation on his face showed clearly. Sir Richard Bennett was not amused.

His body was terse as he wrapped himself with the towel and covered himself with the short black kimono. Chomping on his trademark cigar, finishing his cocktail, munching his own food, Sir Richard Bennett still packed a punch where his good looks and his body were. He still found time to exercise, and by now going on in years, he still held firmly that six-pack flat stomach, which now was covered by the kimono. His eyes shone, going all white as he irritably says, "Whatever it is, tell them to meet me at the office."

The majordomo didn't flinch. "Sir, it's a lady. But I think you should at least..."

"Ogle her," he finished the sentence. "Do they know that it is my fucking day off? It's fucking Sunday. At least they can see this." He was fuming now.

The majordomo said, "She said she'd wait."

Sir Richard Bennett shook his head, winced in pain and threw the cocktail glass against the wall in sheer irritation. The naked Thai ladies, covering their bodies, ran out of the room in panic, shrieking. When their boss blew up, he blew up.

"So fucking don't stand there. Let me finish my bath." At that, he pressed the button and the jacuzzi splashed out. He stayed inside the jacuzzi for a while, with his eyes closed and still smoking his cigar. On his return then, the majordomo brought Sir Richard his light blue tracksuit and runners. His boss.

Composing himself, Bennett used his hands to sleek his thick and grey hair to the back, coming out of his "Paradisiacal Resting Room" and climbing up the stairs up to the first floor.

The majordomo by now pointed at the lady.

She was looking at her surroundings, the beautiful Sydney's breathtaking views from all the angles from where she was standing at the terrace. Naturally, Sir Richard Bennett's residence bespoke a great deal about him. The majordomo knew how to look after her.

She was served coffee and homemade tasteful biscuits. When Bennett turned up, the majordomo announced his presence. The woman turned around. Sir Richard Bennett shook in thorough disbelief when his eyes rested on her face and her main frame.

Her hair was thinning. It looked like if she was wearing a wig. Her face was haggard. She covered the blemishes with heavy makeup. Her eyes, big and round, heavily painted, were lifeless, but you could look into them and feel them piercing into your soul. She looked sick, and her body looked like it was made of wax. And even though she did make an effort to dress up, she not only walked with a heavy limp, she also walked with two sticks aiding her.

The body moved, but the legs were heavy. Bennett felt the pressure and the oppression on her. It gave him anxiety, but she managed. The shoes were black, the likes that one wears in conjunction with a uniform. Bennett sat down, taking in such a poor renaissance of life. This toppled it all. She was wearing a bland outfit of a jacket and skirt, a most stifled grey combination. He couldn't see past her. The woman, what was she in reality?

"Hello." She spoke in a raspy German accent with her empty unfocused eyes staring at Richo.

Sir Richard stared at her blankly. "Have we ever met..." Then mumbling, he whispered, "before?"

The woman stood erect. She was frighteningly commanding and fearsome, resting on both of her sticks.

"Nein," she retorted. "Est ist eine Freunde, sie kennen Zulernen." "Der dick treffen will."

She stated. He saw her so straight that he thought that she would raise her hand and salute him in the Gestapo's way. But she stood erect (here is a friend who wants to meet you), or words to this effect, approaching him. The soles of her shoes noisily hitting the white tiles, with her wooden sticks striking heavily on the tiles making the sounds hard to hear, a terrible noise, leaving behind dark marks on the tiles. She continuously limped. Dicko regarded her not too friendly and amusing. The woman looked lost.

Sir Richard Bennett continued, "Wie und warum sind sie hier?" (How and why are you here?) He asked, looking incredulously.

"Ich wollte dich sehen und mit dir sprechen." She replied daringly. "I wanted to see you and talk to you."

The sparkling blue eyes of Sir Richard's glinted like diamonds. Both of his eyebrows lifted, and the grin returned as he continuously stared at her. His grey and white moustache tweaked.

"Oh? Was von." (Oh? What of.)

"Über eine Frau." (About a woman?) She flatly said it. But the monotone was there.

Sir Richard looked at her, waved at his majordomo and asked for a drink. Curious.

"Kaffee, bitte, Creme, Sache, Zucker, danke." (Please, coffee, cream and sugar.)

"Und für die Dame. Bitte kommen Sie vorbei." (And for the lady too. Please come over.)

As the majordomo went about making the coffee and some finger food for both of them, Richo was now amused. She looked like a Gestapo, SS Hitler's Furies, to be more exact. And if so, what was she doing here? "Was? Von?" (Who. What?)

"Welche Frau, und wie ist ihr Name?" (What woman, and what is her name?)

"Du kennst sie!" (You know her.) She said it convincingly but harsh. Unapologetically, she approached as she now waited for her second serve of coffee.

Then after looking at him with both of her piercing black eyes, she responded.

"Sie wissen, dass ihr Name Sara, Sara Adams." She concluded triumphantly.

(You know her. Her name is Sara. Sara Adams.)

"Vorherige Bridget Adams. Nein, Sara. Bridget A.D.A.M.S., der Jude." (Previous Bridget Adams. Bridget A.D.A.M.S., the Jew.) She almost spat. The dislike was profound.

She knew now that she had his attention. Her hatred, real or deluded, was there.

"Setz dich." (Sit down.) Sir Richard commanded.

The lady now sat rigorously in front of where Sir Richard was. Too late, the majordomo tried to pull out the chair for her, failing to do. He proceeded to pour the coffee into her cup and Bennett's, producing more but freshly made yummy sandwiches, handing over to her the serviettes. He managed to let her know that they were finger food.

For a long time, Sir Richard observed, trying to read the woman and to find out how the woman was and what the implications of her status would be in the near future. He solemnly regarded her with a very peculiar smile dancing on his lips. Then after his long surveying, he asked,

"Was ist dein Name und wer du bist?" (What is your name and who are you?)

"Mein Name ist Cara de Rhe, Dritter Reich Leutnant est Ravensbrück." (My name is Cara de Rhe, Third Reich SS Lieutenant in Ravensbrück.)

She proudly announced her name and status, then she bit into her sandwiches. She was hungry. That was the first thing he noted.

“Geheimdienste. Geheime Staatspolizei...” (Nazi Intelligence... Nazi German Police)

“Sehr beeindruckend.” (Very impressive.) Bennett replied. “Sie scherzen. Wir sind jetzt in den 60er Jahren.” (Gestapo SS Secret Services. You are joking? We are in the 60s.) Bennett drily reminded her as he noted how ravenous she was. She was intensely hungry.

“Du hast nicht gegessen? Dachte ich, der Majordomo hat dich bereits gefördert.” (You haven’t eaten? I thought that majordomo fed you?) He was amused, and mind you, she was ravenous.

“Kekse. Fütterten sie an die Vögel.” (Biscuits. Fed them to the birds.) Drily she retorted.

He found her funny now. With all the hype gone, he was highly impressed with her.

“Warum bist du hier und sprichst Englisch?” (Why are you here and do you speak English?)

“Ja, ich spreche Englisch.” (Yes, I speak English.)

“Warum sprechen Sie alle zu Deutsch?” (So why are you speaking all in German?)

She bit into the other sandwiches and waited until she swallowed and then replied.

“Hier drüben spricht nicht viele Deutsch.” (Over here not many people speak German.)

Sir Richard Bennett smiled and came to rest at the back of his chair. He thought the woman intelligent and clever, and he voiced his opinion.

“Gescheit, sieht intelligent. Wie kommen Sara Adams ins Spiel?” (Clever, very smart. So how does Sara Adams come into play?) Bennett asked again.

"Wir spielten mit ihr." (We played with her.) She replied matter-of-factly. He was impressed. Again, Bennett looked back at the majordomo who was listening, with his eyes asking the question, "Can you believe this?" in silence. The majordomo smiled and looked the other way.

"Wie kann ich ihnen vertrauen?" (How can I trust you?) Relaxed, he asked. When anyone interrupted his short "holidays", Bennett would show it. He felt rested. Any news about the Blighs was good news. His eyes were slits, stretching like the cat who was watching his rat, errr, his prey. One had the impression that his tail, if he had any, was waving and slashing from side to side.

"Ich habe ausgezeichnete Informationen." (I have excellent information.) "Nachweise und Nachweisen." (Proofs and evidences.) She wiped her mouth with the back of her hand.

He nodded. These were good news. He doesn't know them yet, but the woman sitting in front of him could give him thorough insight. She looked desperate, dishonest and vengeful. She would be of good use for him against the Blighs.

"Wo bleiben Sie?" (Where are you staying?) he asked, now with a formulated plan.

"Kann ich Ihre Adresse und Telefon Nein haben?" (Can I have your address and your telephone no.?) he asked again, this time softly. The majordomo lit his cigar.

"Nein. Ich habe keine. Du bist meine letzte Ressource." (No. I haven't got any. You're my last resource?) She looked at him and retorted, not drily now, humbly.

He lit another cigar and offered it to her. She declined, stating, "Ich liebe Zigarren, ja? Aber nicht heute." She now smiled with her skin all waxy-like. (I love cigars, but for today, no.)

She looked at him, expecting him to reply about her staying.

"Du bist letzte Ressource." She again repeated. (You're my last resource.) She bravely attempted to be his charity.

"Ich? Es muss ein großer Fehler sein." (Me. There must be a big mistake.) Bennett amusingly replies. "Warum?" (Why.)

"Ich habe nichts." (I have nothing.) Looking at her, smilingly. The smiling assassin.

"Lügner. Du bist so reich und mächtig." (Liar. You are rich and powerful.) She accused.

"Du schuldest alles." (You have everything.) She was now getting aggressive.

Bennett regarded her intensely. He was highly amused with these silly cat-and-mouse games. Maybe there was something useful for her. She was good for him. Her information was gold. It was too early and too soon, too sudden for him to organise something to do with Cara, but now it would be of most important that he needed to know about her. For all of her claims and her morbid indication on how much she hated Sara Bligh, she still needed to be confirmed with her own status, something that he could come up with, something that she could actually do for him. Her acid hatred against Sara Adams. He still needed to manoeuvre this slightly off-the-base woman. Why? A war. He looked at Cara and why? Bennett has been a spy too during the Second World War, and he decoded many secrets, and he also suspected that it was not her real name.

"Jetzt benötige ich Ihre Identifikation." He said. (Now I need your identification.) He demanded.

"Hier." (Here.) She responded. "Damn, wo werde ich bleiben hier?" (So I shall be staying here.) She was happy now to actually be in his team.

He took at the ID card, looked at it, then he became attentive to her.

"Interessant. Nein, Sie werden in einem Hotel übernachten." (No, you will be staying at the hotel.) His sparkling blue eyes became serious now. They were dark, and he meant it.

She looked at him incredulously and added, "Warum nicht hier?" (Why not here?) She repulsely and indignantly asked again.

He was losing his patience with her. Finally, he snapped.

"Weil ich hier lebe und nicht einmal meine Familie bleibt bei mir." (Because I live here. Not even my family lives with me.) She noted Richo's deep irritation with the quick change from that amicable and generous old man to this. His face changed colour, and his eyes chipped.

"Sie sind in Australien, daher werden Sie Englisch sprechen." (You are in Australia, therefore you will speak English.) He now commanded. "Du arbeitest für mich." (You work for me.) "Sie werden tun, was Ihnen gesagt wird." (You do as you're told.) He continued, watching her confidence melting down. "Keine Fragen gestellt." (No questions asked.) Then he thundered on, "Ich bin der Chef." (I am the boss.) Bennett reinvigorated his command. His voice was dry without any feeling. He stared her down, dominating her completely. A deep and uncomfortable air remained. It might have been hot outside with the sun gliding down the bay of Sydney's more popular sites. The Sydney Bridge glimmering in the background as now was waking up for the nocturnal trysts and many events. A man played the solo guitar whilst others watched him. The tourists were entranced with the views and the sundown. They all collected food, sitting down listening to the dire strumming of the lonely and solo guitar, all the time laughing and singing along. Lives went on.

"Let's start now. You are to go down with the majordomo. The car will take you to the hotel." Then he looked at her and said, "You also will need to change your clothes. We are now in the sixties, and that is not the colour I want. It is time to change yourself." Bennett was not redundant. He stared at her with those blue eyes of his.

Speechlessly she looked at him.

"Remember always that I am the boss. Don't come over until I summon you. Go refresh yourself and be modern. Don't ever come to me in these drags. Get new cosmetics, and the clothes you are wearing..." He shook his head. "What happened to your hair?" "You will have new clothes. Do your hair. I know that this one is fake. Why are you wearing a wig?" He did not understand why, but would change.

"Terrible," she cracked now in her German accent. "Terrible. No vitamins. Nothing."

"When I see you next time, you will be wearing your own natural hair." He warned. "Do NOT," he raised his voice, "never come over here this way," he said.

"Well, we will discuss this when we see each other. Go change yourself. You work for me and now you have money. I will come and see you. Under no circumstances come over here ever." She might come if she had information, and he was highly curious about the evidence and the proofs related to one Sara Bligh.

Bennett showed that he alone could be even more tyrannical than Hitler.

The majordomo waited for her to shuffle out of the chair, taking her down to the main door. Within minutes she was in the hotel. She loved what she saw. The right time would come when Sir Richard would meet up with the rest of Hitler's Furies. For the time being, she was happy.

But she forgot: Hitler's Furies were a long and distant thing, but for Cara, if she herself existed, they needed to exist. Plus, she had the proofs and evidence. The day would come when she would face up to Sara Adams.

"What interesting stories she would tell him," he thought alone, and then smiled. Sated and happy for everything, but today: "Ein Lied, ein Getränk und für ihn Frauen. Zu meine Gesundheit, und die Hölle Zum Blighs." (A song, a drink and for him a woman. To my health, hell to the Blighs.) He looked sporadically like the cat which got himself the full cream. He was thoroughly elated, ecstatic, fluctuating in seventh heaven.

He looked around and played with the identification card of Lieutenant Cara de Rhe, then he scoffed.

It was a black and white identification photo that had seen better days. The person in there did not look anything like the present Frau (woman). He was wondering if this Cara had a "Mann, Mann-Freund." (Man, husband, boyfriend.)

Speaking German whilst he served in the Australian Army, Bennett, being always smart with the Army needing interpreters and translators to crack codes and their Germans' transcribed messages, was Richard Bennett, who was meant to be a bum living off his parents' wealth, served his purpose by actually learning German, making do with translations and interpretations. Bennett went even further. He cracked codes and encrypted messages. Later on, Sir Richard Bennett received an honorary medal during the ANZAC commemoration day. He was not worth only a mention but his honorary stint for his highly polished dedication, proving therefore that he was a highly recommended and valued Australian soldier serving with dignity, honour and purpose. You win some and you lose some. He lost his brothers, but he inherited them all. Sad, but this was life.

"HaH. Gesundheit, für seine Familie Bennett. Ruhe in Frieden für seine ganze Familie." (To health, for his Bennett's family. Rest in Peace, to his family too.)

"Seine beiden älteren Brüder wurden im Einsatz getötet." (His two older brothers were killed in action.)

A lot of pluses and also lots of minuses in here and there.

He studied the picture intently. Something was not right over here, or it was but he did not believe in Cara, or he simply suspected Cara.

Sir Richard Bennett was a real fox. They did not call him "The Smooth Operator" for nothing. He knew that there was something wrong with the whole concept, and being the fox that he was, he suspected more. And he would use his smoothness to get them. Ah, the operator was now thinking of the best way to go about it.

The majordomo returned and informed Dickie boy that Cara had arrived at the hotel. Food again had been served, and she had been making phone calls.

She had nothing to wear. The majordomo stated, "Should she go naked?" He raised an eyebrow.

"Get my secretary on the phone," he said, to which the majordomo did not need a second command. The next, Dickie boy was talking to his secretary, barking out instructions. His directions were short and curt, requesting an officer of the Commonwealth Immigration to be at his office the next morning. He wanted a few things to be checked and informed about, supplying them with the following black and white photo.

As per usual, what he wanted he always got. He had in his possession the file on "Cara de Rhe? A.k.a. Frau Caritas Von Lar."

CONFIDENTIAL

Cara de Rhe. SS Lieutenant, Third Reich's Hitler's Furies.

Real name: Caritas Von Lar. Date of Birth. Place of Birth. Mother's name and maiden name. Father's name. Father's profession. Caritas Von Lar's education.

Caritas Von Lar. Criminal profile.

An officer ranked in the Hitler's Furies, being one of the official thirty thousand agents who were commended highly for the brutal, cruel and mistreatment of the prisoners in Ravensbrück.

Caritas Von Lar married a high-ranking Hitler's SS Gestapo official whose name was Karl De Rhe, whereby at a later stage was sent to the Ravensbrück Concentration Camp. Caritas, who was called Cara for short, officially changed her name and surname from Von Lar to her married name, becoming officially well known as Ravensbrück's Third Reich SS Officer Lieutenant Cara De Rhe.

Work. Caritas Von Lar was now officially known as SS Lieutenant Cara de Rhe in the Third Reich's ranking, as one of the many terrifying perpetrators in the cruel and brutal treatment of the prisoners of war in the Ravensbrück concentration camp.

Background.

Lieutenant Cara de Rhe, who was then Caritas Von Lar, came from a very poor, destitute family.

She was the second child of numerous members of the family, christened and wore the name of Von Lar, but it is doubtful who the real father was. Her mother, the older Caritas, was well known for her poor health and labour. But she was also beautiful, a trait that her daughter Caritas would later be well known for.

They lived on the outskirts of a simple village where life was all rural. Hard work was expected for both the men and women as they laboured with the difficulties against the elements of a harsh place riddled with dire problems, coupled with infertile ground.

The children had limited education, and the freezing temperature kept them at home, with food usually being scarce. The market was usually closed during the winter blues. Young Carita, who was all curls, blonde and cute, learnt what being famished meant: poor, wearing rags, hand-me-downs, barefooted, hungry and always cold. Her beautiful baby face was usually dirty, tinged with that kind of clear and concise innocence. Cara suffered from sniffles. The barren place has long been gone now, and Cara did not miss a beat of it.

Due to these poor, if not terrible conditions, senior Von Lar decided to move interstate so his family could find a comfortable and warm apartment where everybody could feel safe, sound, find employment and earn those hard Reichsmarks (German currency). At least there would be food, hot water and also protection from the dire elements.

His words were an order. By the following week, all in the village carted off the last of their belongings with only the bare necessities. There was that odd bad feeling in leaving the place behind, but no regrets whatsoever. Fed up and tired, they had exhausted all avenues to stay on into a better settlement. Though there had been some nice and enjoyable times, the place was completely barren, useless for any human living conditions and maintenance. They'd all left together, thinking about their own future and the lucky escape.

The trip went through the highs and lows, with Mother Nature inflicting on them the terrifying elements, besieging the whole family and its followers with nothing but problems, disasters, sickness and devastating tragedies, the breaking down of their caravans and carts as they faced all kinds of strange travesties, facing devastating losses and deaths exacerbated even deeply by the often attacks by the hungry wolves, strange animals that were foreign to them, with the water constantly being frozen taking its time to be defrosted. Coffee and their dry meat needed to wait to be cooked and boiled, with their lives in the mainstream getting harsher and more bitter. But on they went, making do with bread on the double, on a daily basis, the only surviving food. Churning the milk from the cows, making it into cheese and butter, which was very much needed as part of their own diet, which was now totally relied upon.

With them was wide-eyed, beautiful and cute goldilocks Caritas, who could only watch and sense that better conditions were waiting for them.

"Milch, Butter und Käse mit Brot. Mehl, wurde gebraucht und er doppelt an. Honig und Zucker machten sie ihre berühmten. Essen der Teig mit dem Loch in der Mitte. Die berühmten Donuts, alle heiß und tief gebraten." Cara wrote in her diary. Wishful thinking.

(Milk, butter and cheese with bread. Flour was needed and was being used on the double. Honey and sugar, they made their famous food: the dough with the hole in the middle, the famous doughnuts, all hot and deep fried.)

With the desperation came anxiety. There were always brutal fights for one thing or another.

But Caritas's father or grandfather always found a reason to appease the camp and its followers.

After months and months of so much problematic and terrifying endeavour, it was an early spring but cold morning when they finally reached the city of Berlin. At the time it was still the capital of East Germany, but once divided after the war, West Berlin's new capital was now Bonn. But for the Von Lars, it would be a new beginning. They knocked the doors to this "Metzger, und schließlich dicker cremiger Kaffee." (Butcher, and finally thick, rich, creamy coffee.)

They were all filthy, dirty, stinking and also exhausted. But now happy to have arrived at their own final destination, as finally they were carting the last of their belongings up the stairs to a new building. It was such a different tableau of new beginnings. They found out that Berlin was comfortable with many strange and modern technologies, especially the bathtubs and the new toilets and bathrooms. The beds looked immensely cosy, accommodating and so inviting.

All of them were. Cara noted. They were finally home, and already her grand uncle was employing her family. The feast was huge. They were all clean and happy, wearing new, clean and fresh clothes, as they were all seated now for a grand banquet. The meat was fresh, the bread fresh from the oven, the "Wein, Bier, Alkohol, frisches Gemüse und Salate, Desserts, Süßigkeiten und Kuchen, heiße und dampfende Hühnersuppe mit frischem knusprigem Brot." (The wine, beer and liquor, fresh veggies and salads, desserts, sweets, cakes, hot piping chicken soup with fresh crispy bread.) The celebrations went on for days. Her grand uncle stopped at nothing to make sure that all were not only happy in their new environment, but specifically that he, and only himself, along with his own family, could spare the goodwill for all of them. He was indeed happy to see all of his family and more to it, reunited with his whole family. "Oh mein Gott, wie sehr er sie vermisst hat..." (Oh my God, how much he had missed them.)

Where her uncle was, Caritas also observed that he was pretty wealthy. He had apartments that he voluntarily gave away to his family, many of the ones who previously lived in them emigrating into the main extreme to the interior of Europe.

Not only that, her grand uncle also offered and created employment for most of them. He knew the high officials who owed him something here and there, and he got them employment. She came to regard her grand uncle as someone who held a high position in the official state of Berlin.

"Jetzt, ein heißes Bad und saubere Kleidung für eine Abwechslung." (Now, a hot bath and clean clothes for a change.) Cara had noted in her diary. That was what she did right on the first day of arrival, to experience the good life as she lovingly immersed into the hot water tub.

"Schlafen in einem warmen und heißen Bett mit Decken und Wänden, um sie alle Zu wärmen. Cara war glücklich für jetzt." (Sleeping in a warm and hot bed, with ceilings and walls to protect them all. Cara was happy for now.) But she also saw for herself the unhealthy state of the things that were happening politically and unpolitically wise.

It was a new life for her and her family. Her mother Caritas was now bedridden. Her brothers, sisters, uncles, aunties, cousins, relatives and the long list of her family were now living separately in their own apartments. She was left with her bedridden mother who would not rest in her bed, and one of her “many” fathers. Von Lar had a heart problem that prevented him from being employed full time. But he worked for his family’s “keeping” so they’d be well provided for. Cara’s mother persevered. With the money, she could now walk about and do her shopping, but her tasks were lighter. Cara was sent to school locally.

Cara outstandingly started off, becoming a smart student, with the plus of being a beautiful girl.

She grew up to be a popular, bright and beautiful student. Her curly long locks, that beautiful creamy European complexion, those amazing blue eyes made many males, young and old, fall in love with her.

As she was growing up, this little flower was blooming physically, and for a fourteen-year-old girl, Mother Nature bestowed on her a beautiful figure that most women would envy: a small waist, medium bust, a wide hip and long shapely legs.

She would go on winning some local beauty contests but never made it to the Miss Germany (Deutsche Frau) Schönheitswettbewerb. (But not enough to compete worldwide or universally.)

Cara missed the opportunity to represent her country proudly for lack of sponsors, and her family refused to back her up where monetary or finance was needed. She also failed to make it into the modelling agencies, and for a time worked as an assistant to a secretarial entrepreneur where she used typing and served coffee to all in the office. But still, money was lacking. By then, other agencies and other sponsors had other newer and younger girls who they would support. They also had money, and they also, much to Cara’s chagrin, were able to enrol in modelling schools. Cara missed all of these opportunities for lack of money, status, and she had nothing to prove or to live for. Naturally, she felt resentful, terribly odious about a world that was not working for her at all.

As she was growing up, she was becoming far more disenchanted with life every day, every week, every month. Financially, she worked hard and kept her finances in tow.

The world was hitting its limits. On a daily basis, there was so much in the news about what Hitler was doing. Adolf Hitler rose to power when he became the Chancellor, and that made him feel all powerful and mighty.

With him came recruitments for major establishments, also youth orientation. He also produced his own manuscript of Mein Kampf, his own struggles during his life's journey.

But Hitler's recruitment came forth. Cara bid her parents goodbye and ventured herself into a new life of extremities. True, with Hitler it was everything or nothing.

She was now wearing the full SS uniform after days, weeks and months of brainwashing work and studies. Where she was concerned, now she could face in full view that she alone was not the only one with creamy complexions, blue-eyed vixens with blonde straight or curly hair.

At the beginning, these blonde vixens were just plain recruiters, volunteers. It was during this time that she came into contact with a tall, dark and handsome "Führer's" disciple and a powerful Gestapo officer.

Her days of living in poverty and eyeing the others with deep envy, missing the odd opportunities, were now going out of her life. Overnight, Cara found gold in this handsome and rich man, and not only became rich and respected, she also gathered an official title that later on would be banished by Hitler.

Now she was seen, beautifully dressed and enchantingly clad in the trendy fashion of the times. She had money for everything, and she would indulge in it the way she saw fit.

Now her curly hair was all done in the trendy fashion of "coronets". She could afford to paint her nails and her lips. She also now had cosmetics, applying herself to all that was hard and expensive to others, but for her it was just a short trip or per se a long trip to the beauty salon, where now she was more than happy with her own massive amount of expensive creams, bought at inordinate prices. Now she also painted her eyes with long strokes of eye-liner, with fake eyelashes with lashes of mascara showered on them. Furthermore, she loved the expensive perfumes and the nylons that she could choose at her own pace, time and expense. Cara's new position, regarded as her royal highness the Viscountess, the power, the status bringing her unlimited privileges, barking orders to all who were at her own beck and call: maids, cooks and a butler. Now life was good. Caritas was now her Ladyship, the Viscountess Cara de Rhe, living in palatial castles and mansions all at her command, travelling in luxury in a car driven by her own chauffeur.

They both fell in love madly. Primarily they were living in a one-room apartment outside Berlin, as he was posted for various positions and needed to vacate and leave quickly, but for the then Carita's pleasure, her husband Gestapo SS De Rhe took her to their castle. Caritas was beyond herself.

Cara's husband was very good looking, handsome, oozing charm and "alpha" male appeal. The women fell for him like bees to "Zucker" (sugar) or "Honig" (honey), and he would take them as they came. He enjoyed their company, and later on, as they both were sent into separate duties, going into different concentration camps, Cara was unhappy and totally devastated. But remember, he explained to Cara: "Ihr seid jetzt die Hitlers' Furies, behandeln Sie sie entsprechend." He sweetly voiced, "You are now the Hitler's Furies, treat them accordingly," he stated after their night of gentle and soft lovemaking. Caritas was in tears. Painful, bitter.

By then in her mid-thirties, with a new status and money, but without her husband, and having suffered so many disappointments previously due to their own lack of money and status, Cara began to suffer from a case of "inferiority complex" and more so the bitterness of knowing that her current husband had taken on a few mistresses, with pictures of him and the dandy ladies falling into her hands through anonymous letters.

But unbeknown to Cara, he was under official duties and worked for the SS. These beautiful and glamorous women were wealthy and married to rich overseas “merchants”. He was like an ancient James Bond who was under Hitler’s orders and of course the Gestapo to do the unthinkable. It was espionage of the best. For all of her own beauty and her supposed intelligence, she really flipped, with deep psychological problems.

Sick of these blows, nothing worked as she wanted. One moment she was on a high, but she also forgot one minor thing. By revenging what she saw as her husband’s betrayal, she never revealed to him about her own pregnancy.

The baby was sent away, but she did send money for the upkeep of her baby. She did mourn the feelings of being a mother. That alone was another hard and devastating blow for her, causing her more torment and torture of what could have been, adding already more devastation to an already exhausting mind, planting roots of evil in her mentally insane mind. She found only satisfaction when she made the women suffer, as she had suffered badly, bitterly, sorrowfully and immensely. Now the women at the camp would suffer too.

Now that she was in the Ravensbrück Concentration Camp, she callously planned, working out an evil timetable. Having a husband who cheated on her with those half-naked “Huren” (whores), she actually took all of her hatred and sexual frustration out on the more beautiful girls, pubescent girls, teenage girls, women in their mid-thirties, forties, fifties, and the elderly. The most beautiful suffered the most horrid treatment. Later on, Cara added to her own vestibule the whipping, earning her the name of the Whipping Witch, making her far more resolute in her ways of discriminating and finding even more ploys to work against them.

Her psychotic episode created more problems inwardly, driving her completely mad. That was the beginning, leading her to the end. She became the authority and also the officer in charge of practically everything: the timetable, the gas chambers, always diminishing their rations by half. If they had breakfast, they would not eat until supper. Food, rapes, paedophilia (they also raped and killed little girls), the slaughtering and killing of newborn babies. She delighted in watching the women going through the terrible and excruciating pain during labour, like she did when she gave birth to her own, laughing hysterically at the bawling and wailing when removing the babies from them. These women, who were already weak and in the process of giving birth, were too weak to fight back. Cara, following her husband's instruction, always thought that they were not called Hitler's Furies for nothing, continuing having a party whilst sending them, still in their post-pregnancies, crawling, wincing in pain, working in the harsh and bitter cold conditions in the camp at nighttime when the temperature fell below zero, while the Furies drank their delicious warm Glühwein and munched on hot fried doughnuts. These women were sent to cultivate only their own deaths, wearing still their torn shifts, barefooted and almost naked. For Cara, that barren, cold and freezing place brought the sad and starving memories of her once-upon-a-time childhood back then in those old wintry blues in her then-village, so much so that even the name was wiped off the map.

That and many other appalling treatments, with many dying of frostbite, others of sickness such as influenza, pestilences, being eaten alive by bed lice, dysentery, starvation, the conditions with the accommodations being all dirty, smelly and putrid. Hence, to stop feeding the women, the nurses called Angels of Death would turn up at the camp's quarters giving the following sick women vaccinations: lethal injections with the sole purpose of killing. But some of the sick women refused to be vaccinated as the injection had a strong smell of petrol.

No hot food. No medical aid. Cara enjoyed denying them everything, even when they needed to use the bathrooms and toilets. No baths or showers, only the gas chambers. She would laugh herself silly, and the whip in her hand was also her best friend.

Not forgetting that these women were human, bleeding internally and externally.

Curtailing their necessities meant that they would venture out, facing the terrible and freezing cold, dressed in those tattered and flimsy see-through nightgowns, barefooted (like she was when she was a kid) and famished. Dozens perished in these appalling conditions. The bitter cold would have been enough to kill anything, let alone humans. If they would not die of one thing, they would have been dead by another. Mumps and poxes followed. None were ever sent to medical centres to be treated. Their bodies wrecking in terrible fever, as in the concentration camp the plague was now raging, with the prisoners all left to die in unconstituted places. That was not the only thing pervading them. The prisoners that survived told of the cold, insipid soup, which was just plain running water, that was fed to all in the nefarious concentration camp.

Much to their amusement and incredulity, the Hitler's Furies also came up with a thorough idea by creating a brothel using the women prisoners in Ravensbrück, where the entertainment was beating and whipping them into submission, raped consistently by both sides, males and females, mercilessly. Each day they would come up with something "refreshingly" odd to subjugate the prisoners.

The SS officers paid no money to the women whom they'd raped but paid their money to the Furies. They made a fortune where it was concerned, thus disposing of the favourites.

The Furies felt highly important, proud and completely honoured for being Hitler's Furies, entertaining themselves due to the fact that Hitler himself honoured these sickos, the SS women officers, personally, as he constantly, and when able, met these cold, hard and cruel women as the Hitler's Furies, gave them all the rights and the authority to continue on their cruel rampage, now making huge money through the selection of the best-looking or beautiful, sending them to be used, abused, beaten, starved, whipped, raped, then killed, or toiling in the outside labour in the freezing conditions. Sometimes, as a special treat and extra punishment, these prisoners were sent out completely naked into the freezing temperature, day or night, being exposed to the awful, dreadful, inhumane conditions, or per se being chased by the equally voracious, wild, famished dogs who would attack and devour the prisoners. None of them stood a chance.

The more beautiful, younger or older version of the prisoners, sometimes were killed the moment they arrived at the camp, so the Nazi males wouldn't see them and fall for them. Giving them the same ordeal by repeating what they would have done, with Lieutenant Cara, who by now was not only getting older, unwiser, sadder, but after her post-pregnancy,

Cara put on considerable weight. She was getting puffier, older and slower. Her drinking bouts and the good food, which was an extreme privilege, made her take duly trips in and out of the Concentration Camp's logistics to collect bigger uniforms and bigger shoes, and now she was wearing extra-size nylons. Her resentment grew even further when she was called fat and podgy, with the prisoners weakening, the famished getting skinnier, bony and fleshless, which for Cara was detrimentally obscene. Her madness knew no fury. Her resentment blinded her totally.

Some of the girls were still virgins, others barely out of their pubescent years, others fresh out of their kinder (children). But that did not stop the Hitler's Furies from doing as they pleased.

Dozens of them fell pregnant, and their babies were slaughtered in a vicious ritual, always saluting Hitler and laughing like the devils that they all were. All babies were made into sacrificial rituals, and that is where the term Holocaust comes from, from the Greek meaning "burnt". At the time, most bodies were burnt into cinders, what we all know now as cremation.

Please note:

(Historical background. Hitler was very much imbued in the occult, and he also created the myth of the new coming of the Aryans. He himself was born under the star and zodiacal sign of Aries, the Ram. His date of birth was on 20 April 1889, and he died on 30 April 1945 by suicide. He was 56 years old. With him was his wife for one day, Eva Braun.)

Ravensbrück Concentration Camp was the second largest camp for the prisoners of war, mainly women, children and girls, and the others were treated like sacrificial lambs. These Hitler's Furies would never stop at anything to do the "right" thing for the Führer. The Führer held a special spell on them. It had never occurred to them that at any stage they were committing criminal acts of such repudiating shape and form. They held onto their own dire convictions, of their own serfdom or servitude to the Führer, as he held all of them under a bastion of some kind of bewitchment, entrancing all of them. By himself, he had induced in them the total belief of them as the Furies. They were now so proud in becoming such a part of an eclectic military organisation, besides being all powerful, as Hitler added them all into his plans which included total dominion and the purging of the Jews. Blinded by their own wrong judgement, they did everything accordingly to their "rights." Suffice to say, for the outsiders, there were notes by and large of the signs of jealousy and narcissism, which led to the debaucheries being committed by these Furies who, under the name of Hitler, were nothing but criminals and murderers. At the trial, where these so-called servants to Hitler were called sadists, with the judgement against them, all the applicable crimes ever to be committed, hence called the Holocaust, as their abuse went as far as to actually commit sexual acts against children: paedophilia, which I am afraid pretty much existed.

But for the good news, some of the babies survived as the doctor ingeniously devised a good plan in making them survive.

Testimony of their vile debaucheries, inhuman treatment, abuse of power, paedophilia, rapes of women, slavery and killing them were noted during the trials, adding up the tales of starvation, brutal beatings, and the wild dogs chasing after the prisoners that they would later be facing.

"The whippings went on a daily basis." "The women were punished for anything, even for sneezing," as Cara enjoyed the sound of the whippings. Overnight, many of the Furies became rich in everything, from the material possessions of the prisoners, keeping their jewellery, the money being paid by the Nazis for the "virgins", the beautiful women, with some of them with "Kinder." The Germans were rich, and now the Furies even richer. Many who knew poverty could afford whatever luxuries they wanted, with ladies' toiletries and their new brigadier of evil. The Furies' women were known for ferocious nicknames such as Angel of Death, the Beautiful Beast, with Cara having the definition of "The Whipping Fury" or "The Whipping Witch." Now she was respected and feared by her own hand.

Their fun ways to entertain were now a novelty game. Due to the diseases and the plague of lice, the Furies took into their hands the pleasure in cutting and shaving the women's hair.

They would wrench their hair, cut it in different styles and have a good laugh. However they did it, the women prisoners would still remain beautiful, much to their chagrin.

Therefore, the Furies found more inventive ways to torture these poor women.

One of them that Cara took notice of, coming to really hate her, was one Jew.

(She was plain to look at, but still blonde-haired and with blue eyes. And she was a Jew?)

"Sie war blond behaart und blauäugig und sie war ein Jude?"

"Sie war einfach anzusehen." (She was plain to look at.)

"Ihr Name wurde Bridget, über Brück, ihr Pass war ursprünglich australisch." (Her name was Bridget, her passport was originally Australian.)

"Aber, sie haben sie Sara genannt. Sie war stolz, ein Jude zu sein, sie war schwer zu knacken." (But they called her Sara. She was a proud Jew, and was hard to crack.)

So the Hitler's Furies had a tough nut to crack. But Sara Adams remained defiant.

She proudly quoted, "Not by might, nor by power, but by my own spirit." True.

Sara suffered the most as Hitler's Furies went all the way after her: rapes, constant beatings, shoving her, starving her, putting her in the isolation black room. Anything to break her, but Sara would always recite the Hebrew Psalms, pray to her God and always use the same motto. Humiliation, embarrassment, shaming her, the babies were killed in front of her, and they sent the dogs chasing after her just for the fun of it all.

Throughout it all, Sara, who would later suffer from Post Traumatic Stress Disorder, felt nothing as she decided that whatever came, she would put up with it. There was no point in living when she didn't have anything to live for. But somewhere along the line, Sara Adams was human, and she really lost the plot. She suffered a mental and nervous breakdown and was committed.

Her husband René was already dead, or so she thought, and her babies, born of the rapings, were also gone. But living or dying, it did not make any difference. But it did. What Sara didn't know was that she would have a second go at life.

Sir Richard Bennett read unexcitedly the information about Cara and then about Sara.

He looked at the majordomo and said, "Unbelievable. What is Cara up to? I know all about Sara in the Concentration Camp. So what is she trying to prove?"

The majordomo smiled and made another cocktail.

"Who did she ring from the hotel?" He asked the majordomo again.

The majordomo picked up the phone and dialled.

Then he came over to the table and handed over a pad with a few names and numbers.

"Interesting. I wonder who they are?" Dickie boy took a few sips and lit a cigar.

The majordomo replied, "I think one would call them Hitler's Furies."

Dickie boy replied nonchalantly. "Hitler's Furies. Hmmm, we are now in the Swinging Sixties. Hitler is already dead. Germany lost not one war but a couple. West Berlin belongs to the Allies. We have a Queen sitting on the British throne, Queen Elizabeth the Second." That made him think of "Queen Elizabeth Bligh of Camelot's Kingdom." The old matriarch Bligh.

"And do they know, these Hitler's Furies, about the new century? Or a new decade, a new era?"

The majordomo smiled and said, "She seems to hate this Sara mortally. I think that they might have a plan. Why don't we wait and see? I think that she is waiting for the return of the Aryans."

"Zu sehen und zu fühlen." (To see and to feel.)

Dickie boy continued, "Are they dangerous?"

"Sind sie gefährlich?" He repeated. "Are they dangerous?"

The majordomo replied in German, "Wütend, verrückt, sauer, toll, böse, bekloppt." (Mad, crazy, unstable, clunky.)

Dickie boy was impressed. "You know all these 'bekloppt'? Now this is serious."

"She sure looked like it," he says, referring to Cara.

"What do you think of these photos of Cara?" Inquired Dickie boy.

The majordomo came close to the table and took a good look at the black and white fading, completely covered with lines and creases.

"Ist diese Cara?" Inquired the majordomo. (Is this Cara?)

"Was denkst du von ihr, schön oder nicht?" (What do you think of her, beautiful or not?) Again asked Dickie boy.

The majordomo replied, "Nein, sie ist nicht einmal hübsch." (No, she's not even pretty.)

"Warum nicht?" (Why not?) Inquired Dickie boy.

The majordomo replied, "Sie ist sehr stattlich. Sie sieht schon aus. Sie ist sehr männlich." (She is very handsome. She already looks it. She is very manly.)

"She was trained to act and behave like this," Dickie boy replied.

"Sie tut nichts für mich," the majordomo replied. (She does nothing for me.)

"Do you know something that I don't?" he asked suspiciously.

"Ich mag sie nicht." (I don't like her.)

"Sie schaut mir große Probleme. Sie ist bekloppt." (She is for me big trouble. She is mad.)

The majordomo stopped for a moment and resumed his explanation. He knew trouble when he saw one, and he had seen many in his entire lifetime.

"Bitte Herr Bennett, vergessen Sie Cara. Sara oder keine Sara ist nicht wichtig." (Please, Sir Bennett, forget about Cara. Sara or no Sara is not important.)

"Cara, Cara ist verrückt. Bekloppt. Verrückt." The majordomo expressed his feelings. (Cara, Cara is mad. Insane. Mad.)

"Und sie schaut es. Nichts Gutes kann dabei herauskommen." (And she looks it. Nothing good can come out of it.) Calming himself down, he gently resumed his speech.

Dickie boy replied, "Sie machen sich Sorgen." (You are worried?)

The majordomo replied. Presently he was behind the kitchen's bar, working on something else. Seriously, he wanted to have his message go through to his master. He loved his master. Sir Richard Bennett had always been good to him. Dicko had plucked him out of nowhere, even though he was of German roots. They always spoke in German, but he knew when his master was completely taken by the likes of mad women as Cara was. Dicko had had a few of them, but this Cara certainly took the cake.

"Denken Sie darüber nach, Herr Bennett. Cara ist eine Furie, alte Geschichte. Warum sollte sie zu Ihnen kommen? Cara ist bis zu etwas. Und wenn sie es ist, kann sie alles alleine." (Think about it, Sir Bennett. Cara is a Fury, ancient history. Why would she come to you? Cara is up to something. And if she is, she can do it all alone.)

"Cara benutzt uns, um sich an Sara zu rächen. Du weißt nicht, was im Kriegsgefangenenlager passiert ist. Hitler ist tot. Wir sind jetzt in den vollen Schwingern der Sechziger Jahre. Was spricht Cara über?" (Cara is using us to get revenge on Sara. You don't know what happened in the POW camp. Hitler's dead. We're now in the full swing of the Sixties. What is Cara talking about?)

"POW? Sara was in Ravensbrück," said Bennett now.

"She was fighting against the Nazis. They all belonged to the Allies, captured and taken to Ravensbrück, like many others. But she was also Jewish."

"Ein Ort, den ich nicht gewagt hätte zu gehen." The majordomo revealed. (A place I would not have dared to go.)

He shook his head. "Von dem, was ich gehört habe, war es ein höllischer Ort. Ich bin Deutscher und stolz darauf." (From what I've heard, it was a hellish place. I am German and proud of it.) "Aber Ravensbrück, Auschwitz, sind nicht meine Überzeugungen." (But Ravensbrück, Auschwitz, are not of my beliefs.)

The majordomo laughed at the posters written on the concentration camps.

"Arbeit macht frei." (Work sets you free.) As Dicko boy handed the majordomo a few of the black and white photos.

The majordomo quoted, and again shook his head sadly.

"Diese armen unschuldigen Menschen." (Those poor innocent people.)

Bennett looked at his majordomo, and he could have sworn that for once his cool, calm and collected majordomo was reduced to tears.

"Take a few days off," Bennett demanded. "It's obvious that you are exhausted with all of these memories," he softly told his majordomo.

"Sir Bennett, please don't do what I am thinking you are going to do. Whatever it is, let the Blighs be." Now he spoke in English, and now it thoroughly betrayed his German ancestry. He spoke with no accent.

Bennett looked at his majordomo and said, "You go and get some rest, for about two weeks. Shall see you then. Meanwhile, get Candace, beautiful Candace, to come over. She will fit my bill."

The majordomo bowed and left. Two hours later, Candace turned up: tall, fresh-faced, dark-haired and with an easy and available personality. Bennett sent her to spy on Cara.

The lady did not ask any questions. She just booked into the hotel, looking modern and rich.

Two different ladies. Let's see how their wits would be matched.

Both were highly trained in intelligence. The question is, who is spying on whom? What has Sara Adams got to do with this SS Third Reich Officer Cara de Rhe? Where does Candace fit into this bill? Who is she? Why is she here? Where is she from? Dicko's eyes sparkled like sapphires. "Well, well and well."

Three women. One a Holocaust survivor. One a Hitler's Fury. And Candace, the spy.

BOOK 2. A PLACE TO CALL HOME "The Forensics" will be continuing in the other further editions. Cara de Rhe will not let go of Sara Adams. See both of them battling it out.

Hoping to see you all then.

Chapter 13: Elizabeth Bligh. Queen of Camelot of Broken Dreams.

"You Bligh women, it's either your way or the highway." Matthew Goddard to grand Elizabeth Bligh. His voice shook, controlling his emotions, feeling rage and bitterness. He was defeated. But he decided one last time to insult and demean the grand Elizabeth Bligh, now Goddard.

"I guess you had Dad under your leash." Matthew Goddard, sorely and painfully, acknowledged his defeat. He saw the mighty power of the impossible and the Bligh women's determination. It was impossible to fight them on or off. He needed to go. The bitter taste of being toppled was just that: totally bitter, tasteless, harsh.

Camelot's Kingdom of broken dreams.

The mystical realm, the castle where the Blighs' Dynasty originated and ruled, with their ways, shapes and regulations. Secretly, socially, secretly and socially being out of sight from the present public eye and scrutiny, thus creating an aura of mystique, a legend, a place that actually conjures up the fantasy of faeries, goblins, pixies, kings and queens, princes and princesses, dames and maids, knights in shining armour, serving by pledging themselves willingly and ably on their own accord, their own serfdom, or forcibly continuing on with their lives, submitting themselves, the loyalty, faithfully blinding them to everything and anything, insidiously facing anything with bravery, dignity and courage, even dying for them with honour. Such gallantries, such passion, such commitment. Magical indeed.

But with the good comes, of course, the bad. Such is life and vice versa. If it is mystical living in a medieval castle, then naturally there would be magicians, jokers, adding up to the witches and warlocks, unleashing their evil, discomfort, hatred, resentment, chaos, mayhem and suffering.

A Place to Call Home

Once upon a time (era uma vez) in the land of fantasy, the obscure, the foggy, the mystical, not to mention a most elusive place. Beautiful in all of her natural glory, a farcical village amidst all the heavy greenery, covered by the subliminal hanging of the cypresses, the long-standing weeping willows, the soft-coloured scented magnolias, the beautiful gardenias, as opposed to the hot pink fuchsias, and the blending of the colourful roses peeping here and there, created an existing myriad of colourful ambience spreading its joy and goodwill all over the fantabulous states of Inverness (down in NSW's Camden in Australia), in which a very neat tapestry was intricately woven, comprising the added touches of gold and silver, embellishing it with colours befitting the glamour and the natural picturesque gravure, scenically inviting, showing the lovely and the lively land, thus adding its more subtle, delicate and fragile touches, generating thus a captivating kingdom named Camelot, where the present people and passers-by would stop, gawked in awe at such a splendidly neat, precisely woven tapestry, or a vivid and lively painting, so idyllic, where the meeting of the mystical, the magickal, inviting thus the cruel world to mingle, creating a story of a Peter Pan's Never Never Land, thus a kingdom was created, sparkling different avenues of stories that came alive by the simple touch or the flicking of a finger, and everything would undergo the seismic cultural self-style where lust, love, romance, hmmm, yes, hmmm, the epicentre of a kind of energy that swirled like smoke, covering it with dense fog, creating the subtlety of what was and was not, blurring the real thing into the fantastical ones, so deep, isolated, so far and distant, forbidden, capturing anyone's imagination throughout it all, generating the curiosity afforded to anyone normal by any standards but highly abnormal towards the ones who seemingly lived inside.

Camelot's Kingdom stretches far and wide with rolling green land, fanned by the huge leafy trees, animals grazing peacefully, boasting an impressive sprawling into a giant land without boundaries, or does it? With the horizon mingling together with the blue sky, connecting them both together, thus one could pretend to touch the horizon with one's finger. The plentiful blending with the sweet harmony of nature, a sight for sore eyes. It was a dream, waking up to the many fantasies and tales all woven into the fabricated legends. This was it.

Camelot's Kingdom had manicured rose gardens, surrounded by beautiful ivory and also mythical statues, depicting them in different and various poses, silent witnesses of the immense privileges and the ostentatious luxuries, with the privacy, the beauty coupled with the splendour, bespeaking by itself, crowing with the impressive wealth that the occupants residing in it could, by and large with one's gaze, fall upon the prestigious and picture-perfect maintained garden where one finds and marvels, immersing into another world just by walking on the soft velvet green lawns. The soft scents of the sweet and inviting fragrances of those beautiful tended roses, so much loved by the matriarch. They say that roses bespeak of romance and endless love, but it can also mean death and sorrow. This place was a double-edged sword.

Camelot, a mythical place, catered for and possessed cattle and horses, whose owners enjoyed galloping at full speed, shaking the grounds with the huge thundering thuds, fogging the air with its sand and dust, enjoying the calming benefits of the fresh air away from the far-polluted modern cities. Camelot could extend its pleasure-seeking people, inviting them to dip into the natural cool crystalline lake where the owners see fit in making picnics on the side. If anything, this kingdom had everything of the best, as most would be happy, outsiders or insiders, taking the time to really rest and enjoy the place by immersing themselves into the cold, refreshingly gentle streams of one gigantic place like this around Camelot's Kingdom, endlessly finding anything, and if anything. But looks can be highly deceiving.

In the midst of it all stood, tall and imperative (no, I am not screaming), majestically, proud, defying it all, was this beacon of light, shining with dignified, beautiful and handsome at the same time, in its sturdy, hard-core foundation. The unique, palatial, grand manor, the Blighs' Palace (for many it is called Ashpark), but for the more romantic ones, this huge and tall building bestowed with such admiring architecture, was in the fictional constraints of Inverness, well known as Camelot, in its own kingdom. Alone, remote, distant, a desired but lonely place, with so much of the cover-ups, innuendoes and forbidden love.

Not forgetting that the name Bligh meant in both languages "Luminoso" or "Lumière," simply and directly "light," meaning be the light.

This magnificent place, where it was ruled only and solely by women, had two sides to it, alas a triple or even more. But for the time being, I am focusing on two sides.

(As I was meant to write it in Sara Adams' Chapter, Book 1, A Place to Call Home, "The Forensics", Chapter 10, but did not, due to it being too long. So here is an excerpt of what originally was supposed to be in the Sara Adams' Chapter.)

(Women, like Sara Adams, walk amongst all of us. There are so many Sara Adams who faced so much misfortune, sadness and heartbreaks, but still conducted themselves and carried on with their work, onwards, facing it all bravely. Having said that, Sara Adams could also be dangerous. Sara was involved in wars and revolutions. In her later years she would fight to earn a place to reign as the new Queen of Camelot's Kingdom, becoming then, but not for very long, who, like the structure itself, changes and modifies as the weather with the harsh elements thrown at them changes. From that tall and majestic building that stands out imperiously, interestingly watching the world through, overseeing the small town of Inverness, beaming its shining light (town, village, city, all three that could be easily called), being the pride and the glory implying the more higher status of the rich and the privileged, the grandiose, the beacon, enhancing all the goodies that entail the members of Camelot's Kingdom and Inverness City to enjoy the bright, sunny, jolly structure. But on the days which were cloudy, smoggy and dark, the building being blown and shaken by Mother Nature's own furious strong winds, changing it completely, scary, dark, evil, completely menacing, autocratic, malevolent, like the previous owners: the grand Elizabeth, then the mad Regina and now Sara. While Mother Nature compels to destroy it with her own fury, sending lightning, flood and thunder, crushing and eliminating everything on her way. Therefore, this palatial building depicts the many moods of anyone exacting, projecting its dark side, the light side, the sun and the moon, the left and the right, the yin and the yang, the black and the white, the ups and downs, the female and the male.

One questions, as easily describing these three previous and future ladies of this same manor (not forgetting the other ladies too: Caro, Anna, Olivia, the indomitable Little Lizzie, along the way Little Lizzie's two daughters Amethyst and Begonia, her son Louis, Little Elaine, with the next Queen being the future David's wife, joining the above dynamic ladies but by then all of the Blighs residing in a new place). Now that you have mentioned where the above-mentioned queens with their split personalities, driving them as insane as they could be, nearly breaking them down, the bursts of their malevolent and evil energies, intentionally venomous ways of hurting and harming anyone crossing their paths, played by the sudden attacks of so much mainstream of regrets, show in itself a very much dark and unbalanced side to their own state of minds. Yet in here, surviving is the key.

With the breaking and the bursting of the dams, with the powerful water exploding all over Camelot's vast terrain, bring us to solicit the true veneer of the residents of Camelot of broken dreams.

Exactly how morbid, eccentric but oh so righteous and imperative this tall majestic edifice was significantly for anyone is, of course, anyone's guess. It is all for sure your own opinion, as in everyone else's. Remember that this is only a fictional and farcical novel, a unique fairy tale with huge connotations, with the fun and fanfare lives that were ruled rigidly by the social standards and the self-serving "protocol." At the time, it could have been the real thing.

She knew all about them: pressures, betrayals, coercions, double dealings, manipulations, double standards. She was brought up through it all, thus she actually learnt to live with them.

The Blighs' family on Elizabeth's husband's side were filthy rich, wealthy, bespoken and almost royalty, but all conniving, constantly changing their ways, stories and their families' traditions.

Respectable gentry that young Elizabeth was brought up to believe. The woman we all came to loathe, hate, love and pity, but sadly too late understood, became so incensed and then a control freak, bearing almost to the point of lunacy. And more to it, when jealousy strikes, as Sir Richard Bennett stated, "it's game over." How true, especially when they cannot do as he says. "I don't like failures," he warned Regina about her being so smug to the point of actually losing the grip on George and the Blighs, badly needing her as the foot soldier to continue what he had actually gathered to in future use for the sole destruction of the Blighs. Man, he was right at it, with or without Regina. Richo always had a plan.

But Elizabeth was not jealous of the other women per se. She was jealous of how the other women felt about having love and a trustworthy man who they could rely upon. By her own admission, she said that "she has never thought that a man could be stronger than a woman." Was she right or wrong? I think that she was wrong. A woman can be stronger than a man anytime, anywhere. But then again, that is my own opinion.

Elizabeth has never learnt, neither did Sara, that "differences which cannot be ignored," quoted Elizabeth in self-defence. She had every opinion and every reason, excuses to actually explain anything, even if she had to lie. Which both did. Elizabeth and Sara. Both had a great deal to hide.

Elizabeth also used Regina, who was used and abused. Sara was nothing but a newcomer. She was still trying to survive still. All three and even more oozed that kind of irresistible charm, charisma, intelligence, foxy astuteness, in addition beauty, class and elegance, sophistication at its peak. "Enchanting," as Douglas Goddard chimed, "What a charming lady." He, without knowing it, instituted it in front of Elizabeth Bligh. And the look on Elizabeth's face: jealousy, disbelief? Or something far more sinister? With Elizabeth, a very much complexed personality, perhaps, as no one could tell. Elizabeth blew hot and cold. One never knew about what to expect when it came about her own personality, character, vices, love, likes and dislikes, which made her the best, the worst, with nothing in between. Just like the towering building and the supposedly beacon of light. Camelot of broken dreams.

However, Elizabeth in herself was the broken one. So was Sara. So was Caro. So was Anna. So was Livvy. So was Little Lizzie.

As Regina put it out clearly and spitefully to Elizabeth Bligh, "You and I are cut from the same cloth," and Reggie was so right.

It was due to Regina, at the behest of Elizabeth, who found that René was still alive and kicking. It was meant to be a blessing in disguise. Bigamy. But now, even dead, Regina was creating havoc by charging George, who was still married to Regina, as his divorce was never annulled. None cared, and no one gave Regina the benefit of the doubt. The now-dead Regina was still causing hell with raptures, inflicting nightmarish events on the Blighs. With Richo smiling incredulously, with his old and near-sighted blue eyes chirping in true grit, with his white moustache tweaking, whilst his cracked skin on his face deepened.

Regina flipped? No thanks to Elizabeth. Her own beauty turned against Regina herself. Poor Regina, being beautiful, thinking that the world owed her everything, or is it because she suffered from a serious case of maladies? Some suggested limerence, a term that means it was an illusive trade, her own. She believed that she was interacting with George and that he loved her. But was it really? But there is something highly suspicious about the whole event: Regina's death. Why would Regina kill herself? Especially me, but let's hear what Queen's Counsel Little Lizzie Bligh will prove and make out of that in Book 2, A Place to Call Home, Regina's Death, Chapter Four: "Homicide." The Bennetts vs the Blighs.

Regina's predictable words: "One day you will come to regret this," when Sara Adams failed to thank Regina for signing the divorce "legal" and "official" documents. Okay, now the dye has been cast. And let's see what comes out of it. But one word though: Sara Adams always found a solution to some of her minor and major problems, but not all of them worked beneficially for her and the Blighs. If anything, presently it was giving them more trouble.

For Elizabeth, Sara Adams at a time was a lost cause. The freaking Jew, that somehow "enchanted" her ways into the Blighs' family and sexually enticed George Bligh. "Some things cannot be ignored," telling Caro, who, like Sara, was fighting for her own survival.

Sara knew how to go about it. She and George were lust, animal, primordial, wild lust, which brings us to the present moment. Lust or not, he married the lady, yes?

As Regina put it, "She's not really something. I don't see anything special about her." No, but there was such a thing called love, when both Regina and Elizabeth plotted the downfall of Sara, in which Elizabeth commanded, "Find something, anything, that will rid us of her permanently and forever." But by then, Elizabeth was at a crossroads when she alone tried to get rid of Regina.

Exactly my point. Elizabeth had so much to live for, but she had even more reasons to cover up the secrets of the Blighs' dynasty, and on issuing that command to her detriment, Elizabeth tried everything to hide all the secrets. Secrets that not even Regina knew, but her cunning would, so she could blackmail Elizabeth. Get the picture?

The more Elizabeth's dark thoughts about Sara and the more she wanted to rid of Sara, the more Sara, wittingly or unwittingly, denied Elizabeth the pleasure, bringing chaos, confusion and, to such an extent, the division between a family. As Elizabeth related to Caro when Caro turned up in Inverness, with all three of them having flights of fancy, they each fancied being something or rather, which ultimately would bring Sara down, with the charges being made against Sara for many reasons other than bigamy, with the Immigration Office to face up on.

She was away for so long from Australia, then she converted to Judaism, her passport being Jewish.

She returned to Australia as the new Jew. The Immigration Officials charged Sara with illegally entering Australia on the Immigration Act 1958, therefore she would need to wait for her visa to re-enter Australia. The Immigration Officials calmed the Blighs down: it was just an oversight.

George is allowed to return home to Sydney, and so was her son David, but Sara, being the "red commie whore" married to the rich and powerful

Cattle Baron George Bligh, was not going to improvise at all, with the bigamy charges coming through.

Elizabeth grows anxious as more detailed facts are uprooted, with Sara and George not being able to return home to Inverness at all at the time. George would never leave Sara by herself in Israel, with George now being the original fodder for the Blighs' family. Under the circumstances, with Sara now having more panic and anxiety attacks and being admitted into the hospitals, George was now a miserable old man, trying to make sense out of it all. David was growing into a tall, handsome, dark, straight, long-haired man. His eyes shone piercingly blue, and his symmetrical face spelt Bligh. He was so much like his dad, as Elizabeth stared at him from afar. Elizabeth was trying to predict his fate.

Sara went from that warrior to the mere regretful mea culpa, sad feelings assailing her, the sufferings, the reminder of those terrible nightmarish days that would see her all curled up in a foetal position, shaking inside the closet. Darkness surrounding her, terrible headaches plaguing her, hard breathing intensifying her anxiety attacks, but now coming up with physical pain, her bones cracked during the hard beatings and whippings in Ravensbrück.

"I have killed. I have poisoned." She would continually over-say it, sickeningly repeating herself to the others. It was the inflection of her own self. She was suffering hallucinations and delusions. By the time Sara returned to Australia with the Resident's Visa, George suffered a heart attack. All that she had lost once, gained again, was now lost again. The palatial residence in Camelot's Kingdom seems to have its own perfidious magic, and it never stopped inflicting the more painful acts on anyone. Sara might be the present queen ruling it, but it would never be at her disposal at all. She was not to live as the eternal Queen of Camelot's Kingdom of broken dreams, period. But it was to be inherited by her own son Master David Bligh, who would sell Camelot of broken dreams, moving the Blighs' family entirely into a new, refreshingly domain into which the past would disappear. Not. Little Lizzie would stay behind in Camelot's Kingdom, with the sad saga continuing.

Ascending to the throne would be a couple of Elizabeths. Elizabeth Alexandra Bligh, daughter of Lewis George Bligh and Elizabeth Bligh, aka Little Lizzie, and Elizabeth Regina Bligh, daughter of Regina Margaret Bligh and George Robert Bligh, and her own twin brother George Robert Bligh the Second, with Sir Richard Bennett hovering around with his youngest son, Richard Bennett the Third, the son of Regina Margaret Bligh and Sir Richard Bennett the Second. The son that Bennett had with Reggie as an insurance policy.

In the middle of it all is the grand Elizabeth Bligh (Goddard). She exhales a deep sigh. Thank goodness Elaine was not another Elizabeth. She was Elaine Elizabeth Bligh, daughter of Anna Bligh and also Henry Fox. And if anything goes by, these were only the beginning, but there was still Little Lizzie to be considered and her three kids. With the Blighs, things couldn't get better, neither could they be bad. But I tell you this much: if it could go down, down it goes.

The shadow of Regina Bligh hovered assiduously, creating deep emotional shadows all around Camelot's Kingdom, and the shadows made them quake in cold feverish fear and freezing cold. That said, it was time for them to move. David had his share of problems, and his family needed a new beginning. He looked at his exotic beautiful wife and surveyed his kids again. The last was born. The oldest was Brannargh, the twins Iris and Calypso, with the youngest one Patrick. He found the real estate and the new place for him to move.

It was a mild day in the midstream of early September. Young Elizabeth, like any young, bright and stay-at-home lady, was embroidering. Time and again she would lift her head to check on her lovely surroundings. Early springtime arrived with some sunny shades, refreshing breezes, and Elizabeth was so happy to watch her beautiful roses blooming. The green lawn now curiously was a spectacle carpet, inviting her for her picnics, almost ready.

The scent and the perfume emanated from everywhere, and especially the bouquet of her own roses implanted in the coloured pink vase, assiduously reminding young Elizabeth of how perfect, fragile and dainty they were, pretty much life in itself.

It grew to be a beautiful day. The maids had just served her an early lunch, and tea was now being served with their delicate sandwiches.

She stopped and again surveyed around the place from her porch. Somehow, she could not shake it off. By the way, where was George?

Out. Where is Caro? Out. And where is Little Lizzie? Out, riding her beautiful purebred, all black and glistening horse. He was a beauty, and she called him just that: Black Beauty.

Where was Lewis? There was no answer. He'd be out again, yes, for sure. She was alone.

Elizabeth shrugged her shoulders and sat right back, accommodating herself, twisting her mouth as she so often did when something displeased her.

The tea was poured and she drank it. She shared her beverage with the extra sweets.

It was so quiet and peaceful. It was harmony at its best.

Nature at her best. There was no music or any sound except for the early buzzing of the bees and the noisy cicadas hovering on all sides of Camelot's. The peaceful atmosphere was broken by the annoying sound of the phone ringing. The call came through, and someone, her maid, mentioned to Elizabeth in a manner of urgency that it was an emergency, some kind of accident. Through it all, they brought her son George home. He was found completely mute and distressed. One of the employees spoke to them both, that George was in a state of shock, fright and incoherence. All shaken was one thing, but the other was that Elizabeth's husband Lewis was dead from an accident. She, as usual, remained cool and distant. But her heart stopped momentarily. It can't be. Lewis was dead. She heard the distant hooves of her younger daughter's horse galloping at full speed, trying to reach home to Camelot. Still Caro was not home, but George was. He was shaking wildly, with hard tears coming down his cheeks. His words were muffled. Elizabeth was no stranger to these kinds of chaos, but she prayed for her son to recover. Caro returned home only to find out the fate of her father. Little Lizzie was being excluded. She was a minor, and older Elizabeth did not want her anywhere near them all.

Through it all, Elizabeth made sure that the funeral arrangements were made and done. Lewis would be buried in the ancestral ground of the Blighs. After the services, light refreshments were served, then the codicil was drawn at her home in privacy.

Her children along with Elizabeth attended the private meeting. They all wore black, and Elizabeth was all elegant in her own petite ways. She sat with her children and with a newcomer by the name of Jack Duncan, in front of the lawyer who was reading out the will.

"And since there is no one outside my own Blighs' family, as I am the only surviving son of the elderly Blighs, and being Lewis Bligh the Second, it is for me to leave everything that belongs to the Blighs, my ancestral home, money, jewelleries, bonds, shares, with anything connected with me. I, Lewis George Bligh, do bequeath everything to my lovely wife Elizabeth, whom I love dearly and who is the mother of my children: George, Caroline and young Elizabeth (Little Lizzie). May they enjoy the best in their lives and in so doing, hoping that they will serve their purposes well in life. I am happy and content that I know my wife Elizabeth Bligh, who inherits everything, will also be the fine and prime Executor of my Will and of the Blighs' inheritance. This Will is to be followed to the letter and without any delays upon my death."

It was signed by Lewis George Bligh and his two attorneys and witnesses.

Everything went to Elizabeth. Now she was the absolute power, the absolute rule, to reminisce and discern. Elizabeth was the sole authority, issuing the rights to implement them. Her in-laws and other parties belonging to the Blighs were thrown out of the door. Elizabeth had enough of them, their lies, their two-faced existence. Now she was the Queen, and thus she would reign as the Queen of Camelot's Kingdom of broken dreams. Too late, Elizabeth saw that.

A Queen Is Crowned: Queen Elizabeth Bligh.

Elizabeth rose on her own. The terrible, difficult years were now behind her. It was so hard to understand where Lewis came from and went, but now she was relieved of her unsubstantiated morals and duties. She predicted something really odd and out of the ordinary was going to happen. If it did not happen one time, it would happen some other time. She was frightful for the truth to be revealed, as this was a frightening society to deal with, imagining the harsh outcome if they had found out that their father favoured males instead of females. Elizabeth needed to take a hard, steely grip on herself. All of those years, the terrible nightmares assailing her on a daily and nightly basis, luckily they were all paid off after a few days, or for that matter they would disappear by the ruthless hands of her own husband. It was not safe to have them blabbing their mouths at all. Money was never a problem. Lewis was the problem.

The farcical Blighs had him marry her to cover up for his "perverted" ways. The honeymoon was not that bad. Lewis did make an effort, being loving and very gentle, as she was still a young virginal bride. She, of course, would always show her support no matter what, more so when both were blessed by little Georgie, the male heir to the Blighs' Dynasty, within one year of their marriage. For all intents and purposes, the male Bligh was functioning. Lewis was happy. His own efforts paid off.

To be fair to Lewis, he was a loving husband and mostly a loving dad. He would stay with mother and baby son for a few months, then would go off into his own long sojourns: big business meetings, his make-believe long and hard travails, where he seemed to be lost in a world of his own, returning home in a foggy, lazed-out stupor, anxious and unhappy. As Elizabeth put it in her way, "he loathed himself for what he was." But away he went again after a few days, leaving Elizabeth and her older son alone in a huge, gigantic, cold, dark and sombre house, where the sun shone few and far between, and where human cosiness and enclosure with feelings of love and cherishing were missing. But Elizabeth was a very strong and determined woman: bitter, disappointed, hardly showing her emotions, hardly feeling any condescending love for her ex. Her smile was dire, hard and empty, and they were all just self-esteem and vacuous. Living in Camelot's Kingdom was no easy matter.

In the mainstream it was either day or night, ebb and flow, everything was then in a flux. Elizabeth's own place to call home.

Lewis returned home to his kids and herself, addicted to the other adventures. For many, he was a "maverick," but he never was. He hid and closed shop. One day, he left and stayed away for over a year.

By the time he returned, Elizabeth had already delivered their third child. But no one raised an eyebrow, and Lewis was so happy with the third little girl and so much "in love" with his wife that he named her Elizabeth. He'd always called her "Little Lizzie." The little girl grew up cute and spoilt, perhaps the favourite of her own distant father.

Elizabeth was born into a wealthy and privileged Australian family who could be royals themselves. In grand mansions all over Australia and palaces overseas, spending her long holidays in places that only one could sigh and dream about, different from her granddaughter Anna and her youngest daughter Little Lizzie, who thought all of these highly official things to be terribly tedious but socially highly privileged. She'd seen poverty with the Great Depression after World War II.

The family favoured her. Elizabeth was educated with a firm hand and at the time with the discipline that most young and wealthy-born ladies then were.

Like anyone at that time, she had long, very long curly mahogany hair. Half of the time it would be covered with ribbons, and also wearing the French beret that most girls in those days wore, with their coats and those buttoned boots, de rigueur.

She was taught French, protocol and also etiquette. She was taught haute couture fashion.

Her clothes were expensive, and she wore them with flair, dignity and elegance. Time and again, as she was growing up, with her flair and discernible tastes, would lend a hand in her being sophisticated, being the one whom the boys would ask for her hand.

She was petite, with long glorious mahogany wavy and curly hair tumbling down. Her face was such a beautiful one that no one could resist falling in love. Her skin was pale, with slanted blue eyes, the high cheekbones that were so becoming of the Blighs' ladies stood out, with a welcoming mouth which she would paint in pink. The jutting of her jaw expressed to viewers that her disposition was detrimentally assiduous and stubborn.

She attended a very convenient and most decorous school for ladies, and what struck the teachers was that Elizabeth was indeed a most determined young lady, and everything she put her mind to would therefore be accomplished. She was very social and quite popular but private. She would rise to any occasion but was hardly the person to show her true colours. Intelligent and savvy but never afraid to speak her mind, those trying years made Elizabeth resolute and independent. If she didn't marry, she would become the principal of the college. But when she returned home to her stately home at the age of eighteen, her parents told her the good news.

Her hand was asked in marriage by the fabulously wealthy Blighs. They had a son who was the epitome and the essence of everything. Tall, dark and handsome was Lewis Bligh.

They'd come for afternoon tea, as it was de rigueur, with Elizabeth returning from her rehearsal, the debutante ball. She was now chosen to be married.

She chose her beautiful "de rêve" white gown, the satin shoes, the basket, the gloves and also beautiful Beau Blume flowers that so much indicated how romantic she was. Beautiful flowers attached around her hair, bringing peace and tranquillity, adding the soft and gentle touches of romance. More now that Elizabeth was getting engaged and married, the blue flower meant desire, love and the metaphysical striving for the infinite and unreadable. It also symbolised hope and the beauty of things to come. She also showed what a dreamer she was, as it was not a flight of fancy or the surmises of blanked blubber. As per usual, the lady was très chic in her elementary endeavours, and she wanted "her new journey" to be eventually a good start for the long road ahead. Discernible and very much her own independent self, Elizabeth already showed that what she wanted, she would get. She was a force to be reckoned with.

Her debutante ball was a huge success. Who's who in the mighty and powerful Australian society attended the Bennetts, with the glamour, glitterati, the sophistication and the elegance of the time, the era, compounded into one evening of such entertainment, a glitzy affair that of course was well spoken of for years to come. That evening, Elizabeth became legally and officially the bride-to-be to the Blighs. Within six months, as was to be expected, she was the lady of everyone's dreams. Apart from a few stolen kisses here and there, and on their announcement, Elizabeth even cried, as Lewis slipped the beautiful sapphire ring onto the third finger of her left hand, to a multitude of sounding ovations with the deafening, endless clapping from all who were there, with champagne flowing and the night afterwards becoming blurred, misty and foggy. It was a most beautiful event, and it was no kosher, not in the surmises of blanked blubber, where one could afford to write something out of the phantasy land.

Their happy pictures were all over the elite magazines and the newspapers, and many would in the long run copy the style and the fashion of young and beautiful, demure Elizabeth. Now she was for all intents and purposes the next Mrs Bligh to be, a very happy bride indeed.

Everything worked like clockwork. Now she was picking her wedding dress from the modiste, choosing her shoes, the gloves, the flowers and the headpiece. She was constantly trying it on and wearing it, trial and error, and of course predictably afraid to put on weight, going on a nice diet, counting as all brides would, for the special day to come. Elizabeth was excited to be married into the Blighs' family and moving into that palatial palace that she had only seen once.

When it did happen, Elizabeth was so chuffed, totally exalted, as she triumphantly walked down the aisle with her handsome beau on her arm, and in her left hand on the third finger glittered her gold wedding band. Finally. She was Mrs Elizabeth Bligh, the Australian Royal Family.

Now she was the exalted one, reigning supremely in her role of the princess, the role and the lady as one of the Blighs' family. Moving into

Camelot's Kingdom was another dream come true. Now she was the one who looked outside from the inside.

For her, Lewis was perfect. Tall, dark and handsome, and the epitome of grace and charm. Lewis, who was wealthy beyond anyone's imagination, was also a surplus. Already the Blighs' name and prominence were very much connected with the high hiatus of British history.

Historical background: The Blighs are a name cognisant with Australian and English history. With it comes the controversy and the fights, the misunderstanding, the whole shebang that naturally goes with anything connected with world history.

William Bligh, who later became Vice Admiral of the Blue FRS-RN, married his wife Elizabeth Betham in 1781. He was one of the major ones that caused the upheaval in the Mutiny on the Bounty, known to have a terrible temper. His timing and bad luck led him to the ones actually involved in mutinies, starting with the Mutiny on the Bounty, when his best friend Fletcher Christian led a mutiny against him, Captain William Bligh. But more were to follow.

But whatever has happened, being him the laughing stock, it seems that William Bligh being a tough and firm disciplinarian was rewarded when he was offered the job of Governor of New South Wales, being paid the handsome sum of two thousand pounds a year. He was appointed by the previous Governor Phillip Gidley, and the new Governor William Bligh arrived in Sydney to take up his post on 6 August 1806.

William Bligh had a dry and cold character that didn't make him popular with anyone. It was unduly funny that he was best friends with Fletcher Christian, due to his inflexibility. When he was arrested then deposed in 1808, he passed away in Plymouth back in 1818, ten years after returning to England. He was dispirited with so much upheaval that he alone created.

Universal history shares that Elizabeth Bligh and these Blighs over here in New South Wales, where two centuries ago the British Blighs came to the shores of Australia, were indeed prominent for their ambitions and bravery. They and the Australian Blighs have nothing to do with one another. Whereas William Bligh was a real person and is part of history, these Blighs are a totally different kettle of fish. Nonetheless, one searches for something that is affordable and supposedly links these two families, but only thus. Elizabeth Bligh's and William Bligh's families have nothing to do with or in common with each other whatsoever. The Australian Blighs were wealthy cattle owners. The British Blighs earned their stripes by cruising the world at sea. Plus, the Australian Blighs are a fictional, farcical tale, a novel to be precise, and this is no kosher. It is a woke, and not a biased woke. It is a woke truth.

From the outside looking into the ancestral, sprawling estate, naturally one would call it a fairy kingdom. Thus, the name of Camelot's Kingdom harnessed anyone's powerful imagination, making it far more complete with tall tales of bravery and knighthood, with princesses, maids and knights in shining armour. One was given to the wild imaginations, entertaining oneself in living in these places that were so dreamy, like this aristocratic, majestic piece of elaborate architecture.

She stood imperiously overlooking the whole state of Inverness. The land bespoke by itself with the opulence, the vastness, wealth and the natural beauty, between the night and the day, the ebb and the flow. One listens to the sound of the more serene singsong of the soft splashing of the lake that was near their estates, as life went around in its various stages.

With such an estate, Elizabeth understood now that the style and status came with their own high standards and the price. But that alone did not encompass the duress where more realistic, believable or unbelievable theories or projectable ideas would encompass a far more ideal of what Camelot's Kingdom was all about. Therefore and undoubtedly, one kingdom so mystical and so magical would have needed the creation or the birth of something out of mystery. Thus, the honourable Mrs Elizabeth Bligh became the Queen of Camelot's Kingdom. Of course, she wore many hats and hair pieces, hair garlands. Twice in her life she wore a real pearl tiara, which was cost-effective in that being profitable and valued for its own money. After all, her family was wealthy, and now she was the mythical Queen Elizabeth of Camelot's Kingdom, but broken dreams to be exact. Right from the beginning, Elizabeth found to her disbelief the dire facts of the Blighs' family. She wept for days on end, for she was led into a marriage that was a false start for the beginning of her unblissful wedded union, a life of torment, of doubts ensued. Then the nightmarish start to her everyday fear of being discovered: the shame, the humiliation, the high embarrassment. Oh, Elizabeth shook and trembled with the idea of the Blighs' terrible secret being found. She lived for each day, each night, petrified by the developing events that if found could have serious, but really serious, developments. Elizabeth was strong. However, in doing so, George, Caro and Little Lizzie thinking in keeping her family out of trouble, but being the new Queen, faced nothing but an oncoming of troubles, obstacles, deaths and sickness. Everything, and of course the terrible secret that could make and break anyone. That Lewis's death came through on that day, Elizabeth didn't know how to tackle it, if it was a relief and a real blessing in disguise.

Camelot has been synonymously covered by the misty fog, shrouding it into more mystery, an existing realm of magic and mysticism, a fairy lake, the sword with magic, adventure, an age of chivalry, of challenges, and of course the search for the Holy Grail, where once upon a time existed a King Arthur of Pendragon and the Knights of the Round Table. Being a kingdom, mystical or not, exoteric or not, magical or not, a realm, a kingdom called Camelot comes with all the intricacies, the beauties, with lovely and beautiful princesses, ladies in waiting, warrior women, along with also knights in shining armour, conjuring the best and the worst, such as a fae and also a wizard. One was the half-sister of King Arthur, whose name electrifies one with its powerful dynamism. Beautiful and smart, she was a warrior before she became the ethereal witch who fought for Camelot and defeated Merlin the powerful wizard, fighting for her own birth rights so she too could wear the gold and ruby-encrusted crown of Camelot's reign. Nonetheless, for her to ascend to the throne, Princess Morgana, or Lady Morgana, fought hard and fiercely for what she thought could be hers through her birth rights. But against her, in this enchanting tale of high love and treason, romance and betrayal, of delightful magic, fascinating tradition and culture, the fashion lore and all that is connected to it. On further analysis, Camelot has practically everything that one could sit down and watch it display all its features in front of anyone. It was, or it is, a bewitching lore entwined with all the angst and sufferings of the day-to-day humans who go through elementally everything: the pain, the sadness, health issues. But they try to survive at their own perils, fighting amongst themselves. To be a ruler comes to an end as King Arthur dies, supposedly in the Isles, and Camelot in Avalon destroys itself.

With the legend going on about if and when Britain is being attacked, King Arthur along with the Knights of the Round Table will rise and go into battle. Whether Sir Lancelot de Lac comes into it, no one knows.

Into this effect, Princess Guinevere, the future wife of King Arthur and the young daughter of the then current rulers of Avalon, Queen Anya and King Jared, was bold and graceful, charming and beautiful, always ready to face up to the challenges that await our Guinevere as the Queen rides the wings of her destiny to vanquish evil and, of course, to detrimentally secure her rightful place as the future Queen of this magnificent but so obscure, misty, cloudy, foggy fairy-tale realm and kingdom. (Starla. Fandômsi.) (In mist, foggy, legends.)

The comparison of one Australian Camelot and of the mystical British Camelot is incredibly uncanny. Both are farcical and fictional. So when one reads Camelot and is in Australia in the turn of the last century, one starts thinking on how close and far these accounts go. Practically the same ideology, the same theory and different practices. It existed in a time of forbidden love, as Guinevere was married to King Arthur but fell in love with Sir Lancelot du Lac (or Lancelot of the Lake), as he was originally from the Lake Lady of the Shallots. He was one of the best Knights of the Round Table, an excellent jouster and also a supreme swordsman, whose first wife Elaine bore him a son who at a later stage would become Sir Galahad. And even though Elizabeth Bligh fell in love with Jack Duncan's father, she stood by Lewis until the end, through fear and foe, determined to do everything she was set out to do. Her children came first. Not as Sir Richard Bennett stated, "You will never win a Mother's Day award. You who for years treated your daughter for the slut that she was," or words to this effect. Being a parent was not Sir Richard Bennett's forte, but his dreadful obsession and hatred against the Blighs were always deep and highly pronounced. He would always be ready to strike the Blighs. Was also highly inventive and ordained in his ways. More of his "naughtiness" is yet to come.

But Elizabeth was the mother, was a wife, the queen. Those days were the woman's duty to actually fulfil all of these trends. In those days, a woman's "place" was home and in the kitchen. Then her extras were to clean, iron and look after her kids, tending to everything for the master or the husband, which was laughable.

A woman suffered all kinds of prejudicial and radical tension, and if she was not married but a working girl she was then a social outcast. These were then the lay-out of what a woman's thorough duties of being married was. But Elizabeth Bligh, as she vehemently stressed, "I never thought that men in general could be as strong as a woman," made sense. But for the others, that was some kind of irrational revelation. It was a woke bias. No judgement. Nor was she deemed out of touch, especially as Elizabeth put it, "We have a woman sitting on the throne." Whatever, Elizabeth might have been the suffragette in those days, but she had started a strong response in being a feminist. Not ideal, but highly plausible. Terribly ignorant but totally in high standards. It was no surmises of the irrational thinking and the coverings of blanked blubbers, and it was no kosher either. It was all real. It was a woke, with the same patina, but she failed to see it in the beginning.

Elizabeth was the eclectic personality but uncommonly colourful, as she wouldn't have wanted to bring or seek the outsiders' attention to her own family, to avoid the scandal and the embarrassment that would in the distance be the cause of such bitter humiliation. But in each and every turn she was undone by her both rebel daughters, Caro and Little Lizzie. To add to her own torments and nightmares, suffering in silence, for Lewis might have been a cold fish but he sired three children. But nothing was ever concrete and everlasting: pretentious, social, activist, tall, dark, handsomely rugged. In public, he was the adoring husband, the doting dad, but that was that. Once the "movie" was finished and the camera stopped rolling, he would kiss her and bid her goodbye. She wondered in fact if anyone knew about it.

The fearful, authoritative, far cold and distant figure. For those who didn't know her, the folklore abounded that she was a non-smiling witch, always too busy for anything and always jumping and judgemental. Once her own beauty was well spoken of, la joie de vivre, as her youngest daughter Little Lizzie was. Elizabeth was hard, manipulative, always using her own powerful status for her own factual fights and tall renditions. She would never ever lose face again. No one would make her suffer fools. She was no pushover but she was being highly sensible. No one would come near the fence of her family. No one would discover the secrets. Those brought her heart attacks.

By trying to do her best, Elizabeth failed somewhat. She was highly critical, always judgemental and bitter to a point of her own self-description, pushing her into isolation. She saw her tears, how lucky she was by marrying into the Blighs' family. What she saw, she felt: tasteless. And when she could taste it, it was bitter. She felt so incomplete, being a Bligh. She felt so cheated. One moment she was grabbed by these convulsions of errors, and the next she totally felt sorry for herself and more. Sometimes the anxiety and depression set in, and the world was never the same, as she lashed her frustration into the world and its people.

She could have had plenty of males if she so wanted. But males and her were always in a collision, with the man coming from Mars and women like her disdainfully coming from Venus. It thoroughly irritated her to the utmost of everything.

Ever since Lewis passed, Elizabeth's life increased and decreased. Now that her wayward husband was not here, she had her three kids to bring up, taking her time and energy to look after them. She could now concentrate with full force, integrity and focus completely on what she most loved: her own family. When she looked around her, seeing for herself that practically the world was her oyster, but she didn't know how to live up to her own status. These were not the surmises of blanked blubbers. Her life was simply empty and vacuous. They were not koshers, but now it was a woke, not a wake-up call but a woke.

Elizabeth protected, cajoled and covered up everything when it came to her family, like the lioness that she was, making herself scarce too and hidden from the austerity of the vox populi so no one could really read her. Socially, she attended some events, but that was all. She kept herself quiet, with updates, and the updates of her own kids. As for the world, "So tired and exhausted of the changes," or words to this effect. That she was.

The excited young and hopeful girl that looked at the world with so much expectancy, walking into the Camelot's Kingdom palace, full of hope, love and so eager to start a new life as the new Mrs Bligh, a perfect candidate. But all the same, she was an outsider, for Lewis's side of the family were obtrusive. They belonged to another world. They never warmed themselves to her, and vice versa. She, like Olivia, avoided Lewis's family like a plague, and when Lewis passed over, she absolutely cut herself and the kids off from the other Blighs. Now she reigned supreme in her own kingdom, flicking out the other Blighs. Caro always wondered if they had a very extended family. There were never cousins, uncles and so forth.

With her long curly mahogany hair tumbling down, with her skin glowing, those beautiful blue eyes that bespoke, the high cheekbones, the small contrived mouth, brimming with such happiness, so exalted, completely elated, walking on cloud nine, climbing the seventh heavens. Her naivety, her youthfulness, her own beauty. But within months, her fairy-tale wedding crumbled. Elizabeth picked up the pieces: her beauty, her hopes, her longings, all for nothing.

On the day that she arrived at Camelot's Kingdom, the weather was not perfect. It was cast with the sky dark and grey, something that she came to learn about Inverness weather. It was also cold even though they were in summer, with the cold wind blowing. She shivered with no apparent reason on the day of her arrival. The maids, the cooks and the then-majordomo waited on her and Lewis. Now she thinks how lousy it was on that memorable day, one that had she taken notice of, were the signs, the omens that were showing her the impending future. When her dreams and wishes crumble, as Anna, her future granddaughter, said, "This house breathes deceit."

She survived it all. But will she survive the new future, the new decade and the bitter onslaught of what would be coming?

Now she is called Queen Elizabeth of Camelot's Kingdom of broken dreams. Yes.

Even with the other ladies waiting for the succession, once in a weak moment, Elizabeth told Olivia that "she was so much like her."

Yes, both were raised by wealth along with the positions that came with both of them.

Both were tricked into being married into a rich but stuffed, high-powered family with so much to hide.

Now more tests should be coming. Olivia as the new Mrs Andrew Swanson. Little Lizzie finally returning. But more.

Presently, Camelot's Kingdom was being tended by Little Lizzie, Elizabeth Alexandra Bligh. One questions now who is the new Queen, with the original Elizabeth Bligh now being Mrs Elizabeth Goddard.

Sponsors

Sir Stanley Ho, the powerful casino magnate of Macau. RIP.

James D. Packer, Australian business entrepreneur.

Hugh Jackman, Australian actor.

Chuck Norris, seven-time world karate champion.

With full authorization from Bevan Lee.

Further sponsors:

My Home and Gifts, 182–186 Victoria St., Richmond VIC 3121.

China Bar, 80 Victoria St., Richmond VIC 3121.

Singapore Street Hawker, Victoria St., Abbotsford VIC.

YoHOME, Massage and Myotherapy, Shop 17/313 Victoria St, Abbotsford, Vic 3067.

General Joao and Filomena Almeida Bruno Foundation.

Macau Club in Melbourne, Australia — the only Macanese-Australian club in Australia.

Thank you,

Filomena Maria de Almeida Bruno

Australia's Golden Angel

www.ingramcontent.com/pod-product-compliance
Lightning Source LLC
Chambersburg PA
CBHW071528030726
47598CB00001B/36

* 9 7 8 1 7 6 4 4 8 3 1 8 6 *